The Privileged Sex

Also by Martin van Creveld

Wargames: From Gladiators to Gigabytes

The Age of Airpower

The Land of Blood and Honey: The Rise of Modern Israel

The Culture of War

The American Riddle (in Russian)

The Changing Face of War: Lessons of Combat from the Marne to Iraq

Defending Israel

Moshe Dayan

Men, Women and War

The Art of War: War and Military Thought

The Rise and Decline of the State

The Sword and the Olive: A Critical History of the Israeli Defense Force

Airpower and Maneuver Warfare

Nuclear Proliferation and the Future of Conflict

The Transformation of War

The Training of Officers: From Professionalism to Irrelevance

Technology and War: 2000 B.C. to the Present

Command in War

Fighting Power: German and U.S. Army Performance, 1939-1945

Supplying War: Logistics from Wallenstein to Patton

Hitler's Strategy 1940-1941: The Balkan Clue

The Privileged Sex

By Martin van Creveld

DLVC Enterprises

Library of Congress Cataloguing-in-Publication Data

Van Creveld, Martin, 1946 -
The Privileged Sex / Martin van Creveld
p. cm.
Includes bibliographical references and index.

1. Women—History. 2. Men—History. I. Title.

First Edition: 2013
ISBN-13: 978-1484983126

DLVC Enterprises
POB 2766
Mevasseret Zion
90805 Israel

For Eldad, my son.

"In every respect the burden is hard on those who attack an almost universal opinion. They must be very fortunate, as well as unusually capable, if they obtain a hearing at all."

John Stuart Mill, *The Subjection of Women*.

Table of Contents

Preface to the English Edition

By the time I began working on this edition of "The Privileged Sex" in early 2013, a decade had passed since I first published the book, in German. I expected that extensive changes would be needed in order to bring it up to date, but was surprised to find that this was not the case. Though some of the details had changed, the essentials had not. In fact, today women are arguably *more* privileged than they were when I first began investigating the subject. In the early 1990s, for example, 300 million people lived in countries where men's life expectancy was higher than that of women. Today, the number is practically zero. In today's Europe, to cite another example, several countries have in place quotas reserving a minimum percentage of seats in parliament for women. The result has been far more women winning seats than would have been the case if elections were truly open and fair. One of those who owed at least part of her meteoric rise to this system is German Chancellor Angela Merkel. These are but two examples, and consequently this edition needed little beyond occasionally updating statistics and acknowledging those who have helped me in my research since "Das Bevorzugte Geschlecht" came out in 2003.

Now as ever, many feminist claims concerning the alleged oppression of women by men at various times and places are unfounded. Now as ever, both biologically and socially, becoming and being a man is in many ways harder than becoming and being a woman. Now as ever, men work longer hours, performing harder, dirtier and more dangerous work than women and suffering proportionally far more industrial accidents. Throughout history it was husbands who supported their wives, not the other way around. And in 9 of 10 households today, this remains the case. Women also receive proportionally far more welfare benefits. Around the world, the law in many ways treats men much more severely than women. In armed forces that admit women — and by no means all do — men proportionally suffer nearly 10 times more casualties than women. Women, meanwhile, receive far more medical attention, which helps to explain why, as mentioned above, women's life expectancy exceeds that of men. And in many other ways, women continue to enjoy a better quality of life. Yet none of these facts has prevented feminists from shedding tears over their lot. A man who "yammers" — in the words of the late "mother of feminism" Betty Friedan — is certain to be despised or ridiculed. But a woman doing the same — and that is indeed what many feminists have done — is much more likely to get what she wants.

Ever since I started writing about women and feminism in the late 1990s, my views on these subjects have gotten me into endless trouble. Those troubles have taught me that Freud was, in fact, wrong. The strongest human drive is not sex — it is the desire to make others shut up. As a man who has dared disagree with feminist myths, however incredible and foolish they might be, I have learned over the past dozen years just how strong that desire is among the guardians of feminism. In publishing this new version of "The Privileged Sex," I invite readers to study the facts and come to their own informed conclusions.

Jerusalem, March 2013

Introduction

Like most books, this one was born out of curiosity. Long ago, I read Simone de Beauvoir. She once pointed out that though the world had always belonged to men, no one could offer a sufficiently good explanation of why this was the case. I found the idea striking, and decided to search for a sufficiently good explanation. The riddle that she, the woman of letters, had posed, I, the male historian, would solve.

Born in 1946, I reached maturity in a world constructed around the ancient tale of women's oppression. As the mythology has it, once upon a time there was a golden age when people lived in extended families and tended their gardens. Both men and women worshipped earth-goddesses and were blissfully unaware of fatherhood. What government existed was in the hands of women, with men content to live under, or at any rate with, it. This Garden of Eden was eventually overthrown, however. Women's benevolent rule was ended, and the wicked reign of men took its place. With women's defeat came materialism, competition, hierarchy, war and countless other societal calamities. They ranged from the commodification of sex to rape and from meat-eating to the destruction of the environment. For millennia on end, women chafed under patriarchy. Then, the dam gave way and the torrent broke through. Modern feminism appeared in all its glory and the world was changed forever. *Vive la révolution!*

If this tale were indeed true, I wondered, then precisely when, where and why was matriarchy overthrown? How did women's oppression begin, and how did it grow and develop? How could the 50 percent of humanity who are men impose their will upon the remaining 50 percent, and continue to do so at all known times and places? If women are oppressed and rebellion against patriarchy is the answer, why do so many indulge in the "illusions of post-feminism" and so few follow the feminist call to arms?[1] Why is it that in the

---

[1] See Vicki Coppock et al., *The Illusions of "Post Feminism": New Women, Old Myths*, London, Taylor & Francis, 1995, chapter 1; Sherrye Henry, *The Deep Divide: Why American Women Resist Equality*, New York, MacMillan, 1994, pp. 1-36; also Jean J. Mansbridge, *Why We Lost the Era, Chicago*, University of Chicago Press, 1986.

United States, only one in three women call themselves feminists, and many others are outright hostile to feminism? Why is it that many well-known women, from Florence Nightingale to Simone de Beauvoir to former Hewlett-Packard CEO Carly Fiorina have declared that they never suffered from the liabilities supposedly associated with their sex?[2] Why do polls among women of several nationalities show that most do not feel they have been discriminated against?[3] And last but not least, to the extent that women have rebelled, why has their rebellion not led anywhere significant, and why is a brave new society nowhere in sight?

After a few months of work, so many problems and contradiction were jostling each other that they seriously threatened my mental balance. It was at this point that my wife suggested that I take a walk. I had scarcely reached the street when I realized that I had been asking the wrong questions. Perhaps my assumption, and that of countless other before me, was wrong. Perhaps, I considered for the first time, women are not in fact oppressed. If women are not in fact oppressed, it could explain why no convincing account of the origins and perpetuation of their oppression has ever been produced. If women are in fact the privileged sex, it could explain why most women seem to be more or less satisfied with their lot, why more women have not cast off their cosmetics and started working jobs like garbage collection. Today, as in yesteryear, women generally continue to do what they can to seek out men, to attract them, to marry them, to make love to them, and to have children by them. Certainly the proposition that women are content with their privileges is more convincing than the claim, by at least one leading feminist, that generations of women have been "mistaken about truth, morality, or even their self-interests"[4] — as condescending a slur as any ever directed against women.

---

[2] For Florence Nightingale see Gertrudee Himmelfarb, *The De-Moralization of Society: From Victorian Virtues to Modern Values*, New York, Vintage Books, 1994, p. 102; for Simone de Beauvoir see her own *Force of Circumstance*, Harmondsworth, Middlesex, Penguin, 1968, p. 199; for Carly Fiorina see S. Shuler. (Winter 2003). "Breaking Through the Glass Ceiling Without Breaking a Nail," *ACJournal*, 6, 2, retrieved from http://ac-journal.org/journal/vol6/iss2/articles/shuler.htm

[3] For the United States see Dahlia Moore, *Labor Market Segmentation and its Implications: Inequality, Deprivation and Entitlement*, New York, Garland, 1992, pp. 145-67; for Germany see "Das Rattenrennen nicht Mitmachen," *Der Spiegel*, 10/1998, p. 112; for the Ukraine see Solomea Pavlychko, "Conservative Faces of Women in the Ukraine," in Mary Buckley, ed., *Post-Soviet Women: From the Baltic to Central Asia*, Cambridge, Cambridge University Press, 1997, p. 226.

[4] Alison Jaggar, *Feminist Politics and Human Nature*, Totowa, NJ, Rowman & Littlefield, 1983, p. 44.

Lest there be any mistaken assumptions drawn by readers of this book, let me clarify just exactly what I mean when I speak of the "privileged sex." To employ this phrase is not to deny that nature, by giving women weaker physiques and making them carry the burden of menstruation, pregnancy, delivery and lactation, has in some ways made their lot harder than that of men. Nor is the phrase meant to imply that their lives are a rose garden. What the "privileged sex" *is* meant to imply is that there is another face to the matter — that for every disadvantage under which women labor, they enjoy a privilege that is equally important to their lives, if not more so. Far too many female authors, because they are determined to see oppression everywhere, and far too many male ones, because they have been made to feel guilty by their female colleagues, ever mention these privileges. Yet without them much of social life becomes incomprehensible. In what follows, I endeavor to set the record straight.

The outline of the book is as follows. Chapter 1 sets the stage by examining several central beliefs about the oppression of women at various times and places in history, and then exposing them for the myths they are. Chapter 2 deals with the different paths that lead toward, respectively, manhood and womanhood, and shows how both nature and society have conspired to make it much harder to become, and to be, a man than a woman. Chapter 3 investigates the privileges women have historically enjoyed, and continue to enjoy, with respect to work. Chapter 4 explains how, because women have traditionally done less and easier work than men, different societies at different times and places in history have sought to ensure women's economic welfare through support by men. Chapter 5 looks at women's position with respect to crime and the law, and shows how laws are often drafted and applied specifically to help women. Chapter 6 shows how women have been freed from participation in war, as well as looks into the attempts to protect them against its horrors. Chapter 7 deals with the results of women being granted their privileged position, including women's more comfortable existence, the greater attention paid to their welfare, and the longer lives they enjoy. Chapter 8 examines why women, in spite of their many privileges, continue to bemoan their lot. And finally, Chapter 9 presents my conclusions.

When I first embarked on the project, I initially feared that finding evidence concerning women's privileges would be as hard as distilling a few ounces of gold from tons of rock. My fears not only turned out to be unfounded, it soon became clear that the challenge was not a shortage of material, but an almost incredible surplus. Gathering, sifting, indexing, evaluating, digesting, arranging and writing down all this material would have required the lifetime not of a single Methuselah, but of a hundred. I can only ask my readers' indulgence for having undertaken this enormous task, and hope that the numerous gaps in my research will be filled by others better qualified than I.

To those who helped me in my work on "The Privileged Sex," please let me express my appreciation. My gratitude to the Alexander von Humboldt Foundation, which financed my stay in Potsdam, Germany, during the first year of my research. My appreciation as well to the Margaret and Axel Johnson Foundation and its director, Mr. Kurt Almqvist, who provided money with which to buy books. And last but by no means least, my thanks to those who helped find material, to those who listened to me discuss my research, and to those who reviewed my manuscript, who in so doing saved me from countless errors and misinterpretations. They are, in alphabetical order: Ms. Kate Aspy, Dr. Yuval Harari, Ms. Margalit Israeli, Dr. Chaim Kahana, Dr. Martina Kayser, Dr. Jonathan Lewy, Dr. Miriam Liepsma, Mr. Amit Perl, Prof. Israel Shatzman, Ms. Ella Shofman, Mr. Paul Spier, Ms. Varda Schramm, and Prof. Ben Ami Shillony. I do not know where I would have been without you; thank you, thank you, all.

Finally, the usual special thanks are due to Prof. Benjamin ("Beni") Z. Kedar. Though he is a medievalist by training, very often I have drawn on his advice as if he knew everything — which, in some ways, he does. Long familiar with my theories, he was skeptical at first. Whether or not I succeeded in convincing him, I do not know. However, his doubts did not prevent him from providing everything that I have become accustomed to receiving from him over the past three decades. His conversation, his encouragement and his criticism amount to the very definition of friendship, and for that he has my sincere gratitude.

Jerusalem, March 2001

Chapter 1: Three Legends

1. The Myth of Oppression

This chapter seeks to dismantle several of the myths concerning women's oppression at the hands of men. Those myths start with the claim that men in developing countries shorten women's lives by robbing them of food and medical care. In fact, in nearly all countries (both developing *and* developed), women outlive men. These myths also include the belief that "hard" professions like engineering feature so few women because men "steer" women away from such work;[1] in fact, not even Stalin was able to force female students to study technological subjects.[2] Some myths about women's oppression are simply foolish, such as the claim that the ubiquitous QWERTY keyboard has remained in use for more than a century because it makes life harder for female typists.[3] And some are outright preposterous, such as the argument that physicians at the turn of the 20th century who persuaded mothers to breastfeed their babies and thereby cut child mortality rates were guilty of "male imperialism perpetrated on females."[4]

In this chapter I shall focus on three case studies, selected for inclusion here because they have led to some of the shrillest denunciations. The first is the claim that ancient Greek men confined ancient Greek women to the home and seldom permitted them to leave their rooms. The second is the claim that early

---

[1] See Gordon Weil, "Gender Analysis of Dismantling the Command Economy in Eastern Europe: The Case of Poland," in Valentine M. Moghadam, ed., *Democratic Reform and the Position of Women in Transitional Economies*, Oxford, Clarendon, 1993, p. 287.

[2] Bernice Glazter Rosenthal, "Love on the Tractor: Women in the Russian Revolution and After," in Renate Bridenthal and Claudia Koonz, eds. *Women in European History*, Boston, Houghton Mifflin, 1977, p. 389.

[3] Juliet Webster, *Shaping Women's Work: Gender, Employment and Information Technology*, London, Longman, 1996, pp. 38, 59, 60.

[4] Anne Lokke, "Philanthropists, Mothers and Doctors: The Philanthropic Struggle against Infant Mortality in Copenhagen, 1860-1920," in Birgitta Jordansson and Tinne Vammen, *Charitable Women: Philanthropic Welfare, 1780-1930*, Dense, Odense University Press, 1998, p. 154.

modern misogynist European male witch-hunters arrested, tortured and executed countless women simply in order to preserve patriarchy. The third is that the Nazis persecuted women almost as much as they did homosexuals, gypsies, Jews and others.

2. Were Greek Women Secluded?

The debate over the position of women in ancient Greece, particularly Athens, is now more than two centuries old. Some, like Rousseau, held up Greek attitudes toward women as a model. Others rejected that model, claiming that it oppressed women and was inherently evil. Though seclusion is only one out of many bad things Greek men are accused of having done, its role in the attack on patriarchy is crucial. In the words of one historian, if women were to be oppressed, then it was first necessary to ensure that they "scarcely ever left the women's apartments." If women "seldom crossed the thresholds of their own front doors,"[5] then surely they were oppressed.

The above argument consists of two parts. The first is that women were confined to their own quarters inside the home; the second, that they were forbidden to leave it. However, if women were in fact allowed to go out into public, then confining them to certain rooms inside the home would not have made much sense. The main source "proving" that women did not go out is usually given as Xenophon's *Oeconomicus*. More an exercise in rhetoric than a description of real life, the book purports to explain how the ideal wife should run a household while her husband goes about his business. The second is a passage from Euripides in which a woman is made to say that "leaving the house and walking about" is "one act which swings scandalous speech [in women's] way beyond all else."[6]

There also exist numerous shorter references with relevant figures of speech, such as Plato's "to cower at home like a woman," and from Pericles' funeral speech for the dead of the Peloponnesian War, "the best woman is one about whom nothing is ever said, neither favorable nor unfavorable."[7] However, these phrases should be understood as expressions of a cultural ideal, rather than as simple descriptions of reality at the time. Likewise, while a

---

[5] E. L. Flacliere, *Daily Life in Athens at the Time of Pericles*, London, Weidenfeld & Nicolson, 1965, p. 55.

[6] *Trojan Women*, 646-7.

[7] Plato, *Republic,* 579b; Thucydides, *The Peloponnesian War*, 2.45.

Jewish proverb has it that "a king's daughter wears her honor inward," this does not prove that Hassidic women were confined to their homes.

Starting our inquiry with mythological females, clearly they were *not* secluded.[8] At one point in the *Iliad* Zeus confined the gods to Olympus so as to help the Greeks. Though this policy applied to males as well as females, his wife, Hera, subverted it. First she made love to him; next she slipped away to help the Trojans. Neither did Thetis, a sea-goddess, have any trouble visiting her son Achilles or going on various errands on his behalf. The same goddess also abandoned Achilles' father, Peleus, because he was not sufficiently sexy.[9] This hardly sounds as if she were sequestered. In the *Odyssey*, Aphrodite was able to get away to enter into an adulterous liaison with Ares. Athene both helped Achilles in front of Troy and welcomed Odysseus as he was coming home. Goddesses roamed the fields, including Daphne, Persephone and Persephone's powerful mother Demeter. One goddess, Artemis, haunted forests and mountains and never even had a home in which she could have been confined.

The same applies to the human heroines of Greek epics. During the siege of Troy, Helene mounted the city walls to watch her two husbands, Menelaus and Paris fight. Far from being rebuked, she got an explanation of the proceedings from her father in law, Priam.[10] Andromache met her husband at the gate of Troy and often visited her friends in the city. During the final duel between Hector and Achilles, Hector's mother Hecuba and her ladies also mounted the wall to watch. In the *Odyssey*, Nausicaa and her female servants went to the spring to do their laundry. When Odysseus recounted his adventures in the hall of King Alcinous, both the latter's wife and his daughter were present. Penelope's husband being absent, she preferred to stay at home. However, there was nothing to prevent her from appearing in public whenever she wanted to. Greek tragedies, too, abound with such cases; had women really been sequestered, then the vast majority of Greek myths would have been impossible.

Furthermore, goddesses belonged, by definition, to the upper classes, as did the ladies of myth because they were normally the relatives of powerful men. Though several spun and weaved, none were supposed to work outside the home. For this reason, and also because they had servants of both sexes whom

---

[8] See Ken Dowden, "Approaching Women through Myth: Vital Tool or Self Delusion?" in Richard Hawley and Barbara Levik, eds., *Women in Antiquity*, London, Routledge, 1995, p. 56.

[9] Aristophanes, *Clouds*, 1067-70.

[10] *Iliad*, 2.140-242.

they could send on errands, if anything they were *more* sequestered than ordinary women. Most people were middle or low class and, at best, could only afford a few slaves. They lived not in the town but in the countryside, working in agriculture. In fact, evidence about women working outside the home is overwhelming.[11] Greek women went to the fountain to fetch water or wash clothes. Others acted as nurses or midwifes or as courtesans, entertainers and prostitutes. Others took wages to do agricultural work. Women even worked as vendors, as is made clear by the fact that Athenian law made it an offense to rebuke any citizen, male *or* female, for selling in the market.[12] Aristotle wrote that preventing poor women from going out was both impossible and unfair. After all, he noted, they did not have slaves who could go on errands or accompany them.[13]

Women also left home, the literature shows, to visit their favorite soothsayer,[14] participate in some public ceremonies,[15] admire works of art on the Acropolis,[16] visit men in prison,[17] argue their case before arbitrators,[18] and attend courtrooms to rouse the sympathy of juries for their male relatives.[19] Women also listened to public speeches; one, Elphinike, reproached Pericles after the latter gave a speech in honor of the Athenians killed in the war against Samos.[20] Plato says that refined women preferred tragedy to comedy; from this, as from two other passages, it appears that women frequented the theater as well.[21] Not only did women participate in their relatives' funerals, but without them those funerals could not be carried out at all. Women were active in religion.[22] They could become priestesses; indeed, some priesthoods were

---

[11] See David Cohen, "Seclusion, Separation and the Status of Women in Classical Athens," in Ian MacAuslan and Peter Walcot, eds., *Women in Antiquity*, Oxford, Oxford University Press, 1995, pp. 138-40.

[12] Demosthenes, 57.30-1.

[13] *Politics*, 1300a, 1323a.

[14] Theophrastus, 11.9-10 and 16.2.

[15] Thucydides, *The Peloponnesian War*, 2.46; Aristophanes, *Acharnanians*, 253.

[16] Plutarch, *Pericles*, 13.9-10.

[17] Andocides, 1.48; Lysias, 13.39-41; Plato, *Phaedo*, 60a.

[18] Demosthenes, 40.11.

[19] Aeschines, 2.148, 152; Plato, *Apology*, 34c-35b; Demosthenes, 19.310, 21.99 and 186, 25.85, 54.35; Aristophanes, *Wasps*, 568-9, *Plutus*, 380.

[20] Plutarch, *Pericles*, 28.

[21] *Laws*, 658a-d, 817a-c; *Georgias*, 502b-e.

[22] See Leena Vittaniemi, "*Partheneia*—Remarks on Virginity and Its Meanings in the Religious Context of Ancient Greece," in Lena Larsen Loven et al., eds., *Aspects of Women in Antiquity*, Sweden, Astron, 1998, pp. 51-4.

reserved exclusively for women. Some religious rites in which women participated were carried out daily, while others focused on festivals held on fixed dates. Some of the festivals were mixed, with others reserved for women. None could have taken place if women had been confined at home. And that is not to mention the feast of Dionysus, during which women not only left their homes but the city as well, making for the mountains instead.

Thousands of works of art show women engaged in all manner of activities. Some of the activities portrayed, such as getting dressed, putting on jewelry, weaving or eating at a table, undoubtedly must have been carried out indoors. Others, however, such as playing a game of knucklebones, minding a child or spinning, could have been carried out either indoors or outdoors. This even applies to having sex; one vase has a picture of a woman masturbating near a fountain with another woman and a man looking on. And others activities, such as encountering a satyr, carrying water, playing ball, making a sacrifice or dancing ecstatically, could take place *only* on the assumption that women went outside. Had art been the sole evidence available, then any speculation about women's alleged seclusion would have quickly been laid to rest.

Art is not, of course, the sole available evidence. Xenophon's aforementioned *Oecomenicus* is arguably the single most important account of the lives of Athenian housewives early in the fourth century B.C. His treatise, it must be noted, was one of a series intended to present reality as it should have been — not as it actually was. One of the characters, Isomachos, explains that human children are tender and require shelter. In order that they would be raised indoors, the gods made women love small children more than men do. By contrast, men's bodies are fit for "traveling and military campaigns." Human laws reflect those the gods had made. Men and women are praised or blamed according to whether they follow their respective natures. Isomachos compares his wife to a queen bee, declaring that if she deserts the home, the home will collapse.[23] However, the fact that his wife's main function was in the home does not mean he prohibited her from leaving it. Drawing such a conclusion is as erroneous as it is to claim that, since it was considered shameful for a man to spend too much time indoors, men lived out in the open like beasts.

If women were free to go out of the home, then obviously it did not make sense to confine them inside it, let alone in women's quarters. The sources do contain a few references to women's quarters. Closer examination, however,

---

[23] *Oeconomicus*, 7.3-5; 9.3-4.

reveals that a number of these women's quarters were in fact those of female slaves. Female slaves, Isomachos says, occupied separate quarters, in order for their master to control their reproduction. It is true that for a stranger to enter the inner rooms of a house without being invited was considered rude. In an extreme case it might lead to violence, and even be mentioned in a lawsuit.[24] Yet a man was perfectly able to visit a friend's house and talk to his wife.[25] Even today, many otherwise modern people would not like visitors to their home peeking into their bedrooms; few would suggest that this proves that those rooms are being used for locking up wives and daughters. At most, one could find evidence that women were more likely to be found at home.[26] One could also find evidence that modesty may have dictated that women leave the dining room and retreat into the inner rooms when male guests visited.

Faced with overwhelming evidence to the contrary, some modern historians have resorted to wild casuistry to support the claim that ancient Greek women were secluded. If Greek beds are narrower than present-day American ones, then obviously Greek men and women did not sleep together and women occupied separate quarters which men seldom visited.[27] If Isomachos' wife has the run of the house, then this is only because Xenophon "resists the conventional Athenian role for his wife."[28] If countless paintings show women engaged in all sorts of outdoor activities, then those women must have been either courtesans or slaves. If the women of myth and drama for the most part move about just as they please, then this proves that imaginary women did what real ones could not.[29] If the evidence concerning women appearing in public during the decades following the Peloponnesian War is overwhelming, then this is because the end of that war led to a vast, though entirely undocumented, social revolution.

---

[24] Demosthenes, *Lysias*, 3.

[25] See David Cohen, *Law, Sexuality and Society: The Enforcement of Morals in Classical Greece*, Cambridge, Cambridge University Press, 1991, p. 156.

[26] *Epidemics*, 6.7.

[27] See Eva Keuls, *The Reign of the Phallus*, Berkeley, CA, University of California Press, 1993, p. 212.

[28] Sarah Pomeroy, *Families in Classical and Hellenistic Greece*, Oxford, Clarendon, 1997, p. 297.

[29] Dyfri Williams, "Women on Athenian Vases: Problems of Interpretation," in Cameron and Kuhrt, eds., *Images of Women in Antiquity*, pp. 103-4; Helene P. Foley, "The Conception of Women in Athenian Drama," in Helene P. Foley, ed., *Reflections of Women in Antiquity*, New York, Gorden & Breach, 1981, p. 151.

In truth, the question before modern historians is not whether Greek women were secluded. Rather, it is how to account for such a determined unwillingness to look the facts in the face.

3. The Great Witch Hunt

Over the past four decades, an enormous amount of literature has been produced on the early-modern European period of witch-hunting (ca. 1500-1650). In the English-speaking world, interest in the field was triggered by the work of Keith Thomas' *Magic and the Decline of Religion* (1971). It offered new interpretations and set new standards of scholarship in the field. Thomas himself wrote that "the idea that witch-prosecutions reflected a war between the sexes can be discounted."[30] However, this and other denials did not prevent scholars from claiming that witch-hunting originated in male hatred for women. One scholar went so far as to argue that the phenomenon constituted "not merely the reflection of an age-old stereotype, not merely the by-product of a patriarchal society; the witch hunts were a part of, and one example of, the ongoing mechanism for social control of women."[31]

Just how and why patriarchy translated into witch-hunting at this particular time and place is by no means clear. Rather than attempting to answer that question, I shall endeavor to show that witch-hunting was *not* simply a matter of female-hating men conjuring up the most horrible crimes in order to burn some women and put the rest in their place. First, it must be underscored that contemporaries, both men and women, firmly believed in witchcraft.[32] Just as few people doubted that there was a God, or that the sun revolved around the earth, so too there was little question about the existence of witches. Contemporaries would have scoffed at the notion that witchcraft was "a crime without criminals," as some modern historians have called it.

---

[30] Keith Thomas, *Religion and the Decline of Magic*, London, Weidenfeld & Nicolson, 1971, p. 586.

[31] Marianne Hester, "Patriarchal Reconstruction and Witch-Hunting," in Jonathan Barry et al., eds., *Witchcraft in Early Modern Europe*, Cambridge, Cambridge University Press, 1996, pp. 288-89. Also see Catherine Belsey, *The Subject of Tragedy: Identity and Difference in Renaissance Drama*, London, Methuen, 1985, pp. 185-86; and Karen Newman, *Fashioning Femininity and English Renaissance Drama*, Chicago, University of Chicago Press, 1991, p. 69.

[32] See Gerhard Schormann, *Hexenprozesse in Nordwestdeutschland*, Hildesheim, Vanderhoeck & Ruprecht, 1977, p. 1.

The mythology of witchcraft was put together over several centuries, and was substantially complete by 1480. Some witches swore formal allegiance to the devil or were possessed by him. Some witches were visited by the devil in their own homes, while others mounted broomsticks and flew to orgies known as Sabbaths. At these orgies, which were held in secret and were reachable only to the initiated, witches ate, drank, danced and had promiscuous sex. In return for the devil's promise to give them power over people and things, they renounced Christianity and defiled its symbols.

According to the mythology, witches were guilty of committing *maleficia*, or evil deeds. These *maleficia* were regarded as a real menace, both to individuals and to society. *Maleficia* were not merely a matter of malicious intent, but of actual death and destruction. Some witches brought about natural disasters such as storms, hail or flooding. Others killed people and livestock, as well as caused a variety of diseases, many of them never heard of before or since, such as making women give birth to rabbits. Some witches prepared love potions to attract new lovers and bring back unfaithful ones. They could also make men impotent. Thanks to being allied with the devil, witches could do things that ordinary criminals never could.[33] Thus there was as much, if not more, reason for society to oppose witchcraft as there was to fight crime in general.

Throughout history, there have been both male and female witches. In 1484, when Pope Innocent VIII issued his Bull against witchcraft, he explicitly stated that it was being practiced by "many persons of both sexes." In 1572 the Elector of Saxony ruled that "sorcerers, man or woman, shall be executed with the sword."[34] Even in England, where the percentage of women among the accused was unusually high, the law always referred to "persons." Pictures of Sabbaths regularly show the devil attended to by both men and women. One expert, the Puritan minister William Perkins, went so far as to blame Moses for his use of the feminine gender in ordering that "thou shalt not suffer a witch to live."[35] In truth, he said, the Bible "exempeth not the male." Many other experts agreed with him in this respect.[36]

---

[33] See Richard Kieckhefer, *Magic in the Middle Ages*, Cambridge, Cambridge University Press, 1990, p. 176.

[34] See Wolfgang Behringer, *Hexen und Hexenverfolgung in Deutschland*, Munich, Universität Tübingen, 1988, p. 157.

[35] *Leviticus*, 20.57.

[36] "Sermon Preached by Mr. James Hutchinson [on Witchcraft]," 13.4.1697, in Brian D. Levack, ed., *Witchcraft in Scotland*, New York, Garland, 1992, pp. 379-80; Barbara Rosen, *Witchcraft in*

So uncomfortable did contemporaries feel about the "fact" that most witches were female that they time and again questioned why it was so. Even King James I of England felt obliged to reflect on the question.[37] Precisely because witchcraft was considered real and not something society had invented, the reason had to be sought in the nature of women themselves. Most experts agreed that women were more malicious than men. Their nature was weaker and their minds not as clear; as a result, the devil was able to ensnare them "after only a light skirmish."[38] Female writers who addressed the issue tended to agree with their male comrades.[39] The authors of the most famous handbook on witch-hunting, the *Malleus Maleficarum*, claimed that the word "feminine" itself derived from "fe-minus," "less faith."[40] But this did not prevent them from including 10 pages on male witches.

An instructive modern analogy is the crime of murder. While the crime is committed by both men and women, more than 80 percent of convicted murderers are men. When we look for an explanation for this fact, we do not say that murders were invented by a man-hating society in order to execute men or put them behind bars. Rather, we seek the reasons in qualities that are innate to men: for example, the much higher levels of testosterone that make them more aggressive than women. In other words, it is not necessarily true that those whose job it was to deal with female witches hated women — no more true than the argument that those who claim that violence is a defining male characteristic hate men. All the witch-hunters were trying to do was what criminologists, sociologists and psychologists of both sexes are doing today — namely, explaining a social phenomenon they found puzzling.

England, Amherst, MA, University of Massachusetts Press, 1969, pp. 51-60; Gaskill, "Witchcraft in Early Modern Kent," p. 274.

[37] See Christina Larner, *Witchcraft and Religion: The Politics of Popular Belief*, Alan Macfarlane ed., Oxford, Blackwell, 1984, p. 20.

[38] Peter Burke, *Culture and Society in Renaissance Italy, 1420-1540*, London, Batsford, 1972, p. 164; also see George Mora et al., eds., *Witches, Devils and Doctors in the Renaissance: Johann Weyer, "e praestigiis daemonum*," Binghampton, NY, Medieval and Renaissance Texts and Studies, 1991, pp. 181-2.

[39] Rachel Speght, *A Muzzle for Melastomus* (1617), quoted in Sara Gamble, ed., *The Routledge Critical Dictionary of Feminism and Postfeminism*, New York, Routledge, 2000, p. 7.

[40] Heinrich Krämer and Jacob Sprenger, *Malleus Maleficarum*, London, Pushkin, 1948 [1495], p.44.

Some historians have claimed that, in persecuting witches, men were trying to suppress female sexuality.[41] This is nonsense. As Shakespeare could have said, "t'is mighty strange" that most of the accused were older women. Some were very old indeed. The oldest on record, a woman by the name of Isabeau Blary, was already past her 100th birthday. Subjected to interrogation, Blary "confessed" that she had been sodomized by the devil.[42] Needless to say, the argument makes no sense, no more so than, say, the fact that young, single men are over-represented among violent criminals proves that society is out to suppress their hormones. All it means is that such men are more inclined to break the law, and less afraid of the consequences, than either older men or women.

In Italy, clerics were perhaps even more at risk of being accused of witchcraft than women were. In Germany, where it was often a question of forcing a witch to identify her accomplices so as to get at the latter's property, prominent men were among the accused. The same applied to Sussex.[43] Typically persecution would start at the level of the village or the neighborhood, usually after the suspect had acquired an unpleasant reputation. The breaking point would come when he or she asked for a favor, such as food, lending a hand or a small loan. Upon being rebuffed, not always politely, she might retaliate by uttering a curse or a threat.

Once the threat or curse appeared to come true, gossip would spread the news, and the authorities would get involved. Quite often it was up to the authorities, who were male, to put the brakes on local outbreaks of witch-hunting. In 1597 James VI of Scotland, as he was then known, abolished the general commission against witchcraft he himself had appointed specifically because people were using it to settle scores.[44] In the second half of the 17th

---

[41] Marianne Hester, *Lewd Women and Wicked Witches: A Study of the Dynamics of Male Domination*, London, Routledge, 1992, pp. 4, 108, 114.

[42] Robert Muchembled, *La sorcière au village xve-xviii siècle*, Paris, Gallimard, n.d., p. 181.

[43] Ruth Martin, *Witchcraft and the Inquisition in Venice, 1550-1650*, Oxford, Blackwell, 1989, pp. 226-7; Walter Rummel, *Bauern, Herren und Hexen*, Göttingen, Vanderhoeck, 1991, p. 317; Cynthia B. Herrup, *The Common Peace: Participation and the Criminal Law in Seventeenth Century England*, Cambridge, Cambridge University Press, 1987, p. 33.

[44] Christina Larder, "Crimen Exceptum? The Crime of Witchcraft in Europe," in Brian D. Levack, ed., *The Witch-Hunt in Early Modern Europe*, London, Pearson, 2006, p. 87; Jim Sharpe, "The Devil in East Anglia: the Matthew Hopkins Trials Reconsidered," in Barry, ed., *Witchcraft in Early Modern Europe*, p. 254.

century, when belief in witchcraft among the elite began to decline, popular persistence in bringing accusations led to many acquittals.[45]

It is true that there were few women among the intellectual elite that wrote about witchcraft and held the trials. On the other hand, female rulers were as apt to persecute witches as were male ones. In the Netherlands, persecutions peaked during the first half of the 16th century, when the country was governed by three successive female regents acting for Charles V: Margaret of Austria, Mary of Hungary, and Margaret of Parma.[46] Later, when William the Silent took over, the persecutions declined. Similarly, in France persecution peaked late in the 16th century under the rule of Catherina de Medici. The Scottish Witchcraft Laws, meanwhile, were enacted during the reign of Mary, Queen of Scots. In 1547, 9-year-old King Edward VI of England, acting on the advice of his male entourage, had all the penalties against witchcraft repealed. Sixteen years later Elizabeth allowed Parliament to reinstate them in even worse form. The reign of "Good Queen Bess" marked the high point of persecution. Under her male heir, both the number of cases and the conviction rate went down.[47] These facts hardly confirm the claim that the objective of witch-hunting was to reestablish patriarchal control.

Women participated in witch-hunts at least as much as men did. Most *maleficia* were directed by women at women.[48] It was mainly women who accused other women of violating normal standards of conduct, insisting that their husbands or other male relatives take action against suspected witches.[49] It was mainly women, bewitched by other women, who suffered from convulsions and fainting fits. It was mainly women, bewitched by other women, who vomited pins, needles and toads and whose statements to that

[45] See Larner, *Witchcraft and Religion*, p. 32.

[46] Marijke Gijswijt-Hofstra, "Six Centuries of Witchcraft," in Marijke Gijswijt-Hofstra and Willem Frijhoff, eds., *Witchcraft in the Netherlands*, Rotterdam, University of Rotterdam Press, 1991, pp. 29-30.

[47] C. L'Estrange-Ewen, *Witch-Hunting and Witch Trials*, London, Kegan Paul, 1929, p. 112ff.

[48] Hester, "Patriarchal Reconstruction and Witch-Hunting," p. 298; MacFarlane, *Witchcraft in Tudor and Stuart England*, p. 160, table 15. One admittedly small sample from the Netherlands shows that bewitched females outnumbered males two to one: Hans de Waardt, "At Bottom a Family Affair: Feuds and Witchcraft in Nijkerk in 1550," in Gijswijt-Hofstra and Frijhoff, eds., *Witchcraft in the Netherlands*, p. 137, table 1.

[49] Deborah Willis, *Malevolent Nurture: Witch-Hunting and Maternal Power in Early Modern England*, Ithaca, NY, Cornell University Press, 1995, pp. 13, 97.

effect might or might not be believed by the responsible male officials.[50] The first Englishwoman tried under the Elizabethan statute, Elizabeth Lowys, was accused mainly by women.[51] The last English witch to stand trial, Jane Wenham, not only was accused by another woman, she herself implicated three other women. All were acquitted. Wenham herself was convicted by the jury, but promptly pardoned by a skeptical judge. Unable to return home, she found refuge on the estate of a male landowner.[52]

Women also played an important role in cases that, rising above the level of neighborhood rivalry, were referred to the courts. Some women initiated proceedings against others. And since prostitutes, who were otherwise barred from providing testimony in court, were permitted to testify in cases involving witchcraft, women may actually have been over-represented among witnesses. In addition, just as modern police forces now employ women to deal with female offenders, early modern women often guarded suspected witches in jail. Others joined men in acting as witch-prickers, professionals who used pins to probe body marks to check if the victim would indeed bleed. One well-known pricker, a Mr. Patterson of Scotland, turned out to be a woman in disguise.[53] Whether because of personal animosities or because they were tortured, the accused women cooperated, implicating other women. Others brought accusations out of jealousy because the devil had preferred some other, more prominent, woman to themselves.[54]

Since there were no women among those who tried witches, had accusations of witchcraft really involved male hatred for women one would expect a higher proportion of female witches to be convicted than male ones. That, however, did not happen. In Scotland a larger proportion of female suspects were executed than male ones, but a larger proportion of female suspects were also acquitted. In Geneva the situation was the reverse. In Italy the vast majority of female witches turned over to the all-male Inquisition

---

[50] See G. Geis, "Lord Hale, Witches and Rape," in Brian D. Levack, ed., *Witchcraft in England*, New York, Garland, 1992, pp. 54-7.

[51] See Alan R. Young, "Elizabeth Lowys: Witch and Social Victim, 1564," in Levack, ed., *Witchcraft in England*, pp. 79-86.

[52] Ian Bostridge, *Witchcraft and its Transformations c. 1650-1950*, Oxford, Clarendon, 1997, pp. 132-4; Phyllis J. Guskin, "The Context of Witchcraft: The Case of Jane Wenham," in Levack, ed., *Witchcraft in England*, pp. 94-117.

[53] W. N. Neill, "The Professional Pricker and His Test for Witchcraft," in Levack, ed., *Witchcraft in Scotland*, pp. 278-9.

[54] See Richard von Dülmen, "Imagination des Teuflischen," in Richard von Dülmen, ed., *Hexenwelten, Magie und Imagination*, Frankfurt/Main, Fischer, 1987, p. 114.

ended up with very light penalties or none at all. A clear bias against women — in the sense that fewer were acquitted *and* more executed — can only be detected in the trials conducted by the circuit courts in England.[55] However, England had relatively few executions. And of those that did take place, by no means all were ordered by the circuit courts.

Contrary to uninformed present-day opinion, the problem of witchcraft did not stand on its own. Rather, it formed part of a much larger complex of "spiritual" offenses that included heresy, apostasy and blasphemy, among others. All were considered to be crimes against God and religion, and all deserved to be punished as harshly as witchcraft. Consequently, witchcraft comprised only a small fraction of the cases brought before the Inquisition. In Venice, the figure amounted to just over 20 percent, and the vast majority of those involved received very light sentences, if any.[56] But whereas most of those accused of witchcraft were women, most of those charged with other spiritual offenses were men. Thus, the same qualities that caused women to be disproportionally indicted on charges of witchcraft — namely, their supposed lesser intelligence — often meant that they were not held accountable for related crimes. This is one reason why women accounted for only 10 percent of all those executed during the period in question. Indeed, far fewer women were executed for witchcraft than for those twin archetypical feminine crimes, infanticide and poisoning.[57]

In describing the witch-hunts, most historians have focused on the period from 1500 to 1650. However, this is misleading. Before 1350, nearly three times as many men as women were tried for witchcraft.[58] In northern France between 1351 and 1400, the number of defendants of both sexes was roughly equal.[59] For Europe as a whole, between 1300 and 1499 the number of accused men is said to have nearly equaled that of accused women.[60] In the Netherlands,

[55] J. K. Swales and Hugh V. McLachlan, "Witchcraft and the Status of Women: A Comment," *British Journal of Sociology*, 30, 3, September 1979, pp. 48-9.

[56] Ruth Martin, *Witchcraft and the Inquisition in Venice, 1550-1650*, Oxford, Blackwell, 1989, appendix, table 1.

[57] Wolfgang Behringer, "'Erhob sich das ganze Land zu ihrer Ausrottung...': Hexenprozesse und Hexenverfolgungen in Europa," in Dülmen, ed., *Hexenwelten*, p. 143. Also see Richard von Dülmen, *Frauen vor Gericht*, Frankfurt/Main, Fischer, 1990, p. 95.

[58] E. William Monter, *Witchcraft in France and Switzerland*, Ithaca, NY, 1976, p. 23.

[59] Muchembled, *La sorcière au village*, p. 176.

[60] Joseph Klaits, *Servants of Satan*, Bloomington, IN, Indiana University Press, 1985, p. 52; Peter Brown, "Sorcery, Demons and the Rise of Christianity from Late Antiquity to the Middle Ages," in Mary Douglas, ed., *Witchcraft Confessions and Accusations*, London, Tavistock, 1970, pp. 17-45.

"before the persecution of witches was seriously undertaken some authorities had already begun to punish cunning men."[61] In Finland, too, the older native traditions usually saw witches as men.[62] In the British Isles during the period in question, men comprised 59 percent of those accused. In the Swiss canton of Neuchatel they accounted for 80 percent and in Wallis 78 percent; in Switzerland as a whole, the figure was just under 50 percent.[63] Concentrating on the period from 1500 to 1650 also conceals the fact that subsequently in Germany the stereotype was reversed. Persons accused of witchcraft were no longer mainly old women, but mostly young men.[64]

Indeed, even the term "early modern period" as used in reference to witch-hunting is arbitrary. Both before and after that period the balance between males and females was quite different. The same is true about the term witchcraft itself. Had historians treated it in conjunction with other "spiritual" offenses, as contemporaries did, then the proportions of those people belonging to either sex who were either accused or executed would have shifted. Women believed in witchcraft just as much as men did. Their contribution to witch-hunting was as important as that of men. In certain respects it was more so. Very often it was women who decided that a particular individual should be accused of witchcraft, women who provided the evidence, and women who implicated others. In fact, it seems that the further removed from neighborhood disputes the male authority responsible for witch-hunting was — and therefore the fewer women were involved — the more fair the treatment witches were likely to receive.[65]

In short, no more than the fact that most present-day murderers are male proves that men are being hunted by matriarchy, does the fact that most early modern witches were female prove that patriarchy targeted women as women. If anything, it proves that when contemporaries said they were out to hunt and eradicate witches of both sexes, they meant what they said.

---

[61] Hans de Waardt and Willem de Blecourt, "'It Is No Sin To Put an Evil Person to Death,'" in Gijswijt-Hofstra and Frijhoff, eds., *Witchcraft in the Netherlands*, p. 69.

[62] Bengst Hennigsen and T. Kervinen, "Finland: The Male Domination," in Bengst Ankerloo and Gustav Henningsen, eds., *Early Modern European Witchcraft*, Oxford, Clarendon, 1990, pp. 31-8.

[63] Richard Kiekhefer, *European Witch Trials*, London, Routledge, 1976, pp. 100, 147; Monter, *Witchcraft in France and Switzerland*, p. 26.

[64] Behringer, "'Erhob sich das ganze Land zu ihrer Ausrottung…'", pp. 167-8.

[65] Larner, *Witchcraft and Religion: The Politics of Popular Belief*, p. 28.

4. Nazi Treatment of Women

The idea of presenting the Nazis as the oppressors of women *par excellence* goes back to Betty Friedan. In 1959 she attended a gathering of magazine editors, all of them male, who were discussing subjects that might interest American women. What she heard did not please her. "As I listened to them, a German phrase echoed in my mind — '*Kinder, Küche, Kirche*,' the phrase by which the Nazis decreed that women must once again be confined to their biological role."[66]

Friedan's accusation against the Nazis was taken up by some of the most important pioneers of modern feminism, including Kate Millett, Germaine Greer, Susan Brownmiller and Andrea Dworkin; Friedan herself repeated it in her memoirs.[67] These feminist scholars endeavored to prove that the Nazis persecuted women almost as much as they did homosexuals, gypsies, Jews and other "inferior" people. Others claimed that the Nazi idea of womanhood represented a form of "secondary racism."[68] Others still argued that anti-feminism was as basic a part of National Socialism as was anti-Semitism, save for the deadly results.[69] The fact that the Nazis constructed "polarized identities for males and females" and did not accept the feminist dogma about men and women being similar in every respect was said to be one of their worst misdeeds. In the Nazis' attitude toward women, one scholar even argued, lay "the roots of genocide."[70]

What was the real position of women in Nazi Germany? To answer this question, it is best to start by looking at German feminism before Adolf Hitler's rise to power in 1933. There were, as it so happens, a wide variety of feminist groups in Germany: a Catholic *Frauenbund*, a Protestant *Frauenbund*, as well as conservative, liberal, socialist, communist, colonial and Jewish *Frauenbünde*, to name but a few of the 230 or so women's organizations active

---

[66] Kate Millett, *Sexual Politics*, Garden City, NJ, Doubleday, 1970; Betty Friedan, *The Feminine Mystique*, New York, Del, 1983 [1963], p. 37.

[67] *The Female Eunuch*, New York, McGraw Hill, 1970, p. 302; Susan Brownmiller, *Against Our Will*, New York, Simon & Schuster, 1975, p. 394; Andrea Dworkin, *Scapegoat: The Jews, Israel and Women's Liberation*, New York, Virago, 2000, p. 30; Betty Friedan, *Life So Far*, New York, Simon & Schuster, 2000, p. 262.

[68] David Schoenbaum, *Die Braune Revolution: eine Sozialgeschichte des Dritten Reichs*, Berlin, Kippenheuer & Witsch, 1961, p. 426.

[69] Richard Grunberger, *The 12-Year Reich: A Social History of the Third Reich*, New York, Holt, Rinehart & Winston, 1971, p. 252.

[70] See Claudia Koonz, *Mothers in the Fatherland*, New York, St. Martin's, 1987, pp. 6, 17, 405.

at the time. Some were in favor of equal rights for women. Others opposed them in the name of motherhood and blamed the Weimar Republic for having enfranchised women. Some supported abortion rights, while others opposed them, and yet others advocated the compulsory sterilization of "unfit" persons.[71] Over time the socialist and liberal women's movements, which demanded equal rights for women, lost power and adherents, while those promoting motherhood grew in stature. By the final years of the Weimar Republic, the label "feminist" itself had become anathema to many women.[72]

The organization that claimed to speak for all the rest was the *Bund Deutscher Frauen* (BDF), a loose confederation of many different groups. Its head was Gertrude Bäumer, a veteran campaigner for women's rights.[73] Before 1914 she had opposed both abortion and contraception. In 1919 she helped rewrite the program of the BDF, injecting it with a right-wing, nationalist ideology. By 1932 the organization was advocating the abolition of democracy and the establishment of a corporate state modeled on fascist Italy. It called on women to help undo the consequences of the Great War, as World War I was then known, by having as many children as possible. Conversely, the societal ills allegedly associated with the Weimar Republic — sexual libertarianism, pornography, abortion and venereal diseases — were to be combated and defeated.

Much of what the BDF had to say found an echo with Hitler. The Nazi objective was to save women from being debauched at the hands of Jews, modernists, internationalists and other enemies of Germany. Healthy values were to be restored, and women would be judged primarily by the number of children they had given the Reich. The objective of girls' education should be to "prepare them for motherhood." Marriage was merely a means for "multiplying and maintaining the race." Childless women (and men) were regarded as harmful to the *Volk*, though ultimately the only measure taken against them was heavier taxation.[74] "By nature," a man was destined for the world, for society. "By nature," a woman was destined for her husband, her

[71]See Ann T. Allen, *Feminism and Motherhood in Germany, 1800-1914*, New Brunswick, NJ, Rutgers University Press, 1991, pp. 197, 201, 202.

[72] Christine Wittrock, *Weiblichkeits Mythen*, Frankfurt/Main, Sendler, 1984, pp. 81-4.

[73] See Richard J. Evans, *The Feminist Movement in Germany, 1894-1933*, London, Sage, 1976, pp. 157, 235, 237, 247.

[74] See Hans Peter Bleuel, *Sex and Society in Nazi Germany*, Philadelphia, Lippincott, 1973, pp. 26-8.

family, her children and her home.[75] Female intellectuals were, in the eyes of contemporaries, a pain in the neck. Like most people at the time, Hitler believed that women who did not have children would eventually become mentally ill.[76] His closest collaborators, including Arthur Rosenberg, Robert Ley, Gregor Strasser, and Gottfried Feder, agreed with him on this point. Women's main task was motherhood, and they had to be protected from having to work outside of the home.

How did the Nazis' views on women's place in society go down with German women? The answer is, perhaps surprisingly, better and better. From its very inception, the party succeeded in attracting women. Most were matrons who liked its fiery young leader. One, Countess von Reventlov, called Hitler "the coming Messiah." Others gave him expensive presents. As if to confirm Nietzsche's famous words, they even competed among themselves to see who could give him the most elaborate whip. One woman, whose name has since been lost to history, produced the first experimental design of the swastika flag.[77] Another woman, Gertrude von Seydlitz, raised the money needed to turn the Nazi newspaper *Der Völkischer Beobachter* into a daily. Other women financed Hitler's November 1923 Putsch. After it failed, it was a friend's wife, Helene Hanfstängel, who prevented Hitler from committing suicide, knocking a gun out of his hand and lecturing him on his duty to live for Germany. During his 13 months in prison he was visited by many women. As Hitler wrote in *Mein Kampf*, during this difficult period it was women who kept the Nazi Party from disintegrating. Indeed, even the paper on which Rudolf Hess took down the Führer's autobiography was provided by a woman, Winifred Wagner, the famed composer's daughter in law.

The Nazis were out to seize power, if not by actual violence then by "the conquest of the streets." As a result, Nazi women were probably *less* tied down to the traditional feminine role than in most other societies at the time. They marched, held meetings, raised money, distributed propaganda and faced hecklers. Others sewed uniforms for S.A men, bandaged their wounds and ran soup kitchens for them. In the decisive elections of 1930, 45 percent of Nazi voters were female. The voting pattern later became even more pronounced. Observers of Nazi rallies noted the way women always occupied the front

---

[75] 1934 speech to the National Socialist Women's Association, printed in Max Domarus, ed., *Hitler, Reden und Proklamationen 1932-1945*, Würzburg, Löwit, 1963-4, vol. 1, p. 449.

[76] Henry Picker, ed., *Hitlers Tischgespräche*, Stuttgart, Goldmann, 1963, p. 11, entry for 1.4.1942.

[77] Adolf Hitler, *Mein Kampf*, Mumbai, Jaico, 1988 [1924-6], p. 411.

rows.[78] Hitler's own basic belief was that women were governed by emotions, rather than by intellect, and that they reserved their greatest admiration for the strong. And he knew exactly how to talk to them. They, in turn, cheered him as loudly as anyone, often while weeping uncontrollably.

If anything, women's worship of Hitler intensified after 1933. The crowds that followed him wherever he went were made up partly of women. Other women made the pilgrimage to Berchtesgaden to give the Nazi salute or to hold out their children for him to touch. For his birthdays, women used to send him acres of scarves, pillow covers and blankets, all embroidered with swastikas of every size, color and variety. He, in turn, was careful not to disillusion them. Once he rhetorically asked a crowd of women what he had given them, and then answered his own question with "The Man."[79] It was for their sake that he remained single and kept secret the fact that he had a mistress. Nothing was allowed to disturb the love affair between German women and their Führer. And until the fall of Hitler and the Third Reich, nothing did.

Following the Nazis' rise to power, women's organizations saw their numbers swell. In 1933 alone, 800,000 new members joined the Nationalsozialistische Frauenschaft (NSF). Membership in the women's league eventually reached 3.5 million. It included some groups, such as domestic servants, who had previously been excluded and who were brought in against the wishes of "respectable" women. The NSF, like nearly all other organizations in the totalitarian Nazi state, wielded little real power. However, it received an enormous amount of funding, as well as substantial leeway in its own areas of activity. The NSF primarily focused on women's welfare and education, particularly the kind of education needed to raise the "racial quality" of the German people. State backing enabled the NSF to pursue its agenda on a scale seldom dreamt of by any women's organization before that time. Forty years later, the leader of the Frauenschaft, Gertrudee Scholz-Klink, was still proud of how she and her assistants, all female, had beaten the "feminists" at their own game, doing as they pleased without interference from men.[80]

Female opponents of the regime were often treated with kid gloves. During the "wild" early days of the Third Reich, only one woman was killed, the Social-Democrat Reichstag member Minna Cammens. Out of some 150 concentration camps built before World War II, just one, Möringen, housed women. It was only in 1938 that the regime carried out its first "legal"

---

[78] Herman Rauschning, *The Voice of Destruction*, New York, Putnam, 1940, p. 265.

[79] Quoted in Otto Strasser, *Hitler and I*, London, Cape, 1940, p. 78.

[80] Koonz, *Mothers in the Fatherland*, pp. xxiii-xxv.

execution of a female victim, the socialist Lieselotte Hermann. Accused of passing classified information to the headquarters of the banned German Communist Party in Switzerland, she was convicted of treason and guillotined along with three of her male colleagues. Certainly life in Ravensbrück, the main concentration camp for females, was far from a picnic. Still, it was not nearly as bad as in some of the camps. Indeed, some women were transferred to Ravensbrück from Auschwitz precisely because the mortality rate in the latter was deemed to be too high. Until the beginning of 1945, when deteriorating conditions led to severe malnutrition and outbreaks of infectious diseases, "only" around 3 percent of the women in Ravensbrück died each year.[81]

Meanwhile, the Nazis began pursuing their dream of creating a pure Aryan race by instituting a series of practical measures designed to encourage women to marry, stay at home and have children. Symbolic measures directed toward the same end were also enacted, such as the celebration of Mother's Day and the awarding of medals to fertile women. Some of these measures either antedated Nazi Germany or were not unique to it. Others, such as child allowances and tax deductions for families with children, were part of the contemporary, near-universal drive toward a welfare state. To assist working mothers while at the same time alleviating female unemployment, the regime permitted taxpayers to deduct a certain sum for child care.[82] This privilege was retained when the Federal Republic of Germany was established in 1949. In the United States, by contrast, it was only introduced into law by the Reagan administration.

Perhaps the best-known Nazi incentive for mothers to settle down and have a family was marriage loans. At the time, a similar measure was adopted in Social-Democratic Sweden. Provided both mother and father were of Aryan stock, a German couple was eligible for a loan if the bride undertook not to take up paid work for two years after the wedding. For each child a quarter of the sum was written off. Later the demand that the woman not work was quietly dropped so that all mothers enjoyed the benefit.

Then there was the *Lebensborn* Institute, a unique type of Nazi welfare organization aimed specifically at women. At the time and later, rumor described the Institute as a stud farm where unmarried women could be impregnated by S.S men. Its real mission was much more prosaic. S.S commander Heinrich Himmler's views were pro-life, provided that the life in

[81] Grit Philipp, *Kalendarium der Ereignisse im Frauen-Konzentrationslager Ravensbrück, 1939-1945*, Berlin, Metropol, 1999, pp. 103, 107, 150, 180.

[82] Reimer Voss, *Steuern im Dritten Reich*, Munich, Beck, 1995, p. 80.

question should be Germanic and free of heritable diseases. One objective of the *Lebensborn* institutes was to offer suitably Aryan pregnant women an alternative to abortion. Another goal, according the S.S. leader, was to remove some of the stigma that "ridiculous blockheads" had imposed on single mothers in Germany. The association provided the women with temporary shelter at extremely cheap rates. Mothers-to-be spent the last weeks of pregnancy at *Lebensborn* institutes under medical supervision, then gave birth, recovered and obtained basic training in how to care for a baby.

Most Nazi measures aimed at helping mothers proved to be immensely popular. The leader of the Catholic German Women's Association, Antoine Hoppman, called them "a stroke of genius."[83] Less popular, but still acceptable to the vast majority of women, were the negative aspects of Hitler's policies. Along with a considerable portion of contemporary public opinion in Germany and abroad, the Fuehrer saw women as delicate creatures unsuited for the rough and tumble world of politics.[84] He detested lawyers in particular. While realizing that he could not do without them, he never stopped calling lawyers "traitors," "idiots" and "absolute cretins." The idea that women should be sheltered from the seamier side of law and politics led to the dismissal of female politicians, senior civil servants and judges, as well as the professional disqualification of some 300 female lawyers. These measures were supported both by the head of the Nazi Women's Association — who rejoiced in Hitler's promise to liberate women *from* work[85] — and by the *grande dame* of German feminism, Gertrude Bäumer.[86] In any case, they only affected about 1 percent of all working women. And most of those who lost their jobs, including female school principals, were transferred to other positions. The rest received full pensions.[87]

Nazi beliefs concerning women in academia resembled those held by contemporaries all over the developed world at that time. Such beliefs began with the argument that women were by nature creatures of emotion rather than of intellect, and as such were less suitable for academic life than were men.

---

[83] Koonz, *Mothers in the Fatherland*, p. 278.

[84] See Dörte Winkler, *Frauenarbeit im Dritten Reich*, Hamburg, Hoffman and Campe, 1977, pp. 187.

[85] Clifford Kirkpatrick, *Nazi Germany: Its Women and Its Family Life*, New York, Bobbs-Merrill, 1938, p. 207; Hilde Browing, *Women under Fascism and Communism*, London, Lawrence, 1943, p. 9.

[86] Gertrude Bäumer, *Des Lebens wie der Liebe Band*, Tübingen, Wunderlich, 1956, p. 135.

[87] Winkler, *Frauenarbeit im Dritten Reich*, pp. 49-50.

Women in academia were also believed to be far more likely than their male colleagues to be unhappy and fall prey to mental illness. And female scholars were understood to be far less likely to get married or have children, than non-academic ones. The first two beliefs could not be statistically proven. However, the third certainly could be.[88] Absent comprehensive figures concerning the fate of female academics during the Third Reich, those originating in the University of Hamburg are instructive. When the Nazis came to power there were 22 women in a faculty of 330 academics. Of those 22, seven lost their jobs — but not because of their gender. Five owed their misfortune — the term being used relatively here, as four of the five were able to leave the country and thereby escape the Holocaust — to the fact that they were Jewish. Of the other two, one committed suicide rather than accept a transfer, and the second resigned rather than join the Nazi Party. At most, one woman may have been dismissed simply because she was a woman, and even in her case the exact cause for dismissal is not clear.[89]

In December 1933, the Nazis took their one and only measure against female students by establishing a *numerus clausus* of 10 percent for women. Once again Bäumer supported the decree. Earlier in her career she had made her name as perhaps the most effective proponent of female higher education in Germany.[90] Now she felt that declining standards called for a partial retreat. In any case, in February 1935 the decree was rescinded. Thus the only female students affected were those in the graduating class of 1934. And even those women could earn retroactive credit, provided they wanted to and provided they had been registered with the university as "listeners."

By the outbreak of the World War II, the policy of steering women away from faculties considered unsuitable for them, such as law and political science, had actually led to a substantial *increase* in the proportion of female students in "practical" fields such as pharmacy, physical education and journalism.[91] By that time, too, the government had started paying female students who gave birth — whether married or not — a "delivery allowance" of 50 Reichsmark.

[88] Calculated from Charlotte Grätz-Menzel, "Über die rassenideologische Wirkung der akademischen Frauenberufe mit besonderer Berücksichtigung der Ärztinnen und Zahnärztinnen," *Archiv für Rassen- and Gesellschaftsbiologie*, 27, 1933, p. 143, table 10.

[89] Astrid Dageförde, "Frauen an der Hamburger Universität 1933 bis 1945: Emanzipation oder Repression?" in Eckart Krause, ed., *Hochschulalltag im "Dritten Reich,"* Berlin, Reimer, 1991, pp. 256-7.

[90] James C. Albisetti, *Schooling German Girls and Women: Secondary and Higher Education in the Nineteenth Century*, Princeton, NJ, Princeton University Press, 1988, pp. 222-3.

[91] Bleuel, *Sex and Society in Nazi Germany*, p. 67.

That was a privilege never equaled in any country before or since. From 1939 to 1944 the proportion of students who were female went up seven-fold, reaching 49.3 percent of the total student body. Many women at the time took the opportunity to enter nontraditional fields. Women came to dominate the natural sciences, rising from 10.8 percent to 63.5 percent of all students. In engineering and technology, the rise was from 0.7 percent to 11.7 percent, while in medicine women's representation more than doubled, to 35 percent. In law, the jump was more than six-fold, from 2.5 percent to 16.4 percent.[92] By the end of the war medicine had become women's favored field of study, even surpassing the humanities. If there ever was a regime that did *not* "steer" its female students toward the "softer" subjects of the humanities, it was the Nazi Party during the final years of World War II.

In 1933, proportionally far more German women worked than their American counterparts.[93] At the time Germany, like the rest of the world, was suffering from the Great Depression. One widely adopted solution to the problem of unemployment was dismissing women in double-income families. Austria, Belgium, Britain, France, Italy, Luxembourg, the Netherlands, Spain, Sweden and the United States all either passed similar measures or contemplated them. In Germany, the only such bill that made it into the books was passed not by Adolf Hitler, but by Weimar-era chancellor Heinrich Brüning. That law had little effect, and few women lost their jobs. Within a year of the Nazi's rise to power, attempts to implement it had ended.

By this time whatever ideological reservations the Nazis may have had concerning the presence of women in the labor force had vanished. As early as 1932, Joseph Goebbels noted that the Führer regarded woman as the "comrade" of man at work. "That's how it has always been, and that's how it will ever be... Man is the organizer of life, woman his helpmate and right hand."[94] At a later date, he added that, "we would be fools not to draw on women in the common task of building our nation."[95] As the Nazis' other measures against unemployment began to bear fruit, the number of women paying social

[92] Jacques R. Pauwels, *Women, Nazis and Universities*, Westport, CT, Greenwood, 1984, pp. 101-5; also see Michael H. Kater, *Doctors Under Hitler*, Chapel Hill, NC, University of North Carolina Press, 1989, p. 99.

[93] Koonz, *Mothers in the Fatherland*, p. 45.

[94] Joseph Goebbels, *Vom Kaiserhof zur Reichskanzlei*, Munich, Zentralverlag der NDSAP, 1939, p 72.

[95] 1932 speech, quoted in Werner Siebert, *Hitlers Wollen, nach Kernsätzen aus seinen Schriften und Reden*, Munich, Zentralverlag der NSDAP, 1937, p. 105.

insurance rose from 4.6 million in 1932 to 4.75 million in 1933 and 5.05 million in 1934.[96] By the late 1930s, a larger percentage of German women were economically active than in any other European country except France.[97] As in other countries, the nature of women's participation in the labor force changed. Increasingly they were drawn into white-collar occupations such as secretarial work, communications, commerce and the professions.[98] As has been said, "five years of Nazi rule in some ways did more to help professional women than a decade of feminist pressure in the Weimar Republic."[99]

As in other countries, German women during the Nazi period earned less than their male colleagues. As in other countries, the main reasons were the reluctance of their families to invest in their professional education, as well as their own tendency to drift in and out of the labor force with interruptions for childbirth and other family obligations. On the other hand, the authorities in the Third Reich tried harder to protect women than their opposite numbers in any other country did. One law prohibited employers from requiring women to work on pedal-operated machinery. Others prohibited women from working underground, dealing with poisonous materials or carrying heavy weights. Nor could they be employed on shift work or night work. In the late 1930s, however, a shortage of labor forced German employers to woo their female employees. As a result, their wages rose faster than those of men. Women began receiving equal wages with men in industries such as textiles, mines, metal, electronics and bricks. Of this achievement, the *Arbeitsfront*, the Nazi trade union, was very proud.[100] There were also arrangements designed to help working women, including special facilities for mothers at work, a "birth premium" and a "breastfeeding premium," as well as free nursing services, medical treatment and medicine. Many proved so advanced that they remained part of German law long after 1945.

The man in charge of Germany's economic preparations for war was Hermann Göring. Among other measures, he developed plans for registering women for compulsory labor. It was to no avail, however, as hundreds of thousands of women found ways of avoiding it. From 1940 onward, other key

---

[96] *Statistisches Jahrbuch des Deutschen Reiches, 1935*, Berlin, 1935, p. 474.

[97] Renate Bridenthal, "Something Old, Something New: Women between the Two World Wars," in Bridenthal and Koonz, eds., *Becoming Visible*, p. 426, table 18-1.

[98] Winkler, *Frauenarbeit im Dritten Reich*, pp. 55, 64-5; Bleuel, *Sex and Society in Nazi Germany*, p. 63.

[99] Evans, *German Feminism*, p. 263.

[100] Winkler, *Frauenarbeit im Dritten Reich*, p. 74.

leaders of the economy and of industry exercised pressure in the same direction. Again, it was to no avail. As Hitler told his plenipotentiary for labor, Fritz Sauckell, "long-limbed" German women were not suited for heavy labor. They could do such work only at very great physical expense and psychological hardship. As he saw it, during World War I the state had failed to protect women. It caused them to undergo "untold suffering," which in turn damaged morale and contributed to defeat. That was an error Hitler vowed he would not repeat. Furthermore, if only because this was something their uniform-wearing "husbands, fiancées, fathers and brothers had a right to expect," "at all costs" working women had to be defended against "maltreatment, overburdening, insults or moral damage." Unfortunately, the war did not permit for protecting women to the full extent appropriate. But looking forward, "the goal remained to ensure that, in 20 years' time, no woman would be obliged to work in a factory."[101]

Social reality reflected these views. With millions of men called up and unable to help women carry out their domestic tasks, between October and December 1939 the number of working women declined by 300,000. By May 1941 there were 500,000 fewer women in the workforce than in May 1939. One reason for this was that German provisions for maintaining the families of members of the armed forces were much more generous than those of other countries. In October 1939, a law was passed which explicitly permitted soldiers' wives to stop working. A British wife with two children received 38 percent of her absent husband's income, while an American one received 36 percent. Their German sisters, by contrast, got 75 percent. Alone among all the belligerents of World War II, Germany provided pensions to the fiancées of fallen soldiers and also to the mothers of their illegitimate children.[102]

Later during the war, the trend toward a smaller female labor force reversed itself. However, the vast majority of newly employed women found work in public administration, where their numbers rose from 954,000 in May 1939 to 1,746,000 in 1943.[103] Proportionally, there were fewer German women than Allied women tasked with heavy work in factories, mines and transportation. And for those who did such labor, conditions were relatively good. In the United States in 1943, 50 percent of all employed women worked night shifts; in Germany, the restrictions against women working late hours were only lifted in January 1944. Germany also provided far more subsidized kindergarten

[101] See Winkler, *Frauenarbeit im Dritten Reich*, pp. 110-9.

[102] Bleuel, *Sex and Society in Nazi Germany*, p. 155.

[103] Winkler, *Frauenarbeit im Dritten Reich*, p. 123.

places for children of working women than did either the United States or Britain.[104]

Another reason why German women had it easier in some ways than their sisters elsewhere was the use of foreign slave laborers. The relative comforts that German women enjoyed during the war were partly due to the exploitation of both women and men. There were an estimated 10,000,000 male slave laborers toiling for the Third Reich. Working in mines and factories, they died like flies. There were also an estimated 2,000,000 female slave laborers. Nearly all these women were taken from the east; the Germans in the occupied west did not forcibly take women, as they did men. Of the 2 million female laborers, several hundred thousand were brought in specifically to assist German women whose menfolk had been drafted.

While most German women enjoyed the perks of their position, the regime went to considerable lengths to promote and publicize the exploits of a few particularly industrious women, as examples for the rest of society. The best known of them, Leni Riefenstahl, produced the most famous propaganda films ever made for a political movement. Meanwhile, at a time when British and American women were only permitted to fly aircraft on transport missions behind the front, at least three German women became test pilots. One, Hanna Reitsch, flew the world's first helicopter. Another, Melitta Schiller, flew no fewer than 1,500 missions testing Stuka dive-bombers, as well as test flying the world's earliest jet and rocket planes. A third test pilot who flew jets and rockets was Flight Captain Beate Köstlin. After the war, when she was known as Beate Uhse, she became rich and famous by establishing a very successful company dealing in pornography and sexual aids.

How did German women confront the more criminal measures of the Nazi regime? The answer is that, to the extent that they had the opportunity, they supported such measures. Some *Frauenbünde* began expelling their Jewish members even before they were officially required to.[105] Later the leaders of the NSF spent considerable energy educating women on the need to maintain racial purity. And as previously mentioned, some *Frauenbünde* long favored compulsory sterilization. Since the sterilization program depended almost entirely on denunciation, women were found both among the informers and in the service of the police. During the war, 40 percent of Gestapo personnel in

[104] Leila J. Rupp, *Mobilizing Women for War: German and American Propaganda, 1939-1945*, Princeton, NJ, Princeton University Press, 1978, p. 171.

[105] Koonz, *Mothers in the Fatherland*, pp. 161, 246.

Vienna, and perhaps in other cities as well, were female.[106] Often the proceedings were initiated by female social workers who visited women in their homes.

Female doctors helped examine candidates for sterilization and carried out some of the operations. Others performed compulsory abortions on female concentration camp inmates.[107] Female nurses killed thousands of mentally and physically handicapped people, of all ages. Women, most of them lower class but including some middle class ones as well, comprised 10 percent of concentration camp guards. Surviving inmates remembered them as being particularly vicious. At Auschwitz, female guards were known to crowd around peepholes to watch as gas chambers were filled with cyanide and the victims entered their death throes.[108] At Ravensbrück, a female doctor, Herta Oberheuser, carried out horrific medical experiments on female inmates.[109] She was not the only Nazi doctor to do so.

In summary, early on certain Nazi leaders had peculiar ideas concerning women's place in society. This did not prevent women from working for the Party, campaigning for it, and increasingly voting for it. Later on, far from attacking feminism, Hitler adopted the goals of many of its leaders, from Bäumer on down. He saw German women as the most precious asset of the *Volk*, an asset that had to be protected "at all cost." This protection had both negative and positive repercussions. The negative aspects affected only a very small number of women, mainly in the civil service, academia and the legal profession. Even so, by 1945 far *more* women were studying law than in 1933. In all other respects, Nazi policy was expressly designed to help women in the field most of them had long considered their primary occupation, motherhood. Many of the relevant measures resembled those instituted by other countries during this period. Most received high praise from German women. Perhaps the only exception was *Lebensborn*, which was surrounded by all kinds of unsavory legends. Its real fault, though, was that it threatened to erase the distinction between pregnant women who had husbands and those who did not.

As in other countries, the Nazis tried to overcome unemployment by firing women in double-income families. However, the attempt was half-hearted and went nowhere. Earlier than in other countries, once the Depression was over the

---

[106] Franz Weiss, "Die Personelle Zusammensetzung der Führungskräfte der Wiener Gestapoleitstelle zwischen 1938 und 1945," *Zeitgeschichte*, 20, 7-8, 1993, p. 247.

[107] Philipp, *Kalendarium*, pp. 101, 122, 123.

[108] Koonz, *Mothers in the Fatherland*, p. 404-5.

[109] Kater, *Doctors under Hitler*, p. 110.

Nazis started encouraging women to take up paid employment. Less than in other countries during World War II were German women compelled to enter the labor force. More than in other countries, those who did enter the labor force were mostly employed in white-collar work. Meanwhile it was non-German slave laborers, men and women, who did arduous work in the fields and factories. German women were protected by various laws and regulations. They also enjoyed benefits, such as allowances and subsidized kindergartens, which would have been the envy of their non-German sisters. No wonder most German women retained their loyalty to Hitler to the very end. Far from being persecuted, to the extent that they were permitted to they cooperated in persecuting others.

5. Conclusions

These three myths are but a few of the many modern feminists have spun to "prove" men's oppression of women. A detailed examination has shown that all three are false. As best we can tell, ancient Greek women were *not* secluded, either to the home or inside it. The witch craze of the period between 1500 and 1650 was *not* simply a mechanism invented by patriarchy to control women who did not stay in their place. Among other things, it was often used by women to get at other women, which may be one reason why the majority of witches were female. Finally, had the Nazis set out to oppress German women, they would scarcely have attracted German women's enthusiastic support. Rather, Nazi policy was mainly designed to help women perform what they *and* their own leaders had long considered their principal task, namely motherhood. In many ways the policy succeeded in doing exactly that, both in its own right and in comparison to other countries. As the Nazis themselves pointed out, for the implementation of racial policies, women's cooperation with National Socialism was at least as important as that of men.

In many other cases, too, the notion that female-hating men have discriminated against women, oppressed them and subordinated them is a myth. In fact, very often the opposite is the case. In many ways, both society and nature have conspired to make women's lives easier than those of men. Far from being discriminated against, in many ways women have been and still are exempt from many of the burdens placed on men. This is true from the moment they are born to the moment they die, to say nothing of the longer lives they lead in between. To convince him or herself of these truths, all the reader has to do is to peruse the pages that follow.

Chapter 2: Masculinity and its Troubles

1. The Forgotten Sex

In the wide body of feminist literature, no accusation is more frequently found than the claim that men tend to treat themselves, and are themselves treated, as the standard sex against which women are measured. This claim is not without some basis in fact. In many languages, the term "man" is a synonym for "human being." However, there is another side to the coin. Precisely because men *are* considered, and consider themselves, standard, being female is to be put into a niche which is seen as particularly interesting. Conversely, being male often means that, *as a man*, one is taken for granted and one's very existence is ignored. A search at the Library of Congress will show that books with the word "women" in their titles outnumber those with "men" 12 to one. At Amazon.com, there are four times as many "women's guides" as men's. On the same website, books on "women" and "exercise" outnumber those concerned with men nearly five to one.

Possibly because so many women do not enjoy sex, the staple fare of sexology is said to be the "narrative of the (female) orgasm." By contrast, "there is little literary concern for the male's orgasmic experience."[1] A major work on female psychology was published by Helene Deutsch in 1944 and remained the standard for several decades. Since then it has been followed by those of Nancy Chodorow and Carol Gilligan (both 1989), among others. However, to this day there is no equally authoritative work on that of men. It is as if male-specific psychological problems do not exist. Similarly, in the field of education, the body of material on the special needs of girls can only be called staggering. But when it comes to those of boys, the silence is almost deafening. As one female historian has written, given that there is no book on

[1] William H. Masters and Virginia E. Johnson, *Human Sexual Response*, St. Louis, MO, Reproductive Biology Research Foundation, 1966, p. 217; also Andy Metcalf and Martin Humphries, eds., *The Sexuality of Men*, London, Pluto, 1985, p. 49.

ancient Egyptian men, a reader might question the justification of writing one on ancient Egyptian women.[2] Needless to say, that observation did not prevent said female historian from going right ahead with the book.

In part, the neglect of men may be traced to institutional arrangements that discriminate against them. Before the advent of so-called "second-wave feminism" around 1970, this was because men were taken for granted. What everybody knows, or believes he or she knows, does not need to be studied. Since then it has been done by design, as part of the campaign against "patriarchy," which threatens to turn any attempt to focus on men's needs and men's requirements into a court case. Whenever fewer women than men study a subject, then this fact is immediately seen as a problem. However, when fewer men take up a subject than women, as is the situation in fields such as foreign languages, most of the liberal arts, and some of the social sciences, nobody seems to care. As one author has written,[3] a visitor from outer space exploring our libraries and our academic life might be excused for concluding that there exists only one gender: the female one.

This chapter will argue that, in fact, becoming and being a man is *much* harder than becoming and being a woman. I start with a brief summary of the bio-psychological basis of the problem from the moment of conception on. Next, I examine the way men compete for and support women, as well as some of the consequences of their failing to do so. Next I show the way society, claiming to prepare young men for the greater burdens that they will have to carry as adults, makes their lives harder still. The last section sums up these problems and explains how, on top of everything else, men are prohibited from talking to others about these very same problems.

2. The Bio-Psychological Basis

Why has nature created two sexes instead of one? Today most biologists would answer that the function of sexual reproduction is to enable each generation to create new life.[4] Life is seen as a process of deterioration, as some genes undergo spontaneous mutation and develop anomalies. Others suffer damage from ultra-violet light. By recombining two strands of DNA, each of them

---

[2] Gay Robins, *Women in Ancient Egypt*, London, British Museum Press, 1993, p. 11.

[3] Terrell Carver, *Gender Is Not a Synonym for Women*, Boulder, CO, Riener, 1996.

[4] See R. E. Michod, *Eros and Evolution: A Natural Philosophy of Sex*, Reading, MA, Helix, 1998, chapter 6.

originating in a different parent, sex causes the errors to be canceled out, much as one can make a new car by dismantling two wrecks and joining the undamaged parts from both.

To form a new organism, two sex cells, each with half the normal number of chromosomes, must merge. Next, sufficient nutrition must be provided to carry the zygote through the earliest phase of life. In theory, the two requirements could be met by two cells coming from two different organisms, each of which is equally mobile (for seeking out the other) and equally nutritious. This solution, known as isogamy, is found in certain mushrooms. However, it is like building an aircraft that is both a transport plane and a high-performance fighter. The resulting hybrid is unlikely to fill either function very well. Like aircraft, the overwhelming majority of sexually reproducing species have developed differently. Some of the parent organisms produce small, mobile sex cells (sperm) and are known as males. Others produce larger, less mobile but more nutritious cells (eggs) and are known as females.

It is the female that is the primary sex. He exists to service her, not the other way around. Since the blueprint of every fetus is either female or sexually undifferentiated, the Bible got it wrong. Males are built on a female chassis, so to speak. To be formed into a male organism requires an extraordinary event: namely, the appearance from somewhere of a Y chromosome that will trigger the process. Otherwise the zygote, taking the path of least resistance, will develop into a female.[5] Nor is conception the end of the story. In many species, such as turtles and crocodiles, the sex of the young is determined by the temperature at which the eggs are incubated. Here, too, nature is said to show "a striking female bias."[6] With humans, even though a Y chromosome is present, hormonal disturbances can still result in the baby looking and behaving like a female. So hard is it to become a male that, in all species for which information is available, once the sex of the fetus is determined, more males than females are aborted.[7]

Biologically speaking, becoming female is taking the path of least resistance. Since society permits girls to follow straight in their mothers'

---

[5] Jared Diamond, *Why is Sex Fun? The Evolution of Human Sexuality*, London, Weidenfeld & Nicolson, 1997, p. 41.

[6] E. H. Herre et al., "Sex Allocation in Animals," in S. C. Searns, ed., *The Evolution of Sex and Its Consequences*, Basel, Birkhäuser, 1987, p. 222; also David Crews, "The Organizational Concept and Vertebrates Without Sex Chromosomes," *Brain Behavior and Evolution*, 42, 1993, pp. 202-14.

[7] I. Waldron, "What Do We Know about the Causes of Sex Differences in Mortality?" *Population Bulletin of the United Nations*, 18, 1986, pp. 59-76.

footsteps, psychologically speaking becoming female also means taking the path of least resistance. Like girls, boys are born to women and spend the first years of childhood under their care. Unlike girls, boys must at some point renounce their mothers, start identifying with their fathers and grow into men. This may be because the father threatens them with castration, as Freud thought. Or it may be because the mother is seen as big and threatening.[8] Or, as some feminists have claimed, it may be because boys, forced to witness the sufferings their fathers inflict on their mothers, will do whatever it takes not to share them.[9] One way or another, men labor under an Oedipus complex. On pain of remaining forever in a state of childhood, they must resolve it; doing so may be the hardest thing they are called on to do in their lives.

Since a single male can impregnate a very large number of females, the great majority of males are not needed to begin with. Once they have donated their sperm, they are needed even less. All this suggests, in the words of one biologist, that males are nature's way of creating additional females, and a rather wasteful one at that.[10] In reality, all that is needed are a syringe and a few cubic centimeters of semen. Should current experiments with fertilizing eggs with DNA taken from other eggs be extended from mice to humans, soon we will not even need that. The fact that the necessary techniques were invented by men merely adds offense to injury. It is as if each time men try to help women along, men only make themselves *more* superfluous.

Male dispensability is most obvious in the case of the mantis and the black spider. The females of these species actually eat the males even as they copulate with them. In addition to donating his sperm, the male also gives away the rest of his protein. Where mammals are concerned, nature's solutions are less radical and less deadly. However, the same principles apply. Whether male animals understand their own dispensability, we do not yet understand. Yet the spectacle of young males of some mammals, such as baboons and zebras, sacrificing themselves to defend females and their young suggests that, at some level, they do. Among humans the fact that "man is the unfruitful animal," in the word of Friedrich Nietzsche, is evident to all. In many cultures, it is

---

[8] Nancy J. Chodorow, *Feminism and Psychoanalytic Theory*, New Haven, CT, Yale University Press, 1989, pp. 32-41; Walter Ong, *Fighting for Life*, Ithaca, NY, Cornell University Press, 1973, p. 71.

[9] Andrea Dworkin, *Pornography: Men Possessing Women*, New York, Plume, 1991, pp. 49-51.

[10] Michod, *Eros and Evolution*, p. 41; Diamond, *Why is Sex Fun?* p. 46.

hammered in from infancy on. Even as children, girls are told they will one day have babies, whereas boys are told they must become men.[11]

As if to confirm this line of argument, a society consisting solely of women is not only conceivable but has often been conceived.[12] Consider the myth of the ancient Amazons. For our purposes, the most important "fact" about them was not that they were warriors "equivalent to men" and capable of fighting and conquering them. Rather, it is that they lived on their own without men. Just how they managed to do this and still have offspring was the subject of several legends, most of them dating to a comparatively late period.[13] So powerful was the impact of the Amazon legend on people's imagination that it led to countless imitations. Thus, Mary E. Bradley in *Mizora* (1890) describes a world of blond, powerful, Brunhildes whose discovery of "the Secret of Life" permitted them to eliminate all men.[14] In Charlotte Perkins Gilman's *Herland* (1915), women, having somehow rid themselves of "their brutal [male] conquerors," lead an isolated life on an Amazonian plateau. At first they expected their race would perish, owing to a lack of offspring. But thanks to some unforeseen miracle, not only did they start reproducing by parthenogenesis, the resulting offspring consisted solely of females.[15]

The second wave of feminism in the 1960s and 1970s generated a fresh crop of such tales. In Joanna Russ' *The Female Man* (1975),[16] most men were killed by a mysterious disease that affected only their gender. The rest were dispatched by Jaël, a man-hating fury with retractable steel fingernails. Children were created by bringing ova together. In *The Wanderground* (1978), Sally Gearhart achieved the same feat by "implantment" and "egg merging." Children had the good fortune of being brought up not by one mother but by seven.[17] Other women's utopias suggest that children be brought up by machines, so as to leave their mothers free to attend to their own spiritual development. In fact, it is not impossible that one day the sperm-less

[11] Margaret Mead, *Male and Female: A Study of the Sexes in a Changing World*, New York, Mentor, 1949, pp. 68, 72-3.

[12] See Frances Bartowski, *Feminist Utopias*, Lincoln, NE, University of Nebraska Press, 1989.

[13] See Josine H. Blok, *The Early Amazons: Modern and Ancient Perspectives on a Persistent Myth*, Leiden, Brill, 1995, pp. 155 ff., 167, 173, 223 ff.

[14] New York, Dillingham, 1890.

[15] Reprinted New York, Pantheon, 1979.

[16] New York, Bantam.

[17] Watertown, MA, Persephone.

fertilization of eggs — based on triggering the genetic code present in any cell of the body — will become a reality.[18]

Until such advances are realized, it might occur to women to keep a few men around in cages for the purpose of reproduction, as well as for sexual enjoyment. Gearhart suggested that they be limited to 10 percent of the population. Monique Wittig, for her part, was prepared to let a few men live.[19] Provided, that is, they accepted a feminist society of primitive communism, laid no claim to any children they might beget, and wore their hair long. Other feminist visionaries suggested that men be given injections to induce lactation, or else be taught a Pavlov-like response to "the sweet pealing of bells" so as to produce an erection on demand.[20]

Male writers, by contrast, have hardly ever sought to rid the world of women, partly because they realized that women are indispensable and partly because they liked them so much. Men's greater need for women may be a function of the reproductive mechanism itself.[21] The difference in size between egg and cell varies, but the egg is always far bigger, six to twelve orders of magnitude bigger, and sometimes even more. Hence each egg requires the female to make a vastly greater investment than each spermatozoid requires from the male. This applies even if one calculates in terms of complete ejaculations. A human male during his lifespan can ejaculate thousands of times. However, a woman will only ovulate some 400 times. Of those eggs, only a small proportion will be fertilized, whereas the rest will be lost in a natural way. The largest number of children known to have been begot by a single man, an early 19th-century king of Morocco by the name of Ismail the Bloodthirsty, is 700, daughters not included. But no woman on record ever had more than 69 children; the lady in question was a Russian who specialized in triplets.[22]

Add the need to gestate the new organism, and the difference becomes so vast that it can hardly even be calculated. Most healthy men short of middle age

---

[18] Marc Goldstein, "Of Babies and the Barren Man," *Scientific American*, 10, 2, summer 1999, p. 79.

[19] Sally M. Gaerhart, "The Future—If There Is One—Is Female," in Pam McAllister, ed, *Reweaving the Web of Life*, Philadelphia, New Society, 1982, pp. 266-84.

[20] Marge Piercy, *Woman on the Edge of Time*, New York, Knopf, 1976; Nelly Kaplan, "Husbands, I Salute You," in Françoise Thébaud et al., eds., *A History of Women in the West*, Cambridge, MA, Bellknap, 1994, vol. 5, pp. 595-7.

[21] Robert L. Trivers, "Parental Investment and Sexual Selection," in Bernhard G. Campbell, ed., *Sexual Selection and the Descent of Man*, Chicago, Aldine, 1972, pp. 136-79.

[22] Diamond, *Why Is Sex Fun?*, p. 38.

can have sex at least once a day, possibly leading to additional offspring. Each time a woman has sex, however, there is a chance that she will become pregnant. Once she does, her ability to conceive will be out of action for at least nine months. Even after delivery has taken place, the mother will remain infertile for as long as she lactates. Depending on the society, that period can last from a few months to three years. The relatively small number of times she can conceive during her lifetime, and her vast investment in each child both before and after birth, give her the strongest possible interest to ensure that each one will survive and grow to maturity. This causes women to be "stingy with their vaginas," as tribal wisdom in Papua-New Guinea puts it.[23] Experiments show that men are much more ready to seek pleasure in the arms of strangers.[24] The same applies to the males of other mammalian species.[25]

Society's arrangement for regulating sexual behavior is known as marriage. However, marriage means different things for people of each sex. As proven by both surveys and the existence in Western societies of an immense industry surrounding brides, women who marry are following their inclinations and fulfilling their dreams.[26] Not so men, who have little to gain by an arrangement whose purpose is to limit them to one or, in non-Western societies, a few women; and who might indeed stand a better chance of evolutionary survival if they remained single. The imbalance explains why a magazine entitled *Groom* and devoted to selling top hats and striped pants has not yet been invented. Instead, we witness stag parties that provide a last fling at sexual freedom; or, in the form of a stripper, a third-rate imitation of it.

Much has been written about female fear of intercourse and the physical and mental consequences that may follow if initiation is not carried out as it should. This is to overlook the other side of the coin, which is no less important.[27] In having sex, as in so much else, a woman is permitted to participate passively. Indeed, in most societies women were traditionally

---

[23] See David D. Gilmore, *Manhood in the Making: Cultural Concepts of Masculinity*, New Haven, CT, Yale University Press, 1990, p. 85; Thomas Gregor, *Anxious Pleasures: The Sexual Lives of an Amazonian People*, Chicago, Chicago University Press, 1985, pp. 200-1.

[24] See Natalie Angier, *Woman: An Intimate Geography*, New York, Anchor, 1999, p. 367.

[25] R. P. Michael and D. Zumpe, "Potency in Male Rhesus Monkeys: Effects of Continuously Receptive Females," *Science*, 200, 1978, pp. 451-3.

[26] Arland Thornton and Deborah Freedman, "Changing Attitudes Toward Marriage and Single Life," *Family Planning Perspectives*, 14, November-December 1982, pp. 297-303.

[27] See Ethel Person, "The Omni-Available Woman," in Gerald I. Fogel et al., eds., *The Psychology of Men*, New Haven, CT, Yale University Press, 1996, pp. 82-3; Roger Horrocks, *Male Myths and Icons: Masculinity in Popular Culture*, New York, St. Martin's, 1995, pp. 9, 14-5, 18.

required to do so; any movement on her part was considered unladylike, and liable to decrease the chance of conception. Not so men, who are expected to perform and without whose performance the act cannot take place at all. As Betty Friedan, a self-proclaimed "bitch" not otherwise known for her solicitude for men, wrote in her memoirs: "It would be terrible to have that pressure [of getting it up] all the time."[28] The result is that men approach the first encounter, and by no means only the first one, with fear and trepidation. Wishing to avoid contempt, they cannot admit ignorance to people of either sex. Often they are driven to lie about their level of experience.

Focusing all its attention on the difficulties faced by girls, modern society demands that boys cope on their own. Not so previous ones, which paid much attention to the problem and tried to deal with it in ways which, however misguided they may seem to some of us, at any rate show that it was taken seriously.[29] Often they made special arrangements for young men. In some societies, boys received instruction from their elders, as among Orthodox Jews to the present day.[30] In other cultures, boys were initiated by an experienced older woman. She might be an unmarried servant who lived with the family, or else a prostitute. In France, Italy, Spain and Latin America, it was customary for fathers to take their adolescent sons to a brothel so as to spare them future embarrassment. In Thomas Mann's *Royal Highness*, which describes the way these things were done among the upper classes in late 19th-century Germany, a royal charge is brought by his tutor to a friend's mistress, who receives in return a memento.

Failure to perform in bed may mark a man's life just as much as it does a woman's. More so, in fact, since the one thing more likely to attract opprobrium than an anorgasmic woman is an impotent man. Whereas the former can be and often is concealed, the latter may not. A woman who blames her failure to enjoy sex on her husband will likely be commiserated with. But a man who accuses a woman of "castrating" him will be ridiculed. The difference may explain why, even in societies where divorce was hard to get, a woman

---

[28] *Life So Far*, p. 313.

[29] Patricia Crawford, "Sexual Knowledge in England, 1500-1700," in Roy Porter and Mikulas Teich, eds., *Sexual Knowledge, Sexual Science: The History of Attitudes to Sexuality*, Cambridge, Cambridge University Press, 1994, pp. 97-8; Roy Porter and Lesley Hall, *The Facts of Life; The Creation of Sexual Knowledge in Britain, 1650-1950*, New Haven, CT, Yale University Press, 1995, p. 213.

[30] A sample of the written instructions in Hebrew to an Orthodox Jewish bridegroom may be found in *Pi Ha'aton*, 1.1.2001, p. 10.

whose husband could not fulfill his "marital duty" was usually able to obtain it if she could prove her claim. Medieval and early modern court records document the methods used to obtain the proof; one hardly needs to explain how humiliating, even self-defeating, they were.

Even if everything goes as it should, a man will find woman's sexual capability superior in some respects. Whatever she may feel, she is always ready. She may come and come, whereas he cannot. Add the problem of premature ejaculation, said to afflict 30 percent of men, and it becomes understandable why, for many of them, the gap in performance represents a constant source of anxiety. The anxiety may turn out to be all too justified. One *Cosmopolitan* magazine poll showed that about half of its married female readers had had an affair. Since *Cosmo* readers tend to be young, this probably underestimates the likelihood that a woman will have an extramarital fling at some point during her life. [31]

Worse still for husbands, research suggests that women are more likely to conceive when they commit adultery than when they have sex in their marriage bed.[32] DNA tests show that between 5 percent and 30 percent of babies born to American and British married women are sired by men other than their husbands.[33] In Germany, the figure is said to be approximately 10 percent. Since the law only allows the results to be used as evidence if the tests have been carried out with the woman's consent, this is likely to be an underestimate.[34] Not for nothing is the identity of Jewish children always determined by way of their mothers. Not for nothing are attempts to change this rule meeting with determined opposition by from Orthodox rabbis. They fear, and with very good reason, that in case paternity tests are carried out the number of Jewish children will undergo a dramatic decline.[35]

In summary, simply becoming male is a risky enterprise. Even when it is successfully accomplished, men remain the superfluous sex both before coitus and after it. Of this fact, most men are acutely aware. The outcome has been an entire literature on worlds without men; whereas the number of attempts to create women-less worlds is very near zero. As Darwin argued, biological

[31] L. Wolfe, "The Sexual Profile of the Cosmopolitan Girl," *Cosmopolitan*, September 1980, pp. 254-65. See Metcalf and Humphries, eds., *The Sexuality of Men*, p. 116.

[32] See Robin Baker and Mark A. Bellis, *Human Sperm Competition: Copulation, Masturbation and Infidelity*, New York, Chapman & Hall, 1996.

[33] Diamond, *Why Is Sex Fun?*, p. 80.

[34] *Abendzeitung*, 9.4.01, p. 5.

[35] Interview with Pnina Mizrachi, head nurse at Hadassah hospital in Jerusalem.

factors make women pickier in having sex than men.[36] Since men will feel a stronger urge to have sex with as many women as possible, marriage itself entails a much greater sacrifice for them than for women, especially where monogamy is the rule. With or without marriage, "phallic power is an unrelenting treadmill that threatens to collapse at any moment."[37] And finally, woman's sexual performance is superior to men's — to say nothing of her ability to have offspring whose paternity could rarely, until recently, be established with any certainty.

3. Compete and Provide

In all animals, male sex cells must seek out the less mobile female ones, either inside the body, as with mammals, or outside it, as with fish. Heaven forbid lest this be understood as proof that female sex cells are less "active" than male ones; rather, the *kind* of activity they engage in is different. Spermatozoids compete as they try to reach the eggs. Eggs stay in place, using finger-like structures on their walls, to "decide" which ones to admit and which to refuse. Thus, for male sex cells life itself starts with a competition; out of tens of millions that enter the race, just one will live.

To deposit their sperm, males must first compete to gain access to one or more fertile females and monopolize them insofar as is possible. The mathematics of the competition varies by species, but the principle itself is widespread. Male ants and bees compete with each other for the queen. Many kinds of male fish compete for the females' attention by chasing them and displaying brilliant colors. Many kinds of male birds and mammals do the same. Many develop special displays such as canine teeth, manes, antlers or brilliant colors. Always it is the female who, unless she is raped (which is not entirely unknown among animals either)[38] stands and watches. The competition over, she will express her approval by mating with the victor.

The male imperative to compete for females often comes at a heavy cost. In some mammals, such as kangaroos, mountain sheep, deer and sea elephants, it leads to fights that can result in life-threatening injuries. At a minimum, the

[36] *The Descent of Man and Selection in Relation to Sex*, New York, Random House, 1962 [1871], p. 579.

[37] Metcalff and Humphries, *The Sexuality of Men*, p. 61.

[38] See Barbara Smuts, "Male Aggression against Women: An Evolutionary Perspective," *Human Nature*, 3, 1992, pp. 1-44.

loser can expect a drop in status as well as eviction from the most favorable feeding grounds, leading to a shortened life expectancy. Moreover, sexual selection often operates at cross-purposes with other evolutionary forces.[39] A male who develops disproportionately sized organs, or displays brilliant color, or emits certain sounds, may well lose some of his mobility or become more vulnerable to predators. Trying to attract a female, in other words, may cost him his life.

Furthermore, developing organs or engaging in activities whose sole purpose is sexual display can be very expensive in terms of biological resources. Famous examples are the peacock's tail and the stag's antlers, which have to be shed and re-grown each year.[40] Males, in other words, present their biological fitness by engaging in types of display that are *not* essential for survival;[41] the greater the biological cost of a color or organ, the more it proves the owners' ability to bear that cost. The human analogy is a man who drives a shiny new Mercedes. Though such a car is not essential for transportation, it demonstrates its owner's clout in a way that a humble Chevy or Volkswagen never could. By driving his Mercedes, the owner is telling the world that he commands a financial surplus — one which, women hope, he will share with them and their offspring.

In almost all cultures, a man must invest in a woman in order to attract and keep her. To attract and keep a man, a woman must invest in herself.[42] Few if any men can make their way simply by virtue of their looks or by being good at socializing. Those who do are labeled as hustlers. Not so women, for whom beauty is often the fastest way to advance and for whom social skills may be enough to maintain their lifestyle. In American department stores, the square footage dedicated to women's accessories, jewelry and cosmetics is seven times that allotted for comparable men's products.[43] Not by accident, most magazines that deal with self-enhancement are read by women.[44] Not by accident, most of those which explain how to get ahead are read by men. How

---

[39] See Charles Darwin, *The Descent of Man and Selection in Relation to Sex*, p. 579.

[40] S. J. Arnold, "Quantitative Genetic Models of Sexual Selection: An Overview," in S. C. Stearns, ed., *The Evolution* of *Sex and its Consequences*, Basel, Birkehäuwer, 1987, p. 290.

[41] Amotz Zahavi, "Mate Selection—A Selection for a Handicap," *Journal of Theoretical Biology*, 53, 1975, pp. 205-14; *idem*, "The Cost of Honesty," *ibid*, 67, 1977, pp. 603-5.

[42] D. M. Buss, "Sex Differences in Human Mate Preferences: Evolutionary Hypotheses Tested in 37 Cultures," *Behavioral and Brain Sciences*, 21, 1989, pp. 1-49.

[43] William Farrell, *Why Men Are the Way They Are*, New York, Berkeley, 1988, p. 238.

[44] See Farrell, *Why Men Are the Way They Are*, pp. 18-23.

exactly a man succeeds is immaterial — the reward is always women with parted lips and deep cleavages. Thus competition among men, even if it involves self-enhancement as in the case of bodybuilding, will end up by leading them toward giving. In the end, men will be measured largely by their pockets. By contrast, competition among women consists mainly of self-enhancement. The purpose of such efforts is to make a man pay for them — an act that is by definition egocentric.

In many societies, control over a woman's reproductive capacities rests with her family. A young woman may give herself to a man out of infatuation, as Julia did to Romeo. Not so her parents or other relatives, who are much more likely to have practical considerations in mind. The legends of many peoples tell of rulers who organized competitions for their daughters' hand. In the Irish epic *The Tain*, the hero Cuchulainn must kill 24 men — and risk being killed by each of them — to gain the right to travel the "sweet country" of his beloved's breasts. Later in the epic, a woman, Medb, promises her daughter to seven different suitors simultaneously, a case of fraud if there ever one was.[45] Many of the men who lost the competitions ended up being killed in a variety of exotic ways. Nor are situations in which women were bestowed, or bestowed themselves, on the best fighters limited to myth. As long ago as ancient Rome, successful gladiators received the same kind of attention from women as today's soccer stars. In many tribal societies, and by no means only tribal societies, warriors are able to translate their prowess into sexual favors, whether temporary ones before the wedding or permanent ones after it.

Another way in which men are made to compete for women is bride-service. The biblical Jacob was made to serve Laban for seven years before obtaining the latter's daughter Leah, and another seven before finally obtaining his true love, Rachel. In our own day, bride-service continues to be practiced by many black African tribes, as well as in parts of Oceania and Australia. It may be of a symbolic nature and last for just one day, as among the Ngondi of Rhodesia and the Baganda of Kenya. It may also last as many as 20 years and drain away a man's resources, as among the Goba of the Zambezi Valley.[46] The

---

[45] *The Tain*, Thomas Kinsella, trans., Oxford, Oxford University Press, 1969, pp. 27, 215.

[46] For Australia, see Phyllis M. Kaberry, *Aboriginal Woman: Sacred and Profane*, London, Routledge, 1939, p. 97; For Ngondi, see J. A. Barnes, *Marriage in a Changing Society*, London, Rhodes-Livingstone Papers, No. 20, 1951, p. 67; For Baganda, see Lucy P. Mair, *African Peoples in the Twentieth Century*, London, Russell & Russell, 1934, p. 82; For Goba, see Chet S. Lancaster, "Brideservice and Authority among the Goba (N. Shona) of the Zambezi Valley," *Africa*, 44, p. 51.

period in question is stipulated in advance and starts years before the wedding can take place. Nor is there any guarantee that the young man will get what he wants, since either the woman or her parents may change their mind.

Some see bride-service and brides-wealth as a system old men use to control younger ones. Others think it is meant to reassure "insecure" husbands that their wives will not run away during the earliest stages of marriage.[47] Focusing on Japan, others see a link between the low rate of divorce in the country and the fact that, ere a wedding can take place, the groom or his family must fork out as much as 30,000 (1999) dollars.[48] Whatever the explanation may be, in all societies it is men, not women, who must work and pay to marry. In this, as in so many other ways, they are humanity's beasts of burden. Not only did Cuchulainn have to risk his life 24 times, he also had to perform "the salmon's leap" while carrying "twice his weight in gold."[49]

Stimulated and abetted by women, the competition is likely to shape a man's entire life. The winner may gain power, riches and a rise in his self-esteem. However, even for the victor the rewards are bittersweet. The very qualities needed to win, such as aggression, craftiness and ruthlessness, are likely to isolate the victorious ones, making it almost impossible for them to have real relationships with either men *or* women. Often the man at the top is the one who has the fewest friends. Joseph Stalin, to cite one example, was perhaps the most powerful man who ever lived. He made even his closest Soviet cronies cringe, and abroad he achieved the same effect by threatening to use his 500 army divisions and, later, atom bombs. Contrast that with the Stalin shown in a documentary film watching a private performance by a famous ballerina, glass of vodka in hand. After the show he did not even bother to sleep with her; after all, doing so would not have proved anything.

For Stalin and his ilk, providing for the family was no problem. However, for many other men, then and now, doing so presents the hardest thing they will do in their lives. Some, but by no means all, male birds are monogamous and feed their females during courtship or while the latter are roosting.[50] Even among such birds, however, this is a temporary arrangement, not one that lasts

---

[47] Jane F. Collier, *Marriage and Inequality in Classless Societies*, Stanford, CA, Stanford University Press, 1988, p. 231; Wahiduddin Khan, *Woman Between Islam and Western Society*, London, Islamic Center, 1995, p. 230.

[48] Lionel Tiger, *The Decline of the Male*, New York, St. Martin's Press, 1999 p. 154.

[49] *The Tain*, p. 27.

[50] See Diamond, *Why is Sex Fun?*, pp. 37, 55, 56, 58, 72, 107; also Konrad Lorenz, *On Aggression*, London, Methuen, 1967, pp. 108-9.

throughout their life. By contrast, the males of most mammalian species simply wander off after they mate, having provided their offspring with nothing but their genes. Only a few, including gorillas, gibbons and saddleback tamarin monkeys, provide any form of paternal care at all. Yet even this consists of little more than playing with the young, if and when the males are in the right mood to do so. In no primate except man is there any question of the father providing for his offspring.

Compared with the size of their mothers' bodies, human babies are enormous. This fact, plus the fact that bipedalism caused the human birth canal to become relatively narrower than that of any other mammal, made giving birth both difficult and dangerous.[51] Once delivery has taken place the newborn of no other mammalian species is more helpless or takes a longer time to raise. This is true both absolutely and in relation to the overall life span. Even the most precocious youngsters, living in the simplest societies, will hardly complete the process before entering their mid-teens.[52] Almost certainly this is why our hunting-gathering ancestors developed the arrangement, found in no other species, by which males provide long-term economic support not only to their offspring but to the mothers as well.

To this day, all other things being equal, a mother or father who tries to raise children by herself or himself faces a severe handicap. He or she will find it much harder to raise healthy, well-adjusted children.[53] To help women cope, men's support of them has been made essentially permanent. It lasts from the wedding to the grave, and beyond. Regardless of whether marriage is monogamous or polygynous or polyandrous, regardless of whether it takes place among hunter-gatherers or in a post-industrial society, regardless of whether those who enter into it are Christian or Muslim or Buddhist or animist, regardless of time, place and culture with perhaps the sole exception of the short-lived Communist experiment, it has almost universally meant that one male supports one (or sometimes more) women and their offspring. The exception, polyandry, is found in less than 1 percent of societies. In the vast majority of cases, men marry one or more women. Having done so, they are expected to give up much, perhaps most, of their subsistence to them. For most

---

[51] William Leutenegger, "A Functional Interpretation of the Sacrum of Australopithecus Africanus," *South African Journal of Science*, 73, 1977, pp. 308-10.

[52] See Sherwood L. Washburn, "Longevity in Primates," in James L. McGaugh and Sara B. Kiesler, eds., *Aging: Biology and Behavior*, New York, Academic Press, 1981, pp. 11-29.

[53] See Judith S. Wallerstein et al., *The Unexpected Legacy of Divorce*, New York, Hyperion, 2000, pp. 35-8,107-9, 250, 297.

modern Western men, abandoning their families will result in increasing their dispensable income by as much as three quarters.[54] In the whole of nature, there is no arrangement that is more demanding and more altruistic.

Given the immense burden under which they labor, it is hardly surprising that some men find it hard to deal with life all of the time, or that nearly all find it hard to deal with life some of the time. Depending on culture and personal inclination, a range of solutions to the problem have arisen. Several such solutions will be discussed here, in the order of the danger they pose, both to men themselves and to society.

First there is fantasy. It can take many forms, from reading the *Iliad* to playing a computer game. At all times and places, both men and women have dreamt of he-men, albeit for different reasons. What he wants to be, she wants to have. From the Roman games through medieval tournaments to the modern-day Super Bowl, the function of spectator sports has been similar. They provide men with heroes with whom to identify themselves, thus taking attention away from reality, at least temporarily.

Pornography, too, can be understood as a subspecies of fantasy. Often it is used by men who feel unable to obtain the women whom they want, establishing a kind of universe in which they are all-seeing, all-knowing and all-powerful.[55] It may also represent an attempt to penetrate the mystery of womanhood — "the great gulf of nothingness," as American author Henry Miller once put it[56] — or to stimulate a flagging performance in bed. It is true that women resort to pornography as well, sometimes in the company, or at the insistence, of men whose interest they hope to stimulate in this way. However, one need only go to the nearest newsstand to see that the number of those who do so is much smaller than that of men. Gay pornography is plentiful and has often resulted in the most magnificent art.[57] Lesbian pornography, by contrast, hardly exists. Nor, if psychoanalysts are to be believed, do women respond to pornography in the same way. In particular, they do not seem particularly keen on scenes in which force and compulsion are used.[58]

Another solution is crime. All over the world, far more men than women become criminals. To cite but one example, in Britain during the 1990s men committed 84 percent of all recorded crimes, 92 percent of violent ones and 97

[54] Lester Thurow, "Companies Merge, Families Break Up," *The New York Times*, 3.9.1995.

[55] Metcalff and Humphries, eds, *The Sexuality of Men*, pp. 53, 55, 57, 59, 161.

[56] *Tropic of Cancer*, New York, Grove Press, 1961, p. 140.

[57] See Camille Paglia, *Vamps and Tramps*, New York, Vintage, 1994, pp. 122-6.

[58] Person, "The Omni-Available Woman and Lesbian Sex," pp. 73-4, 75-8, 83-4.

percent of burglaries. By the time they were 25 years old, one-quarter of all men had been convicted of one offense or another.[59] The question is why.[60] Part of the answer may be biological and rooted in men's hormones. However, many sociologists believe that the criminal propensities of young men reflect the greater difficulties they face in trying to find their place in the world. As we shall see in the next section, men's greater criminality may also reflect the harsher treatment they receive at the hands of society from the moment they are born.

Men's problems may be compounded by the fact that modern urban life does not allow them to fully take advantage of their most important advantage over women: their physical courage and prowess. In simpler societies, these qualities enable males to establish adult status. Presented with hard if not impossible goals, handicapped as to the means that they may use to attain them, and branded as wimps or losers if they do not succeed, it is scant wonder that some of them turn to illegal ways. All other things being equal, the less affluent their background, the more likely this is to be the case. Conversely the need to have money to spend on girls is said to be one of the driving engines behind the drug trade.[61]

One crime that needs to be discussed in this context is rape.[62] In the case of people who know each other — so-called date rape — the cry of "rape" may result from a misunderstanding. The importance of this fact consists in that even the most determined female opponents of rape admit that 50 percent of the women in question were attacked by people whom they knew.[63] Some studies put the figure much higher. A man may have what he thought was consensual sex with a woman and parted from her on the most friendly of terms, only to find himself accused of rape the next day, or even years later. No wonder that, according to police officers with experience in the matter, virtually all of those arrested for this crime seem to be very surprised to hear the accusations

[59] Jeff Hearn, "Troubled Masculinities in Social Policy Discourses: Young Men," in Jennie Popay et al., eds., *Men, Gender Divisions and Welfare*, London, Routledge, 1998, p. 44.

[60] See James W. Messerschmidt, *Masculinities and Crime: Critique and Reconceptualization of Theory*, Lanham, MD, Rowman & Littlefield, 1993.

[61] See Carl S. Taylor, *Dangerous Society*, East Lansing, MI, Michigan State University Press, 1989, p. 60.

[62] See Paul Pollard, "Sexual Violence Against Women," in John Archer, ed., *Male Violence*, London, Routledge, 1994, pp. 186-7; N. A. Groth, *Men Who Rape: The Psychology of the Offender*, New York, Plenum, 1979.

[63] Brownmiller, *Against Our Will*, p. 400.

directed at them.[64] In some cases, the charge of rape means no more than that a woman asked for sex and was rejected. Think of the biblical Joseph and Potiphar's wife. As one female scholar put it, false allegations are "an old, old female strategy."[65]

Even taking these possibilities into account, there are undoubtedly cases when rape means just that. Both American and British reports claim that the vast majority of rapists are single, working-class, unskilled and unemployed.[66] If this is true, then rape may well be a method by which unsuccessful men gain access to women who despise them and who do not want to have sex with them. In other cases, especially those involving violence and various kinds of sadistic acts, rape may represent a way for a man to use a woman to avenge himself on other women.[67] Whatever the motive, very often rape points to the perpetrator's inability to attract love, his insecurity, his dissatisfaction and his powerlessness.[68]

The final option men have is to give up on life. When statistics on suicide began to be collected during the 19th century, it was found that men were more likely to cause their own death than women. Other men may waste away, as is perhaps best told in Herman Melville's short story, "Bartleby the Scrivener."[69] Bartleby, a copywriter working on Wall Street, one day stops working and caring for himself. His condition starts deteriorating, much to the horror of his employer, who acts as the narrator and whose own gloom increases as he tells the tale. Having resisted his boss' entreaties to pull himself together, Bartleby ends his life curled up in "The Tombs," as the Manhattan Detention Complex was nicknamed at the time.[70] There, refusing to eat, he dies of starvation. The story has likely struck a chord with many men in the century and a half since it was published. Men's lot in life is endless hard work whose fruits will be consumed largely by others. The more men bring in, the greater the demands.

---

[64] Menachem Amir, *Patterns in Forcible Rape*, Chicago, University of Chicago Press, 1971, p. 70; Barbara Toner, *The Facts of Rape*, London, Arrow Books, 1982, pp. 176-7.

[65] See Eileen B. Leonard, *Women, Crime and Society: A Critique of Theoretical Criminology*, New York, Longman, 1982, p. 45.

[66] Richard Wright, "The English Rapist," *New Society*, 17.7.1980.

[67] See Diana Scully, *Understanding Sexual Violence*, Boston, Unwin Hyman, 1990, pp. 162-3; V. Greendlinger and D. Byrne, "Coercive Sexual Fantasies of College Men as Predictors of Self-Reported Likelihood to Rape and Overt Sexual Aggression," *Journal of Sex Research*, 23, 1987, pp. 1-11.

[68] Metcalff and Humphries, *The Sexuality of Men*, p. 107.

[69] Herman Melville, *Billy Budd and Other Stories*, New York, Penguin, 1986 [1853].

[70] Thanks to Jonathan Lewy for bringing this little-known fact to my attention.

Should men fail, they may lose both what they made and those to whom they gave it. Perhaps the most terrifying thing about Melville's story is that, at times, Bartleby's behavior and fate can tempt even the most active and successful man.

In the end, the only way men can escape their burden is to grow old. In Plato's *Republic*, it is an old man, Cephalus, who opens the discussion. Responding to a question, he explains how glad he is to be rid of the "raging and savage" passion of sex;[71] at long last, he is able to live a quiet life and sacrifice to the gods. Similarly, in Chinese art, a famous motif is that of bald, fat, smiling, old men sitting comfortably in the lotus position. They have reached a point where they have nothing to worry about except eating as much as they please; in the best examples of the genre, they almost seem to be floating in the air. But then reaching such a comfortable old age depends on the ability to shoulder the burden and survive the competition. Among humans, as among apes,[72] the road to tranquility is littered with male corpses.

To sum up, the mathematics of reproduction turned women into the choosy sex. The same mathematics created in men a desperate need to possess women and compete for them. Hundreds of thousands of years of evolution have firmly programmed this competiveness into their genes.[73] The competition is especially ferocious in polygamous societies which, historically speaking, have always formed the great majority. In such cultures, many men may only be able to marry late, if at all. Starting soon after puberty, the competition lasts during most of their adult life. It may take the form of fighting, or of working, or of payment. Irrespective of the form it takes, in almost all cases it will involve the burden of economic support. Whether in terms of risk, resources, wealth or health, the price men pay for engaging in this competition is staggering. No wonder that, in some cases, they either resort to unconventional means or simply drop out.

---

[71] *Republic*, 3.3.c.

[72] Diamond, *The Third Chimpanzee: The Evolution and Future of the Human Animal*, New York, Harper Collins, 1992, p. 132; Charles E. Oxnard, *Fossils, Teeth and Sex: New Perspectives on Human Evolution*, Seattle, WA, University of Washington Press, 1987, 252-4.

[73] Margo Wilson and Martin Daly, "An Evolutionary Psychological Perspective on Male Sexual Proprietariness and Violence Against Wives," in *Violence and Victims*, 1, 28, February 1993, pp. 271-94.

4. Growing Up Male

In everything except pregnancy, delivery and lactation, men are the sex with the heavier burdens to bear. As youths they must be more or less forcibly separated from their mothers so that they may grow into the adult male role — uprooted from the maternal paradise, as one psychiatrist has put it.[74] Next they will find themselves doomed to compete against other men for the favors of women, whether in terms of risk-taking and achievement or by providing them with economic support. In a certain sense, they will always remain the superfluous sex. Like an erection, manhood cannot be taken for granted, but must be reasserted until old age makes it irrelevant. Given all this, how does society treat men? Does it assist them and smooth their way? Or, to the contrary, does it place even more obstacles in their path?

First, the dreaded break with the mother. Listen to Simone de Beauvoir: the child, she says, can expect "a second weaning, less brutal and more gradual than the first... the boys especially are little by little denied the kisses and caresses they have been used to. As for the little girl, she continues to be cajoled, she is allowed to cling to her mother's skirts, her father takes her on his knee and strokes her hair. She wears sweet little dresses, her tears and caprices are viewed indulgently, her hair is done up carefully, older people are amused at her expressions and coquetries — bodily contacts and agreeable glances protect her against the anguish of solitude. The little boy, in contrast, will be denied even coquetry; his efforts at enticement, his play-acting, are irritating. He is told that 'a man doesn't ask to be kissed... A man doesn't look at himself in mirrors... A man doesn't cry. He is urged to be 'a little man;' he will obtain adult approval by becoming independent of adults. He will please them by not appearing to please them." "Many boys," she continues, "frightened by the hard independence they are condemned to, wish they were girls." No wonder that "certain of them held obstinately to the choice of femininity, even to the point of urinating in a sitting position."[75]

The process of gender differentiation starts even before birth. Told that they are pregnant with boys, women are much more likely to report the fetus' stirrings as "vigorous" than those carrying girls.[76] The greater vigor ascribed to

---

[74] Horrocks, *Male Myths and Icons*, p. 15; also Metcalff and Humphries, eds., *The Sexuality of Men*, p. 147.

[75] *The Second Sex*, p. 252.

[76] Carole R. Beal, *Boys and Girls: The Development of Gender Roles*, New York, McGraw-Hill, 1994, pp. 27-8.

boys may explain why, as infants, they are much more likely to be restrained, disparaged, threatened and ordered about.[77] Later on, parents are more likely to push boys to actively explore their surroundings and, in so doing, take a certain amount of risk.[78] The male young of many other species face similar pressures; perhaps the method of making greater demands on males is built into our genes.[79] By contrast, girls tend to be sheltered against danger of every kind, be it climbing trees, using swings, riding bicycles or going out alone at night. They are also more likely to enjoy better living conditions than boys. In Britain, for example, class by class boys are more likely than girls to suffer from overcrowding, lack of amenities and poor psychological support.[80] Nor are boys slow to understand either the fact that parents make life harder for them or the rationale behind this fact. By the time they are 4 years old, research shows, they already want to be "tough."[81]

Worse still for boys, should they be perceived as "difficult," which is often synonymous with "vigorous," then the difference in their treatment will increase accordingly.[82] The *same* behavior which may cause adults to support and comfort a female toddler may cause them to chastise or discipline a male one. Conversely, failure to perform is much more likely to be tolerated in girls but denounced, combated and punished in boys. Boys are also four times as likely to have their aggressive acts responded to by teachers as are girls.[83] In the words of one psychologist, for them "the cycle of child difficulty and...

[77] L. Cherry and M. Lewis, "Mothers of Two Year Olds: A Study of Sex-Differential Aspects of Verbal Interaction," *Developmental Psychology*, 12, 1976, pp. 272-82.

[78] Beal, *Boys and Girls*, p. 77.

[79] See B. Mitchell and E. M. Brandt, "Behavioral Differences Relate to Experience of Mother and Sex of Infants in the Rhesus Monkey," *Developmental Psychology*, 3, 1970, p. 149; also C. M. Berman, "Variation in Mother-Infant Relationships: Traditional and Nontraditional Factors," in Meredith F. Small, ed., *Female Primates: Studies by Women Anthropologists*, New York, Liss, 1984, pp. 17-36; and J. R. Walters, "Transition to Adulthood," in Barbara Smuts et al., ed., *Primate Societies*, Chicago, University of Chicago Press, 1987, pp. 19-35.

[80] See Hilary Graham, "Socio-Economic Change and Inequalities," in Ellen Annandale and Kate Hunt, eds., *Gender Inequalities in Health*, Buckingham, Open University Press, 2000, p. 103, figure 4.6 and p. 104, figure 4.7.

[81] R. Omark and M. S. Edelman, "A Comparison of Status Hierarchies in Young Children: An Ethological Approach," *Social Science Information*, 14, 1975, pp. 87-107.

[82] P. J. Turner, "Attachment to Mother and Behavior with Adults in Preschool," *British Journal of Developmental Psychology*, 11, 1993, pp. 75-89.

[83] Susan Golombok and Robyn Fivush, *Gender Development*, Cambridge, Cambridge University Press, 1994, p. 125.

responsiveness is more robust."[84] All these are merely euphemisms for saying that, starting practically at birth, males are proportionally much more likely to get a push than a hug.

Many societies use initiation rites to separate boys from their mothers. As some tribespeople put it, the objective is to excise their "female substance."[85] Accordingly, as long as women do not share in them, the precise nature of the rites does not matter much. The first step may be to take the novices from their mother's hut and prohibit them from ever entering it again.[86] Next they are brought to a hallowed place outside the village, or else locked into a house that no woman may enter. There they will be presented with male "secrets" they must never afterward divulge, even to the women who are nearest and dearest to them.[87] Having graduated, the youngsters are presented with special clothing, ornaments and implements that henceforth mark their new status as men.[88]

A second, and closely related, aspect of initiation is to test the boys' mettle prior to granting them full male status. As carried out in countless societies around the world,[89] they may have to endure humiliation by having their hair, and sometimes pubic hair, shaved. They may be made to strike ludicrous poses, recite self-mocking formulae, or strip naked in front of their elders. Other ordeals may include subjection to hunger, thirst, cold and sleep deprivation, or having one's bodies cut, mutilated and tattooed at the cost of "terrible" pain.[90] In Papua New Guinea, the men of some tribes were known to climb a tower, have a rope tied to their legs, and then plunge downward head first. The rite is said to be the origin of bungee jumping, but the traditional practice was hardly as safe as the modern one, making the plunge a test of mettle indeed.

---

[84] L. S. Carli, "Biology Does not Create Gender Differences in Personality," in Mary R. Walsh, ed., *Women, Men and Gender*, New Haven, CT, Yale University Press, 1997, p. 49.

[85] Fitz John Porter Pole, "The Ritual Forging of Identity," in Gilbert H. Herdt, ed., *Rituals of Manhood*, New Brunswick, NJ, Transaction, 1998, p. 123.

[86] Gilmore, *Manhood in the Making*, p. 85.

[87] Gilbert H. Hertdt, "Fetish and Fantasy in Sambia Initiation," in Herdt, ed., *Rituals of Manhood*, p. 79.

[88] Deborah B. Gewertz, "The Father Who Bore Me: the Role of *Tsambunwuro* during Chambri Initiation Ceremonies," in Herdt, ed., *Rituals of Manhood*, p. 298.

[89] See above all Elisabeth Badinter, *XY: On Masculine Identity*, New York, Columbia University Press, 1995, chapter 3.

[90] See Jürg Schmidt and Christin Kocher Schmidt, *Söhne des Krokodils: Männerhausrituale und Initiation in Yensan, Zentral-Iatmul, East Sepik Province, Papua New Guinea*, Basel, Ethnologisches Seminar, 1992, pp. 114-6, 143, 158.

In many places around the world, the focal point of male initiation consists of circumcision or some other form of genital mutilation. Except among Jews, usually the ceremony is carried out on boys ranging in age from 6 to 12. Since the objective is to prove that the boy can endure the operation without flinching, it is deliberately made painful. Should he fail the test, he will disgrace both himself and his family. Tribal women in Australia told one researcher that they would refuse to marry a man who had not undergone it.[91] One 19th-century visitor to Arabia claimed to have witnessed a ceremony whereby a youth, standing straight, had the skin of his penis peeled off in the presence of his bride. Crouching and playing a drum, she had the right to refuse him if he so much as stirred or moaned.[92]

In the literature, first-hand accounts of female initiation rites are comparatively hard to come by. Those that do exist suggest that they tend to be comparatively mild affairs. There is little humiliation — the most a girl may be required to do is to strip in the presence of other women. Nor is there any question of inflicting pain. Usually all that takes place is that the initiate, having menstruated for the first time, is secluded for a few days. When she emerges she is washed, anointed and presented with female articles of dress and decoration that henceforth mark her status as a marriable woman.[93] Some societies mark and mutilate the female genitals in various ways. However, once again there is a crucial difference between the sexes. Whatever its purpose may be, female circumcision is not meant as a test of character or strength. Those who undergo it are permitted, even expected, to scream like hell.

In places as far apart as Imperial China, medieval Egypt and Christian Europe from the early Middle Ages onward, high class boys aged 6 to 8 were often assigned to special institutions. The institutions were likely to be military, or monastic, or some combination of the two. Modern schools of this type often resemble prisons or concentration camps. They come complete with barred windows, assembly grounds, walls and fortified gates. Candidates may be made to undergo tests of courage, endurance, or both. For example, Nazi schools for the elite made admission of 12-year old boys conditional on their swimming 10

---

[91] Kaberry, *Aboriginal Woman*, p. 82.

[92] J. L. Fischer, "Semi-Castration on Ponape," *Seventh International Congress of Anthropological and Ethnological Science*, 8, 1965, p. 95.

[93] See Gisele Simard, "The Case of Mauritania: Women's Productive activities in Urban Areas—A Process of Empowerment," in Parvin Ghorayshi and Claire Belanger, eds., *Women, Work and Gender Relations in Developing Countries: A Global Perspective*, Westport, CT, Greenwood, 1996, p. 159.

meters from one gap to another under the ice.[94] Never in history has anything similar been demanded of girls.

Once admitted, the boys were humiliated by having their hair shaved, being dressed in strange and uncomfortable clothes, and the like. Regardless of whether their vocation was religious or military, these ordeals were followed by years of training. Some of the training was corporal, including sleep deprivation, forced fasting, physical punishment and strenuous exercise. To this was (and is) added mental exercises such as meditation, mastering foreign languages, learning difficult or incomprehensible texts by heart, and repeated confession of one's most intimate thoughts. And in addition to all that, there was always constant supervision, denial of privacy and harassment. So rough was the Spartan *agoge*, or education course for males, that Artistotle thought it was more suitable for beasts than for men. Then as now, many of the exercises served no purpose except creating hardship pure and simple. This was done both as a means of "character building" — itself often a euphemism for abuse — and to help students bond with each other and the institution.

Other boys often had to undergo some kind of schooling as well. Now that most modern countries have adopted coeducation, schools may not appear as particularly threatening institutions. But historically, in schools intended for boys alone, the situation was often quite different. In both Greece and Rome, "the leaders of youth," who were either slaves or freedmen, made liberal use of the stick to force what knowledge they possessed into the heads of their charges. In ancient art, the rod became the schoolmaster's trademark. Exaggerating as was his wont, the Roman poet Martial compared the noise of beatings to "that of bronze being beaten on an anvil when a smith makes an equestrian statue for some orator", as well as to the cheers of a crowd in the amphitheater.[95] In medieval England, schoolboys were known as "unbroken young colts" and were regularly beaten.[96] One of those who experienced this kind of discipline first hand was Erasmus of Rotterdam (1466-1536). Later he wrote an entire book on the need to abolish it.

Partly because they were regarded as less difficult and more compliant — and partly because, as 18th-century German handbooks on education suggested,

---

[94] Johannes Leeb, *Wir waren Hitlers Eliteschüler*, Munich, Heyne, 1999, p. 62.
[95] *Epigrams*, 9.68.
[96] James B. Given, *Society and Homicide in Thirteenth-Century England*, Stanford, CA, Stanford University Press, 1977, p. 196.

beating girls was simply not nice[97] — girls of all classes were much less likely to receive physical punishment. Not for nothing have the soft and unblemished skins of upper class girls in particular become proverbial. They took their first lessons, and often all their lessons, from their mothers or other female members of the household. In Europe during the early modern age, and in some places into the 20th century, the daughters of the really well-to-do were given private tuition at home.[98]

Yet another type of education for boys consisted of apprenticeship. Journeymen were commonplace across Europe from the Middle Ages onward, but historical accounts seldom mention any journeywomen. Even when young women did leave home, they tended to stay close by so as not to lose touch with their families.[99] Having been apprenticed, perhaps against their will, boys entered a strange household. There they might spend many years doing the most menial jobs for little or no pay.[100] Whatever the precise arrangement, clearly it was capable of giving rise to much unhappiness. It was young men of this lot who are said to have invented the term "homesickness" early in the 19th century.[101] Girls, too, might be apprenticed. However, as long ago as the Middle Ages, more girls were privileged to stay behind.[102] All over Europe, the later the date, the fewer female apprentices there were to be found.[103] Perhaps reflecting these differences, until recently proportionally twice as many American girls as boys remained at home until getting married.[104]

---

[97] Peter Petschauer, *The Education of Women in Eighteenth-Century Germany*, Lewinston, NJ, Edwin Mellen, 1989, pp. 486-7.

[98] Barbara Miller Solomon, *In the Company of Educated Women: A History of Women and Higher Education in America*, New Haven, CT, Yale University Press, 1985, p. 64.

[99] Theodor Penners, "Bevölkerungsgeschichtliche Probleme der Land-Stadtwanderung," *Braunschweigische Jahrbuch*, 37, 1956, p. 68.

[100] Robert Campbell, *The London Tradesman*, London, Gardner, 1747, p. 23.

[101] Harvey S. Graf, *Conflicting Paths: Growing Up in America*, Cambridge, MA, Harvard University Press, 1995, p. 34.

[102] Steven A. Epstein, *Wage Labor and Guilds in Medieval Europe*, Chapel Hill, NC, University of North Carolina Press, 1991, p. 118; P. J. P. Goldberg, "'For Better or Worse': Marriage and Economic Opportunities for Women in Town and Country," in P. J. P. Goldberg, ed., *Woman is a Worthy Wight: Women in English Society, 1200-1500*, Phoenix Mill, England, Sutton, 1992, pp. 111, 112.

[103] Debora Simonton, *A History of European Women's Work, 1700 to the Present*, London, Routledge, 1998, pp. 51, 53; O. Jocelyn Dunlop, *English Apprenticeship and Child Labor*, London, Unwin, 1912, p. 151.

[104] Farrel, *Why Men Are the Way They Are*, pp. 168, 292.

Like boys, some girls were able to obtain some form of formal schooling without having to leave the home. And like boys, some girls were educated outside the home in convents and the like. In the 13th century Maimonides referred to classrooms filled entirely by girls.[105] Visiting the Indian city of Hinawr during the early years of the 14th century, Arab traveler Ibn Battuta noted it had 23 schools for boys and 13 for girls;[106] the women, he says, all knew the Koran by heart. This was even truer in Germany from the time of the Reformation on. Following Luther's call to provide "instruction in German or Latin," boys' and girls' schools developed in parallel from the time of the Reformation onward. Each time a municipality or community founded an institution for boys, it was only a question of time before an equivalent one was established for the girls whom they expected to marry.

Beginning with Erasmus, a vast amount of literature was devoted to the subject. By 1800, according to one expert, "the number and variety of educational opportunities available for girls inside and outside their parental or other households defie[d] the imagination."[107] Reflecting the preferences of parents, not just fathers, fewer girls were made to attend school than were boys. Reflecting the demands of society, about the only kind of education closed to them was cadet schools. Most of the schools in question originated during the 1740s. Taking in boys from the age of 12 up, they were notorious for their Spartan character and their ferocious discipline. If girls were excluded from them, then it was in order that ferocious discipline and a Spartan character might be maintained. Now that military academies have become coed, their former harshness is largely gone.[108] Instead we get scholars who do not know the first thing about war telling us that, in training for war, Spartan methods are "arbitrary and unnecessary."[109] No wonder that, over the last few decades, almost every time Western troops were sent to fight in the "developing" world they were soundly defeated.

Most schools for girls were modeled on school for boys. Until well into the 19th century, the principal subject taught to youngsters of both sexes was

---

[105] See Shlomo D. Goitein, *A Mediterranean Society*, Berkeley, CA, University of California Press, 1971, vol. 5, pp. 183, 185.

[106] *The Rehlah of Ibn Battuta*, Mahdi Hussain, trans., Baroda, Oriental Institute, 1953, p. 179.

[107] Petschauer, *The Education of Women*, p. 105.

[108] See Brian Mitchell, *Women in the Military: Flirting with Disaster*, Washington, Regnery, 1998, pp. 61-2, 64, 227-8.

[109] Virginia Valian, *Why So Slow? The Advancement of Women*, Cambridge, MA, MIT Press, 1999, p. 253.

religion. Next came the so-called "three Rs," reading, writing and arithmetic. Middle-class girls were supposed to assist their future husbands by means of bookkeeping and the like, hence much of the instruction was similar for both sexes. The difference consisted in that both the admission standards girls had to meet and the curricula designed for their use tended to be less demanding. At the lowest levels, they might be taught to read but not to write. Since historians usually judge literacy rates by counting those who could sign their names, they may have exaggerated the educational differences between the sexes.[110] Girls were not required to study difficult subjects such as Latin, Greek, mathematics or the natural sciences. But that does not necessarily mean that such subjects were out of bounds. For parents who wanted their daughters to study them, the corresponding schools were easily available.[111]

What all girls' schools did have in common was a relaxed atmosphere. In the words of the great feminist Mary Wollstonecraft, who at one point headed one such school, it was here that pupils were "first spoiled."[112] Boys had their mettle tested, often with barbaric cruelty. With girls, by contrast, the more difficult a subject, the more likely it was to be offered on a voluntary basis and less intensively. This was as true in the United States as it was in pre-revolutionary Russia.[113] Grading, too, was carried out differently. Being forced to repeat a class was hardly unusual for boys. Before coeducation came along, though, it was rarely applied to girls. A teacher who made "the flesh of the girl tremble under the rod or ferule... [was] liable to be charged with undue severity."[114] All this explains why the memoirs of 19th-century female students, unlike those of male ones, rarely contain expressions of fierce hatred for school.[115]

Many of the differences in education can be ascribed to the fact that girls' schools were not supposed to prepare them for university, which with rare exceptions were closed to women. Acknowledging this fact, however, is not to

---

[110] Walter H. Small, "Girls in Colonial New England," *Education*, 22, 1902, p. 533; Walter H. Small, *Early New England Schools*, Boston, Ginn, 1914, p. 278.

[111] Anthony Fletcher, *Gender, Sex and Subordination in England, 1500-1800*, New Haven, CT, Yale University Press, 1995, p. 373.

[112] *A Vindication of the Rights of Woman*, Mineola, NY, Dover, 1996 [1792], p. 130.

[113] Albisetti, *Schooling German Girls and Women*, p. 109.

[114] Charles W. Moore and George P. Sanger, *School Committee Report*, Charlestown, MA, 1848, quoted in David Tyack and Elisabeth Hansot, *Learning Together: A History of Coeducation in American Schools*, New Haven, CT, Yale University Press, 1990, p. 92.

[115] Albisetti, *Schooling German Girls and Women*, pp. 23, 51, 52; Petschauer, *The Education of Women in Eighteenth-Century Germany*, pp. 370-1.

suggest that higher education was directly discriminating against women. First, until the second half of the 20th century, the vast majority of men did not attend university either. Second, and more importantly, universities were meant for those who had to earn their living. As a result, the sons of the truly great and rich did not attend them any more than their sisters did. Conversely, and except for a Grand Tour on which women, for fear that they would be seduced and return home pregnant, could not embark, the education those sisters did receive was often quite as good, or as bad, as that of their brothers.

During the 19th century, the United States became the first country to adopt coeducation. Other countries eventually followed, as well as began adopting universal, compulsory schooling from about 1850 onward. In the process, the teaching profession became overwhelmingly feminized. By 1900, three-quarters of all public school teachers in the United States were female. Twenty years later, the figure was no less than 90 percent.[116] For the first time in history, large numbers of boys began to be taught by women; the more integrated the school, the more likely they were to be treated like girls. The result was that boys were, quite simply, put at a disadvantage — whether because they developed more slowly, or because they were physically more active and found it harder to spend endless hours in class, or because having to compete with girls was experienced as a humiliation.[117]

By the second half of the 19th century, girls were outperforming boys in elementary school.[118] Since then the same has become true in the high schools of almost all modern countries.[119] And the same trend is currently being observed in universities as well. At the same time, the significance of grades has been eroded. Nineteenth-century foreign visitors noted that American

---

[116] Nancy E. Durbin and Lori Kent, "Post-Secondary Education of White Women in 1900," in Julia Wrigley, ed., *Education and Gender Equality*, London, Palmer, 1992, p. 72; Tyack and Hansot, *Learning Together*, p. 149.

[117] W. O. Eaton and L. R. Enns, "Sex Differences in Human Motor Activity Level," *Psychological Bulletin*, 100, 1986, pp. 19-28.

[118]Tyack and Hansot, *Learning Together*, pp. 46, 101, 102, 114; G. R. Johnson, "Girls Do Better than Boys in Schools," *School and Society*, 47, 1938, pp. 313-4.

[119] Tyack and Hansot, *Learning Together*, pp. 114, 179; S. Klein, ed., *Handbook for Achieving Sex Equity Through Education*, Baltimore, MD, Johns Hopkins University Press, 1985; also Ingrid Jonsson, "Women and Education from a Swedish Perspective," in Wrigely, ed., *Education and Gender Equality*, p. 64, table 3.2; Jeff Hearn, "Troubled Masculinities in Social Policy Discourses: Young Men," in Popay et al., eds., *Men, Gender Divisions and Welfare*, pp. 41-3; Christina Hoff Sommer, *The War against Boys: How Misguided Feminism is Harming Our Young Men*, New York, Simon & Schuster, 2000, pp. 23-34.

schools, which were coed, tended to be less achievement-oriented than European ones.[120] Throughout the developed world today, criticizing a student, let alone marking a paper with an "F," has become taboo. As schools admitted girls, who are on average less competitive than boys, they were compelled to adjust themselves to meet those girls' needs.

Sooner or later, though, the hothouse atmosphere of school, along with the great majority of female teachers, was left behind as the sexes went their separate ways. Unless they came from well-to-do families, and often even then, most boys were pushed to take up paid work while in their early to mid-teens. Not so girls, who, regarded as the bearers of culture, were not supposed to hold jobs. They found it much easier to acquire an education; indeed, education itself was seen as a luxury intended for girls who did not have to earn a living. Boys who dared show their love for learning often earned contempt instead of respect; some were called sissies and punished. These pressures explain why, during the second half of the 19th century, girls began to outnumber boys at elementary school.[121] Among high school students, the gap was even wider. This is not surprising, given that secondary education for girls was sometimes free; by contrast, boys' parents had to pay fees.[122] By 1900, girls in American high schools outnumbered boys three to two.[123]

Take the educational system of St. Louis, which around 1900 was considered a large and progressive city. Twenty-three percent of 16-year-old European-American girls, but only 15 percent of boys of similar age and background, attended school. The figures pertaining to working youths were just the opposite: 73.7 percent of boys, but only 46.9 percent of girls, were employed.[124] Contemporaries were well aware that American women had more opportunities to study than American men;[125] some people thought this was

---

[120] Richard Rubinson, "Class Formation, Politics and Institutions: Schooling in the United States," *American Journal of Sociology*, 92, 1986, p. 521.

[121] See Hunt, *Gender and Policy in English Education*, p. 59.

[122] Tyack and Hansot, *Learning Together*, pp. 124-6, 129. The same also applied in France: Cecile Viela, "Les écoles de charité du bureau de bienfaisance de Bordeaux dans la première moitié du xix siècle," in Bernard Plongeron and Pierre Guillaume, eds., *De la charité à l'action sociale*, Paris, CTHS, 1995, p. 273.

[123] Mabel Newcomer, *A Century of Higher Education for American Women*, New York, Harper & Row, 1959, pp. 35, 42.

[124] Karen Graves, *Girls' Schooling during the Progressive Era: From Female Scholar to Domesticated Citizen*, New York, Garland, 1998, p. 166.

[125] C. F. and C. B. F. Thwing, *The Family: A Historical and Social Study*, Boston, Lee & Shepard, 1887, p. 16.

why boys, "driven from the classroom," focused on athletics as "the only place where masculine supremacy is incontestable."[126] These differences persisted. In 1950, the average years of schooling for the population aged 25 and over stood at 9.6 for women versus only 9 for men.[127] To this day, more girls graduate from high school than boys. Since more female educational institutions are closed to men than the other way around, girls also have more "collegiate options" open to them.[128]

In times and places when girls enrolled in separate schools, they were usually admitted on easier terms. They also enjoyed more comfortable circumstances, took less demanding curricula, were subjected to less severe discipline, and were able to graduate with little effort or none at all. Still not content with these advantages, they or their instructors demanded that subjects such as cooking and cleaning count as much toward receiving grants and being admitted to the universities as Latin and algebra.[129] When girls began to be educated together with boys, they *still* gravitated toward the curricula which were, or which were perceived to be, less demanding. For example, they might study the humanities rather than the exact sciences. That may be another reason why, on average, girls have long received higher grades. If girls were educated separately from boys, it was claimed they were discriminated against. If they were educated together with boys, it was said that their special needs were not being met.[130]

When women began to be admitted to universities, the same pattern was established. Oberlin College, founded in 1833 in order to train priests, was the first in any country to offer tertiary education to women. And right from the beginning, female students were exempted from calculus, which was considered to be the most difficult subject of all. The budding priests studying at Oberlin might have little use for calculus, one could argue, but how they were supposed to do without both Greek and Latin is rather less clear. These measures were not intended to discriminate against women, but rather to attract them. Indeed, as soon as four women asked to be admitted into the full men's

---

[126] Kathleen D. McCarthy, *Women's Culture: American Philanthropy and Art, 1830-1930*, Chicago, University of Chicago Press, 1991, p. 131.

[127] Newcomer, *A Century of Education for American Women*, pp. 47-8.

[128] Roslyn Arlin Mickelson, "Why Does Jane Read and Write So Well?" in Wrigley, ed., *Education and Gender Equality*, p. 153; Solomon, *In the Company of Educated Women*, p. 207.

[129] Hunt, *Gender and Policy in English Education*, pp. 84, 85, 120.

[130] Hunt, *Gender and Policy in English Education*, p. 141.

course in 1837, their request was granted. Nevertheless, the great majority of women continued to enroll in the easier ladies' course.[131]

Other 19th century women's colleges developed their programs similarly. Wellesley, founded in 1875, claimed from the outset to be as good as any male school. But unlike its male counterparts, Wellesley it did not require the "formidable" subject of Greek for admission. Though Vassar and Bryn Mawr both had high admission standards, in neither was Greek required.[132] In fact, of all the early women's colleges, only Smith equaled its male counterparts. Founded in 1871, after just a few years it was left practically without students and had to start cutting corners.[133] As late as the 1950s, only a very small minority of women's colleges mentioned scholarship "in the sense of developing intellectual curiosity and love of knowledge" in the catalogues they used to attract students.[134]

According to Mabel Newcomer, a Vassar professor of economics who studied the question during the late 1950s, "the women's colleges as a whole have provided better dormitory facilities, and more elaborate gardens and grounds, than other colleges. The economizing is done elsewhere. The parlors of the women's dormitories, at least, are apt to be redecorated at frequent intervals by professional decorators, even though the classrooms, which account for more student hours per week than any parlor, remain dingy and unattractive. If faculty resides in the student dormitories their quarters are more elegant than anything their colleagues achieve on their own salaries; and faculty offices tend to be as bare as monks' cells."

Justifying the amenities, Newcomer claimed that they "would be wasted on men" who did not need "white-capped maids" to wait on them but were happy to eat in cafeterias. Though tuition cost more in men's colleges than in women's, when room and board were added the situation was the reverse; men spent more on study, women on leading a gracious life. Not only did living like ladies carry a price, it was a price paid disproportionally by others. At the time two-thirds of college men, but only half of women, contributed to the costs of

---

[131] Elizabeth Seymour Eschbach, *The Higher Education of Women in England and America, 1865-1920*, New York, Garland, 1993, p. 4.

[132] Newcomer, *A Century of Higher Education for American Women*, pp. 83, 85.

[133] See Eschbach, *The Higher Education of Women in England and America*, pp. 62-4.

[134] Newcomer, *A Century of Higher Education for American Women*, pp. 59, 82; Eschbach, *The Higher Education of Women in England and America*, p. 53.

their own education.[135] As late as 1987, women received more financial support for attending college than men did.[136]

Preparing to make a living, men chose fields such as engineering, agriculture and law. Preparing to become housewives or, if they failed to find a husband, to teach, women chose home economics and education.[137] As late as 1961, only a small percentage of American female college students were concerned with making a living.[138] The most they expected to do was to find a nice, clean job in an office where they might meet a future mate. Many passed straight from college into their husbands' homes, if they did not break off their studies in order to get married first. By and large, the same pattern has persisted to the present day. In the United States, as in other countries, men form the vast majority among engineering and natural science students. Conversely, women outnumber men in the humanities and, more recently, many of the social sciences as well.[139]

Feminists have often blamed women's tendency to focus on the humanities on society's "steering" them in that direction. In fact, the opposite is usually the case. Even as children, girls are more likely to be admitted to boys' company than vice versa.[140] In the past, attempts to lure more women into technical work and the natural sciences failed to change the situation.[141] To this day, the most demanding fields in higher education, such as engineering and physics, are

---

[135] Newcomer, *A Century of Higher Education for American Women*, pp. 113, 124, 153, 155, 157.

[136] See Paul Taubman, "The Role of the Family in the Formation of Offspring's Earnings and Income Capacity," in Paul L. Menchik, ed., *Household and Family Economics*, Boston, Kluwer, 1996, p. 35 fn. 22.

[137] Newcomer, *A Century of Higher Education for American Women*, p. 91.

[138] Solomon, *In the Company of Educated Women*, p. 197; Newcomer, *A Century of Higher Education for Women*, p. 175.

[139] For figures relating to various countries, see Sara Delamont, *A Woman's Place in Education*, Aldershot, Avebury, 1996, pp. 97-8, 117; Statistiches Amt der Europäischen Gemeinschaft, *Frauen in der Europäischen Gemeinschaft*, Luxemburg, Amt für amtliche Veröffentlichungen der Europäischen Gemeinschaft, 1999, pp. 61, 64; Rosemary Simmen, "Women in Switzerland since 1970: Major Achievements or Minor Changes?" in Joy Charnley et al., eds., *25 Years of Emancipation? Women in Switzerland 1971-1996*, Bern, Lang, 1998, p. 19; Joan Wolffensperger, "Engendered Structure: Education and the Conceptualization of Gender," in Kathy Davis et al., eds., *The Gender of Power*, London, Sage, 1991, pp. 93-6; and *Der Spiegel*, 2.8.1999, p. 82; Christiane Dienel, *Frauen in Führungspositionen in Europa*, Weinheim, Deutsches Jugendinstitut, 1996, pp. 25-6.

[140] Barrie Thorne, "Girls and Boys Together... but Mostly Apart," in Wrigley, ed., *Education and Gender Equality*, p. 125.

[141] See Jonsson, "Women in Education from a Swedish Perspective," p. 50.

those that have the fewest female students.[142] Barring theories concerning the different intellectual capacities of the sexes, which at the moment are so out of fashion that a president of Harvard was fired for mentioning them, two explanations for this state of affairs come to mind. First, girls' different upbringing may mean that, having been indulged and pampered from birth, they shy away from any subject that is, or is said to be, difficult. They are said to be "extremely ingenious and determined" in doing so.[143] Second, relatively few women expect to feed a family. Consequently the subjects they do enter are often chosen with objectives other than having a lucrative career — in other words, women are freer to study what they like.

Many women enter the humanities and some of the social sciences because these fields are initially considered easy. As the difficulty increases, they often drop out, if not during their studies then later while trying to climb the academic ladder. The remaining ones tend to enter female ghettoes. Among them are two-year community colleges, gender studies departments, and certain other departments staffed and attended[144] almost entirely by women. "Soft" medical specialties, such as pediatrics, psychiatry and general practice, also have more than their share of women.[145] Surveys in several countries confirm that female academics are, on average, considerably less productive than their male colleagues.[146] Women's inability or unwillingness to compete with men

---

[142] T. Loose. (8.1.2013). "Ever Wonder Which Majors Require the Most Study Time?", *Yahoo Education*, retrieved from http://education.yahoo.net/articles/most_demanding_majors.htm?kid_1LCND

[143] Lynda Measor, "Gender and the Sciences," in Martyn Hammersley and Peter Woods, eds., *Life in School*, Milton Keynes, Open University Press, 1984, p. 65.

[144] Evelyn Torton Beck, "To Make Our Lives a Study," in Lie and O'Leary, eds, *Storming the Tower*, London, Kogan Page, 1990, p. 218.

[145] For the United States, see Valian, *Why So Slow?*, p. 208; for Britain and Australia, see Rosemary Pringle, *Sex and Medicine: Gender, Power and Authority in the Medical Profession*, Cambridge, Cambridge University Press, 1998, pp. 150-2; also see Beck, "To Make Our Lives a Study," p. 218.

[146] See Sara Delamont, *A Woman's Place in Education*, pp. 110-2. Swedish women also chose less prestigious occupations: Jonsson, "Women in Education from a Swedish Perspective," pp. 55-6; Diane E. Davis and Helen S. Astin, "Life Cycle, Career Patterns and Gender Stratification in Academe," in Lie and O'Leary, eds., *Storming the Tower*, p. 92, table 6.1. p. 94, table 6.2; Suzanne S. Lie, "The Juggling Act: Work and Family in Norway," *ibid*, pp. 109, 111, 123; J. R. Cole and Harriet Zuckerman, "The Productivity Puzzle," in P. Maehr and M. W. Steinkampf, eds., *Advancement in Motivation and Achievement*, Greenwich, CT, JAI Press, 1984, pp. 217-56; M. F Faver and C. A. Faver, "Men, Women and Publication Productivity," *Sociological Quarterly*, 26, 1985, pp. 537-49.

may explain why, even in the five remaining all-female colleges in the United States, males form a majority of full professors.[147] It also explains why women-only academic contests and prizes have a long history.[148]

Conversely, the few women who do show courage and do enter the "difficult" specialties explicitly deny being discriminated against.[149] Often they do as well as their male colleagues.[150] Still, even in those fields Nobel prizes, which among other things reflect exceptionally great effort and sacrifice, are awarded mainly to men. According to some analyses, the much greater readiness of men to follow paths involving harder work and leading to larger rewards is a direct result of their enforced break from their mothers. Others believe it has something to do with men's hormones, testosterone in particular, which on average make them more aggressive and more competitive.[151]

Be that as it may, we have seen that society's way of preparing men for the heavy burdens they must bear as adults is to put increasingly greater burdens on them, beginning right at birth. The same behavior may cause girls to be pampered, indulged and comforted, while boys are pushed away and scolded. Starting with parents, these differences are reinforced by means of initiation rites and also by whatever school system may be available in the society in question. If only because men wanted to marry suitable women, at any given time and place it was only the most Spartan schools which did not have a female equivalent. The opposite also applied: once women were admitted to such schools, it was only a question of time before they ceased to be Spartan.

Once the schools started admitting girls and ceased being Spartan, boys *still* tended to be discriminated against by the growing number of female teachers. Unable to cope with the boys' greater boisterousness, female teachers did what they could to suppress it.[152] If, during breaks, girls failed to take part in boys' games, then it was said that they were excluded. If they did take part, on the

---

[147] Valian, *Why So Slow?*, p. 227.

[148] McCarthy, *Women's Culture*, pp. 20, 101, 109.

[149] See J. R. Cole and B. Singer, "A Theory of Limited Differences: Explaining the Productivity Puzzle in Science," in Harriet Zuckerman et al., eds., *The Outer Circle: Women in the Scientific Community*, New York, Norton, 1991, pp. 277-310.

[150] See (in Hebrew) Ninna Toren, "Men and Women on the Faculty of the Hebrew University, 1983/1993," figures on pp. 10, 11, 12.

[151] See on this Steven Goldberg, *Why Men Rule: A Theory of Male Dominance*, Chicago, Open Court, 1993.

[152] See Jere Brophy, "Interactions of Male and Female Students with Male and Female Teachers," in Louise C. Wilkinson and Cera B. Marrett, eds., *Gender Influences in Classroom Education*, New York, Academic Press, 1985, pp. 115-42.

other hand, then it was declared that they were being harassed. All this suppression and all this discrimination almost certainly constitute one reason why, at most levels of short of the highest, boys tend to do less well than girls. Conversely, the less challenging and demanding a school, the better girls do in comparison with boys.

When the point is finally reached when they are given a choice, both men and women continue to do exactly what society expects of them. Preparing to become wives whose first duty is to assist their husbands as they make their way in the world, proportionally more women go into fields that will enable them to wend their way through society without undue embarrassment. Nowadays, it must be added, women must also consider how to make a living if they should at some point in the future go through divorce. Proportionally more men, meanwhile, preparing to become husbands whose first duty is to provide for their wives, go for fields that are difficult and require hard work. The more advanced the school, the truer this becomes.

5. Conclusions

Since 1970 or so, a considerable amount of literature has sought to show that women, as women, are disregarded, oppressed and discriminated against by men. The truth, however, is just the opposite. Whether for biological, psychological or social reasons, it is women and not men who are seen as particularly interesting. This was as true around 1300, when pseudo-Albertus Magnus wrote *Women's Secrets*, as it is today. Whether for biological, psychological or social reasons, in almost any field the literature written about women exceeds that dealing with men many times over. This, too, was as true in the past as it is today. At almost every stage in life, both men *and* women have always made life harder for men. Since the same applies to primates, some of it may have genetic roots. However, for the most part it is deliberately planned by people of both sexes. The objective is to prepare men for the hardship of adulthood, and the method is to make life hard for them even before adulthood is reached.

The lesser efforts demanded of women may also have something to do with the psychology of mating. This is because, to gain access to a woman, a man has to perform and pay. All other things being equal, the better his performance and the more he can pay, the more likely he is to impress both the woman and her relatives. This was as true among the Australian aborigines as it is in today's most advanced Western societies. By contrast, one of the best ways for a woman to attract a man is to be lonely, helpless and poor. This is especially true if she is young and good looking, and especially if her plight can be blamed not on herself but on some other man. For every man who has ever "oppressed" a woman, there has been another who was standing ready to save her so as to gain her favors, even at the risk of his own life.

For a woman to make an effort, cope with hardship and gain independence is but one road toward finding a mate. Worse still, such a course of action may actually be counterproductive. Studies show that female undergraduates believe men dislike women whom they see as too smart,[153] and they may be right. As has been said, if it is better for a woman to be good looking than intelligent, this is because men are better at looking than at thinking. Now, as in the 19th century,[154] the better educated a woman and the more successful her career, the less likely she is to be married and have children. Most of the time, girls received their schooling separately from boys, a fact that contemporaries justified by the need to preserve decency. How right they were is proved by the fact that, now that coeducation has become the norm, boys as young as 4 years old risk being accused of sexual harassment;[155] it is as if their teachers, almost all of whom are adult women, want to punish them for being male.

As long as they received their schooling separately from boys, girls almost always had an easier time at it. When this ceased to be the case, either they continued to have an easier time at it or else their "humanizing" and "softening" presence caused everybody to be given an easier time. Boys who, whether because of the harsher treatment they received or because of the lack of challenge, started misbehaving were punished. Nowadays, they are drugged; among children diagnosed with a variety of behavioral problems, proportionally far more boys than girls are prescribed Ritalin.[156] All this was as true in the West as it was on the other side of the world; in early twentieth-century China;[157] at a time when most people only attended a few classes of elementary school, as when forty percent of a given age group enter some sort

---

[153] See Delamont, *A Woman's Place in Education*, p. 12.

[154] Claudia Goldin, *Understanding the Gender Gap: An Economic History of American Women*, New York, Oxford University Press, 1990, pp. 204-5; Lynn D. Gordon, *Gender and Higher Education in the Progressive Era*, New Haven, CT, Yale University Press, 1990, pp. 31, 32.

[155] B. Schulte, "For Little Children, Grown-Up Labels as Sexual Harassers," *Washington Post*, 3.4.2008.

[156] Lawrence H. Diller, *Running on Ritalin*, New York, Bantam, 1999, pp. 35-6.

[157] See Pang-Mei Natasha Chang, *Bound Feet and Western Dress*, New York, Anchor Books, 1996, pp. 47, 59-60.

of academy or college; when most youngsters joined the workforce as teenagers as when "boys" of thirty-something sit for exams and "girls" of the same age have yet to give birth.

Yet sooner or later the moment will come when almost all women want to become pregnant, deliver babies and care for their offspring. The moment will also come when almost all men, on pain of failing to find a female partner or of losing the one they already have, have to assume the extra burden which results from women getting pregnant, delivering babies and caring for their offspring. As people of both sexes prepare for that moment, gaps in education — "human capital," in scholarly parlance — open up. Willy-nilly, most women drop out of the rat race or enter one of several available female ghettoes, where they are largely among themselves and where there is less competition. Willy-nilly, most men either work by the sweat of their brows in whatever jobs they can get, or continue to study to prepare themselves to compete for the higher, more responsible, more difficult and more lucrative positions society has to offer. Though there are some exceptions, most women settle into a life in which they are provided for and protected. Though there are some exceptions, most men step into one in which they provide and protect.

Finally, not only are men doomed to support women but, since resources are always scarce, doing so means that they have to compete with other men. On top of the other hardships it involves, competition prevents men from opening up to each other or to women. The heavy burden they assume, and the harsh treatment they receive, must remain unmentioned. The greater a man's success, the truer this becomes. A man, as the saying goes, is expected to "take it" — irrespective of what the "it" actually entails. If he confesses his difficulties, he will likely find himself despised by men and avoided by women.[158] All this explains why men have a much higher threshold for crying than women do, and why married men in particular are less likely than any group to ask for psychological help.[159] After all, they have responsibilities to shoulder.

Should men fail, then only too often the first to desert them are their wives. The need to compete also explains why occasional attempts to set up men's

---

[158] See Roy Schafer, "Men Who Struggle Against Sentimentality," in Fogel et al., eds., *The Psychology of* Men, pp. 95-110; Jeff Hearn, "The Welfare of Men?" in Popay et al., eds., *Men, Gender Divisions and Welfare*, p. 27.

[159] Virginia Valian, *Why So Slow?*, p. 109; Phyllis Chesler, *Women and Madness*, New York Doubleday, 1972, p. 57; Jessie Bernard, *The Future of Marriage*, Harmondsworth, Middlesex, Penguin, 1973, pp. 309-14, tables 1-10.

movements have not been very successful. As in some fairy tale, the best a man may hope for is to meet a stranger in an inn. He may buy him a glass of wine, pour out his troubles and hope to be presented with some sagacious piece of advice. In one version of the story, a man is reduced to talking to a fish. To some readers, parts of the present chapter — with its emphasis on the much greater hardship of becoming and being a man — may sound maudlin and self-pitying. If so, then this merely proves my case.

Chapter 3: Men, Women and Work

1. A Short History of Labor

In our own day, perhaps the first question a person is asked when meeting a stranger is what work he or she does. The implication is that *not* working is, if not a misdemeanor, then at the very least slightly dishonorable. A man who does not work for a living will probably be called a playboy or a parasite, while such a woman will be labeled a socialite or a housewife.

However, as the biblical tale concerning the expulsion of Adam and Eve from the Garden of Eden makes clear, during most of history work tended to be seen as something unpleasant, hard and even dangerous. Similar attitudes permeate the rest of the Old Testament. In fact, ancient Hebrew does not really have a term for "work;" the modern word for it, *avoda*, derives from the root *avad*, "to serve." Service could be to a god, in which case it was only positive in case it entailed worship of the great and jealous Jehovah. It could also be to a human, in which case its connotations were almost always negative. The Bible tells us countless times of a people being conquered and made to "serve" another ruler. The Israelites called out to God against the "service" forced upon them by the Egyptians. In short, to work was an act that was anything but agreeable. In fact a secondary meaning of the term is "to pay tribute." From *avad*, too, comes the standard word for "slave," *eved*, implying that work equals servitude, and vice versa.[1]

Likewise, the Greek term for labor, *ponos*, can also mean "suffering" or "penalty"[2]; its opposite, *hedone*, can be translated as "ease" or "pleasure." A good example of what *ponos* might involve is provided by the 12 "labors" Zeus imposed on Heracles for killing his brother Eurystheus in a drunken fit. Some

---

[1] See Isaac Mendelsohn, *Slavery in the Ancient Near East*, New York, Oxford University Press, 1949, pp. 96-7.

[2] See Birgit van den Hoven, *Work in Ancient and Medieval Thought*, Amsterdam, Gieben, 1996, pp. 28-30, 31-8; also Paul Ransome, *The Work Paradigm: A Theoretical Investigation of Concepts of Work*, Aldershot, Avebury, 1996, pp. 102-5.

ponoi were humiliating. Others involved working in mountains of filth, whereas others still were life-threatening. As with the Greek *ponos*, the Latin term *labor* also carries secondary meanings of "endurance" "suffering" and "hardship. " It also carries another meaning, "distress," including the kind of physical distress that women suffer in childbirth.[3] The modern English "labor," the Italian "*lavoro*" and the French "*travail*" have retained these various meanings. English, moreover, makes the link between work and suffering doubly clear by suggesting that a person "labors under" this or that difficulty.

In both Greece and Rome, the fundamental distinction was between slaves who worked (and very likely suffered as they did so) and free men who, if they could, did not work. In Buddhist thought, the fundamental distinction was between secular persons and sacred ones. Secular persons were either those who worked for a living, such as merchants or craftsmen, or else ruled over others who did so and supported them by their labor, such as princes and warriors. Sacred ones were also supported by the labor of others. However, rather than taking charge of society, they spent their time praying or looking at their navels. It is true that Taoist thought did not distinguish between sacred and secular persons to the same extent. However, here too the ideal was not work, but meditation. Self-enhancement, understood as freedom from earthly concerns, was and remains the common goal of both religions.

The common language of the Middle Ages being Latin, many of the connotations which that language associated with "*labor*" remained as they were. If anything, Western Christianity, guided by the Old Testament, created an even stronger association between work, sin and punishment.[4] It is often said that medieval society consisted of those who fought, those who prayed and those who worked. Though this is an oversimplification, the fact that those who worked were located at the bottom of the societal ladder speaks for itself. What made the Middle Ages different from the ancient world, and also from biblical times, was the fact that chattel slavery — the kind of slavery in which a class of people were legally the property of others, had no rights whatsoever, and were predestined for nothing but work — was rare. As a result, working was not automatically associated with servitude. At least in theory, it was not considered demeaning either. Particularly if one lived in a town rather than in the countryside, one could engage in work and still be a free person.

---

[3] See N. Loraux, "*Ponos*: Sur quelques difficultés de la peine comme nom du travail," *Annali del seminario de studi del mondo classico*, 1982, pp. 171-92.

[4] van den Hoven, *Work in Ancient and Medieval Thought*, p. 30.

In theory, if not in practice, those at the top of the ladder were not supposed to work. They administered, hunted and fought. And what was the situation of the members of the second estate, monks and nuns? Their vocation in life was to worship God. However, it was recognized that doing so to the exclusion of everything else was unhealthy for both body and mind. A few ascetics apart, there are limits as to how many hours people can spend praying or meditating without losing their minds. In any case, the days when prophets lived in the desert and commanded ravens to feed them were gone. Many monasteries were large and complex organizations. Hence the rule, first instituted by St. Benedict early in the 6th century, that monks and nuns should work — *laborare et orare*, as the saying went — as well as pray.[5]

Later the idea that work is a positive thing in itself was taken up by the lay community, specifically the Protestants. As Martin Luther put it in the first of his 95 Theses, for Protestants "the whole of life [was] penance." Protestantism also did away with prayer, the sacraments and good works as the path to salvation. Faith apart, perhaps the principal way to get to heaven was by means of productive labor. It was performed in the hope that it would lead to riches and prove to the owner that he or she was one of God's chosen ones.[6] The implication was that work as such was hard and unpleasant, and the temptation to abandon it both constant and great. Hence the numerous warnings against idleness that have formed the stock-in trade of Protestant culture from the 16th century to this very day.[7]

Between about 1600 and 1800, the idea that work was good for the soul permeated society at large, as is also shown by the workhouses that began to be established in Amsterdam, London and elsewhere.[8] The next stage was to extend the system to the prisons. Taking the place of other forms of punishment, such as exile, fines, flogging, mutilation and death, prisons began dotting the European countryside from about 1780 on. Once prisons existed, it was not long before work began to be used in society's efforts to reform its

---

[5] van der Hoven, *Work in Ancient and Medieval Thought*, pp. 152-8. For the importance of the Benedictine rule in establishing the ethic of work see also Lynn White, *Machina ex Deo: Essays in the Dynamism of Western Culture*, Cambridge, MA, MIT Press, 1968, p. 63.

[6] See Richard H. Tawney, *Religion and the Rise of Capitalism*, London, Murray, 1960 [1926], p. 108.

[7] See William C. Carroll, *Fat King, Lean Beggar: Representations of Poverty in the Age of Shakespeare*, Ithaca, NY, Cornell University Press, 1996, pp. 4-5.

[8] See J. Bentham, *Panopticon; or, the Inspection House,* London. Payne, 1794; also see J. Mill, "Prisons and Prison Discipline," in James Mill, *Political Writings*, Terence Ball, ed., Cambridge, Cambridge University Press, 1992, pp. 195-224.

criminals. To prevent prisoners from engaging in unfair competition with those toiling outside, often the work they did was completely inane, as with digging holes and then filling them again. However, even in its most inane forms work was supposed to instill such habits as order, regularity and discipline.[9] Incidentally, the same claims were made by the "*Arbeit macht frei*" signs that stand at the entrance to Auschwitz, Dachau and other Nazi concentration camps.

In summary, during most of history and in places as far apart as Western Europe, India and China, labor was commonly viewed as something unpleasant, difficult and demeaning. As a result, it was often inflicted as punishment. To be sure, Protestant attitudes were different. Even in this case, though, it was not so much labor that was glorified, as idleness that was denounced. Indeed, it would hardly be too much to say that Protestantism glorified work precisely *because* it was unpleasant and, therefore, well-suited to doing "penance." It was only during the 20th century that attitudes changed and work began to be seen as something positive in and of itself. Even so, that view did not always extend among the lower classes (or "working classes," as they are alternatively known). For them work remained a harsh necessity to be avoided whenever possible — and with good reason, as anybody who has ever visited a mine or foundry knows.

2. Men's Work, Women's Work

Given these attitudes toward work, some of them purely subjective but others rooted in the hard reality of physical labor, it would seem appropriate to ask how exactly that physical labor has been divided between men and women. Perhaps the earliest answer to the question is provided by the Bible: when God drove the first human couple out of Eden, it was Adam and not Eve whom he punished by decreeing that "by the sweat of thy brow shalt thou eat bread."[10] Why He did so is a matter for conjecture. It may have been because men are stronger and more suitable for physical labor; but it may also have been because God felt that, in this respect, women should not be treated as harshly as men.

---

[9] J. A. Sharpe, *Crime in Early Modern England 1550-1750*, London, Longman, 1984, pp. 178-80.
[10] *Genesis*, 3.17-9.

The story of Sisyphus may have been governed by a similar logic. Sisyphus had successfully tricked the gods and was punished by being made to push heavy stones up a hill. However, no sooner did he reach the top then they rolled down, forcing him to start all over. Provided the stones were lighter, there was no reason why a woman should not have been given similar punishment. Now, Greek mythology has plenty of wicked women who committed sins, and who were made to suffer various punishments, from madness to being turned into a spider. None, however, was made to labor as hard as Sisyphus was.

To the extent that mythological women were made to labor, their work was rather light. Several Greek goddesses spun and weaved. So did Greek nymphs; the *Odyssey* has an idyllic picture of the nymph Circe singing merrily while working the loom.[11] The tales of other peoples, notably German and Russian ones, are similar. Wodan's wife Freya engaged in embroidery. Many fairy tales present us with male heroes sent on impossible missions from which they were not expected to return. By contrast, women's work, even such as was forced, consisted of housekeeping (Cinderella), spinning or sorting various small objects. Such work might be tedious, unpleasant and even impossible, as in the case of the girl who was ordered to spin hay into gold. If the work was not performed on time dire punishment may have been threatened, but rarely did the work itself involve real hardship.

If etymology proves that work has historically been regarded as a burden rather than a privilege, it also shows that men always did the heaviest labor. Thus, the Biblical term *eved*, "slave," only has a male form. The terms for "female slave," *shifcha* and *ama*, are related to the Semitic words for "female" and "family."[12] This reflects the fact that female slaves often served as concubines. Clearly, neither term connotes anything to do with labor. Similarly in Germanic languages, *Arbeiter* (laborer) was originally male and only acquired its female form after 1800. A second word, *schaffen*, is said to be derived from the Old German *scaffan*, "bent double."[13] In addition to its primary meaning of "to create," it also mean "to succeed by hard work," "to toil," or "to slog." The derivative term for "worker," *Schaffer*, is male and often used as a surname. As such, it has no female equivalent.

Reality reflected legends and language, or perhaps things worked the other way around. Proceeding in rough chronological order, in ancient Egypt the

---

[11] *Odyssey*, 10.220-23.

[12] Mendelsohn, *Slavery in the Ancient Near East*, p. 99; Dr. Haim Kahana, letter to the author, 2.7.01.

[13] *Ullstein Lexikon der deutschen Sprache*, Berlin, Ullstein, 1969, p. 767.

100,000 persons conscripted each year to build the pyramids — who, as pictures show, were soundly whipped when they did not pull their weight — were not women, but men. Men, whether prisoners of war or those enlisted by press-gangs, constructed roads, dug canals, erected fortresses and built temples all over the ancient Middle East.[14] According to the Bible, King Solomon used tens of thousands of male slaves to obtain the materials for building the Lord's Temple.[15] Men, not women, built the Great Wall of China, dying by the thousands in the process. Countless male slaves, but very few female ones, worked in the silver mines of Laurion from which classical Athens derived much of its wealth.[16]

Men, not women, sometimes took the place of beasts of burden in turning industrial-scale mills where corn was ground. Much like modern prisons, the places where such work was done were normally considered too unsavory to attract visits by members of polite society. During the second century A.D, however, one of them was inspected by the Roman writer Apuleius, who reported that:[17]

> Merciful gods, what wretched manikins did I see there, their entire skin covered with bluish welts, their backs torn into bloody strips, barely covered with rags, some having only their genitals covered with a piece of cloth, all of them showing everything through their tatters. Their foreheads were branded with letters, their heads half shorn, their feet stuck in rings. They were hideously pale, the dank of the stinking hole had consumed their eyelashes and diminished their sight. Like wrestlers, who are sprinkled with a fine powder as they fight their bouts, they were blanched with a layer of dirty-white flour.

Being a female slave, to be sure, was hardly all fun and games, both because of the nature of their labor and because they were sexually at the mercy of their owners. However, a scrawny prostitute, or one dressed in tatters, or one too frightened to properly play her role, would have commanded a much lower

[14] Mendelsohn, *Slavery in the Ancient Near East*, p. 92.

[15] *Kings*, 5.27-30.

[16] On slavery in these mines see I. Morris, "Remaining Invisible: The Archaeology of the Excluded in Classical Athens," in Sandra R. Joshel and Sheila Murnaghan, eds., *Women and Slaves in Greco-Roman Culture: Differential Equations*, London, Routledge, 1998, pp. 199-211.

[17] Apuleius, *Metamorphoses*, 9.12.

price, if any. Hence workers in the oldest profession are usually well fed, reasonably clothed and tolerably housed. They are also unlikely to undergo physical punishment so severe as to permanently damage their charms. In any case, as references in Petronius, Horace and Seneca show, male slaves were also open to sexual exploitation.[18]

Male manpower, some of it conscripted and some consisting of prisoners of war, built the Roman roads and erected the Coliseum. When the Spaniards in Mexico and Peru instituted the *repartimiento*, or "forced labor," system as a method for working their silver mines, it was once again men and not women who were sent down the shafts.[19] This system itself was based on the Aztec and Inca ones for conscripting men, not women, to build temples, construct roads and act as beasts of burden in societies that neither possessed large domestic animals nor had invented the wheel. In fact, all pre-monetary economies used forced male labor to carry out large-scale public works. Even in Western Europe, *corvées*, which Adam Smith called "one of the principal forms of Tyranny,"[20] persisted until the end of the 18th century. In Eastern Europe, where men were made to work for free on two, three, even four days of the week, it lasted into the 1860s.[21] To the extent that women participated, they worked shorter hours and performed lighter tasks.[22]

In none of these societies was the social and legal position of women equal to that of men. To the extent that attempts were made to balance matters, however, the differences were *still* maintained when it came to work. In the *Republic* Plato created a society that was, sexually speaking, perhaps more integrated than any in history. To enable women to participate fully in the life of the *polis*, families were abolished and newborns taken from their mothers to be raised communally. Men and women trained together in the gymnasium, and ran the city together. And yet, Plato nonetheless has Socrates state that "lighter tasks must be assigned to the women than to the men because of their weakness as a class."[23] Had Plato been alive today, this sentence would undoubtedly have had him labeled a woman-hater. The same could be said of Thomas More,

---

[18] Petronius, *Satyricon*, 75.11; Horace, *Satires*, 1.2.116-19; Seneca, *Controversies*, IB praef. 1. See also Beert C. Verstraete, "Slavery and the Social Dynamics of Male Homosexual Relations in Ancient Rome," *Journal of Homosexuality*, 5, 3, spring 1980, pp. 227-36.

[19] See J. Juan and A. de Ulloa, *Discourse and Political Reflections on the Kingdoms of Peru*, Tulsa, OK, University of Oklahoma Press, 1978, p. 77 ff.

[20] *The Wealth of Nations*, Chicago, Chicago University Press, 1976 [1776], p. 253.

[21] See Karl Marx, *Capital*, Chicago, Kerr, 1932 [1867], vol. 1, pp. 262-3.

[22] August Meitzen, *Urkunden schlesischer Dörfer*, Breslau, Parey, 1863, p. 334.

[23] *Republic*, 457 A-B.

Thomas Campanella, Charles Fourier and countless other utopian writers. Why women have always been assigned the lighter tasks is quite clear.

Thanks largely to the attempts to integrate women into the armed forces of many modern countries, the physical differences between the sexes have been precisely measured.[24] One study found the average U.S. Army female recruit to be 12 centimeters shorter and 14.3 kilograms lighter than her male brethren. Compared to the average male recruit, females had 16.9 fewer kilograms of muscle and 2.6 more kilograms of fat, as well as 55 percent of the upper body strength and 72 percent of the lower body strength. Fat mass is inversely related to aerobic capacity and heat tolerance, hence women are also at a disadvantage when performing activities such as carrying heavy loads, working in the heat and running. Even when the samples were controlled for height, women possessed only 80 percent of the overall strength of men. Only the upper 20 percent of women could do as well physically as the lower 20 percent of men. Had the 100 strongest individuals out of a random group consisting of 100 men and 100 women been selected, 93 would be male and only seven female.[25] Yet another study showed gthat only the upper 5 percent of women are as strong as the median male.[26]

Another definition of women's work was that it did not take those engaged in it very far from their homes or into unexplored territory. In part, the reason why women seldom undertook long travel, a term itself linked to the French word for work, *travaille*, was because once married they would spend much of their time either pregnant, breastfeeding or looking after their children. In part, however, it was because such travel was dangerous. The dangers might come either from the elements, or from people, or from both. Dangers posed by the elements explain why women did not normally join deep-sea fishing expeditions. Nor, except as passengers, did they embark on vessels engaged in maritime commerce. Dangers posed by both the elements and by people explain why they did not often embark on long journeys on land. It was not every ruler who, like Egyptian Pharaoh Ramses III, could boast that women

---

[24] See Brian Mitchell, *Women in the Military: The Weak Link*, Orlando, FL, Regnery, 1996, pp. 141-2.

[25] Desmond Morris, *Manwatching; A Field Guide to Human Behavior*, New York, Abrams, 1977, pp. 239-40.

[26] Presidential Commission on the Assignment of Women in the Armed Forces, *Report to the President*, Washington, Government Printing Office, 1993, p. C-74.

were able to travel safely throughout his kingdom.[27] And even that boast was almost certainly spurious.

Women's physical weakness and their reluctance to move far from home have always dictated the nature of female work.[28] Men hunted big game and were sometimes killed while so engaged; women, by contrast, went for smaller and less dangerous creatures.[29] Men covered long distances running, whereas women proceeded at a leisurely pace, taking breaks whenever it suited them, gathering roots and berries. Men dived for pearls, while women stayed ashore, went for shallow-water clams or processed the catch.[30] Men herded the larger and harder-to-handle animals, such as camels, horses and cattle. Women's charges were smaller domestic animals and poultry.

In the 1830s the French political scientist Alexis de Tocqueville toured the United States gathering material for his celebrated *Democracy in America.* American women, he wrote, were never "compelled to perform the rough labor of the fields, or to make any of those laborious exertions which demand the exertion of physical strength." "No families," he added, "are so poor as to form an exception to this rule."[31] Another visitor was Harriet Martineau, the most famous female economist of her age. One modern female researcher says that she "made more trenchant observations about women than de Tocqueville ever imagined."[32] One thing she observed was that the hair of American husbands "stands on end at the idea of his wife working, and he toils to provide her with money."[33]

In 19th-century America, it was cowboys, not cowgirls, who spent weeks on the trail, sleeping in the open air, unable to wash, shave or change clothes, while driving cattle from grazing ground to market and from market to

---

[27] Miriam Lichtheim, *Ancient Egyptian Literature*, Berkeley, CA, University of California Press, 1975-80, vol. 2, p. 137.

[28] See G. P. Murdock, "Comparative Data on the Division of Labor by Sex," *Social Forces*, 15, 1937, pp. 551-3.

[29] For the island of Vanatinai east of Papua New Guinea, see Maria Lepowsky, "Gender in an Egalitarian Society," in Peggy Reeves Sanday and Ruth Gallagher Goodenough, eds., *Beyond the Second Sex: New Directions in the Anthropology of Gender*, Philadelphia, University of Philadelphia Press, 1990, pp. 180, 182, 202.

[30] See Malcolm Gray, *The Fishing Industries of Scotland, 1790-1914*, Oxford, Oxford University Press, 1978, p. 13; Nancy Dorian, *Tyranny of Tide*, Ann Arbor, MI, Karoma, 1985, p. 33.

[31] *Democracy in America*, New York, Schocken, 1967 [1835-40), p. 252.

[32] See Wendy Kaminer, *A Fearful Freedom: Women's Flight from Equality*, Reading, MA, Addison-Wesley, 1990, p. 39.

[33] *Society in America*, New York, Doubleday, 1966 [1837], vol. 3, p. 106.

railhead. In other societies, too, the less pleasant, the more demanding and the more dangerous a job, the more likely it was to be done by men.[34] In China, both the dominant Confucian ideology and the prevailing unsafe conditions resulted in women being expected to work in or near the home; indeed, one word for wife is *neiren*, "inside person."[35] As a result, they only carried out between 5 percent and 38 percent of all agricultural work. Well into the present century, to see them wielding a hoe was considered shocking.[36] When Communist officials tried to change the system and get women to work with men in the fields during the 1950s, people of both sexes did what they could to resist their demands.

What was true in agriculture was also true in other work. Ancient Egyptian didactic texts describe *all* the trades which men could enter, except that of scribe, as arduous by definition.[37] Men erected houses, while women gathered straw and thatched roofs. (When roofs began to be made up of wood or stone, however, women disappeared from building sites). Women may have baked in the home, but the heavy, hot work of kneading dough and baking bread on a commercial scale was almost always done by men. Women may have spun and combed and carded, but the heavier work of operating looms to produce cloth for sale was done by men.[38] Though it is true that women were everywhere responsible for household work, with most people living at or near the subsistence level, the burden was minimal. Among both hunter-gatherer societies as well as nomadic cattle-herding peoples, housework in our sense barely existed. In most other societies, whether rural or urban, the vast majority of the population ate simple, easy-to-prepare food. Possessing no more than a

---

[34] For a modern example see Tuula Heinonen, "Negotiating Ideal Womanhood in Rural Philippine Households: Work and Survival," in Parvin Ghorayshi and Claire Belanger, eds., *Women, Work and Gender Relations in Developing Countries: A Global Perspective*, Westport, CT, Greenwood, 1996, pp. 109-10.

[35] See Tamara Jacka, *Women's Work in Rural China: Change and Continuity in an Era of Reform*, Cambridge, Cambridge University Press, 1997, p. 22.

[36] R. S. Watson, "Girls' Houses and Working Women," in Maria Jaschok and Suzanne Miers, eds., *Women and Chinese Patriarchy*, Hong Kong, Hong Kong University Press, 1994, pp. 28, 32; Tokyo Yoshida Ch'en, "Women in Confucian Society," Columbia University Ph.D. thesis, 1974, University Microfilms, p. iii; John Buck, *Land Utilization in China*, New York, Council on Economic and Cultural Affairs, 1937, pp. 290, 293.

[37] Robins, *Women in Ancient Egypt*, p. 108.

[38] Theresa M. McBride, "Women's Work and Industrialization," in Bridenthal and Koonz, eds., *Becoming Visible*, p. 285; Simonton, *A History of European Women's Work*, pp. 42, 142, 144-6.

few pieces of rough furniture, often they looked at personal hygiene more as a nuisance than as a pleasure.[39]

Women's physical weakness and their need to stay in or near the home apart, a third reason why men and women did different kinds of work was the way work affected health. Long before modern science was born, the 4th-century B.C Hippocratic text known as *Diseases of Women* warned against making women who had given birth work too hard. The 2nd-century A.D. Greek physician Soranus was fully aware that heavy labor would lead to the loss of a woman's period and, if it lasted too long, her fertility as well.[40] Women were also more vulnerable to the effects of heat and noxious chemicals, and efforts were made to keep them away from trades involving such exposure. In ancient Babylon, female slaves wove and male ones bleached.[41] When Joshua Wedgewood started manufacturing pottery, it was men who were responsible for the dirtier parts of the process, such as handling and firing the clay, whereas women added the decoration.[42]

How justified such concerns are is evident from the fact that, in early 20th-century Japan, during the years that women were allowed to work in mining, 20 percent of those so engaged contracted diseases of the urogenital organs.[43] The greater susceptibility of women to infection explains why it has always been men who were made to do all kinds of dirty work, particularly outside the home. Good examples are charcoal burning, slaughtering large animals and cleaning public sewers. In fact, even though doctors were aware that sweeping chimneys could cause cancer of the scrotum, doing so was made a man's job. To this day in the United States, garbage collection and removal is said to be "the most male of all male jobs."[44]

Not only did women usually do the lighter, less exhausting and more salubrious kinds of work, but their working lives differed from those of men in that they were likely to be both part-time and intermittent. Some societies

---

[39] See Raymond Pahl, *Divisions of Labor*, Oxford, Blackwell, 1984, p. 29; Olwen Hufton, "Women and the Family Economy in Eighteenth-Century France," *French Historical Studies*, 9, 1975, p. 11; Edward Shorter, "Women's Work: What Difference Did Capitalism Make?" *Theory and Society*, 3, 1976, p. 516.

[40] Soranus, *Gynaicology*, 1.22-3, 1.27 and 3.9.

[41] Mendelsohn, *Slavery in the Ancient Near East*, p. 113.

[42] Simonton, *A History of European Women's Work*, p. 43.

[43] Regine Mathias, "Female Labor in the Japanese Coal-Mining Industry," in Janet Hunter, ed., *Japanese Women Working*, London, Routledge, 1993, p. 113.

[44] Sue Headlee and Margaret Elfin, *The Cost of Being Female*, Westport, CT, Praeger, 1996, pp. 18-9.

regarded the menstrual period as "a pleasant interlude."[45] Regardless of what American novelist Pearl Buck wrote about Chinese women returning to work within hours of having given birth, the fact that pregnant women or women who had recently delivered could only do light work has always been recognized.[46] Until the introduction of kindergartens, a late-19th-century innovation, women with young children could not work full-time either. In short, whereas men throughout their life worked full-time, or were expected to do so, in the case of women this applied only to the young and unmarried and to widows.[47] Economic laws and regulations often reflected this reality. For example, in 17th-century England, day-rates for women were only quoted on a seasonal basis.[48]

The aforementioned principles appear to have applied to practically all societies at almost all times and places. This, of course, did not preclude considerable variation, both among different societies and within the same society at different times. Whereas nowadays knitting is seen almost exclusively as a female job, before roughly 1800 it was often shared by people of both sexes. In Tibet, weaving carpets was men's work. Particularly during the busy agricultural season, urgent tasks were often carried out jointly by people of both sexes. But even at such times, a division of labor prevailed: normally the heavy work, such as loading the product on wagons, was done by men. Except when the men were absent — whether permanently, as emigrants, or temporarily, as soldiers — women rarely performed the hardest tasks of all, such as plowing. When circumstances did force them to undertake such work, the outcome was a sharp drop in productivity, as in Germany during World War I. In other cases the land would lay fallow, as happened in the Soviet Union during the 1920s.[49] In China during the Great Leap Forward, the attempt to make women do agricultural work while men produced iron in back-yard furnaces led to mass starvation.[50]

---

[45] Lepowsky, "Gender in an Egalitarian Society," p. 190.

[46] See Angier, *Woman*, pp. 337-9.

[47] For the Middle Ages see M. Kowaleski, "Women's Work in a Medieval Town: Exeter in the Late Fourteenth-Century," in B. A. Hanawalt, ed., *Women and Work in Pre-Industrial Europe*, Bloomington, IN, University of Indiana Press, 1986, pp. 147-8; also Helena Graham, "A Woman's Work: Labor and Gender in the Late Medieval Countryside," in Goldberg, ed., *Woman is a Worthy Wight*, pp. 135-6.

[48] Clark, *Working Life of Women*, p. 66.

[49] Wendy Z. Goldman, *Women, the State and Revolution: Soviet Family Policy and Social Life, 1917-1936*, Cambridge, Cambridge University Press, 1993, p. 177.

[50] Jacka, *Women's Work in Rural China*, pp. 36-7.

The Israeli *kibbutzim* provide another illustration of what happens when the physical differences between men and women are overridden or ignored. Partly because they were short of capital, and partly for ideological reasons, the earliest settlements tried to support themselves almost entirely by agriculture. Partly because of their socialist outlook, partly because the harsh conditions in a new and unknown country made it imperative to use every pair of hands, they carried the doctrine of equality between the sexes to extremes rarely seen before or since. Pictures of that time often show women, with scarves around their heads, wielding the shovel or the hoe, though even then they tended to be assigned the lighter tasks.

To make equality possible, they were largely relieved of housework. That included cooking (meals were taken in common), laundering (done by the *kibbutz* laundry) and looking after children (who lived in their own homes and only saw their parents for several hours each day). The difference consisted in that mothers, but not fathers, were given an hour off work each day.[51] Even so, within a few years most women could no longer keep up. Those who tried paid the price by aging very fast; the figure of the *kibbutz* woman who looks as if she could have been her husband's mother used to be a familiar one in Israel. The rest started withdrawing into the kitchen, kindergarten, school, laundry, communal sewing plant, secretariat and clinic, causing those occupations to become standard for *kibbutz* women for decades to come.

In summary, women have always been privileged with respect to work. Partly this was because of their relative physical weakness. Partly it was because they had children to carry or look after, and partly because the risks to their health were understood. Partly, too, it was because, being less able to defend themselves, they tended to stay nearer the home. Conversely, the participation of women in male activities could itself be one sign that those occupations were no longer dangerous. A good example is provided by medieval and renaissance ladies who went hunting, either shooting specially-made small crossbows or flying the falcon. A more modern example can be found in the recent fashion for cowgirls. With few exceptions, the fact that women were privileged in respect to work was as true when women were free as when they were slaves or serfs, when they worked without pay, when they assisted their relatives or when they labored for strangers in return for wages.

[51] Alison M. Bowes, *Kibbutz Goshen: An Israeli Commune*, Prospect Heights, IL, Waveland, 1989, pp. 81-2, 90, 93.

Lest there be any misunderstanding, this is not to say that women's lives were necessarily easy, or that they had much leisure time, or that the work they did was always pleasant, or even that they did not have to do certain kinds of work considered degrading. Nor does it mean that women's work was not important. In subsistence economies that did little or no trading, the distinction between the paid work of men and the unpaid work of women was itself unknown.

What it does mean, however, is that the really heavy labor — the *ponos* — was always and everywhere reserved almost exclusively for men.

3. Industrialization and Its Impact

Whereas women have always done less and lighter work closer to home than men, the effect of the industrial revolution was to make many of them stop working entirely. Behind the change was the mechanization of two processes, production and transport. Mechanical manufacturing resulted in a massive shift from numerous small businesses to a far smaller number of large factories. Mechanical transport, meanwhile, assisted the change by permitting far more people and goods to travel with unprecedented ease and speed, to unprecedented distances, at unprecedentedly low prices.

The separation of the workplace from the home affected men and women in different ways. Men started to commute, leaving the home in the morning and returning only after the day's labor was done. Women, having a household and children to look after, were left behind. Previously most women had done at least some productive work at some time during their lives. It was around this time that the category of the full-time mother and housewife was invented. This development took place at a time when domestic servants were both cheap and regarded as an indispensable part of life, even in lower middle class households. As urbanization spread, fertility began to decline, making the lives of married women easier still.[52] The higher their social status, the less likely they were to earn their keep, either before marriage or after it.

Not all women, it ought to be noted, ceased working at the same time, and some never did. That was especially true on the farm. The first labor-saving devices, such as steam engines to haul plows, were meant to ease the hard labor of men. Women's work was both lighter and, since it did not involve bulk

[52] See McBride, "Women's Work and Industrialization," p. 282.

commodities, harder to mechanize. Inventing a grain harvester is much easier, relatively speaking, than inventing a machine for picking tomatoes. Indeed, another century would pass before machinery started affecting the traditional tasks of women, such as gardening and looking after livestock.[53] Cultural factors also played a role. Dutch women stopped working earlier than most; conversely, women were associated with dairy work long after they had left other agricultural occupations.[54] The really heavy work, as well as that involving long journeys away from home, continued to be all but monopolized by men.

Most employed women worked in domestic service, an area of employment in which they greatly outnumbered men. In the mid-19th century, 18 percent of the women in London over the age of 20 worked in domestic service. Such workers accounted for 43 percent of all women in London listed as having an occupation. In the United States, they accounted for half of the female labor force as late as 1940.[55] In part this was because they were unqualified to do anything else. In part, however, it was because the work had its attractions. Then as now, some people saw factory work as being irreconcilable with femininity. Work in a household was considered both more pleasant and less impersonal.[56] It also tended to be steadier, leading to low unemployment.

Another advantage was that a working woman's basic needs, including lodging and at least some of her clothing, were provided by others. The same was true with food; domestic servants ate better than other workers did. It has been calculated that in no other type of employment could unskilled women of the lower classes earn as much. The hours were long and free time was scarce, but this made saving one's wages easier. Most women only served for a relatively short time before leaving their positions and getting married. Those who did elect to make service into a career were very likely to gain promotion. In Hamburg, for example, only 1 percent of women in domestic service stayed

---

[53] Simonton, *European Women's Work*, pp. 113-5; also see Annelies Moors, "Gender, Property and Power: *Mahr* and Marriage in a Palestinian Village," in Kathy Davis et al., eds., *The Gender of Power*, London, Sage, 1991, p. 117.

[54] Hetti A. Pott-Butter, *Facts and Fairy Tales About Female Labor, Family and Fertility, a Seven-Country Comparison, 1850-1990*, Amsterdam, Amsterdam University Press, 1993, pp. 285-6.

[55] For London, see 1851 Census, vol. 3, London, *Parliamentary Papers*, 87, 1852-3, p. 8, table 2; for Britian, see Simonton, *European Women's Work*, p. 98, figure 5.1; for the United States, see Rosalyn Baxandall and Linda Gordon, eds., *America's Working Women*, New York, Norton, 1995, p. 200.

[56] McBride, "Women's Work and Industrialization," pp. 288-90.

at the lowest rungs. The great majority became skilled housekeepers, companions and cooks, among other more advanced positions.[57]

As the nineteenth century progressed, in the towns at any rate it was only the wives of the very poor who worked. Even more than today, for a man to be supported by his wife was considered incompatible with his pride. Friedrich Engels' maudlin description of "poor Jack" sitting at home and shedding tears of humiliation while trying to mend his wife's stockings is a true period piece.[58] Even that great advocate of women's rights, John Stuart Mill, thought that "it is not... a desirable custom that the wife should contribute by her labor to the income of the family."[59] At most, such labor was seen as a reserve to be called upon in extreme need. Married women only took casual employment, returning home just as soon as they could.[60] Over time, this even applied to the wives of unskilled workers and immigrants.[61]

Among industrial workers, women comprised only a small minority. In England, the most industrialized country by far, female workers numbered just 8,879 in 1841. In the Dutch city of Tilburg, young male factory workers outnumbered female ones five to one.[62] Women comprised between 3 percent and 4 percent of the workforce in mining, a field they had started leaving as early as the 1780s. And the women that did work in mining rarely went into the tunnels, instead toiling above ground, sorting coal and preparing it for transport.[63] As a French proverb had it,[64] mining areas were hell on horses which went down the shafts and never got out. They were purgatory for the

---

[57] Katharina Schlegel, "Mistress and Servant in Nineteenth-Century Hamburg," *History Workshop*, 15, 1983, p. 75.

[58] Friedrich Engels, *The Condition of the Working Class in England*, Harmondsworth, Penguin, 1993 [1844], p. 154.

[59] Mill, *The Subjection of Women*, p. 47.

[60] See S. Alexander, "Women's Work in Nineteenth-Century London," in Juliet Mitchell and Ann Oakley, eds., *The Rights and Wrongs of Women*, Harmondsworth, Middlesex, Penguin, 1976, pp. 59-111; also Louise A. Tilly and Joan W. Scott, *Women, Work and Family*, London, Methuen, 1978, pp. 19-30, 135.

[61] For unskilled workers, see Michael Hanagan, "Family, Work and Wages: The Stéphanois Region of France, 1840-1914," in Angelique Janssens, ed., *The Rise and Decline of the Male Breadwinner Family?* Cambridge, Cambridge University Press, 1998, pp. 137-8; for immigrants, see Teresa Amott and Julie Matthaei, *Race, Gender and Work*, Boston, South End Press, 1996, p. 113.

[62] Angelique Janssens, *Family and Social Change: The Household as a Process in an Industrializing Community*, Cambridge, Cambridge University Press, 1993, p. 40.

[63] Angela V. John, *By the Sweat of Our Brow: Women Workers at Victorian Coal Mines*, London, Croom Helm, 1980, pp. 24-5.

[64] Hanagan, "Family, Work and Wages," p. 135.

men who made the journey every day, and paradise for the women whose only contact with the dust and grime was to help wash it off the bodies of their male relatives.

Even these minuscule numbers led to an outcry about the "corrupting" effects of industrial work on women. In 1844, the first Factory Laws were passed in England. Later they spread to other countries including Belgium, France, Germany and the United States. Step by step, working women were provided protection. It included limits on the trades in which they could be employed, the hours they could be required to work, the conditions under which they could be employed, and the shift work they could, or could not, be made to do. By 1908, future justice Louis Brandeis was able present the United States Supreme Court, in *Muller v. Oregon*, with more than 100 studies on the need to protect women against overwork. The strategy worked, and state regulation of women's work was declared to be constitutional. Yet notably, just three years earlier another court had rejected similar regulation of an industry in which men bore among the heaviest burdens, namely baking.[65] At any rate, by 1917 no less than 40 states in America had passed some kind of protective legislation for women.[66] It would only be much later that men, which included male children aged 11 or older, were given similar protection. When legislation for men did finally pass, it was modeled on the existing regulations for women.[67]

By the 1880s, clean gas and electricity were beginning to take the place of coal as the main source of energy. As a result, at least some branches of industry shed off some of the dirt and grime that had characterized Dickens' "Coketown" at its worst. Large corporations expanded their internal administration, creating an insatiable demand for secretaries and receptionists. More white-collar positions were created by the expansion of government, including social insurance, healthcare and compulsory universal education.[68] Others owed their existence to technological advances, such as the telegraph, telephone and teleprinter. Previously work in household service or in factories

---

[65] Lynn E. Winer, *From Working Girl to Working Mother: The Female Labor Force in the United States, 1820-1980*, Chapel Hill, NC, North Carolina University Press, 1985, p. 72.

[66] Mimi Abramovitz, *Regulating the Lives of Women: Social Welfare Policy from Colonial Times to the Present*, Boston, South End Press, 1996 [1988], p. 188.

[67] Mary Lynn McDougal, "Working Class Women During the Industrial Revolution," in Bridenthal and Koonz, eds., *Becoming Visible*, p. 262; Kaminer, *A Fearful Freedom*, p. 67.

[68] See Martin van Creveld, *The Rise and Decline of the State*, London, Cambridge University Press, 1999, pp. 213-21.

had been below the dignity of the typical middle class young woman, who spent her years before marriage learning how to sing, embroider or paint. Now they flocked to take up temporary employment in jobs which, if often unexciting, were at least clean, safe and not too demanding in terms of effort or skill. Thus it came to be that in 1887, three-quarters of female workers in large American cities were under 25 years old. No fewer than 96 percent of them were single; in Berlin the situation was similar.[69]

Wherever easy, clean work was available, vast numbers of women flocked to it. In the United States, women comprised 4 percent of clerks in 1880. A decade later, the figure had risen five times over, to 21 percent. The overall number of office workers jumped from 504,000 to 750,000.[70] In Germany between 1882 and 1907, the number of female white collar workers in commerce, transport, the civil service and the professions tripled.[71] The prevailing 19th-century wisdom was that women were weak, delicate souls. The further away from home they were, the greater the danger that they might be corrupted by men, losing their manners if they were lucky and their virginity if they were not. Most employers shared these concerns. Even if they did not, to attract female workers they had to protect them. Pictures often show halls filled by young, neatly dressed women working at their desks with hardly a man in sight.[72]

These attempts to make the lives of working women easier notwithstanding, they only entered the labor force to a limited extent. In 1851, about one-quarter of English women worked. Sixty years later, the figure was still the same.[73] Whereas 83.7 percent of men aged 10 or older were in the labor force, the same only applied to 31.6 percent of women.[74] And that figure does

---

[69] Amott and Matthaei, *Race, Gender and Work*, p. 115; Rosemary Orthmann, "Labor Force Participation, Life Cycle, and Expenditure Patterns: The Case of Unmarried Factory Workers in Berlin, 1902," in Ruth-Ellen B. Joeres and Mary Jo. Maynes, eds., *German Women in the Nineteenth Century: A Social and Literary History*, Bloomington, IN, Indiana University Press, 1986, pp. 29-36.

[70] Baxandall and Gordon, eds., *America's Working Women*, p. 207.

[71] August Bebel, *Die Frau und der Sozialismus*, Berlin, Dietz, 1923 [1883], p. 216.

[72] See Gregory Anderson, "The White Blouse Revolution," in *idem*, ed., *The White Blouse Revolution: Female Office Workers since 1870*, Manchester, Manchester University Press, 1988, pp. 1-26.

[73] MacDougall, "Working Class Women During the Industrial Revolution," in Bridenthal and Koonz, *Becoming Visible*, p. 267; Alice Kessler-Harris, *Out to Work: A History of Wage-Earning Women in the United States*, New York, Oxford University Press, 1982, pp. 75-107.

[74] See Gail Braybon, *Women Workers in the First World War*, London, Croom Helms, 1981, p. 25.

not tell the whole picture, because many women who did enter the workforce did so because, given the demographic imbalance that emigration had created, they were unable to find men. The situation in Continental Europe resembled that in Britain.[75] In the United States, where there was a surplus of marriable men, only one in 20 married women took up paid work.[76] And even that figure does not fully reflect the reality at that time. A turn of the century survey of "married" working women in Philadelphia revealed that of the 728 women polled, 237 were in fact widows, 146 had been deserted by their husbands and 12 were divorcées. Just 333 of the 728 women actually had a husband at home.[77]

When World War I broke out, it was at first thought that the disruption of economic life would lead to unemployment among people of both sexes. This, indeed, was what happened during the first few months. Industries in which women were active, particularly those manufacturing luxury articles, suffered from reduced demand or were forced to close.[78] As a result, nearly half of British working women experienced unemployment at some point in 1914.[79] However, as early as the winter of 1914-1915, the situation reversed itself. As millions of men left for the fronts, they had to be kept supplied with millions of tons of materiel of every kind. Before the war the authorities had believed that their main job would be to provide for the unemployed. Instead, they soon found themselves screaming for labor — male or female — to take up positions that had been left vacant or had been newly created.

As usual, women were concentrated in industries where the work was comparatively light and clean. The most important ones manufactured shoes, boots, hosiery, uniforms, webbing, kitbags, harnesses and other such articles.[80] Next, women started taking men's places in jobs that brought them into contact

---

[75] Michael R. Haines, "The Demography of Life-Span Transitions: Temporal and Gender Comparisons," in Alice S. Rossi, ed., *Gender and the Life Course*, New York, Aldine, 1985, p. 52, table 3.3 (1890 figures).

[76] Valerie K. Oppenheimer et al., "United states of America," in Hans-Peter Blossfeld, ed., *The New Role of Women: Family Formation in Modern Societies*, Boulder, CO, Westview, 1995, p. 142.

[77] Leslie Woodcock Tentler, *Wage-Earning Women: Industrial Work and Family Life in the United States*, 1900-1930, Oxford, Oxford University Press, 1979, pp. 165-6.

[78] See M. B. Hammond, *British Labor Conditions and Legislation during the War*, Oxford, Oxford University Press, 1919, chapter 3.

[79] Simonton, *European Women's Work*, p. 186.

[80] I. O. Andrews, *The Economic Effects of the World War upon Women and Children in Great Britain*, Oxford, Oxford University Press, 1921, chapter 4.

with the public, and in which, again because of their supposedly delicate souls, they had previously engaged seldom, if at all. Women staffed counters at post offices and in banks. Women collected bus and tram tickets, and drove taxis and even vans. In 1916, some women, attracted by high wages, started entering munitions factories as well. Still, even at the peak of the war in April 1918, when Britain's armies were reeling under the most powerful offensive ever launched by any army in history up to that point, the workforce remained almost two-thirds male. At that time, notwithstanding the fact that three and a half years had passed since the outbreak of the war, the total number of British working women only went up from 3,276,000 to 4,808,000.[81]

Other countries resembled Britain in this respect. By 1916-1917, female workers in several countries — Germany, Italy, France and Britain itself — were earning such excellent wages in the munitions factories that men accused them of turning the war into a grand old time,[82] at a time when men were dying by the hundreds of thousands. Even so, the really heavy work in mining, forestry and transportation, among other fields, continued to be done almost entirely by men. Such men were either unqualified for military service because of age or health, or had been released from service because their jobs could not be performed by women. For example, at Wigan Pier, later to be made famous by George Orwell, women formed just 5.5 percent of the work force. Of them, not a single one worked underground.[83]

The war over, most women happily returned home. Normally the question was not whether a married woman would stop working, but how soon. Working men, influenced by left-wing ideologies, often considered the question from the point of view of the class struggle. They felt proud that capitalism, though it had succeeded in enslaving them, had failed to lay its hands on their wives. Conversely, those whose wives worked tended to be looked down upon.[84] In the United States, only 15 percent of married women worked and only 20 percent people of either sex even thought women should work. By 1939, the

---

[81] See A. W. Kirkaldy, *Industry and Finance*, London, Pitman, 1921, vol. 2, section i.

[82] Françoise Thébaud, "The Great War and the Triumph of Sexual Division," in Thébaud, ed., *A History of Women in the West*, p. 37; Sandra M. Gilbert, "Soldier's Heart: Literary Men, Literary Women, and the Great War," in Margaret R. Higonnet et al., eds., *Behind the Lines: Gender in the Two World Wars*, New Haven, CT, Yale University Press, 1987, pp. 204-12.

[83] Diana Condell and Jean Liddliard, *Working for Victory? Images of Women in the First World War, 1914-18*, London, Routledge, 1987, p. 72.

[84] John R. Gillis, *For Better, for Worse: British Marriages, 1600 to the Present*, New York, Oxford University Press, 1985, p. 252.

latter figure had dropped to 10 percent.[85] As one company vice president wrote at the time, freedom from work was "God's greatest gift to woman and her natural birthright." In all countries except the Soviet Union, both the proportion of working women and their share in the labor force stagnated. In 1929, 40 percent of all married women in the United States had *never* worked outside the home.[86] At no time, and in no country, did they comprise more than 36.1 percent of the labor force.[87] To the limited extent that women did take up work, they continued to hold the less strenuous and less unhealthy jobs.

When the Great Depression struck, men bore the brunt of it. The net effect of the Depression was to make it much harder for both men and women to find work. However, it did not hit the two sexes equally. Focusing on the United States, since fewer women worked, and since they generally earned less, proportionally fewer women lost their jobs than did men. As the decade wore on, the labor market rebounded faster for women — in clerical work, in services and in light industries — than it did for men, who found themselves undercut by women.[88]

The impact of unemployment on the two sexes also differed. For women it often meant deprivation, while for men it meant both deprivation and emasculation. As youths they were prevented from becoming men. Particularly if their families could not afford to keep them in school, they might end up becoming bums or hobos. As adults they stayed at home or left it in search of work, only to return empty-handed. Their social connections were cut, their status was reduced, their self-esteem was undermined, and their marriages were destabilized.[89] All of this applied to women, if at all, only to a much smaller extent. Photographs show thousands of men lining up, three or four abreast, in

[85] Gallup polls quoted in Baxandall and Gordon, eds., *America's Working Women*, p. 239; William H. Chafe, *The American Woman*, New York, Oxford University Press, 1980, p. 56.
[86] Solomon, *In the Company of Educated Women*, p. 173.
[87] Bridenthal, "Something Old, Something New," in Bridenthal and Koonz, eds., *Becoming Visible*, p. 426, table 18-1.
[88] Kessler-Harris, *Out to Work*, pp. 258-9; Samuel A. Stouffer and Paul E. Lazersfeld, *Research Memorandum on the Family in the Depression*, New York, Social Science Research Council, 1937, pp. 28-35.
[89] See M. Komarowsky, *The Unemployed Man and His Family*, New York, Dryden, 1940, *passim*; David Wadinger et al., "'All Jumbled Up': Employed Women with Unemployed Husbands," in Jennie Popay et al., eds., *Men, Gender Divisions and Welfare*, London, Routledge, 1998, pp. 231-4.

front of soup kitchens. As was noticed at the time,[90] bread lines did not contain any women. Few women wound up in flophouses or slept in the park. However bad their suffering, somehow women always managed to find a meal and a roof over their heads.

World War II was a repetition of its predecessor. Once again, millions upon millions of men were conscripted. Once again, governments called upon women to fill the gap, first in services and white-collar work, then in light industries, and finally in heavy industry. Still, with the exception of the Soviet Union, women continued to enjoy many privileges. It is true that Britain and the United States employed large numbers of married women, but even in those countries women usually did the easier work. For example in Britain, even at the peak of the war in 1943, 10 million women did not work. On average, these women had less than one child each to care for. At no time during the war did women comprise more than 38.8 percent of the labor force. Thus, after 5,000,000 men, as compared to just 450,000 women, had been put into uniform, working men still outnumbered women almost two to one. Only toward the end of 1943 did the authorities finally start "directing" women with no children under the age of 14 toward war-related work. As it was, fear that the scheme might lead to rebellion by women and men alike caused it to be applied quite cautiously.[91]

In 1945, out of 52 million American adult women only 19.5 million held jobs. Among married women, only a quarter did.[92] Though the image of Rosie the Riveter dominated propaganda, its link to reality was tenuous. In metal-working plants of all types, male workers outnumbered female ones more than three to one.[93] A 1945 poll sheds light on women's decision as to which jobs to fill and which ones to avoid. It turned out that three quarters of employed women expected to go on working after the war. If possible, they hoped to do so without leaving their chosen fields. Only in war industry was the figure much lower. Yet it was there that women obtained the highest pay of all, the

[90] Meridel Le Sueur, "Women Are Hungry," in *Ripening: Selected Works, 1927-1980*, Old Westbury, NY, Feminist Press, 1982, pp. 137-8.

[91] British data from Celia Briar, *Working for Women? Gendered Work and Welfare Politics in Twentieth-Century Britain*, London, UCL, 1997, pp. 76-8.

[92] Kessler-Harris, *Out to Work*, p. 276; Chafe, *American Women*, p. 56.

[93] U.S. Department of Labor, *Industrial Injuries to Women*, Washington, 1947, Government Printing Office, 1947, p. 4, table 1.

difference between them and female workers in other fields being around 50 percent.[94]

So why did women want to leave precisely those industries that paid best of all? Another series of statistics provides an answer. The largest concentrations of women were found in industries with the smallest number of accidents. In such industries, women outnumbered men nearly four to one. Conversely, in the most dangerous places, there were hardly any women at all.[95] Overall, the injury rate experienced by male industrial workers was more than double that of their female counterparts.[96] No wonder women disliked the male-dominated branches of industry. In spite of the exceptionally high wages paid, most planned to leave such work as soon as they could. To wit, most did so as soon as their menfolk returned and resumed the burden of supporting them.[97]

In summary, the separation of the workplace from the home that started during the 19th century had a profound impact on the working lives of women. Only on the farms did women continue working as before. Elsewhere the effect was to cause very large numbers of women, married ones in particular, to cease working altogether. Partly because they did not want to do heavy or dangerous work, partly because the law increasingly prohibited them from doing so, those who remained in the urban work force generally did the easier and safer work. The resulting pattern prevailed during most of the first half of the 20th century, and in some countries, such as the Netherlands, all the way into the 1960s.[98] Whether because governments tried to protect women or because of opposition from women themselves, that pattern not even two world wars could change.

4. The Great Transformation

As was noted earlier in this chapter, during most of history work was seen as a burden imposed on man as a punishment — one which, monks and Protestants

---

[94] U.S. Department of Labor, *Women Workers in Ten Production Areas and Their Postwar Employment Plans*, Washington, Government Printing Office, 1946, p. 41, table II-7, and p. 44, table III-1.

[95] U.S. Department of Labor, *Industrial Injuries to Women*, p. 5, table II.

[96] U.S. Department of Labor, *Industrial Injuries to Women*, p. 4, table I.

[97] U.S. Department of Labor, *Women Workers in Ten Production Areas*, p. 48, table IV-2.

[98] See Jenny de Jong Gierveld and Aart C. Liefbroer, "The Netherlands," in Blossfeld, ed., *The New Role of Women*, p. 108. It turns out that women's participation in the workforce was actually lower in 1960 than it had been in 1900.

apart, most people tried to avoid as much as they could. During the 19th and 20th centuries, this view began to die out. The change can be traced back to the late 17th-century English philosopher John Locke. Locke's argument was that, in the state of nature, everybody had as much right to everything as anybody else. The origins of private property were to be found in labor; if some owned much more of it than others, then ultimately this was because they or their ancestors had worked harder and done more to transform raw nature into products consumable by man.[99] To the young Marx, productive work was the cardinal difference between man and other animals.[100] In the hands, or rather mouths, of subsequent socialist leaders, work became the foundation of the social order. Going further still, Soviet biologists declared the hand, rather than the brain, to be the prime human characteristic. Thus, not only did work form the essence of man, it had actually caused his evolution.

Previously most men had preened themselves on their wealth, social status and education. Most women, incidentally, had also preened themselves on their husbands' qualities. But now capitalists and socialists alike were starting to praise work. As a result, being a man of leisure became socially unacceptable, so that even those who did not need to work began doing so, or at any rate pretended to do so. Gradually they came to regard work as the essence of their lives. Once work had ceased to be seen — on the declaratory level, at any rate — as a burden and started to be regarded as a privilege, it was not long before men, claiming to speak on behalf of women, started suggesting that women share in it.

As the writings of John Stuart Mill show, the problem of emancipating women from their husbands' economic despotism was very much in the air. The most important author to suggest that the instrument of emancipation should be work was Friedrich Engels. The way he put it in *The Origins of the Family, Private Property, and the State*, under "primitive communism" men and women had been equal, sharing the fruits of the earth in common. However, technical progress and the invention of herding and subsequently agriculture led to private ownership over the means of production. Economically speaking, the shift made men's work much more important than

---

[99] John Locke, *An Essay Concerning the True Origin, Extent, and End of Civil Government*, in *Two Treatises of Government*, Peter Laslett ed., Cambridge, Cambridge University Press, 1960, pp. 305-7.

[100] Karl Marx and Friedrich Engels, *The German Ideology*, London, Lawrence & Wishart, 1970 [1845-6], p. 42. See also Karl Marx, *Capital*, London, Lawrence & Wishart, 1954 [1867], vol. 1, p. 174.

women's. Worse still for women, it led to a situation in which property, which was no longer owned in common, had to be passed to a man's sons. The combination of inheritance and private property proved deadly to the position of women in society. The one way to break women's economic, and therefore social, dependence was for them "to take part in production on a large, social scale." By this Engels meant paid work outside the home. The unpaid work they had previously done was, in his view, unproductive by definition.[101]

Partly out of a genuine concern for women, partly in the hope that women would join the movement or persuade their husbands to do so, other socialist leaders endorsed these ideas. The most detailed program was put forward by the founder of the German Social Democratic Party, August Bebel.[102] In Bebel's telling, women's history was a sorry tale of subjection and degradation made possible by women's lack of economic independence. Under socialism, he proclaimed, women would be liberated. In fact, the right to participate in productive labor and be remunerated accordingly was the essence of liberty. Women's economic dependence having ended, people of both sexes would be free — for the first time in history — to choose their partners for love alone.

In many ways, Bebel's work formed the basis for the policies adopted by the Soviet Union from 1918 onward. Having seized power in a country ruined by war and revolution, the Bolsheviks' most immediate concern was to restore production. They believed that the fastest way to achieve this goal was to draw upon what they saw as the country's chief untapped source of manpower: the vast number of unemployed women. It was primarily in order to enable, not to say compel, them to do so that the nascent Communist state carried out some of the most thorough reforms in women's history.[103] The nature of the reforms was outlined by two women, Alexandra Kollontai and Lenin's wife Nadezha Krupskaya, both of whom echoed Bebel without giving him due credit.

For Kollontai in particular, labor on behalf of society was the most important thing in life — so important, in fact, that she was barely prepared to grant women the time needed to deliver another "unit of labor." To enable women to work, "the kitchen was to be separated from marriage." Women's traditional chores, such as cleaning, cooking, laundering, mending clothes and even child-raising would be communized. In her more radical moments, Kollontai even predicted that one-family housing would disappear. Its place

[101] Friedrich Engels, *The Origins of the Family, Private Property, and the State*, Harmondsworth, Middles, Penguin, 1972 [1884], pp. 83, 199.

[102] *Die Frau und der Sozialismus*, Stuttgart, Dietz, 1910 [1879], pp. 169-82.

[103] Vladimir I. Lenin, *Married Women in the Labor Force*, New York, Harvester, 1966 [1921].

would be taken by huge dormitories. Indeed, plans for such dormitories were still being produced by architects during the late 1920s.[104]

Had these plans been realized, they would have turned the Soviet Union into a vast, impersonal *kibbutz*. If only because women refused to have their children taken from them as the Communist Party wished, little came of such ideas. In the end, the most thorough reforms were the ones introduced into family law. Men's position as the heads of households was officially terminated, and with it went the distinction between legitimate and illegitimate children. Expecting women to work for a living on equal terms with men, the government made divorce so easy that the family itself was all but abolished. With it went alimony, now understood as the lynchpin of the old system. It was believed at the time that such monetary payments robbed women both of their economic independence and their pride.

The results, not least a skyrocketing divorce rate, quickly revealed themselves. The number of deserted wives and children desperately trying to survive without male support — that is, in the main, without any support at all — rose into the millions.[105] Poverty bred crime. A generation of youngsters was thrown into the street, forced to live by theft or prostitution. In the late 1920s, the authorities performed an about-turn. The family was restored to its place of honor as the basic unit of Communist society. The prewar provisions that had subordinated women to men were left off the books, but alimony was restored to the law to make sure divorced men continued to support their wives and children. Kollontai's works disappeared from the libraries, and several of the men responsible for drafting the earlier laws were shot. In the end, perhaps the most important part of the original program to be realized was precisely the one that concerns us here — namely, the effort to push women into paid work.

Before the Revolution, the vast majority of people in the countries that would comprise the Soviet Union made their living by agriculture, which meant that women had always worked both in the home and around it. That was to change by the late 1920s, when a vast effort to draw women out of agriculture and into other professions was underway. The share of women in the labor force rose. It reached 24 percent in 1928, 26.7 percent in 1930, 31 percent in 1934, and 35 percent in 1937. As in other countries, the first women to be hired were those without a man to support them. As late as 1936, by which time the

---

[104] On Krupskaya see Alena Heitligner, *Women and State Socialism*, London, MacMillan, 1979, pp. 42, 108; on Kollontai Rosenthal, "Love on the Tractor," pp. 377, 388.
[105] Goldman, *Women, the State and Revolution*, pp. 65, 119-22.

Communist regime was firmly entrenched, fewer than half of married women worked.[106]

At first, nearly the entire increase took place in sectors that had traditionally employed women. These included light industry — food, tobacco, textiles, leather and paper — as well as services such as teaching and commerce. Beginning in 1930, however, a determined drive was launched to push women to work in nontraditional fields. By 1930-33, 44 percent of recently-added construction workers, and as many as 80 percent of industrial ones, were female. The share of women among all workers in large-scale industry jumped from 28 percent in 1930 to 40 percent in 1937. In the largest industrial cities, such as Leningrad, the figure was higher still.[107] A select few women who succeeded in their new fields became the foci of extensive propaganda campaigns. Some even earned the greatest prize of all, a meeting with the Father of the Peoples himself. Others were driven by draconian labor laws. Still, even in this brave new world, the leaders' own wives did not work.

Millions of other women entered Soviet universities and obtained a professional education. Often they did so in fields previously reserved for men, such as engineering,[108] though not to the extent that the state would have liked. However, no more than their male comrades were women able to overcome the intolerable rigidities of the regime and its tendency to stifle any initiative, economic or otherwise. In the end, the Communist hierarchy of labor — including, after 1945, that which prevailed in satellite countries such as East Germany and Czechoslovakia — came to resemble that of all other countries. Most women worked in a handful of occupations that had few men. The most important ones were teaching, low-level administration, personal services and retail.[109] Soviet women were concentrated in the less prestigious, low-paying positions. Women may have been well represented in medicine and law, but that is in large part a reflection of the mediocre income and prestige of

---

[106] Rosenthal, "Love on the Tractor," pp. 380, 386, 387, 389, 392, 395.

[107] Goldman, *Women, the State and Revolution*, 123, 310-2.

[108] William M. Mandel, *Soviet Women*, New York, Anchor Press, 1975, pp. 124-40.

[109] For the former Soviet Union, see Rosenthal, "Love on the Tractor," pp. 392, 395; for East Germany, Juta Gysi and Dagmar Meyer, "Leitbild: berufstätige Mutter—DDR-Frauen in Familie, Partnerschaft und Ehe," in Gisela Herwig and Hildegard Nickel eds., *Frauen in Deutschland 1945-1992*, Bonn, *Bundeszentrale für politische Bildung*, 1993, pp. 236-7; for Czechoslovakia, Alena Heitinger, *Women and State Socialism*, London, Palgrave, 1979, p. 148.

professionals in those fields. In the economy as a whole, the higher up one went the fewer the women one encountered.[110]

Cramped housing, the need to spend hours queuing for the simplest consumer goods, and the continued burden of housework made the lives of many women intolerable. And from the 1930s onward, they responded by having fewer children. In the Soviet Union, contraceptives were always of doubtful quality, in short supply and, at times, officially discouraged or even prohibited. Hence the main method of birth control consisted of abortions, both legal and illegal. It has been estimated that, during the last years of the regime, two-thirds of all fetuses were aborted.[111] Even under the best of circumstances, abortion is a traumatic experience. In the Soviet Union, where it was often carried out under difficult conditions and with little or no anesthetics, it was more so still.[112] It would scarcely be too much to say that, over the 70 years Communism lasted, its attempt to emancipate women by making them work on equal terms with men caused their very will to live and give life to be extinguished.

It was only around 1980 or so that the regime understood it had a problem on its hands.[113] Seeking a solution, it began by closing 450 of the harder and more hazardous occupations to female workers. Next, women got permission to work part time. Other women were allowed to do certain kinds of work at home so as to combine work with child care. This was followed by longer periods of paid and unpaid parental leaves.[114] Finally, Mikhail Gorbachev launched a "back to the home" campaign that would have made the fathers and mothers of socialism spin in their graves.[115] Soviet women had learned their lesson,

---

[110] Joel C. Moses, *The Politics of Women and Work in the Soviet Union and the United States*, Berkeley, CA, Institute of International Studies, 1983, pp. 32-6; Heitinger, *Women and State Socialism*, p. 158.

[111] L. Remennick, "Epidemiology and Determinants of Induced Abortion in the Soviet Union," *Social Science and Medicine*, 33, 7, 1991, pp. 841-8; *International Herald Tribune*, 16.2.2001, p. 1.

[112] See Goldman, *Women, the State and Revolution*, pp. 279-81, 290-9, 333-5; also Mary Buckley, "Glasnost and the Woman Question," in Linda Edmondson, ed., *Women and Society in Russia and the Soviet Union*, Cambridge, Cambridge University Press, 1992, p. 208.

[113] Moses, *The Politics of Women and Work*, pp. 22-3.

[114] Jo Peers, "Workers by Hand and Womb: Soviet Women and the Demographic Crisis," in Barbara Holland, ed., *Soviet Sisterhood*, Bloomington, IN, Indiana University Press, 1985, p. 135; Sue Bridger, "Young Women and Perestroika," in Edmondson, ed., *Women and Society in Russia*, p. 191.

[115] Mikhail S. Gorbachev, *Perestroika*, London, Fontana, 1988, pp. 117-8.

refusing point blank to enter manual trades.[116] Some women swore at feminism, which they held responsible for forcing them to work. But it was too little, too late. By the time Communism collapsed, so hard had women's lives become that Russia's population was declining by 1 million each year. During the 1990s alone, the population of St. Petersburg contracted by 10 percent.

In the 1960s, the idea that work was both a privilege and an indispensable tool for woman's emancipation reached the capitalist West. Ideologically speaking, this was a revolution. In 1930, Sigmund Freud declared that the "natural" human propensity was to shy away from work.[117] Well into the 1950s, the expression "wage slave" continued to be used. It described the kind of man who spent his entire life working for corporations that not only controlled him but seldom hesitated to fire him at a moment's notice. Women made clear they had no intention of participating in such servitude any longer than necessary. In 1945 and 1946 alone, 3 million American women stopped working and returned home.[118] In Britain after World War II, the platforms of all three major parties called on women to continue working. Women, however, had other ideas. Far from enjoying "their new independence," as one researcher found, women, and married women in particular, had been "made miserable by the wartime interruptions of family life" and "fervently wish[ed] themselves back into their prewar home routine."[119] The outcome was a short-lived baby boom. Meanwhile, to take the place of those who had left the labor force, foreign workers had to be imported.[120]

In the ensuing decades, the situation steadily changed. The first factor behind the transition was longer life expectancy, which meant that the average woman would spend a greater part of her life without having children to look after. A second cause was the reestablishment of the long-term trend toward declining fertility, which led to the same result as greater life expectancy. Yet another reason was better education opportunities for women, which made many of them wonder if being a housewife was not, in fact, a colossal waste of their knowledge and skills. The result was what Betty Friedan called "the problem without a name." Women, she claimed, were confined to the mind-numbing routine of the home. They spent their time cleaning floors, dusting

[116] Mandel, *Soviet Women*, p. 110.
[117] Sigmund Freud, *Civilization and Its Discontents*, London, Hogarth, 1930, p. 34.
[118] Winer, *From Working Girl to Working Mother*, p. 95.
[119] See Denise Riley, *War in the Nursery*, London, Virago, 1983, pp. 141-4.
[120] Briar, *Working for Women*, p. 95.

cupboards and, by way of supreme achievement, baking cookies. Bored and isolated, they became mentally ill, or took to the bottle, or found a lover.

Encouraged by Friedan's message, legions of married women in all Western countries started leaving home to take up paid work. By the last decade of the 20th century, in most developed countries the percentage of women who were in the labor force was beginning to approach that of men.[121] Most middle class women — by this time, the majority of Americans in particular described themselves as middle class — sought work that would be light, pleasant, clean and not too demanding in terms of time. Thanks to the fact that working hours had fallen by nearly one-third (from 59 to 40), millions of them were able to find precisely such work. An important role was played by the rise of the service sector. To a large extent, the process became self-reinforcing. Most women continued to do housework and mind their children as well as do their jobs. The solution was to contract out domestic functions they had previously performed with their own hands. Such tasks including minding small children and cleaning the house, as well making, mending and laundering clothes. It also included a growing reliance on prepared food for consumption both in the home and outside it.

The needs of working women led to the rise of an entire new branch of the economy known as "household services."[122] Almost all of those performing the services were themselves women. Women, in effect, created work for other women, who in turn created work for yet more women. For example, in Britain between 1985 and 1996, the sums spent on domestic service doubled, making it the fastest-growing part of the entire economy.[123] In the United States during the early 1990s, women accounted for 97 percent of all nurses, 97 percent of childcare workers, 73 percent of teachers, 84 percent of elementary school teachers, 97.8 percent of pre-kindergarten teachers, and 68 percent of social workers. The division of labor in many other services has been equally slanted.[124] Thus, in a great many cases, the effect of women going out to work

[121] Suzanne Gordon, *Prisoners of Men's Dreams: Striking Out for a New Feminine Future*, Boston, Little Brown, 1991, p. 125.

[122] Sven Illeris, *The Service Economy*, Chichester, Wiley, 1996, p. 36.

[123] "Holding the Baby," *Economist*, 31.1.1998.

[124] For the United States, see Andrea P. Baridon and David R. Eyler, *Working Together: The New Rules and Realities for Managing Men and Women at Work*, New York, McGraw-Hill, p. 42, figure 1-14; for Europe, see Isabella Bakker, "Women's Employment in Comparative Perspective," in Jane Jenson et al., eds., *Feminization of the Labor Force: Paradoxes and Promises*, New York, Oxford University Press, 1988, p. 20; for Britian, see Juliet Webster, *Shaping Women's Work: Gender, Employment and Information Technology*, London, Longman, 1996, p. 108; for Japan,

has been not so much to change the nature of their tasks as to make them do for strangers, and outside the home, what they had always done for themselves and their relatives inside it.

Insofar as the vast majority of women entered work that neither demanded heavy physical labor, nor required long distance travel, nor involved risk or danger, women still remained the privileged sex. Insofar as pressure by feminist organizations has caused most of the previous restrictions on female labor to be dropped, women have become doubly privileged, being literally able to have their cake and eat it too. Meanwhile, in all developed countries almost all the really hard work continues to be done by men. Just as was the case a century ago, women in such fields as mining, construction, utilities and transport constitute a very small minority.[125] Just as it was a century ago, it is almost exclusively men who work in forestry and heavy industry. Men plow the fields, dig the canals, lay the tracks, build the roads, and move heavy loads (hence those twin expressions, "manhaul" and "manhandle"). They also construct buildings, operate and maintain large pieces of machinery,[126] put out fires and hunt violent criminals. In most countries it is almost exclusively men who drive trains, trucks, vans and taxis, to say nothing of piloting sailing ships and, until recently, commercial aircraft.

The reason why men do these and other hard jobs is, of course, because for them they are not as hard as they are for women. When women *do* enter men's work, it is usually only a question of time before they get out again.[127] Thus much of the training they receive is wasted. If these problems are to be avoided, then men's work must first be made easier, as happened when the introduction of computers turned printing from a dirty, messy job into a clean and efficient one.[128] The combination of modern anti-discrimination laws, on the one hand, and women's reluctance to pull up their sleeves, on the other, can lead to strange results. Thus, whereas 80 percent of all clerks in the United States are women, the one "clerical" job that involves substantial outdoor walking — mail

---

Larry S. Carney and Charlotte G. O'Kelly, "Women's Work and Women's Place in the Japanese Economic Miracle," in Katharyn Ward, ed., *Women Workers and Global Restructuring*, n.p., ILR Press, 1990, p. 127.

[125] Simonton, *European Women's Work*, p. 184, figure 9.1.

[126] See Headlee and Elfin, *The Cost of Being Female*, p. 17.

[127] Jonsson, "Women in Education from a Swedish Perspective," pp. 56-7.

[128] For Britain, see C. Cockburn, *Brothers: Male Dominance and Technological Change*, London, Pluto, 1983; for the United States, see Barbara F. Reskin and Patricia A. Roos, *Job Queues, Gender Queues*, Philadelphia, Temple University Press, 1990, pp. 275-98.

delivery — is done almost entirely by men.[129] Even in all-female prisons run by women for women, construction and maintenance work is done exclusively by men.[130] Finally, to the extent that any occupations are still reserved for men, without exception they are those which involve the heavier, less salubrious, work.

In all developed countries, without exception, women spend fewer hours working. In the United States, female doctors work fewer hours than their male counterparts; the same is true for female lawyers.[131] In Japan, nearly one-third of the increase in the labor force between 1960 and 1986 was accounted for by female part-time workers. Since then the figure has continued to grow.[132] In Germany, only one-quarter of mothers of young children work, and only half of those do so full time; fathers of any age who hold part-time jobs, by contrast, hardly exist at all.[133] Young Swedish women work fewer hours than their male peers; the same goes for older Swedish women. The same also goes for married Swedish women, as well as cohabiting ones. Swedish women with children work fewer hours than Swedish fathers; so, too, do Swedish women without children.[134] And fewer than half of Swedish women with preschool or school-age children work full time.[135] Not for nothing is the Swedish welfare state said to be "women-friendly."

The usual reason given for women's shorter hours is the famous double burden. However, upon closer inspection, this well-worn argument falls apart.[136] To be sure, women who do not hold a job spend more time doing housework than do their spouses, but this is only part of the story. Contrary to conventional wisdom, it is simply not true that working mothers devote much

---

[129] Headlee and Elfin, *The Cost of Being Female*, p. 18-9.

[130] Estelle B. Freedman, *Their Sisters' Keepers; Women's Prison Reform in America*, 1830-1930, Ann Arbor, MI, University of Michigan Press, 1981, p. 71.

[131] Valian, *Why So Slow?*, pp. 208, 260; F. M. Kay and J. Hagan, "Raising the Bar: The Gender Stratification of Law Firm Capital," *American Sociological Review*, 63, 1998, pp. 728-43.

[132] Carney and O'Kelly, "Women's Work and Place in Japan," p. 133.

[133] Sybille Meier and Eva Schulze, "Frauen in der Modernisierungsfalle—Wandel von Ehe, Familie und Partnerschaft in der Bundesrepublik Deutschland," in Gisela Herwig and Hildegard Nickel eds., *Frauen in Deutschland 1945-1992*, Bonn, *Bundeszentrale fuer politische Bildung*, 1993, p. 173. For more recent figures, see *Das Parlament*, 21.1.2000, p. 2.

[134] *Women, Men and Incomes: Gender Equality and Economic Independence*, Government Official Reports, No. 87, Stockholm, Ministry of Labor, 1998, pp. 13, 70.

[135] E. Nasman, "Childhood, Family and New Ways of Life: The Case of Sweden," in Lynne Chisholm et al., eds., *Growing Up in Europe*, Berlin, de Gruyter, p. 124.

[136] See Katherine Hakim, *Key Issues in Women's Work: Female Heterogeneity and the Polarisation of Women's Employment*, London, Athlone, 1996, pp. 52, 203.

more time to childcare than do working fathers. Since many children from the age of 6 months up spend much of their time outside the home, looking after them only takes up a tiny fraction of a woman's adult life. The smaller the family, the truer this is. Depending on whether they work part time or full time, mothers in developed countries are said to devote 1-4 percent of total available time to childcare, compared to 2-3 percent for fathers. So limited is the time academic mothers spend raising their children that they actually outperform their colleagues who have never given birth.[137]

Furthermore, work can be defined as any task that one person can entrust to another to do for him or her. Using this approach, a United Nations survey in 13 different countries found that men spent nearly *twice* as much of their total time working than women, 66 percent to 34 percent.[138] As a result, women have more time than men to look after their personal needs, such as eating, dressing, socializing, watching TV and sleeping.[139] If they "value a well-rounded life,"[140] then this is because they have leisure to do so. Women who work part time also enjoy other advantages. They are much less likely to work overtime or at night. They pay proportionally far less taxes,[141] which means that, on an hourly basis, they can earn much more than men holding similar but full-time jobs.[142] Possibly as a result, part-time workers tend to be much more satisfied with their jobs than full-time ones. Part-time female workers with children also enjoy better health than their fully-employed sisters.[143] No wonder only 10 percent of British part-time female workers expressed in an interest in working full time.[144]

One might conclude that, in everything pertaining to work, it is only full-time working women who really measure up to male standards. But even that is not correct. Even when people of both sexes hold full-time, year-round jobs,

---

[137] See Valian, *Why So Slow?*, p. 270.

[138] United Nations Development Program, *Human Development Report*, 1995, table 4.2.

[139] Dominique Anxo and Lennart Flood, "Patterns of Time Use in France and Sweden", in Inga Persson and Christina Jonung, eds., *Women's Work and Wages*, London, Routledge, 1998, pp. 102-3.

[140] See Valian, *Why So Slow?* p. 267.

[141] Joy Hendry, "The Role of the Professional Housewife," in Hunter, ed., *Japanese Women Working*, p. 236.

[142] N. Stockman et al., *Women's Work in East and West*, London, Sharpe, 1995, p. 81.

[143] M. Bartley, "Domestic Conditions, Paid Employment and Women's Experiences of Ill Health," *Sociology of Health and Illness*, 14, 3, 1992, pp. 313-41.

[144] Stockman, *Women's Work in East and West*, p. 200.

men work longer hours than women do. In both Europe and the United States, "full time" means 10 percent more for men than it does for women.[145] In Britain, whereas 28 percent of male full-time employees regularly spend more than 48 hours on the job each week, half of female ones work fewer than 40 hours.[146] Factoring in overtime, the difference is greater still. For example, no sooner did large numbers of women enter the American automobile factories in the late 1960s than they and their representatives demanded that the old system of mandatory overtime be abolished. When that demand was granted and voluntary overtime substituted, they were still not satisfied. They declared that since men were more prepared to do overtime, the *right* to do so discriminated against women. By 1973, women workers' contradictory demands had driven the Union of Auto Workers almost to distraction. As part of its attempts to bring the matter to a close and move on with business, the union endorsed the Equal Rights Amendment. That legislation, however, ended up being rejected by most women.[147]

Since 1970 or so, depending on the country in question, working women have demanded, and often obtained, the following benefits: shorter hours, shorter weeks, flexible hours, flexible weeks, flexible career tracks — which, in the professions, can mean working 35 hours per week instead of 60 — [148] menstrual leave, breastfeeding breaks,[149] hormone breaks,[150] paid maternity leave and unpaid maternity leave with a job guaranteed upon return after months or even years of absence. In Germany, women also have the right to deduct the cost of household help from taxes, similar to American women's right to deduct childcare services. And in Britain, women are guaranteed the right not to do unhealthy work or be moved from one location to another,[151] not

[145] For the United States, see May H. Stevenson, *Determinants of Low Wages for Women Workers*, New York, Praeger, 1984, p. 4; for Europe, see Statistisches Amt der Europäischen Gemeinschaften, *Frauen der Europäischen Gemeinschaft*, Luxemburg, Amt für amtliche Veröffentlichungen der Europäischen Gemeinschaften, 1992, pp. 94-7.

[146] Briar, *Working for Women*, p. 153.

[147] See Nancy Gabin, "Time Out of Mind: the UAW's Response to Female Labor Laws and Mandatory Overtime in the 1960s," in Ava Abron, ed., *Work Engendered: Toward a New History of American Labor*, Ithaca, NY, Cornell University Press, 1991, pp. 355, 351-74.

[148] "Women in the Law Say Path is Limited by 'Mommy Track,'" *New York Times*, 8.8.1988, p. A1.

[149] For Japan, see Carney and O'Kelly, *Women's Work and Place in Japan*, p. 146.

[150] For Silicon Valley, see Karen Hossfeld, "'Their Own Logic Against Them': Contradictions in Sex, Race and Class in Silicon Valley," in Ward, ed., *Women Workers and Global Restructuring*, p. 172.

[151] Katherine O'Donovan and Erika Szyszcak, *Equality and Sex Discrimination Law*, Oxford, Blackwell, 1988, pp. 65-6; Meade-Hill and another v. the British Council [1995], IRLR 478.

to mention employer-supported kindergartens and vouchers to pay for those kindergartens. They are also granted time off for childcare, emergency childcare, care for sick children and care for the elderly.[152] Britain also has special training opportunities, known as mentor programs, to help women climb the corporate ladder.

So numerous and varied are the programs offered by many corporations that keeping track of them has become a job in and of itself. Specially-developed software is utilized to assist women in applying for such programs. To ensure that such benefits do not go unutilized, women demanded, and in many cases obtained, obligatory representation on corporate boards.[153] European corporations call these programs "total E-quality." However, since many of them are open to women only, it is hardly equality in the literal sense of the word. In some cases the language of the law permits men to take equal advantage of such programs, but this rarely occurs in practice. When men enter female-typed occupations, they still tend to work full time.[154] Even in Sweden, only 8 percent of eligible men made use of their right to work part time after the birth of a child.[155]

By contrast, so rarely are women expected to work like men that many of the women officially in the labor force are actually at home enjoying their privileges. Again, this is particularly true in Sweden, arguably the most advanced welfare state of all. Parental leave is granted in Sweden at 90 percent pay for as long as 15 months. In addition, parents are entitled to as much as 60 days of leave per year to look after each sick child. Assuming a working year of approximately 220 days, a woman with two children can take off work more than half the time without suffering any kind of disadvantage. Scant wonder that most of them tend to work for the public sector, where profit is far less of a priority and where productivity is hard if not impossible to measure. Scant wonder, too, that a survey found that only *one in seven* working mothers of young children were present on the job.[156] So inclusive is Sweden's definition of woman's paid work, in fact, that it distorts the country's entire labor

[152] See Baridon and Eyler, *Working Together*, pp. 188-90.

[153] Dienel, *Frauen in Führungspositionen in Europa*, pp. 138-41, and table 36; Bundesministerium für Wirtschaft, ed., *Frauen als Wirtschaftsfaktor in Europa*, Frankfurt, Bundesministerium für Wirtschaft, 1997, pp. 20-1, 97.

[154] Kea Tijdens, "Segregation Processes by Gender: The Case of the Electronic Data-Processing Occupations," in Petra Beckman, ed., *Gender-Specific Occupational Segregation*, Nuremberg, German Institute for Economic Research, 1996, p. 118.

[155] Nasman, "Childhood, Family and New Ways of Life: The Case of Sweden," p. 124.

[156] Pott-Butter, *Facts and Fairy Tales*, p. 208.

statistics. Adjust the data, and much of the increased participation of Swedish women in the labor force since roughly 1950 is exposed for what it is: a myth.[157]

What applies to developed countries also applies, in a different way, to developing ones. Since their economies were based largely on agriculture, until recently the division of labor in these countries was, as one would expect, as it has always been. In all of them, men did the heavy work as well as that which involved journeys away from home. On an annual basis, women spent fewer days working than men. When they did work, they usually undertook the lighter tasks close to the home so as to be able to keep an eye on their children.[158] On the other hand, even in these countries there were at least some comfortable jobs available in administration or the professions. Such jobs tended to be disproportionally held by women.[159]

Industrialization reached developing countries in the 1960s. Often it took the form of foreign-owned plants designed to manufacture items such as textiles, and later on electronics, using locally-available, cheap, mainly female labor. In other cases it was a question of processing data for companies, such as airlines, which were located elsewhere. Such work was repetitive and boring, and as was the case in some industries, the need to spend days poring through a microscope or in the presence of noxious chemicals occasionally made it injurious to health. Still, as the women themselves were the first to admit,[160] it was a lot better than slogging away in the mud, the more so because it paid up to 25 times as much.[161] No wonder it often became the subject of fierce competition. Compared to the work of most men, whether in agriculture or in urban trades like construction and transportation, it was safe, easy and clean.

The outcome was that in countries including South Korea, Taiwan, the Philippines, Thailand, Malaysia, Singapore, Indonesia and Mexico, women began entering the plants by the hundreds of thousands. As in 19th-century

---

157 A. Nyberg, "The Social Construction of Married Woman's Labor-Force Participation: The Case of Sweden in the Twentieth Century," *Continuity and Change*, 9, 1994, pp. 153-4.

158 For China, see Davin, *Woman Work*, p. 149.

159 Jane L. Parpart, "Gender, Patriarchy, and Development in Africa: The Zimbabwean Case," in Valentine M. Moghadam, ed., *Patriarchy and Economic Development*, Oxford, Clarendon Press, 1996, p. 151.

160 See Diane L. Wolf, "Linking Women's Labor with the Global Economy; Factory Workers and Their Families in Rural Java," in Kathryn Ward, ed., *Women Workers and Global Restructuring*, Ithaca, NY, Cornell University Press, 1990, p. 42.

161 Sinith Sittrak, *The Daughters of Development: Women and the Changing Environment*, London, Zed, 1998, p. 93.

Europe, most of those who stitched sport shoes, or assembled computer circuits, were young and unmarried. Very often they lived with their families and were supported by them while contributing little or nothing to household income. Instead, they spent their wages on luxuries such as clothes and cosmetics. Others saved as much as 50 percent of their income.[162] Once the women married and left the labor force, as most did,[163] they continued to be supported, this time by their husbands. *Pace* Western feminists, they refused to "recognize that they are exploited or organize to challenge the sources of that exploitation."[164]

Not only in these countries, but in all countries since the industrial revolution, a disproportionate number of working women were single or widowed. Later on, owing in part to the spread of feminism, these two groups of women were joined by the growing army of divorcees. Married women — both those who do work outside the home and, even more so, those who do not — for the most part still expect their basic economic needs to be provided by men. Recent works on, and by, career women describe the joys of being in the labor force as well as its disappointments. The latter include the need to please one's boss, moving from one location to another, sudden reversal of fortune owing to corporate restructuring, or simply the loss of personal freedom and leisure time to devote to family and friends.[165] Those disappointments and those joys, it would seem safe to assume, affect men just as much as women. Having set out to take the male world of work by storm, sooner or later women were bound to discover its disadvantages as well. When they do discover those disadvantages, however, many women are permitted to do something that men are only rarely able to — namely, stop working and return home.

Periods of unemployment apart, men normally stay in the labor force throughout their working lives. Not so women, two-thirds of whom are constantly drifting in and out of employment. As a result, in most industrialized countries late-twentieth century women were actually *less* likely to work

---

[162] Wolf, "Linking Women's Labor with the Global Economy," p. 43; Sun Joo Oh, "The Living Conditions of Female Workers in Korea," *Korea Observer*, 14, 1983, pp. 185-200.

[163] P. Pongpaichit, "Two Roads to the Factory: Industrialization Strategies and Women's Employment in South East Asia," in Bina Agarwal, ed., *Structures of Patriarchy: the State, the Community and the Household*, London, Zed, 1988, pp. 158-61.

[164] Rita S. Gallin, "Women and the Export Industry in Taiwan: The Muting of Class Consciousness," in Ward, ed., *Women Workers and Global Restructuring*, p. 190.

[165] See Beth Milward, *Working with Men*, Hillsboro, OR, Beyond Words, 1990, pp. 179-276; also see Elizabeth P. McKenna, *When Work Doesn't Work Anymore: Women, Work and Identity*, New York, Delacorte, 1997, chapter 1.

continuously throughout their lives than their sisters before them. In Britain, just 10 percent of women in 1980 remained continuously employed, a drop from 15 percent in 1965.[166] In the United States, working mothers put in slightly more than half as many hours as working fathers into their jobs.[167] Whether or not they are married, over a lifetime career women are likely to work 40 percent fewer hours than men. That is arguably the single biggest reason why their work experience does not, on average, match that of men.[168] In sum, for most women the old pattern whereby they only participate in the economy to a limited extent persists. Perhaps the most important change has been a very sharp drop in the birth rate. Even the few remaining children are likely to spend so much time at day care centers or school that they hardly know their parents; leaving women with less to do than at any other time in history.

As for men, their pattern of employment reflects the fact that they continue to bear the prime responsibility for feeding their families. Lacking a socially acceptable alternative, it is usually the only choice they have.[169] Few people will object if a married woman decides to leave the workforce to spend the rest of her days, say, watering her plants or resolving her internal conflicts. On the contrary: Her "reluctance to forfeit her entire self for the sake of her career" may earn praise as "particularly thoughtful and intelligent."[170] A man who makes the same choice will be devalued by men *and* women. Very often this is true even if his economic future is secure. If his wife continues to work, then this is likely to be doubly true. At some point, the man's wife will begin to wonder why she should carry the entire burden on her own. Once she starts doing so, divorce is usually on its way.[171]

---

[166] Catherine Hakim, "Theoretical Measurement Issues in the Analysis of Occupational Segregation," in Beckman, ed., *Gender-Specific Occupational Segregation*, pp. 76-7; Hakim, *Key Issues in Women's Work*, pp. 117, 134, 140-1.

[167] For 1996, see Council of Economic Advisers, *Families and the Labor Market, 1969-1999: Analyzing the "Time Crunch,"* Washington, p. 4.

[168] Tiger, *The Decline of Males*, p. 121; M. T. Coleman and J. Pencavel, "Trends in Market Work Behavior of Women since 1940," *Industrial and Labor Relations Review*, 46, 1993, pp. 653-77.

[169] See John Money and Patricia Tucker, *Sexual Signatures: On Being a Man or a Woman*, Boston, Little Brown, 1975, p. 199; also see Susan Moller Okin, *Justice, Gender and the Family*, New York, Basic Books, 1989, p. 144.

[170] Liz Roman Gallese, *Women Like Us*, New York, William Morrow, 1985, p. 250-1.

[171] See Sandra Tsing Loh, "The Weaker Sex," *The Atlantic*, December 2010; also see A. Cherlin, "Worklife and Marital Dissolution," in George Levinger, eds, *Divorce and Separation*, New York, Basic Books, 1979, pp. 151-66.

Today, as before, for men to earn their bread by the sweat of their brow remains a duty that the vast majority of them can escape, if at all, only if they are unmarried, childless or both. Today, as before, women who follow a similar path are mainly those who do not have a man to support them. In addition, married women, and to a lesser extent unmarried ones, tend to do easier work, work fewer hours and drop out of the labor force earlier than men. What happens when women are *not* granted these privileges is illustrated by the fate of both *kibbutzim* and the Soviet Union. In the latter, it literally led to the country's collapse. As the number of Russians stagnated and started to decline, Moscow lost its grip over its remaining population. Many of them were Muslim, meaning that women were less likely to be employed and that their fertility remained high.[172] To a lesser but still significant extent, the same was also true elsewhere in the former Eastern Bloc. Such were the consequences of women's emancipation, communist style.

5. Conclusions

When it comes to work, women have always enjoyed many privileges over men. To a considerable extent, these privileges can be traced back to the biological facts that limited the labor women could perform. Certainly if they had children, and to a lesser extent even if they did not, women were also prevented from traveling far from home. Even in the United States during World War II, out of 106,000 women who worked for the railways, only 250 — less than one-quarter of 1 percent — were active in railroading proper.[173] If it is true, as some say, that "it is far easier… to switch from being a wage worker to occupying a domestic role than to do the reverse,"[174] then perhaps one reason for this is because men's work is often *hard*.

Women's privileges changed over time. Each time a technological and economic revolution took place, such as the shift from agriculture to industry, or from industry to services, it affected the work of people of both sexes. Women began working in the fields, and then in the factories. They also began working at home, in offices, and in sales outlet. Wherever men and women worked, however, a clear division of labor always prevailed. Most women were

[172] Moses, *The Politics of Women and Work*, pp. 24, 32.

[173] Doris Weatherford, *American Women and World War II*, New York, Facts on File, 1990, p. 140.

[174] Okin, *Justice, Gender and the Family*, p. 103.

concentrated in a relatively small handful of occupations. Here and there a societal emergency, such as the busy agricultural season or a war, might cause women to join in men's work. However, over time the customary division of labor always reasserted itself. As long as work was considered a burden, women, like men, did their best to avoid it. Much more than men, women were sheltered from work, either by their male relatives, prevailing social attitudes, or both. Sometimes the work of men of earlier generations became the hobby of women, as with horseback riding and pottery. In this sense, too, women represent the leisure class.

Over the past century and a half, first socialist and then feminist writers have declared work to be a right and a privilege. Yet throughout, the situation has remained fundamentally unchanged. Understandably, most women compelled to work by economic circumstance continue to see their jobs as a burden. As turnover statistics show, often they take the first opportunity to escape from their jobs. This, incidentally, is one reason why feminism has only enjoyed limited success among working-class women. As to those women who took up work even though they did not have to, they, too, for the most part have retained their privileges. This includes doing less, and lighter, work; the right to leave their jobs when they so choose; an earlier retirement age; and, as the plum in the pudding, the right to strike a self-righteous attitude toward work by claiming that, unlike men, they are in it not for the money but for the "interest" and "opportunities for self-development" it offers.[175] Now as ever, the higher the class to which women belong — thanks in large part to the work of their menfolk — the truer this all becomes. Among all of Adam's descendants, it is to these women that his curse still does not apply.

---

175 See McKenna, *When Work Doesn't Work Any More*, p. 37.

Chapter 4: From Dowries to Social Security

1. The Great Riddle

If it is true that the origin of all wealth is work, as the philosophers of the Enlightenment in particular believed, and if it is true that women have always done less and lighter work than men, then how did women manage to survive and, quite often, prosper? The answer is simple and well known: to a large extent, the reason why women could survive is because they were fed, clothed, housed and looked after by men. To quote the most important female anthropologist of all time, Margaret Mead: "Somewhere in the dawn of human history, some social invention was made under which males started nurturing females and their young... In every known human society… the young male learns that… one of the things which he must do in order to be a full member of society is to provide food for some female and her young... The division of labor may be made in a thousand ways… but the core remains. Man, the heir of tradition, provides for women and children."[1]

In this chapter, the mechanisms society has devised to make men support women will be explored in some detail. Ignoring childhood as the time when people of both sexes cannot look after themselves, the chapter begins with an examination of the arrangements made to ensure that women should be provided for within the family. That examination is followed by a look at the ways various societies have sought to help women who for one reason or another did not have husbands or male relatives willing and able to take care of them. Next, this chapter examines the way many of these arrangements were taken over, or adapted, by the modern welfare state. From all this it will quickly become evident that the great riddle is not, in fact, a riddle at all. Women have always been supported by men, and a society in which this was *not* the case has yet to be discovered.

---

[1] Margaret Mead, *Male and Female: A Study of the Sexes in a Changing World*, New York, Mentor, 1949, p. 145-6.

2. The Economics of Marriage

In the eyes of the German philosopher Georg Friedrich Hegel, the defining characteristic of the family is that it is based on altruism and love. In this respect it differs from civil society, which is the province of egoism and economic competition. It also distinguished the family from the state, which polices both the family and civil society and allegiance to which provides the spiritual significance of human life.[2] The idea certainly has much to recommend it. Nevertheless, there is no question that no family is, or ever has been, based *solely* on love.

Among other things, the family is an economic institution. As such, its purpose is to guarantee that the woman or women will be provided for. Cases in which the situation is reversed are rare. Where and when they do exist they are expected to be temporary, as when wives see their husbands through school or so-called cougars spend part of their lives with younger men. The ways society makes men look after their female relatives vary. Many societies have long had, and some still have, the levirate, an arrangement that permits and often obliges a dead man's brother to marry his widow. If the Koran allows a man to take several wives, it does so not in order that he may have fun, but as a way of providing for widows. In a society without clear territorial borders or any kind of police force, women were very vulnerable. Not accidentally, the Arabic term *qawwamun*, which describes the position of men vis-à-vis women, can mean either "defenders" or "maintainers."[3] In Reformation Europe, the first thing the authorities did when confronted with nuns who had left the convent was to find men to look after them. One of those who was helped in this way was the wife of Martin Luther.

Very often, before a man can marry he must work and pay, and after joining hands in matrimony he must continue to work and pay. For example, Germanic men in Tacitus' day had to pay a *dos* as a condition for marriage.[4] During the late Roman Empire, men betrothed their wives by means of gifts. An entire body of literature developed around the question of whether or not

[2] See Georg W. F. Hegel, *Philosophy of Right*, Oxford, Oxford University Press, 1942, sections 75, 158, 159, 162; also see Shlomo Avineri, *Hegel's Theory of the Modern State*, Cambridge, Cambridge University Press, 1972, 133-4, 139-41.

[3] M. Muhammad Ali, *Translation of the Holy Quran*, Lahore, Ahhamadyyah Anhuman Ishaat-i-Islam, 1951, 3, 4, 86, and footnote 1.

[4] Tacitus, *Germania*, 28.

the would-be groom was entitled, if the woman did not take the man's hand in marriage, to receive his gifts back.[5] For a Muslim youth to earn the brides-wealth or *mahr* often means having to put in several years of hard work while living away from his native village. No wonder that, when Ibn Battuta visited the Maldives, one of the things he liked best was that the *mahr* demanded of him was small.[6]

Normally the money went to the woman's relatives, usually the father but occasionally the mother. However, the bride-to-be often benefited as well. The *dos* a prospective Germanic son-in-law paid to the bride's father had to be handed over to the bride herself. In 18th-century England, prospective spouses gave presents to each other. A woman whose wedding was canceled was entitled to receive back everything she had given — but a man only obtained half back.[7] In strict Islamic law, a woman is entitled to the whole of the brides-wealth. Until recently in Palestinian villages, a bride-to-be obtained roughly one-third of it. Normally she would invest the wealth in jewelry that she then wore, thus putting her husband's love on show. Now that patriarchal power is no longer what it used to be, she once again gets the entire sum.[8] If the wedding does not take place, she is still entitled to part of the *mahr*.

Yet another form of direct payment was the so-called "morning-after gift." Depending on the time period and the man's circumstances, it could range from a small sum all the way to an entire district, complete with its inhabitants and the income it generated. A French royal decree of 1214 gave a wife the rights to half her husbands' property, both that which he owned at the time of the wedding and that which he subsequently acquired.[9] Likewise in India, such gifts ranged from a trinket to a landed estate.[10] Often it was disguised as a "love gift." In practice it was an obligation that men, and high-class men in particular, owed their wives. Once the gift had been made, it became the woman's inalienable property; it came to be known as her dower.[11] In Germany and

[5] Judith Evans Grubbs, *Law and Family in Late Antiquity*, Oxford, Clarendon, 1995, pp. 175-6.
[6] *The Rehlah of Ibn Battuta*, p. 202.
[7] Anon, *A Treatise of Femme Couverte or the Lady's Law*, London, n.p., 1732, p. 30.
[8] Moors, "Gender, Property and Power," pp. 17-8.
[9] Theodore Evergates, "Aristocratic Women in the Country of Champagne," in Theodore Evergates, ed., *Aristocratic Women in Medieval France*, Philadelphia, University of Pennsylvania Press, 1999, p. 93.
[10] Anjani Kant, *Women and the Law*, New Delhi, APH., 1997, pp. 37, 244-51.
[11] Christine Fell et al., *Women in Anglo-Saxon England and the Impact of 1066*, Oxford, Blackwell, 1984.

perhaps elsewhere, the custom was still in full force during the 16th century.[12] The precise arrangements varied from one society to the next,[13] but what all had in common was that it was men, and not women, who were made to pay.

Once he had been married, a man could expect to support his wife or wives for the rest of his life. This is one reason why, even in societies which permitted men to marry more than one woman at a time, only a small minority did so. Figures from Algiers during the 1860s are indicative. Of the 18,289 married men in the city at the time, fewer than 5 percent had more than one wife, and only 0.4 percent had more than two.[14]

This belief in man's obligation to support his wife goes back to ancient history. In ancient Egypt, the earliest literate society of all,[15] the words of one man to his son make clear the husband-to-be's responsibility:

> If you are excellent, you shall establish your household
> And love your wife according to her standard;
> Fill her belly, clothe her back.
> Perfume is a prescription for her limbs.
> Make her happy, as long as you live!
> She is a field, good for her lord.
> You shall not pass judgment on her![16]

Arrangements also existed to ensure that women would continue to receive support if they were widowed. One such example was permitting a widow to continue occupying the house that had come with her late husband's job. Since daughters were expected to be supported by their husbands, normally a man's

---

[12] See Herbert Helbig, "Die Verlobung im Mittelalter," *Der Herold*, 8, 1988, pp. 253-61.

[13] See Lepowski, "Gender in an Egalitarian Society," p. 180; also Ekong, *Bridewealth*, p. 68; Jack Goody, *The Development of the Family and Marriage in Europe*, Cambridge, Cambridge University Press, 1983, p. 254; Jan Ovesen et al., *When Every Household is an Island: Social Organization and Power Structures in Rural Cambodia*, Uppsala, Uppsala University Press, 1996, p. 57.

[14] See L. Sharp, "The Social Organization of the Yir Yiront Tribe, Cape York Peninsula," *Oceania*, 3, 1932-3, pp. 429-30; H. Gerber, "Social and Economic Position of Women in an Ottoman City, Bursa 1600-1700," *International Journal of Middle East Studies*, 1, 1980, p. 232; Jack Goody, "Polygyny, Economy and the Role of Women," in Jack Goody, ed., *The Character of Kinship*, Cambridge, Cambridge University Press, 1973, pp. 176-82.

[15] See Robins, *Women in Ancient Egypt*, p. 129.

[16] R. B. Parkinson, *Voices of Ancient Egypt: An Anthology of Middle Kingdom Writings*, London, Enchiridion, 1991, p. 55.

heirs were his sons. However, to provide for a childless wife, a man could subvert the law by adopting her as his daughter.[17]

Much later, the Graeco-Macedonian and Roman occupations of Egypt produced many important political, economic and social changes. What did not change in occupied Egypt, however, was the husband's obligation to support his wife. A marriage contract dated 92 B.C. explains how it was done at the time:[18]

> Let Apollonia be the wife of Philiscus, having been persuaded by him that it is fitting for her to be his wife, and let her have mastery in common with him over all their possessions. And let Philiscus provide for Apollonia all the things that she needs and her clothing and the rest that it is suitable for a married woman to have provided for her — and let him do this wherever they live, according as their means allow.

The husband's obligation to support his wife was also written into subsequent Roman wedding charters.[19] Another example is the Jewish *ketubah*, a standardized agreement which has remained unchanged for centuries. In the document, the groom promises to provide the bride's "nutrition, clothing and sexual needs." Should the couple divorce, then the husband is obliged to compensate his wife with a sum specified in the *ktuba.*

The duty of husbands to provide for their wives according to their means is universal. It is can be enforced either by way of public opinion or by that of the courts. Very often it was incorporated into sacred wisdom, as in both the Vedic writings and Islam.[20] In England, the formula "with all my worldly goods I endow thee" has persisted for almost a millennium, in spite of all the changes in the laws that governed its application. To help husbands support their wives, the latter were often given a dowry. Returning to Philiscus and his sweetheart Apollonia, it is possible that she herself provided the money. Normally, though,

---

[17] Robins, *Women in Ancient Egypt*, p. 134.

[18] Marylin Arthur, "'Liberated' Women: The Classical Era," in Bridenthal and Koonz, eds., *Becoming Visible*, p. 75.

[19] See Grubbs, *Law and Family in Late Antiquity*, p. 146.

[20] Julia Leslie, "Recycling Ancient Material: An Orthodox View of Hindu Women," in Leonie J. Archer et al., eds., *Women in Ancient Societies: An Illusion of the Night*, London, MacMillan, 1994, p. 241; Wahiduddin Khan, *Woman between Islam and Western Society*, p. 177.

doing so was the duty of a woman's father; should he die, then it devolved on her brother or brothers.

In return for being allowed to administer the dowry, Philiscus had to agree to several conditions. He was, according to the marriage contract:

> "[T]o take no other wife but Apollonia, and no concubine, and let him have no boyfriends or beget any children from any woman as long as Apollonia is living, nor inhabit any other household but the one over which Apollonia rules. Nor let him repudiate her or do violence to her or treat her badly or alienate any of their property in a way which is unfair to Apollonia. If he is caught doing any of those things... then let him pay back immediately to Apollonia her dowry... By the same token, let Apollonia not be permitted to spend the day or the night away from the house of Philiscus without his knowledge. Nor may she sleep with another man, nor may she squander their common household property, nor may she disgrace Philiscus in the ways in which men get disgraced. But if Apollonia willingly does any of these things, let her be sent away from Philiscus, and let him repay to her the dowry simply within ten days of her departure."

The terms of divorce were striking. If a dissolution of the marriage came about through some transgression of Philiscus, the dowry had to be returned. If Apollonia was the party guilty of bringing about divorce, the dowry also had to be returned.

In ancient Athens, as in all other societies, few fathers or other male guardians would give their female wards to a man who could not support her properly.[21] As in many other societies, the prospective husband expected to receive a dowry to help him in his legal duty of supporting his wife. But the dowry did not become his property. All he could do was administer it on her behalf. If the couple divorced, the dowry had to be returned. Men who failed to return their ex-wives' dowries were penalized a monstrous interest of 18 percent.[22] The relevant lawsuits were handled by a special procedure, known as *eisangelia*, that was similar to the one used for the most serious crimes, such as attempts to overthrow the constitution. From the point of view of the woman

---

[21] Richard Garner, *Law and Society in Classical Athens*, London, Croom Helm, 1987, pp. 14, 85; Just, *Women in Athenian Law and Life*, p. 31.

[22] Just, *Women in Athenian Law and Life*, p. 73.

and her male guardians, *eisangelia* had the advantage that a failed suit did not expose to penalties those who had brought the case. Since Greek justice was agonistic — meaning that anybody seeking to impose a penalty on another would have the same penalty visited on him in case he lost his suit — this was a great privilege indeed.

Dowries also served to regulate the transfer of wealth from one generation to the next. To stay in ancient Greece, daughters received their dowries upon marriage as a sort of "*ante-mortem* inheritance."[23] Dowries were a way of giving daughters their due even though their father was still alive. Similar methods were used in Rome, where a prospective bride might have property bestowed on her by her parents *and* by her husband.[24]. Likewise, dowries were expected among the early Germanic tribes, among Jews from at least the time of the Second Temple onward, and also during the European Middle Ages.[25] By contrast, men were compelled to postpone marriage until after they were able to support families. Often that meant having to wait for their fathers' death.

In Renaissance Italy, dowries were expected even in marriages among the *miserabili*.[26] On average, marrying off a girl cost a father one-seventh of his wealth.[27] One 17th-century English gentleman, Sir Roger Wilbraham, complained that members of his class had to expect four "casualties:" lawsuits, building costs, serving a prince and "marrying a daughter."[28] In late 19th-century Europe, an entire family might pool its resources in order to prevent a bourgeois woman from having to marry below her station. The custom of giving daughters their inheritance years, even decades, before their brothers received theirs remained common all the way through the mid-20th century.

---

[23] Pomeroy, *Families in Classical and Hellenistic Greece*, p. 20.

[24] Grubbs, *Law and Family in Late Antiquity*, pp. 143, 147; O. F Robinson, "The Historical Background," in Sheila A. M. Maclean and Noreen Burrows, eds., *The Legal Relevance of Gender: Some Aspects of Sex-Based Discrimination*, London, MacMillan, 1988, pp. 48-9.

[25] Andree Coutemanche, *La richesse des femmes: Patrimoines et gestion à Monasque au xive siècle*, Paris, Vrin, 1993, pp. 172-5, 294; Shachar, *The Fourth Estate*, pp. 127-8.

[26] See Carol Bresnahan Menning, *Charity and State in Late Renaissance Italy*, Ithaca, NY, Cornell University Press, 1993. p. 155; Samuel K. Cohn, "Marriage in the Mountains, 1348-1500," in Trevor Dean and K. J. P. Lowe, eds., *Marriage in Italy, 1300-1500*, Cambridge, Cambridge University Press, 1998, pp. 184-5.

[27] David Herlihy and Christiane Klapisch-Zuber, *Tuscans and Their Families: A Study of the Florentine Catasto of 1427*, New Haven, CT, Yale University Press, 1978, p. 228.

[28] See Felicity Heal and Clive Holmes, *The Gentry in England and Wales, 1500-1700*, London, MacMillan, 1994, p. 141.

In all the aforementioned civilizations, it was assumed that married women had limited, if any, ability to earn their keep. The idea, therefore, was to help daughters attract husbands by having giving them dowries that would act as an advance on their inheritances. Since it was husbands who had to do the providing, they were given control over the property as long as the marriages lasted. This did not necessarily mean they could do with it as they pleased. If the dowry consisted of land, the husbands might not be able to alienate it. If it consisted of cash, the prenuptial agreement might stipulate that it be put into a bank where it would earn interest and from where the husband could not withdraw it. If divorce came to pass, either the dowry was used as a basis for calculating the amount of maintenance due or else it had to be returned.[29] The same obligation also existed if the husband predeceased his wife.[30]

In theory, the fact that women often received their inheritances in advance should have prevented them from inheriting property. In practice, women in early medieval Europe, Anglo-Saxon England and the Islamic world were often able to get their dowries *and* inherit all or part of their parents' wealth.[31] Regardless of what the law might say, the same was true in ancient Greece.[32] In Sparta, if Aristotle and after him Plutarch may be believed,[33] so many men were killed in war that heiresses were numerous and extremely powerful. By the 4th century B.C women owned two-fifths of all public land and a major proportion of private land as well. When Spartan mothers demanded that their sons return from war, either with their shields or on them, they may have been motivated by more than pride alone.

Socially, and often legally as well, a man whose daughters were married was supposed to leave his property to his sons, whose duty it was to provide for their mother. By contrast, a woman was under no obligation to leave her husband anything at all.[34] Provided her sons were no longer dependent on her, she could often leave it to whomever she pleased. This difference between the sexes emerges quite clearly from an examination of the way women gave to

---

[29] See Linda Guzzetti, "Separation and Separated Couples in Fourteenth-Century Venice," in Dean and Lowe, eds., *Marriage in Italy*, pp. 257-8.

[30] Steven Epstein, *Wills and Wealth in Medieval Genoa, 1150-1250*, Cambridge, MA, Harvard University Press, 1984, pp. 103-6.

[31] See Goody, *The Development of the Family and Marriage in Europe*, pp. 21, 207, 243, 253; Amyu Livingstone, "Aristocratic Women in the Chartrain," in Evergates, ed., *Aristocratic Women in Medieval France*, p. 59.

[32] Pomeroy, *Families in Classical and Hellenistic Greece*, p. 20.

[33] Aristotle, *Politics*, 1270a 23-4; Plutarch, *Agis*, 7.3-4.

[34] Epstein, *Wills and Wealth in Medieval Genoa*, p. 109.

charity[35] and also from studies of French and English wills from the 11th century to the 17th century. In both France and England, women normally named a larger number of heirs than did men. Particularly if they had no male offspring, but sometimes even if they did, they were also more generous to other relatives, especially female ones, as well as to servants, charities and the Church.[36] The single biggest reason was that they could afford to: In early modern England, over half of the widows in one sample bequeathed wealth at least equal to the amount that had been left by their husbands.

Since men regularly earned more than women, it stands to reason that the latter got more out of marriage than they put into it. British figures from the period between 1780 and 1860 lend credence to this theory.[37] A study of 1,350 working-class households from that era suggests that husbands' share in generating family income ranged between 55 percent and 83 percent. Husbands, as long as they were employed, always earned more than all other family members combined. At times they made nearly five times as much. The low of 55 percent was reached in the mid-19th century, during the so-called "hungry 40s." Both before and after that decade, the figure was considerably higher. Of the remaining family income, more was generated by children than by wives. In fact, wives' contributions never exceeded 12 percent, and in some years were as low as 5 percent. No wonder women were valued primarily for their fertility, and derived what power they had from it. Only in families with unemployed children did wives sometimes bring in as much as 41 percent of household income. This exceptionally high figure refers to mining families during the difficult period from 1787 to 1815. In other families, and at other times, wives seldom contributed more than 25 percent.

As the domestic ideal established itself around 1850, the share of household income generated by women declined.[38] The higher the class to which the family belonged, the truer this became. By 1890, women's work in Europe and the United States contributed just 1.9 percent to 3 percent of household

---

[35] Kate Mertes, *The English Noble Household, 1250-1600: Good Governance and Politic Rule*, Oxford, Blackwell, 199, p. 158.

[36] Goody, *The Development of the Family and Marriage in Europe*, pp. 65, 209; Coutemanche, *La richesse des femmes*, pp. 168, 172-5; Amy L. Erickson, *Women and Property in Early Modern England*, London, Routledge, 1993, pp. 213, 215, 217.

[37] Sara Hormel and Jane Humphries, "The Origins and Expansion of the Male Breadwinner Family: The Case of Nineteenth-Century Britain," in Angelique Janssens, ed., *The Rise and Decline of the Male Breadwinner Family*, pp. 31, 32, 35, 47, 60-1.

[38] Horrell and Humphries, "The Origins and Expansion of the Male Breadwinner Family," p. 48.

income.[39] French women in 1914 contributed a surprisingly high 11 percent to 30 percent. However, these figures only apply to the lower middle class.[40] Even in our day, it is only the wives with the most feckless husbands who do not get the better side of the bargain. In Czechoslovakia shortly before its dissolution, women were only responsible for 12 percent to 22 percent of household income.[41] In the Soviet Union during the last decade before its collapse, only 15 percent of women earned more than their husbands.[42] Swedish wives earn an exceptionally high 39 percent of after-tax household income,[43] but as is discussed later in this chapter, this figure can be attributed in part to the fact that Swedish men pay far more in taxes. In other Western countries, women's contribution is much lower.[44]

In the United States, women who put out matrimonial ads are 10 times more likely than men to look for money.[45] And with good reason: In 2010, women on average only contributed 38.5 percent to the income of American families.[46] That figure is itself an improvement over 1940, when it stood at 30 percent.[47] However, these figures refer to any given moment during a couple's life together. Women's careers tend to be interrupted more often than those of men, and normally they retire earlier than men. Hence, over a lifetime the data grossly overestimate women's contribution to household finances. No wonder that in one survey, *all* the employed homemakers interviewed believed "men should be responsible for the financial support of families." To make sure that men met their obligations, 80 percent of people of both sexes said they would ostracize a man who failed to provide for his family as he should.[48]

---

[39] Haines, *Life Cycle, Savings, Demographic Adaptation*, p. 49, table 3.1.

[40] Louise A. Tilly, "Family, Gender, and Occupation in Industrial France: Past and Present," in Alice S. Rossi, ed., *Gender and the Life Course*, New York, Aldine, 1985, p. 203.

[41] Alena Heitlinger, *Women and State Socialism*, London, MacMillan, 1979, p. 155.

[42] Moses, *The Politics of Women and Work in the Soviet Union and the United States*, p. 21.

[43] According to Ann Critenden, *The Price of Motherhood: Why the Most Important Job in All the World is Still the Least Valued*, New York, Metropolitan, 2001, p. 248.

[44] Julia A. Shorab, *Sexing the Benefit: Women, Social Security and Financial Independence in EC Sex Equality Laws*, Aldershot, England, Dartmouth, 1996, p. 23.

[45] Michael Lind, "The Beige and the Black," *The New York Times Magazine*, 16.8.1998, pp. 38-9.

[46] Stephanie Coontz, "The Myth of Male Decline," *The New York Times*, 29.9.2012.

[47] Bianchi, "A Cross National Look at Married Women's Earnings Dependency," p. 4; Hilda Kahn, "Economic Perspectives on Work and Family Issues," in Malkah T. Notman and Carol C. Nadelson, *Women and Men: New Perspectives on Gender Differences*, Washington, 1991, p. 11.

[48] G. L. Staines, "Men and Women in Role Relationships," in Ashmore and Del Boca, eds., *The Social Psychology of Female-Male Relationships*, p. 228.

To earn money is one thing. To spend it, however, is another thing entirely. At most times and places, most agricultural households were, in the main, self-sufficient. If they were not, it was probably the men who worked outside the home and earned money. Upon earning money, men would then spend it on luxuries, often for their wives and daughters, as well as on tools and implements that they could not manufacture by their own efforts. They also spent their earnings on paying taxes. To the extent that the household itself generated a surplus, going to the nearby market and selling it was often the responsibility of women. This would enable them to control the family economy, handling practically all the money that the family possessed. To the present day, this arrangement still exists in rural Cambodia.[49]

In urban contexts, the question as to which spouse would spend most of the household income depended on whether shopping was a male job or a female one. In ancient Greece, the former was usually the case. In Rome, where some husbands praised their wives for being "thrifty with our money,"[50] women probably controlled a considerable part of the family income. Early in the industrial revolution, women's purchasing power is said to have stimulated demand in many industries ranging from textiles to pottery.[51] By Victorian times, middle-class women were known as "consuming angels." Most advertisements targeted them, to the point that men either are not shown at all or else are presented in a marginal way.[52]

Further down the social ladder, most of the earnings of working-class married men ended up in the hands of their wives. Many surrendered their pay packet without even opening it, receiving back only what they needed to buy their daily ration of wine and tobacco.[53] Today, too, women buy 80 percent of

---

[49] For early modern Europe see Simonton, *Women's Work in Europe*, p. 20; for Cambodia see Ovesen, *When Every Household is an Island*, pp. 563, 60, 62.

[50] Pliny Jr., *Panegyric and Letters*, 4.19.2; ILS 8444, printed in Jane F. Gardner and Th. Wiedemann, *The Roman Household: A Sourcebook*, London, Routledge, 1991, p. 54.

[51] See Neil McKendrick, "Home Demand and Economic Growth: A New View of the Role of Women and Children in the Industrial Revolution," in Neil McKendrick, ed., *Historical Perspectives: Studies in English Thought and Society*, London, Europa, 1974, pp. 201-3.

[52] Lori Ann Loeb, *Consuming Angels: Advertising and Victorian Women*, New York, Oxford University Press, 1994, pp. 5, 9, 12, 34.

[53] Pierre G. F. le Play, *Les ouvriers européens*, Paris, A. Mame, 1875, vol. 5, p. 427; Peter Stearns, "Working Class Women in Britain, 1890-1914," in Martha Vicinus, ed., *Suffer and be Still*, Bloomington, IN, University of Indiana Press, 1972, p. 106; Jane Lewis, "Models of Equality for Women: The Case of State Support for Children in Twentieth Century Britain," in Gisela Bock and Pat Thane, *Maternity and Gender Policies: Women and the Rise of the European Welfare States, 1880s-1950s*, London, Routledge, 1991, p. 81.

everything.[54] From the United States and Europe to China and Japan, it is women who do most of the day-to-day shopping. By contrast, major expenditures involving items such as a new house or car tend to be decided upon by men and women jointly.[55] Possibly because men work much longer hours, many of them walk around with only pocket money.

Returning to 19th-century Britain — and America, whose legal system derived from English common law — married women could not own property of any kind, at least in theory. In practice, however, things often worked out quite differently. First, men were obliged to maintain their wives both in this period *and* after the reforms of 1861, 1881, 1920 and 1964. Second, recognizing that wives were the main consumers, the law permitted them to have and spend money for day-to-day use. In many, perhaps most, cases, this meant practically all the money the couple possessed. Third, many lower-class women, in England in particular, did not bother to marry. Instead they lived in common-law marriages, which enabled them to keep their property "separate from that of their husbands from one generation to the next."[56]

Finally, there were legal ways to ensure that a woman's property should not pass into her husband's control, either during her life or after her death. In the words of one female historian: "The concept of separate marital property was firmly entrenched in the Anglo-American legal tradition, far more so than that of a community of goods."[57] Assisted by specialized literature known as "conveyancing manuals,"[58] people drew up prenuptial agreements. Alternatively they set up trusts. So effective were trusts in protecting women's assets that men used to deliberately establish them in the names of their wives or daughters to protect themselves against creditors in case they went bankrupt.[59] After 1880 the protections became even stronger, as several countries passed laws absolving women of liability for their husbands' debts. Meanwhile, husbands' liability for their wives' debts remained universal and absolute. Since it included debts contracted before the wedding, some women got married specifically in order to shift the burden onto their husbands'

[54] See Germaine Greer, *The Whole Woman*, New York, Anchor Books, 1999, p. 145.

[55] See Stockman, *Women's Work in East and West*, p. 132, table 4.8; for China, see Jacka, *Women and Work in Rural China*, pp. 66-8.

[56] See Gillis, *For Better, for Worse*, p. 199.

[57] Basch, *Framing American Divorce*, p. 108.

[58] Erickson, *Women and Property*, pp. 104-5.

[59] Erickson, *Women and Property*, p. 107.

shoulders.[60] The obligation stayed in force even if the couple lived apart, even if he did not have the foggiest idea of where she was — and even if she was sleeping with everybody except him.

So absolute was husbands' liability that it even covered attorney's fees in divorce suits. In other words, women could file for divorce at their husbands' expense. As late as 1966, a New York court ruled that "legal services rendered to a wife in a matrimonial action are necessaries and a lawyer had a common law right to bring a plenary action against the husband for having supplied such services." A year later, another court in the same state ruled that "the legislative intent seems to be to confine obligations to pay the other party's counsel fee to the husband or father."[61] In Kansas in 1984, according to one survey,[62] more than half the men involved in divorce proceedings had to pay their wives' legal expenses as well as their own.

Since marriage is an arrangement by which men provide economic support for women, logically that support should end if the marriage ends in divorce. A man whose wife left or divorced him would, of course, lose everything he had invested in her, both before the marriage and during the time it had lasted. However, women expected to be supported even after divorce. And at most times and places, they received that support. In ancient Egypt, divorce entailed heavy financial penalties for the husband, but none for the wife.[63] Both Hindu and Muslim law oblige husbands to support their divorced wives. In other cases, she has the right to be maintained by her children.[64] In Europe beginning in the Middle Ages, divorce was very difficult to achieve for both men and women. As a result, legally speaking a man might *never* be released from his duty to support his wife — even if the couple had long ceased to share a house and bed, even if she had turned to prostitution, even if they had been formally separated by an ecclesiastical court.[65] In this sense, if perhaps in no other, the declaration "till death do us part" was quite literally true.

---

[60] Peter Linebaugh, *The London Hanged: Crime and Civil Society in the Eighteenth Century*, London, Allen Lane, 1991, p. 141.

[61] See Shirley Wolf Kram and Neil A. Frank, *The Law of Child Custody: Development of the Substantive Law*, Lexington, MA, Lexington Books, 1982, pp. 145, 153.

[62] "What Fathers Tell Us," *The Squire*, 14.6.1984, p. 2.

[63] Anette Depla, "Women in Ancient Egyptian Wisdom Literature," in Archer et al., eds., *Women in Ancient Societies*, p. 35.

[64] Kant, *Women in the Law*, pp. 91, 117, 203.

[65] Randolph Trumbach, *Sex and the Gender Revolution*, Chicago, Chicago University Press, 1998, pp. 525-6.

Between 1850 and 1920, many modern countries introduced legislation aimed at facilitating divorce.[66] To do so, they introduced the concept of "fault." Though the reforms enabled either partner to sue, for the suit to be successful he or she had to show that the other was to blame. The economic bias behind the arrangement was evident from the beginning. Throughout the second half of the 19th century, many wives sued and won their cases because of their husbands' alleged failure to support them. At the lower end of the social ladder, a divorce might not even be necessary. In Wales, a working-class woman whose husband did not provide for her was regarded as free to marry another with or without the formality of returning her ring.[67] As late as the 1960s, in most of the United States a woman could obtain a divorce based on lack of support. It hardly needs to be noted that that the reverse did not apply.

Since married women were not supposed to work, if she divorced him she received alimony as a matter of course. If he divorced her, she also received alimony, almost as a matter of course. Only if she had been caught in flagrant adultery would an exception be made — and even then, not always. As far back as 1721, a certain Mrs. Centreville wrote that "a wound in the reputation of an English woman... only lets in Alimony."[68] Afraid women might be left without support, judges and juries treated adultery as "peculiarly a crime of darkness and secrecy." They demanded such high standards of proof as could rarely be met.[69] As one New York court put it in 1974, the presumption of legitimacy of a child born in wedlock was "one of the strongest and most persuasive in law."[70] Now that DNA tests allow paternity to be established beyond doubt, some American courts *still* refuse to order them or accept their results.[71] Thus not even the presence of children who are clearly illegitimate necessarily infringes on a woman's right to maintenance. No wonder that, as long ago as

---

[66] See Robert E. Griswold, "Divorce and the Redefinition of Victorian Manhood," in Mark C. Carnes and Clyde Griffin, eds., *Meanings for Manhood*, Chicago, University of Chicago Press, 1990, chapter 5.

[67] Gillis, *For Better, for Worse*, pp. 209, 251.

[68] Quoted in *Oxford English Dictionary*, vol. 1, p. 319.

[69] Robert E. Griswold, "Divorce and the Redefinition of Victorian Manhood," in Carnes and Griffin, eds., *Meanings for Manhood*, pp. 106-7.

[70] Quoted in Kram and Frank, *The Law of Child Custody*, p. 86.

[71] Robert Seidenberg, *The Father's Emergency Guide to Divorce-Custody Battle*, Takoma Park, MD, JES, 1997, pp. 16-7.

the second half of the 19th century, American women, realizing their power, filed about two-thirds of all divorce cases.[72]

As the law was interpreted during much of the 20th century, a divorced woman had the right to be maintained "at the level to which she had been accustomed." Often she was given up to 50 percent of her former husband's income for life. This even applied when the couple had no children, even if she was perfectly capable of working, and even if this meant a decade of guaranteed income for every year spent with him. But whereas until the 1840s children stayed with their fathers, who remained responsible for their economic welfare, later in the 19th century mothers began to receive child custody almost automatically.[73] Since few judges were so callous as to throw children into the streets, most also got the couple's home, if not permanently, then at least for as long as the children remained minors.[74] None of this applied to divorced men. If, as rarely happened, they asked for support, they were likely to earn both a refusal and rebuke. As late as 1979, the United States Supreme Court had to strike down an Alabama law that denied alimony to a person simply because he was male.[75]

After 1975, the legal situation changed again. Largely at the insistence of feminists, most modern countries did away with the "fault" clauses, thereby allowing both parties to file for divorce without having to justify doing so. As more married women entered the work force, the arrangement whereby they received alimony but did not share in the couple's joint assets began to look unfair. Partly this was because those assets had been accumulated by the labor of both spouses. Partly it was because alimony, by assuming a woman was unable to fend for herself and perpetuating her dependence on her former husband, was considered injurious to her dignity. The new laws' objective was to bring about "a clean break," meaning a situation whereby neither party would remain dependent on the other.

Normally this was achieved by dividing the couple's assets — other than those which each party had brought into the marriage at the outset — between

---

[72] Judith A. Baer, *Women in American Law: The Struggle Toward Equality from the New Deal to the Present,* New York, Holmes and Meier, 1996, p. 138.

[73] See Maeve E. Doggett, *Marriage, Wife Beating and the Law in Victorian England*, London, Weidenfeld & Nicolson, 1992, p. 102; for New York State see Kram and Frank, *The Law of Child Custody*, pp. 20-6.

[74] Fiona Williams, "Troubled Masculinities in Social Policy Discourses: Fatherhood," in Popay, ed., *Men, Gender Divisions and Welfare*, p. 73.

[75] Leo Kanowitz, "'Benign' Sex Discrimination: Its Troubles and Their Cure," *Hastings Law Journal*, 31, 6, July 1980, p. 1386-7.

husband and wife in proportion to the effort each had put into their acquisition. With women now presumed to be as capable of working as men, alimony went into decline.[76] Since men usually work more and earn more, in case after case it turned out that the husband's share in accumulating the couple's assets was much greater. As couples' assets were divided accordingly, and numerous divorcées received no payments except support for any children they might have, many were forced to fend for themselves. Even as feminists ranted against the "equality trap" they themselves had helped create,[77] many divorced women were said to be sinking into poverty.[78]

As has always been the case, and will surely remain the case until the Day of Judgment, usually the divorced woman's best way of avoiding poverty was to marry another man. Compensating women for their lesser earning capacity has always been among the most important purposes of marriage. The arrangements instituted to accomplish that purpose ranged from bride-service to dowries, from exhortation to the most stringent laws and the penalties attached to them. Some arrangements benefited women directly. Others did so indirectly by way of their male, and sometimes female, relatives. Some were put in place before the wedding could take place, while others were made following a divorce. All applied as long as the marriage lasted. So deeply ingrained was the system that when American couples asked the courts to release husbands from their duty to support their wives, their requests were met with point-blank refusal.[79]

By insisting that women were just as able to make a living as men, the Communists in the 1920s doomed millions of women to poverty. To a lesser but apparently significant extent, the same has been happening in Western countries from roughly the 1970s onward. By insisting, against all experience, that women are as able to make a living as men, feminists ended up destroying or threatening to destroy their sisters' long-held privileges. No wonder that,

---

[76] For the United States see Shirley P. Burggraf, *The Feminine Economy and Economic Man: Reviving the Role of Family in the Post-Industrial Age*, Reading, MA, Addison-Wesley, 1997, pp. 120-33; for Canada see Kristen Douglas, *Spousal Support Under the Divorce Act: A New Direction*, Ottawa, Library of Parliament, Background Paper No. BP-259 E, 1994.

[77] Mary Ann Mason, *The Equality Trap*, New York, Simon & Schuster, 1988, p. 50; Baer, *Women in American Law*, p. 311; Betty Friedan, *The Second Stage*, New York, Summit, 1981, pp. 97-8; Okin, *Justice, Gender and the Family*, pp. 134-69.

[78] See Ruth Sidel, *Women and Children Last: The Plight of Poor Women in Affluent America*, New York, Viking, 1986, pp. 56-60.

[79] See Lenore Weitzman, *The Marriage Contract: Spouses, Lovers and the Law*, New York, Free Press, 1981, pp. 41-3, 71-4.

when the Equal Rights Amendment looked as if it might make women liable for supporting their husbands, most women preferred to keep the situation as it was.[80]

3. Women and Charity

The previous section examined how a woman who has a man to support her is economically privileged. This section looks at how a woman who does not have another person to support her is nonetheless privileged. Rightly regarded as less able to earn a living, such a woman will usually find it easier than a man to obtain assistance. This is especially true if she does not have parents, especially if her morals are in danger; especially if she is a widow, and especially if she has children. The mere fact that a person is female may entitle her to benefits which, had she been male, she could have only gotten if she were sick or incapacitated and thus prevented from working.

In the book of *Deuteronomy*, the Lord designated widows, along with orphans and strangers, as special objects for charity. In a series of curt, sharp ordinances, He commanded the Israelites to take care of them and "damned" those who failed to do so. Early Christianity continued where Judaism left off. As at virtually all other times and places, in Roman Palestine around the time of Christ, providing for women was the responsibility either of their husbands or, in the latter's absence, other male relatives. Women who had joined the early Christian communities, however, were often forced to severe their family ties. They were left without support, which explains why the New Testament mentions them as special objects for charity.[81]

Subsequent Christian societies continued the tradition. In medieval Paris, Saint Louis donated 4,000 francs to set up the *Filles de Dieu*, a refuge for ex-prostitutes he was trying to get off the streets in 1226. Two centuries later, there were at least four other hotels that catered specifically to women. Men could only get similar help if they were sick or leprous. What was true of Paris was equally true of other medieval cities. In Florence from roughly 1350 to 1500, the largest charitable organization was that attached to the Orsanmichele

[80] Andrew Hacker, "What Killed the ERA? A Lack of Concern for the Housewife," *Albany (NY) Times-Union*, 19.10.1980, p. H1.
[81] i *Timothy*, 5.16.

Madonna.[82] Most of its clients were women, particularly those who did not have a man to support them and were either too old or too young to work. Single women comprised the single largest group receiving such assistance, save for the elderly and the widowed.

In early modern French prayer books, prayers on behalf of widows outnumbered those on behalf of widowers four to three.[83] In day-to-day life there were certain forms of charity that only women could obtain. The easiest way to help indigent women was always to hitch them to some man. If necessary, this was done by providing them with a minimum dowry so as to enhance their charms. The Talmud around 200 A.D recommended that orphan girls be given fifty *zuz* out of the public treasury. That was not exactly a fortune, but enough to buy two tunics and a cloak, the minimum outfit every person had to possess if he or she were not to go about naked. Among Orthodox Jews, the commandment known as *hachnassat kalah*, literally "helping a bride enter her wedding canopy," is still practiced. It can involve spending tens if not hundreds of thousands of dollars. The practice was also taken up by Christian Europe. Of the 50 earliest known English wills, several contain clauses providing for girls to be given dowries.[84] Both in medieval Paris and in Byzantium, people who donated or bequeathed money to charity often made specific mention of unmarried girls.[85]

In 14th-century Florence, finding dowries was the task of the Monte di Pieta, a sort of charitable pawnshop which used its profits for that exact purpose.[86] In Bologna, the regulations of the Barracano Conservatory specifically referred to "physically unattractive" girls who were given an opportunity to earn their — quite substantial — dowries by staying in the institution for seven years.[87] In Venice at the beginning of the 17th century, the so-called *Scuole grandi*, or charitable foundations, spent between one-quarter

[82] John Henderson, *Piety and Charity in Late Medieval Florence*, Oxford, Clarendon Press, 1994, pp. 36, 257, 266, 342, 383, 384, and table 9.4.

[83] Allain Tallon, "Prière et charité dans la compagnie de Saint Sacrement, 1629-1707," *Histoire, Économie et Societé*, 103, 1991, p. 337.

[84] F. J. Furnivall, ed., *The Fifty Earliest English Wills in the Court of Probate, London, A.D 1387-1439*, London, Early English Text Society, 1882, p. xii.

[85] B. Germeck et al., *The Margins of Society in Late Medieval Paris*, Cambridge, Cambridge, University Press, 2006, p. 184; also Demetrios J. Constantelos, *Poverty, Society and Philanthropy in the Late Medieval Greek World*, New Rochelle, NY, Caratzas, 1992, p. 95.

[86] Menning, *Charity and State in Late Renaissance Italy*, p. 259.

[87] For this and the following paragraph see Stuart Woolf, *The Poor in Western Europe: The Eighteenth and Nineteenth Centuries*, London, Methuen, 1986, 24-5.

and three-quarters of their budgets on dowries. They gave away 75,000 ducats a year, not including clothing and furniture.[88] A century later, the *Santissima Annunziata della Minerva* annually distributed dowries to 400 Roman girls. In theory it determined recipients by first examining their means, but in practice few questions were asked. The charity extended to young persons tended to be differentiated by sex. Both boys and girls were placed in household work, the former in order to become apprentices and learn a trade, the latter to work as servants and accumulate a dowry. However, girls were much more likely than boys to get their money in the form of an outright gift.

At all times and places, a special emphasis was placed on female sexual purity. Finding a halfway respectable man to assume responsibility for an orphan girl was one thing, but to do the same for a woman who had worked as a prostitute or given birth out of wedlock was quite another. Whether to prevent women from losing their virtue or to help those who had done so already, a variety of relevant arrangements existed across history. They started with shelters for the wives of abusive men, proceeded through attempts to redeem prostitutes, and ended with houses where unmarried but pregnant girls could give birth in secrecy and under halfway decent circumstances. Between 1600 and 1800 some Italian cities even developed their "conservatories" into interlocking municipal systems. They transferred girls from one institution to another, as dictated by the requirements of the moment and the resources available.

Women who could not support themselves but did not wish to marry could be turned into nuns. During the Middle Ages some nunneries were specifically designed as homes for noble but penniless females. Throughout Europe until the Reformation, and in Catholic countries until the French Revolution and beyond, individuals and societies which provided dowries were often equally prepared to help girls take up the veil. The number of women who were assisted in this way may have been considerable indeed. For example, out of 38 nuns in one 18th-century French institute, only 21 had been endowed by their parents. Of the rest, three had benefited from charitable donations and 14 were admitted free of charge.[89]

---

[88] Brian Pullan, ed., *Poverty and Charity: Europe, Italy, Venice, 1400-1700*, Aldershot, Ashgate, 1994, p. IV 1022; IX 19-21.

[89] Marie Claude Guiller and-Champenier, "Les femmes consacrées de l'Anjou et la pauvreté aux xvii et xviii siècles," in Plongeron and Guillaume, eds., *De la charité à l'action sociale*, pp. 83, 88; Pullan, ed., *Poverty and Charity*, p. 4.

Another way to help women was to give them a monopoly over trade in certain commodities. A shortage of wool in Norwich in 1532 offers a telling example. To enable spinsters to survive until the next sheep-shearing season, butchers were ordered to sell skins exclusively to women.[90] Towns and cities might permit women to trade even though they did not possess the privileges of free citizens, thus enabling them to buy and sell such items as eggs, cheese and beer.[91] For example, in 1708 the city of Edinburgh licensed Anny Sempley, Mary McCallum, Jean Murray and Anna Burnet, all unmarried women, to trade "for the space of seven years gratis."[92] Similar arrangements existed in places as far apart as Kingston upon Thames and Geneva.[93]

Finally, in Europe as well as in colonial America,[94] arrangements existed to assist widows and other female relatives of deceased craftsmen. One way of doing this was by means of mutual insurance. Thus, in 18th-century Amsterdam the surgeons' guild spent one-half of all available funds — and fully two-thirds of those set aside for relief — for this purpose alone. Other guilds had similar arrangements, so that the number of women they assisted always exceeded that of persons of all other categories several times over.[95] Another method was to permit them to carry on the trade of the deceased even though they had not served an apprenticeship and even though they were not guild members. Trades that allowed this included "white" ironsmiths, glaziers, candle-makers, saddle-makers and surgeons, among others.[96] Elsewhere similar regulations applied to printers, goldsmiths and many other trades.

Then as now, teaching a youngster a trade and registering him in a guild was expensive. Then as now, exempting a person of either sex from having to bear that expense was a great privilege. The professional status that men could only attain by investing a great deal of sweat and money, women could obtain simply by marrying. If, having outlived their first husbands, they married

---

[90] Alice Clark, *The Working Life of Woman in the Seventeenth-Century*, London, Routledge, 1982, p. 107.

[91] Clark, *The Working Life of Women*, pp. 230-1.

[92] See Elizabeth C. Sanderson, *Women and Work in Eighteenth-Century Edinburgh*, London, MacMillan, 1996, pp. 7, 11, 27, 35, 137, 138.

[93] Simonton, *European Women's Work*, pp. 49, 50.

[94] Mimi Abramovitz, *Regulating the Lives of Women: Social Welfare Policy from Colonial Times to the Present*, Boston, South End Press, 1996 [1988], pp. 94-5.

[95] Sandra Bos, *"Uyt Liefde tot Malcander:" Onderlinge Hulpverlening binnen de Noord-Nederlandse Gilden in Internatinale Perspectief, 1570-1820*, Amsterdam, IISG, 1998, pp. 74-5, 135.

[96] Clark, *The Working Life of Woman*, pp. 161, 184, 194; Boss, *"Uyt Liefde tot Malcander,"* p. 38.

another of the same guild, then so much the better. When it came to the rights of women to engage in trade, the law of almost all cities was prepared to turn some strange somersaults. For some purposes the authorities treated one and the same woman as married and unable to contract debts, but for others as independent and answerable for her deeds.[97]

In 17th-century England, widows (other than relatives) were disproportionally likely to be remembered in the wills of other widows, as were single women.[98] In 18th-century Ansbach, a disproportionate number of old widows were the beneficiaries of pious endowments.[99] In Paris during the same period, the all-female hospital of La Salpetrière sheltered three times as many people as did Bicêtre, its all-male counterpart.[100] In the Oslo Parish of Gronland, widows who received assistance outnumbered widowers three to one.[101] In Copenhagen, the Brondstraedes Hospital took in five times as many women as men.[102] Women's greater ability to receive aid may explain why, in early modern towns, male beggars regularly outnumbered female ones by as many as 4 to 1.[103] Another reason for this figure, it ought to be noted, may have been that early modern parents cut boys off financially at an earlier age than girls, and as a result more boys ended up without a livelihood.[104]

One of the first attempts to create a countrywide "welfare system" was made by the French National Assembly in 1794. A resolution was passed to introduce a "*Livre de bienfaisance nationale*," which was a list of those entitled to pensions from the state. Since statistics covering the entire country were unavailable, each *département* was given a quota and told to fill it as those in charge saw fit. Women, particularly single mothers, occupied an important place in the scheme. They were put on par with wounded or disabled war

---

[97] Clark, *The Working Life of Woman*, p. 153; Mary Beard, *Women as Force in History: A Study in Traditions and Realities*, New York, Octagon, 1976, [1946], p. 208; Merry E. Wiesner, *Women and Gender in Early Modern Europe*, Cambridge, Cambridge University Press, 1993, p. 31.

[98] Erickson, *Women and Property*, pp. 212, 215.

[99] H. Wunder and Th. Dunlap, *He Is the Sun, She Is the Moon*: *Women in Early Modern Germany*. Cambridge, MA, Harvard University Press, 1998, p. 139.

[100] Robert M. Schwartz, *Policing the Poor in Eighteenth-Century France*, Chapel Hill, NC, University of North Carolina Press, 1988, pp. 43-4.

[101] Alfhild Nakken, "La pauvreté en Norvege 1500-1800," in Thomas Riis, ed., *Aspects of Poverty in Early Modern Europe*, Odense, Odense University Press, 1990, p. 72.

[102] Harald Jorgensen, "L'assistance au pauvres au Danemark jusqu'a la fin du xviii siècle," in Riis, ed., *Aspects of Poverty in Early Modern Europe*, p. 25.

[103] Cissie C. Fairchilds, *Poverty and Charity in Aix-en Provence, 1640-1789*, Baltimore, MD, Johns Hopkins University Press, 1976, pp. 110, 113.

[104] Schwartz, *Policing the Poor in Eighteenth-Century France*, p. 103.

veterans. For example, in Montpellier the intention was to assist 1,000 individuals. They were divided into four classes: former soldiers, aged or infirm farmers and artisans, aged widows, and mothers and widows deemed to be overburdened with children. Of the 1,000 who eventually registered, 253 were aged widows, and another 150 were among those overburdened with children. The total, therefore, was 403 women. In practice, however, women's share of the pensions was substantially higher, because few artisans met the stringent preconditions and because far more women than expected applied.[105]

As the National Assembly's inability to obtain the necessary data shows, the *Livre de bienfaisance* was ahead of its time. As a result, during much of the 19th century the old methods remained in use. Especially during the first half of the century, the emphasis on female sexual purity remained. Its importance may even have increased. One outcome was the rise of many charitable societies aimed at protecting single women from the advances of men. They did so by offering them lodging when they moved into a new town in search of work, by setting up clubs where they could spend their leisure, and the like. In Copenhagen, where such arrangements dated to the mid-1870s, it took another 40 years before they were extended to men.[106] A typical club engaged the women in needlework. It also provided a small library, brought speakers, acted as a labor exchange, and offered free coffee and tea. Others acted as temporary homes for prostitutes who had mended their ways, or had promised to. The numbers of women who were, or were claimed to have been, "saved" reached into the tens of thousands. Occasionally a talented ex-prostitute joined her saviors, writing, preaching and visiting her former comrades with the best.[107]

Toward the end of the 19th century the definition of a "deserving" woman began to change. Previously a woman was considered deserving only if she had led a "blameless" life — in other words, if she had not entered into illicit love affairs and if her children were legitimate. After 1880 or so, this requirement tended to be watered down or eliminated. The outcome was that women were more able to obtain charity even if their children had been born out of

---

[105] Colin Jones, *Charity and Bienfaisance: The Treatment of the Poor in the Montpellier Region, 1740-1815*, Cambridge, Cambridge University Press, 1982, pp. 176-8, 202.

[106] Abramovitz, *Regulating the Lives of Women*, p. 187; Vammen, "Ambiguous Performances," p. 129, fn. 15; Kerston Norlander, "To be A Woman Capitalist," in Jordansson and Vamme, eds., *Charitable Women*, p. 173.

[107] F. K. Proschka, *Women and Philanthropy in Nineteenth-Century England*, Oxford, Clarendon Press, 1980, pp. 189-90, 194.

wedlock.[108] Moreover, the spread of the domestic ideal meant that divorced and deserted women could receive assistance even if they did not have any children at all. In short, a poor man received assistance if he *had* a woman, while a poor woman received assistance if she *did not have* a man.

Given these privileges, it is not surprising that, among recipients of relief, women continued to outnumber men. Thus, mid-19th century Gothenburg, Sweden, had several charitable societies. Like those of New York, most of them were run by women. They specifically targeted poor women, either by distributing goods to them or else by teaching them the principles of "tender and moral motherly care."[109] Copenhagen during the same period witnessed the construction of so many shelters for fallen women, pregnant women, postpartum women, lactating women, women with children and elderly women that they began "affecting the city's architectural profile." By 1876, out of 56 housing projects for the poor, 20 specifically targeted single women and did not admit any men.[110] In Stockholm, too, more women than men received subsidized housing.[111] Nor did men have to reach adulthood to discover that, in respect to charity, they were discriminated against. Thus, in Denmark and Sweden, arrangements existed whereby middle-class families provided working-class children with free vacations by inviting them to their summer homes. Whether because boys found it harder to leave their jobs or because families disliked having them, in both countries far more girls benefited from this perk than boys.[112]

In Turin, Italy, in 1885 so many benefactors were prepared to donate money to newly-delivered mothers that raising money for the scheme proved easier than finding women who, in return for a paltry sum, agreed to participate.[113] In late 19th-century Britain, far more women than men received

[108] Pamela Sharpe, *Adapting to Capitalism: Working Women in the English Economy, 1800-1850*, London, MacMillan, 1996, p. 134-40; Vammen, "Ambiguous Performances," p. 103.

[109] Birgitta Jordansson, "Philanthropy in a Liberal Context: The Case of Gothenburg," in Jordansson and Vammen, eds., *Charitable Women*, pp. 72-80.

[110] Vammen, "Ambiguous Performances," pp. 97, 129, fn. 6.

[111] Kerstin Thorn, "Stockholm's Arbertarhem: Building Welfare," in Jordansson and Tinne Vammen, eds., *Charitable Women*, p. 205.

[112] Vammen, "Ambiguous Performance," p. 133, fn. 132; Thorn, "Stockholm's Arbertarhem" p. 210.

[113] Annarita Buttafuoco, "Motherhood as a Political Strategy: The Role of the Italian Women's Movement in the Creation of the *Casa Nationale di Maternità*," in Thane, eds., *Maternity and Gender Policies*, pp. 184-5.

assistance.[114] Across the Atlantic, New York City around 1820 had a whole series for relief organizations specifically designed to assist women. Needless to say, there were no similar organizations for men; even the largest "coed" charitable organization, the Association for Improving the Condition of the Poor, aided 27 percent more women than men.[115] In the 1880s the Charity Organization Society, which had become the largest of its kind in New York and which, like the rest, was run mainly by women, assisted four times as many women as men. Some of the difference can be accounted for by the fact that women were more likely to be burdened with children. On the other hand, one post-Civil War inquiry showed that, of all single women receiving aid in New York State, fewer than one-quarter had more than one child. Of the remaining three-quarters, many had no children at all.[116]

One method for helping needy women was to reserve certain professions for them, a practice still widespread today. At the bottom of the social ladder this applied to domestic service. So thoroughly feminized did it become that male indoor servants all but disappeared. The same was true of teaching. Like domestic service, teaching was safe, clean and only moderately demanding physically. Like domestic service, it was often regarded as the continuation of women's traditional role in the home. To be sure, one reason why women were preferred to men in both occupations was because they only earned one-half to two-thirds as much as their male colleagues. On the other hand, that very fact protected the women in question against the encroachment of men. Such work was arguably treated almost as a form of welfare for women.

As one female editor of a 19th-century American women's magazine wrote, female teachers could not look forward to amassing a fortune. Neither were they "obliged to give from [their] earnings support to the state or government."[117] The tendency to see certain professions as sinecures for women, especially unmarried ones, may help explain why women tended to suffer from unemployment less than men did. Even at the height of the Great Depression, black American female college graduates had what almost amounted to a guaranteed job waiting for them in segregated schools.[118] It also

[114] Proschka, *Women and Philanthropy*, pp. 32, 101, 244.

[115] New York City Association for Improving the Conditions of the Poor, *Fifth Annual Report*, New York, 1852, pp. 20-2; *Ninth Annual Report*, New York, 1858, p. 38.

[116] Abramovitz, *Regulating the Lives of Women*, pp. 158.

[117] Sara J. Hale in *Godey's Lady's Book*, vol. 44, 5 June 1852, p. 99; also see Simonton, *European Women's Work*, p. 65.

[118] Solomon, *In the Company of Educated Women*, p. 145.

explains the ban on married female teachers. Far from being meant to discriminate against women, the ban's strongest supporters were single female teachers. The last thing they wanted was competition from their married sisters. The latter, they claimed, had a man to look after them.[119]

Today forms of relief that favor women over men are alive and well. Whether in the form of homes for unmarried mothers, or of shelters for abused wives, or of legal aid to divorcees, women receive considerable societal attention and funding. By contrast, there are no public institutions open to men only. Indeed any attempt to set up a government-backed male-only institution would surely be squashed by the courts, if not by society at large. In many countries, religious organizations continue to provide women with dowries so that they may marry. Whereas women are almost always entitled to share in any form of charity provided to men, men are not permitted to share in many forms of charity provided to women. This is true even if they are single, even if they are divorced, deserted or widowed, and even if they have a brood of young children to look after.

Even under the best of circumstances, for people to depend on charity or receive relief is no great pleasure. That said, even under the worst of circumstances, for a woman to obtain assistance has always been easier and less humiliating than for a man. Assuming the Pentateuch was compiled around 500 B.C and describes, as it claims to do, the social situation as it existed several centuries earlier, this difference between the sexes existed as far back into history as we are able to look. It still exists today, and presumably will continue to do so as long as there are men and women.

4. Inside the Welfare State

To assist needy people is one thing. To create a countrywide class of persons who, having met certain requirements, are *entitled* to receive it, is another. The former, known as charity or philanthropy or "poor relief," existed in all societies up through the end of the 19th century. Its offshoots, though dwarfed by the welfare state and often supported by it, still exist. The latter is characteristic of the modern welfare state. The one depends on personalities and goodwill, the other on the supposedly impersonal provisions of the law and the rights and obligations it creates.

---

[119] Albisetti, *Schooling German Girls and Women*, pp. 58, 177; Sharif Gemie, *Women and Schooling in France, 1815-1914*, Keele, Keele University Press, 1995, p. 43.

The ultimate cause behind the shift from charity to welfare state was the industrial revolution. As vast numbers of people migrated to towns in search of work, those among them who did not find it, or lost it, or were unable to do it, swamped the ability of private organizations to cope. The contemporary switch from outdoor to indoor relief made the situation worse still. To protect against impostors — in 1838, one writer estimated that in London alone 1,000 false applications for aid were written every day[120] — and cut costs, conditions in the new workhouses were made fairly daunting. Those who lived in them were compelled to work. However, when it came to women that requirement was sometimes waived. No wonder that, particularly in the summer, when work might be available elsewhere, workhouses were populated almost exclusively by women.[121]

In socialist and capitalist states alike, sooner or later the government was compelled to step in so as to alleviate the plight of the poor. In the United States, for example, women were already a favored group by the turn of the 20th century.[122] Some of the first steps were taken in 1906, when several counties in California started providing aid to "deserving" women with children in their own homes. Between 1908 and 1911, Oklahoma, New Jersey and Michigan started providing mothers with financial aid. By that time the idea of "mothers' pensions" was in the air, and spreading rapidly. Like other pensions, those provided to mothers were intended to be continuous and permanent. Unlike other pensions, they neither required an investment of capital nor depended on contributions; instead, the pension was disbursed based on need. In 1911 Missouri became the first state to institute mothers' pensions. By 1935, all but two states had them on the books.

The schemes rested on the belief that the mother was the best guardian of her children and that, to look after them, she should stay at home. As late as 1968, Charles Schottland, president of the National Association of Social Workers, claimed that for a mother of young children to work ran against "a universally-held conviction."[123] That was true even if she was perfectly fit and able to do so but avoided work out of her own free will. Worse still, often she passed the same attitude to her offspring, thus opening the way for generations of welfare recipients. Initially in most states, only widows were eligible for the

---

[120] James Grant, *Sketches in London*, London, Clarke, 1838, p. 4.

[121] Himmelfarb, *The De-Moralization of Society*, pp. 132, 135.

[122] See Winer, *From Working Girl to Working Mother*, pp. 128-30; also see Woodcock Tentler, *Wage-Earning Women*, pp. 193, 200-1, 204-5.

[123] See Abramovitz, *Regulating the Lives of Women*, p. 333.

program. As had also happened in the case of charity, however, the provisions were progressively relaxed.

By 1921, the programs, in all but six of the states which had them, were also open to divorced women, deserted women, single married women, and the wives of men were incarcerated. Initially, to qualify a woman had to prove her "fitness" by means of a demonstrable effort to provide her children with clean, orderly homes. Over time, however, that requirement tended to be dropped as well. As long as there was no evidence of mental illness or abuse, benefits were provided to practically all mothers under a certain income level. To receive benefits, all a woman had to do was to have unprotected sex, conceive and have a child.

In 1935, Congress was asked to consolidate the various state schemes and underwrite their cost in the Aid to Dependent Children program. There was limited interest on Capitol Hill, however, for the simple reason that children cannot vote. Only after it was explained to members of Congress that the program was actually another form of granting mothers' pensions did the nation's lawmakers see the program's political usefulness and pass the relevant legislation. The real purpose of Aid to Dependent Children was to attract women's votes. Had Congress really been concerned with the plight of underprivileged children, it could have assisted them directly by providing free school meals or vouchers to pay for their medical expenses. At the time the program was launched, millions of men were jobless. Since eligibility depended on a woman not having a man to support her, it was clear to more than a few men and women that some wives might be better off without a husband. Some women looked forward to the day their husbands would expire so that they could collect widows' benefits. Indeed, if only to oblige their wives, some husbands left home and disappeared.[124]

Over time Aid to Dependent Children became the principal vehicle by which millions of American women who could not, or would not, work were saved from starvation. Needless to say, divorced fathers, or fathers whose wives had deserted them, or whose wives were dead or in prison, did not get anything. In fact, in the entire United States, the only one state which did *not* discriminate against men in such situations was Colorado. Other states compounded the injustice by permitting female relatives, but not male ones, to receive the benefits if the mother was unable to. Under some circumstances this could create a situation in which fathers were compelled to surrender their

[124] Baxandall and Gordon, *America's Working Women*, p. 213.

children to grandmothers, aunts or sisters. Only in 1975 did the courts finally make men eligible to obtain benefits as well. However, even this victory proved short-lived. In 1980 Ronald Reagan swept the Republicans back into power. Seeking to cut costs by forcing beneficiaries of the Aid to Families with Dependent Children, as the program was known by then, into gainful employment, the administration began raising eligibility standards and cutting payments. Apparently the fact that men had become eligible for a welfare program was enough to put it on the cutting block.

The other important program created in 1935 was Social Security. Like Aid to Dependent Children, Social Security favored women right from the beginning. In part this was because of its contributory nature. Men only got benefits if they worked and contributed. However, married women — forming the vast majority of adult women — received benefits irrespective of work. Also like Aid to Dependent Children, Social Security was built on the assumption that the man in the family was its main breadwinner. Consequently, a widow past retirement age would be entitled to receive benefits. On the other hand, a man past retirement age whose wife had died would get exactly nothing.

Given that the system discriminated against men, one might expect that it would have been men who turned to Congress for help. As it turned out, it was in fact women who fought to change the original structure of Social Security benefits. Their reasoning was that even though some women made more than their husbands, they would, if their spouses died, only receive the benefits deriving from their husbands' contributions. And within three years of the establishment of Social Security, the rules were changed so as to favor women even more. Widows who, as long as their marriages had lasted, had worked and contributed to the system were now able to obtain benefits in accordance to either their own contributions or those of their husbands, whichever was higher. As so often, women were able to have their cake and eat it too. The higher their income relative to their husbands, the more likely this was to be the case. Widowers, as usual, got nothing.[125]

In 1950 another change was made. The rules that discriminated against male breadwinners were relaxed to some extent, but only if a husband could pass a special "support test" that proved his financial dependence on his employed wife. To do so he had to show that, in the year before his wife's death, his income had amounted to no more than one-quarter that of his wife.

[125] Abramovitz, *Regulating the Lives of Women*, pp. 257-8.

The bar was set so high that it effectively excluded all but a few men. Needless to say, no thought was given to the possibility of subjecting women to a similar test. Unless they had been divorced, women continued to enjoy automatic and unrestricted rights to any benefits that had been earned by their late husbands. Having supported their wives during their entire lives, those husbands were expected to continue doing so after their deaths as well.

It was only in 1975, 40 years after Social Security was first instituted, that the Supreme Court finally abolished all these forms of discrimination in favor of women. But as in the case of Aid to Families with Dependent Children, the victory proved hollow. Accidentally or not, 1975 was also the year in which Title XX of the Social Security Act was enacted. The legislation consolidated a vast number of programs and marked the apex of the American welfare state, such as it was. A few short years later, however, the Reagan administration was already at work rolling back those benefits. As with Aid to Families with Dependent Children, an invisible hand seemed to be at work. As soon women's benefits were extended to men, those benefits came to be regarded as unnecessary — yet more proof, if such be needed, that men are truly history's beasts of burden.

Space does not permit for a full examination of the way other 20th-century welfare states have favored women over men. A short survey, however, gives a rather clear picture of how things have developed. In Norway the Sickness Insurance Act of 1909 began to grant maternity benefits as well as benefits to the wives of insured men. Six years later, the state began to provide financial assistance to single mothers, too. In Italy, the very first effective national welfare scheme was the Maternity Insurance Act of 1910. In France, maternity benefits were instituted in 1913, 15 years before the introduction of the first comprehensive social insurance scheme. In all cases, women started receiving benefits years, often decades, before men did. Some of the early schemes were designed to help women who had lost their husbands, while others were aimed at women who had never had one. Over time, however, these distinctions tended to disappear.[126]

Today most modern countries have child allowances, the United States being one of the few major exceptions. Insofar as the declared purpose of child allowances is not to indulge parents but to help them invest more in their children, it is accepted that the system which gives them to mothers and not to

[126] See Bock and Thane, eds., *Maternity and Gender Policies*, pp. 4, 11.

fathers is clearly discriminatory.[127] In some countries, and under some circumstances, it can be doubly discriminatory. For example, widowers who bring up their children can be denied benefits. It may even be possible for a divorced mother to continue to receive benefits while her former husband, having been granted custody, raises the children and pays for their upkeep. These and similar inequalities are leftovers from the period between roughly 1900 and 1980, a time when most people in most countries still took it for granted that women were better suited to act as parents than fathers.

The tendency of modern welfare states to give preferential treatment to women over men is reflected in their own official accounts. Take the case of Sweden. A study submitted to the Ministry of Labor in 1997 showed that, from 1975 to 1994, Swedish women increased both their earnings and the allowances they received from the state. During the same two decades, men, who carried the financial burden, saw their work-derived income *decline* by 14,000 Swedish kronor ($2,000) a year on average.[128] Although in Sweden almost as many women are officially in the labor force as men, in the mid-1990s men paid 61.5 percent of taxes, compared to 38.5 percent by women.[129] As a result, in 1994, as in 1975, men were paying more into the system than they got out of it.

In 1994, Swedish women received three-quarters of all advance maintenance allowances, parental allowances, housing allowances and study grants paid by the state. Even though women worked fewer hours per year than men, they still managed to receive more sickness allowances. Women received four times as much in parental allowances and seven times as much in advance maintenance allowances. Taking all family-related allowances into account, the difference was two to one. Women received 29 percent of their income as welfare payments from the state, men 19 percent. Though women only paid two-thirds as much in taxes as men did, they received 23.5 percent more tax-exempt allowances.[130] No wonder that the taxable wealth of Swedish women was more than one and half times that of Swedish men.[131] In Sweden, as in most other modern countries, feminist pressures caused the relevant laws to be

[127] Jane Bates, "Gender, Social Security, and Pensions: The Myth of the 'Everyday Housewife,'" in Maclean and Burrows, eds., *The Legal Relevance of Gender*, p. 122.

[128] *Women, Men and Incomes: Gender Equality and Economic Independence*, Report to the Committee on the Distribution of Economic Power and Economic Resources between Women and Men, Stockholm, Ministry of Labor, 1997, pp. 36-7.

[129] *Women, Men and Incomes*, p. 12.

[130] *Women, Men and Incomes*, p. 11, table 11; p. 31, table 7; p. 35; appendix A, table 3.

[131] *Women, Men and Incomes*, appendix A, table 40; p. 74.

rewritten in gender-free language. And in Sweden, as in most other modern countries, this has *not* changed the fact that men pay for women.

It is impossible to list all the ways in which the modern welfare state has favored women, is favoring women, and will presumably continue to favor women. Some of the benefits are very minor or even symbolic, as when women are assigned reserved parking spaces, spaces that might just as justifiably go to senior citizens of either sex. Sometimes they are substantial indeed, as when women receive the lion's share of all transfer payments, or when entire bureaucracies are set up to both provide employment mainly to women and to look after their interests almost exclusively. What all have in common is the fact that, should public and even private money be used to extend similar advantages to men, the resulting outrage can only be imagined.

5. Conclusions

The number and variety of mechanisms that society has invented to ensure that women are provided for by men is nothing less than astounding. Many were of an informal nature, but often they were written into formal law. Whether or not legal structures were put in place, these mechanisms were often reflected in sanctions ranging from neighborly censure to imprisonment. Both today as in the past, the only way to avoid such sanctions may well be to give up everything and leave the country. However, even this may either be prohibited or fail to work.

Most of the time it was a question of each man being obliged to look after his female relatives, mainly but not exclusively his wife or wives. Very often women were married off, or chose to marry, specifically in order that they might be supported. Very often some form of economic support was provided, or was supposed to be provided, even after a marriage ended in divorce. Such was the situation in some of the earliest known societies, and today it still prevails in many societies.

At most times and places, women who did not have male relatives to look after them depended on charity. Like men, women might be required to work before becoming eligible for charity. Alternatively, to obtain such assistance, they had to prove that they were unable to work. Still, on the whole they had an easier time of it than men did. This was especially, but by no means only, true if they had children and if they avoided being promiscuous. Sometimes women could obtain charity even if they were fit to work, even if they were promiscuous, and even if they did not have children. For the most part, by contrast, men could only obtain charity if they had women to support.

With the rise of modern welfare systems, many forms of support that used to be the responsibility of husbands, male relatives or charitable organizations were taken over by the state. As before, women have found it easier to get benefits, especially women without a man and with children. Many schemes, in fact, are deliberately designed to benefit women exclusively, or almost so. Meanwhile, men's role as living ATMs has remained unchanged. However, the conditions under which they are made to pay have, in some ways, worsened. As long as the family served as the main mechanism to help women, it was men who called the shots, and it was their own female relatives who benefited from the arrangement. When it was a question of charitable giving men were still able to choose whether to pay and who should receive support.

The advent of the welfare state caused any pretense of voluntarism to disappear. The treasury took over, raking in the necessary money in taxes or as tax-like "contributions" to social security. As a result, today many of the recipients are women of whom men did not know, and perhaps did not want to know, anything. The less careful about birth control an unattached woman is, the more benefits she will get. On the face of it, a husband, a charitable institution and a modern welfare system are entirely different. In fact, though the details differ, the principle is the same: All are designed partly — and some would say primarily — to transfer resources from men, seen as more capable of earning their living, to women, who are seen as, and very often claim to be, less so. Historically, the price women were made to pay, or at any rate asked to pay, was avoiding promiscuity on the one hand and raising their children properly on the other. Now that the welfare state has taken over, very often they are not even asked to do that.

Even little girls playing with their Barbie dolls readily grasp who consumes and who pays.[132] No wonder that "many women in the U.S. today do not understand the feminist position." Contrary to the pretensions of some, these women are neither weak nor foolish. Upper-class women know, and resent, the fact that their and their husbands' tax money is used mainly for the benefit of other women. Women on the receiving end of welfare know who is picking up the bill. Both groups understand that the arrangement under which they themselves are looked after economically, in return for performing the role of

---

[132] See Naomi Wolf, *Promiscuities: The Secret Struggle for Womanhood*, New York, Fawcett Columbine, 1997, p. 16.

mother and homemaker, is often "inequitable"[133] — inequitable, that is, from the point of view of many men.

[133] See Marcia Guttentag and Paul F. Secord, *Too Many Women? The Sex Ratio Question*, Beverly Hills, CA, Sage, 1983, pp. 170-1.

Chapter 5: Facing the Law

1. The Weaker Vessel

Physically speaking, women have always been, as the Gospel of Peter put it, the weaker vessel. And precisely because women are the weaker vessel, when it comes to the law they have seldom been treated in the same way as men, or held accountable to the same extent. The first section of this chapter presents a very brief survey of the way the difference between the sexes was legally handled at various times and places in history. The second, moving to the 20th century, examines how the justice systems of modern countries have systematically and consistently favored women over men at every stage. The third takes a look at the way those same justice systems treat conflicts that arise between men and women.

2. Historical Overview

As far as can be determined, as far back as ancient Egypt women occupied a favored position under the laws of the land, or at any rate under the procedures that were customary in court. A verse from the wisdom literature exhorts a man "not to tell lies against your mother because the magistrates abhor it."[1] Apparently women were also exempt from the most ferocious punishments, including mutilation and impalement.[2]

The tendency to hand down lighter punishments to women is also evident in Greek mythology. The story of Sisyphus, and its lack of a female equivalent, was already noted here. Tantalus, another male who offended the gods by killing a youth and then offering them the victim's flesh, was sentenced to eternal hunger and thirst. Prometheus' punishment for stealing the Olympic fire

---

[1] Lichtheim, *Ancient Egyptian Literature*, vol. 1, p. 191.

[2] Robins, *Women in Ancient Egypt*, p. 117.

and giving it to humankind was even worse. Chained to a rock, his liver was eaten by an eagle. The organ kept regenerating itself, so that the torture could restart each day. For accidentally seeing Athene naked, Theresias was struck blind. He could count himself lucky. Having committed the same offense with respect to Artemis, Acteon was turned into a stag and torn to pieces by his own hounds.

No woman ever suffered a comparable fate. What punishments women did undergo seldom involved pain or endangered their health. The most notorious case was that of Medea. First, to help her husband Jason escape, she cut her younger brother to pieces and scattered his limbs at sea in order to elude her relatives, who were pursuing them. Then, using false pretenses, she boiled her father-in-law alive. Then, in an uncontrollable outburst of jealousy, she killed her own two children, as well as her husband's second wife and the latter's father, the king of Corinth. And what wrath awaited this woman who had killed all those closest to her in cold blood? None, as it turns out. Medea escaped punishment in a chariot kindly put at her disposal by no less a person than the Sun God, Helios.

Shifting from mythology to history, we known of a case in ancient Mesopotamia in which the attorneys of a woman involved in conspiracy to murder tried to get her acquitted by pleading the weakness of her sex.[3] From Greece comes the story of Phryne, a famous courtesan in 4th-century B.C Athens. At one point she was accused of impiety, a very serious crime and one listed among those for which Socrates was executed. She, too, would have been condemned, except that during her trial her lawyer, at just the right moment, tore the clothes off her body and asked the all-male jury whether they really wished to end the life of such a beautiful woman. Needless to say, she was acquitted.

Some six centuries later, Zenobia, queen of Palmyra, rebelled against Rome. Defeated and taken prisoner, she begged Emperor Aurelian for her life as "a mere woman." Instead of being executed in one of the many unpleasant ways reserved for enemies of Rome, she was spared. Zenobia's male adviser, the philosopher Cassius Longinus, took the blame and suffered the consequences. She herself ended as a *grande dame* in a villa near Rome. This good fortune was almost certainly connected to the fact that she was said to

[3] Martha T. Roth, "Gender and Law: A Case Study from Ancient Mesopotamia," in Victor H. Matthews et al., eds., *Gender and Law in the Hebrew Bible and the Ancient Near East*, Sheffield, Academic Press, 1998, p. 178.

possess a beautiful voice and "incredible sex appeal."[4] That is not necessarily to say that the emperor, a tough soldier and capable statesman, fell for her charms. Like many other rulers before and since, he must have realized that executing a woman, especially a good-looking one, makes for bad publicity. Conversely, one reason why early Christian propaganda abounds with stories, real or invented, of women being tortured and put to death[5] is to put the pagans in the worst possible light. From the point of view of the propagandist, whether or not the stories were true was immaterial.

The tradition of treating women better than men was continued under Salic law. Originally issued by Frankish King Clovis between 507 and 511, it was later developed by his successors. For example, for merely touching "the hand or the finger of a freewoman or any other woman" a man could be fined 15 *solidi*. The more intimate the touch, the higher the penalty.[6] Cutting off the hair of a boy "without the consent of his relatives" cost he who was found guilty of it 1,800 *solidi*. Doing the same to a girl cost 4,000. Though minors of both sexes were under the control of their adult relatives, obviously a woman's person was considered more precious. The fine for blocking the road of a free woman or striking her was also three times the sum due for the same offense committed against a man. The penalty for killing a freeman was 600 *solidi*; for killing a freewoman, 1,800. Another clause says that the penalty for killing a freewoman was the same as the one for killing a male count. Other traditional societies maintained similar distinctions. For example, in Yemen the blood money demanded for the death of a woman was *11 times* that demanded for a man. In the eyes of one modern female writer, this rule was part of a "chauvinistic code of chivalry."[7]

To oblige women, many medieval rulers were even prepared to forego the usual penalty reserved for rebels, namely the confiscation of property.[8] In 1333-1347 Joan, countess of March, was able to keep her Irish estates even though her husband, Robert Mortimer, had been executed for not only

---

[4] See Antonia Fraser, *The Warrior Queens*, New York, Vintage, 1988, p. 114.

[5] See Herbert Musurillo, *The Acts of the Christian Martyrs*, Oxford, Oxford University Press, 1972, pp. 22, 24, 115, 129, 133.

[6] *The Laws of the Salian Franks*, Katherine F. Fischer, trans., Philadelphia, University of Philadelphia Press, 1991, pp. 84, 94-5, 125, 131, 144, 162-3, 200, 203.

[7] Sheila Carapico, "Gender and Status Inequalities in Yemen: Honor, Education and Politics," in Valentine M. Mogahdam, *Patriarchy and Economic Development: Women's Positions at the End of the Twentieth Century*, New York, Oxford University Press, 1996, p. 85.

[8] Rowena E. Archer, "Women as Landholders and Administrators in the Later Middle Ages," in Goldberg, ed., *Woman is a Worthy Wight*, pp. 163-9.

committing treason against King Edward III, but also for being the queen's lover. In 1399-1402, Elizabeth Fitzalan, widow of the duke of Norfolk, persuaded King Henry IV to allow her to keep her property. Three years later, Constance Holland, the widow of another duke of Norfolk who had ended his life on the scaffold — it was a time of civil war, unhealthy for dukes — persuaded the same Henry, who was her uncle, to allow her to retain her dower. Each of these cases marked a conflict between the desire to uphold the law and enrich the treasury and the political imperative to avoid treating women too harshly. In each of these cases, it was politics that won out.

Conversely, when a woman bit into the proverbial unripe fruit, it was the teeth of her husband or other male relatives that broke. A good example of the way things worked, this time at the bottom of the social ladder, is provided by the English village of Alweras in Staffordshire.[9] In Alweras, and presumably in many other villages as well, most of those active in illegal brewing were women. But in Alweras, and presumably in other villages as well, most of those fined for illegally selling ale were men. The explanation is simple: Those who committed the offense were actually female. Most females, however, were either the daughters of males or married to them, and consequently it was they who were made to bear the consequences.

In 1634 another English court spelled out the reasoning behind this arrangement. The case in question was that of one Thomas Hellyard. He and his wife Elizabeth were brought before the dreaded Star Chamber to answer for having sold saltpeter — an ingredient of gunpowder — without a license. The charges were serious indeed, comparable in today's terms to a crime like assisting terrorists. Convicted, Hellyard was sentenced to pay the enormous sum of 1,000 pounds sterling, and was subjected to pillory, whipping and imprisonment. Not so his wife and partner, who had sold over 1,000 pounds of saltpeter. Though "the courte was fully satisfyed with sufficient matter whereupon to ground a sentence against the defendant... shee being a wyfe and subject to obey her husband theyr Lord ships did forbeare to sentence her."[10]

In Edinburgh and perhaps other places as well, the practice of saddling merchants with their wives' transgressions continued into the 18th century.[11] Husbands whose wives used dirty language in public were also held

[9] Helena Graham, "A Woman's Work... Labor and Gender in the Late Medieval Countryside," in Goldberg, ed., *Woman Is a Worthy Wight*, pp. 139, 141, 144.

[10] Clark, *Working Life of Women in the Seventeenth Century*, pp. 34-5.

[11] Elizabeth C. Sanderson, *Women and Work in Eighteenth-Century Edinburgh*, London, MacMillan, 1996, p. 10.

accountable.[12] The practice of remanding offending women to their husbands may be one reason why, in France during that period, the vast majority of those subjected to judical torture were men. So small was the number of women involved that the necessary techniques were all but forgotten. When one such case arose in 1778, those responsible for carrying out the unpleasant business had to confront the fact that in the 40 previous years, no woman had been questioned under duress. To learn what to do, they had to consult the archives.[13]

Nor has the practice of punishing husbands for their wives' sins yet come to an end. Here is a verbatim description by an American woman of what happened to her following an illegal abortion she had had:[14] "After I got home [from the clinic], I developed a high fever. I was so sick I was delirious with the pain and fever. My mother took me to the emergency ward. The doctors asked her who had done the abortion. When she didn't tell them, they refused to treat me. They said that they would let me die if she didn't tell them the name and address of the abortionist. Frightened, she gave them a false name and then they started treatment for me. When the police... found out that my mother had given false information, they went to my house and arrested my husband." A case of male chauvinism at work, no doubt.

Pace modern feminist authors, the most cursory research shows that women sometimes held a privileged position even in respect to the laws governing the most intimate aspects of life. Thus, as long ago as ancient Athens it is possible to find cases in which men, but not women, were put on trial and punished for adultery.[15] In Republican Rome, the law permitted a husband to kill his wife's lover but not the woman herself. Later, when punishment was taken out of the hands of the husband and put into those of the courts, this difference still existed.[16] Many centuries later, Salic law applied a similar standard, prescribing a hefty fine for a man "who secretly had intercourse with a free girl with the consent of both." But while the law clearly described the

[12] Gillis, *For Better, for Worse*, p. 77.

[13] Lisa Silverman, *Tortured Subjects: Pain, Truth and the Body in Early Modern France*, Chicago, University of Chicago Press, 2001, pp. 77, 98.

[14] Baer, *Women in American Law*, p. 181.

[15] Demosthenes, *Against Aristocrates*, 23.55, 55.

[16] Gardner, *Women in Roman Law and Society*, p. 129; also Grubbs, *Law and Family in Late Antiquity*, p. 217.

offense as one committed with the consent of "*both*," no similar fine was prescribed for the female partner.[17]

Some of the most interesting evidence on this matter comes from Byzantium.[18] Under imperial law as formulated by Constantine I, a man guilty of fornication was heavily fined or, if he could not pay, mutilated. However, the woman with whom he had fornicated only shared in the same punishment if she was a nun. The underlying logic was that such a woman was not her own mistress, and stood under the guardianship of her relatives. This fact made the woman incapable of giving her consent, a fact of which the man should have been aware and which he ought to have respected. Whether because she was deemed incapable of giving her consent, being under her relatives' guardianship, or because fornication (*stuprum*) was wrong in itself, for an unmarried woman to have sex was an offense. Nevertheless, there was no thought of punishing her. Instead, she benefited from the fine which her paramour had to pay, and which was paid to her and not to the *fisc*. In other words, under this legal system a man would be punished for seducing a woman. By contrast, a woman could actually be rewarded for seducing a man.

Early medieval European statute books were largely silent on the question of adultery. When penalties began to be prescribed early in the 14th century, they applied first to men and only then to women.[19] Nor was the rule that adultery was considered a worse offense in men than in women limited to Christendom. For example, in 1342-1343 Ibn Battuta found himself doing duty as a *kadi*, or religious judge, in the Maldives. Trying a concubine and a slave who had been caught sleeping together, he "chastised" them both but had only the man locked up. When a local ruler interceded on the man's behalf, Battuta grew indignant. He had the man fetched and ordered him "beaten with bamboo rods which are more painful than whips, and I had him paraded through the island with a rope around his neck."[20] In parts of 17th-century Germany, a conviction for fornication also led to much smaller penalties for women than for men. The latter, on top of being made to pay, were also forced to surrender any public offices they might hold.[21]

---

[17] *The Laws of the Salian Franks*, p. 80.

[18] Laiou, "Sex, Consent and Coercion in Byzantium," in Laiou, ed., *Consent and Coercion to Sex and Marriage*, pp. 119, 121, 122. 125, 126, 135, 137, 142, 146, 150-1.

[19] Dean, "Fathers and Daughters: Marriage Laws and Disputes," in Dean and Lowe, eds., *Marriage in Italy*, p. 86.

[20] *The Rehlah of Ibn Battuta*, p. 213.

[21] Wunder, *He Is the Sun, She Is the Moon*, p. 125.

Women's position with respect to other sexual offenses was even more privileged, going back as far as biblical times. *Leviticus* 20.13 and 17 rules that, in cases of incest between brother and sister, "he shall bear his iniquity;" as if cases in which older sisters abused their younger brothers did not exist. The penalty prescribed for male homosexuality is death. *Leviticus* has served as Judaism's primary guide on sexual behavior for more than 2,000 years, and to this day, some rabbis still demand that gay males be severely punished or at least ostracized. Throughout this time, lesbianism was seldom mentioned. The Talmud at one point says that women who "tangle"—later interpreted as "those who rub their genitals together" — should be prevented from marrying the high priest.[22] Another rabbi did not agree, claiming that the activity was just an obscenity and expressly permitting such a marriage to take place.[23] A millennium later, Maimonides condemned lesbianism as "an Egyptian deed." But he did not prescribe any penalties for it.[24]

Roman attitudes toward male homosexuality were relatively relaxed. Later, though, the advent of Christianity caused matters to change. St. Paul in *Romans* 1.27 speaks of homosexuality among men. He says that "working that which is unseemly, they receive in themselves that recompense of their error which was meet." In the previous sentence he mentions the "vile affections" of women; however, he does not say anything about the need to punish them. The Christian emperors Constantine, Constans, Theodosius II and Justinian took him at his word. All four passed ferocious laws against male homosexuality, but lesbians remained exempt.

St. John Chrysostom explained around 390 AD that lesbianism was the devil's work. Roughly three centuries later, Theodore of Canterbury and Bede denounced it as a sin. So did St. Anselm and Abelard in the 12th century. Gratian's *Decretum* of 1140 mentions it as "contrary to nature." This work, incidentally, remained the standard one on canon law until 1917. In 1267-1273 Thomas Aquinas in *Summa Theologica* called lesbianism "an unnatural vice." Though love between women was abhorred, not one of these sources said it should be punished. One monk advised that, when it came to sexual behavior such as lesbianism, masturbation, bestiality, incest and contraception, women

---

[22] *Yebamot*, 56.1. I wish to thank Amichai Borosh for bringing this passage to my attention.

[23] See Louis Crompton, "The Myth of Lesbian Impunity: Capital Laws from 1270 to 1791," *Journal of Homosexuality*, 6, 1, fall/winter 1980/81, pp. 11-3, 15-21.

[24] See Goitein, *A Mediterranean Society*, vol. 5, p. 316.

should be questioned “mildly and gently.” Female sexual offenses merited purgatory, not hell.[25]

A law published in 1265 by the king of Castile, Alfonso X, prohibited both male and female homosexuality. In 1314 Cino da Pistoia, a friend of Dante’s, published a *Commentary* on the Code of Justinian in which he reinterpreted an imperial edict of 587 A.D. as referring to lesbianism. Whether or not his interpretation was correct, it became part of Roman law as studied in Italy, Spain, France, Germany and Scotland. Seeking to disprove the “myth” of lesbian immunity to prosecution, one modern scholar claims to have identified 400 cases of female homosexuals being executed during the late Middle Ages and early modern period. Even according to his count, though, very few victims were women, and most of them met their fate for other reasons. Their main crime was to have dressed as men — sometimes, repeatedly and in spite of several warnings — and to have married other women. One such case took place in Halberstadt, Saxony, in 1721. It involved a woman who had repeatedly dressed as a man to attract women; in the end she married one and used a dildo to have sex with her.[26]

In 1791 the French National Assembly abolished homosexuality as an offense for both men and women. But this was hardly the end of the story in Europe. In English law, anal intercourse had long been a capital crime.[27] Toward the end of the 19th century, the issue became mixed up with contemporary fear of “decadence.” As a result, the law against anal intercourse was tightened even further. Since females could not commit buggery, the only victims were males. Nor was England the only country to follow this policy. In 1911 the Netherlands passed a law criminalizing relations between men. The German Empire, for its part, had on the books the notorious “Paragraph 175.” The police used it to open “pink files” on known homosexuals.[28] Later the Nazis locked up some 10,000 gay men in concentration camps.[29] Singled out for maltreatment at the hands of both guards and other inmates, they suffered from exceptionally high death rates. Others were subjected to medical

[25] Burchard of Worms, quoted in Danielle Jacquart and Claude Thomasset, *Sexuality and Medicine in the Middle Ages*, Princeton, NJ, Princeton University Press, 1985, p. 89; *ibid*, p. 160.

[26] See Brigitte Eriksson, "A Lesbian Execution in Germany 1721," *Journal of Homosexuality*, 6, 12, fall/winter 1980/81, pp. 27-40.

[27] Porter and Hall, *The Facts of Life*, p. 29.

[28] Hans Georg Stümke, *Homosexuelle in Deutschland*, Berlin, Förster, 1989, p. 144.

[29] Rüdiger Lutmann, "The Pink Triangle: The Persecution of Homosexual Males in Concentration Camps in Nazi Germany" *Journal of Homosexuality*, 6, 1/2, fall/winter 1980/81, p. 141-60.

experiments designed to "cure" them, including castration and the implantation of artificial glands.[30] There were many attempts to extend the law to women as well. All were rejected by the Ministry of Justice, which argued that the matter would have to wait until the end of the war.

In Stalin's Soviet Union, male homosexuals were severely punished.[31] The same laws, however, were not applied to lesbians. Later Mao Tze Dong in China took a similar line.[32] To this day in American prisons, homosexual relations between female inmates — and sometimes between them and female guards — are tolerated. One contemporary female scholar suggests that this is because "many of the lesbian relationships reported in prison are based more on affection with a sexual connotation than on actual sexual activity."[33] As so often, a crime is a crime only as long as those who commit it are men. As of 1993, 22 states in America had laws against male gays having intercourse. But lesbian sex was not prohibited by even one of them.[34] Historically, so great has the difference been between the way lesbians and male homosexuals are treated by society that it has given rise to an entire body of literature.

Females accused of spiritual transgressions such as blasphemy and apostasy were also leniently treated. Normally they were remitted to their male relatives. For example, when the German noblewoman Argula von Grumbach wrote on behalf of the Reformation during the 1520s, the authorities, instead of arresting her as they would have done if she were a man, told her husband to take her home and shut her up.[35] The custom of remitting female offenders to their male relatives may be one reason why single women and widows are said to be over-represented among accused witches. In other words, the reason why these women were put on trial was because they had no man to which the law could entrust them, as in the case of von Grumbach and other married women. By way of another example of how women accused of "spiritual" offenses were

---

[30] For "cures" see Günter Grau, ed., *Homosexualität in der NS Zeit*, Frankfurt/Main, Fischer, 1993, pp. 305-21, 345-57; for why women were not persecuted see *ibid*, pp. 39, 102-3.

[31] Rosenthal, "Love on the Tractor," in Bridenthal and Koonz, eds., *Becoming Visible*, p. 388.

[32] Harriet Evans, *Women and Sexuality in China*, New York, Continuum, 1997, p. 208.

[33] Joanne Belknap, *The Invisible Woman: Gender, Crime and Justice*, Belmont, CA, Wadsworth, 1996, p. 112; Nancy K. Wilson, "Styles of Doing Time in a Coed Prison," in John Ortiz Smylka, ed., *COED Prison*, New York, Human Sciences, 1980, p. 159

[34] Data valid as of September 1993; Peter McWilliams, *Ain't Nobody's Business if You Do: The Absurdity of Consensual Crimes in a Free Society*, Los Angeles, McWilliams, 1993, pp. 779-80.

[35] For ancient Rome see Tacitus, *Annales*, 13.32; for the early modern age see Freedman, *Their Sisters' Keepers*, p. 10; Von Grumbach: Wiesner, *Women and Gender in Early Modern Europe*, p. 188.

treated, the English Reformation under Henry VIII cost the lives of eight men but only one woman. Later the situation was reversed and it was Protestantism which became a crime. Some 230 men, but only 50 women, died at the hand of "Bloody Mary;" a percentage one modern authority calls "surprisingly high."[36]

What was true of offenses connected with religion was equally true of secular ones. Figures from 18th-century London show that women standing trial were more likely than men to be acquitted. What is more, given the extreme severity of the law, juries often committed "pious perjury" so as to save people from the worst consequences of their crimes. Apparently twice as many women as men were spared in this way. Pregnant women in danger of being condemned to execution even had the right to be tried by a female jury, rather than a male one. This was known as "pleading the belly."[37] Of the 1,242 people who were hanged in London between 1703 and 1784, only 92 — 7.5 percent — were women.[38] In other countries, too, women often received lighter punishments. This was particularly true if they were virgins, particularly true if they were about to give birth, and particularly true if they had young children[39] — in other words, during a substantial portion of their lives.

Medieval German even had a special term, *Frauenfrevel*, or "women's trifle," for reducing the penalty levied against women. It amounted to 50 percent of the fines imposed on men. Both then and in later centuries, there existed a whole class of sanctions which, regarded as relatively light, were known as "women's punishments." They involved discomfort or humiliation, but not actual pain.[40] To the extent that pain *was* inflicted on them, women also tended to get off lightly. For example, 18th-century female American beggars who returned to towns from which they had been driven away received 25 lashes. Males got 39. Men, not women, were sent to the galleys. In the 1790s, Emperor Joseph II ordered male, but not female, convicts to haul barges along the banks of the Danube. So harsh were conditions that the convicts died like flies.[41]

---

[36] Arthur G. Dickens, *The English Reformation*, New York, Schocken, 1969, pp. 266-7.

[37] J. C. Oldham, "On Pleading the Belly: A History of 'The Jury of Matrons,'" *Criminal Justice History*, 6, 1985, pp. 1-64.

[38] Linebaugh, *The London Hanged*, pp. 85, 91, 142.

[39] Chris Docherty, "Female Offenders," in McLean and Burrows, eds., *The Legal Relevance of Gender*, p. 174.

[40] Wunder, *He Is the Sun, She Is the Moon*, pp. 188-9.

[41] N. Finash, "Zur 'Ökonomie des Strafens': Gefängniswesen und Gefängnisreform im Roer-Department nach 1794," *Rheinische Vierteljahresberichte*, 4, 1989, pp. 188-210.

Finally, to the extent that imprisonment was used to punish and deter, women also suffered less than men. To focus on England, early on prisons normally incarcerated men and women together. Their fates, however, were entirely different. Visiting a 16th -century male inmate, a friend found him "wasted to a skeleton and in a state of exhaustion from grinding at the treadmill, a most pitiful sight. There was nothing left of him except skin and bones and I cannot remember having seen anything like it — lice swarmed on him like ants on a molehill." Other male prisoners might be employed to dig streets and clean sewers. By contrast, female prisoners were made to perform otherwise routine feminine duties, such as cooking, cleaning, operating spinning wheels or, if they worked outside the prison, picking rags. Some women engaged in prostitution within the prison walls. Living like queens, they "were feasted with varieties of wines and delicate meates."[42]

When prison reform started early in the 19th century, again it was men who bore the brunt. The reforms made some improvements in that they imposed strict controls on the arbitrary behavior of guards. They also replaced the old ramshackle structures with new, custom-designed, more sanitary buildings. People's ideas concerning the purpose of the system also changed. Instead of being used merely to punish and deter criminals, it was now supposed to reform them as well. The first step was to isolate each inmate in his own cell. They were only permitted to leave those cells to do hard, but sometimes entirely senseless, work, such as walking the treadwheel or turning the crank. To prevent them from communicating with other prisoners, a rule of strict silence, sometimes lasting for years, was imposed. The outcome was to turn prisons into tombs for the living.

For women, the results were entirely different. Beginning in late 18th-century America, spreading middle-class ideas concerning female modesty caused women to be segregated. Next it was decided that only women were fit to supervise women. As one New York reformer put it, no female prisoner should so much as suffer a male guard approaching her. Instead, they required "the shield of a pure woman's presence — one who could bring to bear a force often found more potent than muscular strength."[43]

Whereas male prisons were strictly regimented, in female ones benevolence and compassion were supposed to prevail. Whereas men were to be reformed by isolation and silence, women were to be educated by living together in

[42] William C. Carroll, *Fat King, Lean Beggar: Representations of Poverty in the Age of Shakespeare*, Ithaca, NY, Cornell University Press, 1996, pp. 58, 112.

[43] See Freedman, *Their Sisters' Keepers*, p. 62.

groups and talking with each other, and with the female staff, to their hearts' contents. Whereas male prisoners were often made to do backbreaking labor both within prison and outside of its walls, employing women in chain-gangs was prohibited. Incidentally, in 1995 a prison commissioner in Alabama included female prisoners in gangs that picked trash from state highways; he was quickly forced to abandon the plan and resign.[44]

By the end of the 19th century women's prisons began to look almost like country clubs. They consisted of cottage-like structures, each housing a group of women, usually in a bucolic setting. The fortress-like compounds that typically housed male prisoners were avoided. Instead of cells, female prisoners were given rooms. Often they had more privacy than male ones, were given greater leeway in decorating their rooms, and lived under much less security.[45] "Good linen and china" completed the picture. Some women's prisons provided considerable liberty in taking trips outside the facilities. Others allowed inmates to wear their own clothes, and others even provided what could almost be called a pleasant lifestyle, complete with outings, dances, picnics and light agricultural work. By 1900, special facilities "suitable for... feminine temperaments"[46] existed in several American states.

On the other side of the Atlantic male guards in female prisons were also gradually replaced by women. In Britain, too, making female prisoners do work that would be both punitive and productive proved difficult and taxed the imagination of those responsible. In Britain, too, punishments regarded as appropriate for male prisoners, such as being put in irons, or forbidden to talk, or whipped, or put on short rations, were considered too severe for women.[47] Conversely, female prisoners received much more education than their male counterparts. Female guards were often left powerless as prisoners wore what they pleased, used the presence of their children — whom they were permitted to have with them — to avoid work, or even vented their anger by emptying chamber pots on them.[48] The incomparably easier regime imposed on female

[44] Medea Chesney-Lind and Lisa J. Pasko, *The Female Offender: Girls, Women and Crime*, Thousand Oaks, CA, Sage, 1997, p. 164.

[45] See Kathryn W. Burkhart, *Women in Prison*, New York, Doubleday, 1973.

[46] Freedman, *Their Sisters' Keepers*, p. 68.

[47] Lucia Zender, *Women's Crime and Custody in Victorian England*, Oxford, Clarendon Press, 1991, pp. 106, 145-6, 169, 175, 209.

[48] Zender, *Women's Crime*, pp. 147, 168.

prisoners may explain why, in comparison to men, far fewer of them were first offenders and why far more of them were rearrested following release.[49]

In both Britain and the United States, people were prepared to see women as *a priori* less culpable. In both countries, the prevailing view was that "women are more often the accomplices of crime, its aiders and abettors."[50] Whereas men were held "strictly accountable," women were assumed to be endowed with an "almost paralytic passivity"[51] and were judged accordingly. To the extent that they participated in crime at all, it was believed at the time, was not on their own initiative, but because of the corrupting influence of vicious men. Whether by making false promises of marriage or by other means, those men had somehow succeeded in robbing women of their independent will. However flawed the logic, the privileges to which it led were very real. In the words of one British journalist, "very properly the law makes merciful allowance in dealing with the female offender when it can be apparent that she has been impelled to commit breaches of the law under masculine influence."[52]

Like Medea, some women were literally able to get away with murder. In late 19th-century Britain, less than one-quarter of those tried for the crime were women. On the other hand, then as now women made up almost all of those tried for infanticide. British juries regarded these women as victims of "puerperal mania." The latter was a fashionable disease that was also believed to cause "extraordinary obscenity in thought and language." Very often, juries would simply refuse to convict. Parliament responded by changing the law so as to separate infanticide from murder and place it in a category of its own. Yet even so prosecutors still found it all but impossible to obtain convictions. Normally they could do so, if at all, only if they agreed that light sentences should be imposed. Even so, rarely did infanticidal women serve out their complete term. This was because, among all those declared to be criminally insane, it was they who stood the greatest chance of being granted an early release.[53]

At practically all times and places, women who ran afoul of the law had an easier time of it than did men. This was as true in mythology as in real life, in

---

[49] Zender, *Women's Crime*, pp. 22, 138, 170, 247; Roger Matthews, *Doing Time: An Introduction to the Sociology of Imprisonment*, London, MacMillan, 1999, p. 182.

[50] *The English Woman's Journal*, January 1859, p. 291, quoted in Zender, *Women's Crime*, p. 19.

[51] Basch, *Framing American Divorce*, p. 165.

[52] Adam Hargrave, *Woman and Crime*, London, Laurie, 1914, p. 4.

[53] Zender, *Woman's Crime*, pp. 38, 78-9; Elaine Showalter, *The Female Malady: Women, Madness and English Culture, 1830-1980*, Harmondsworth, Middlesex, Penguin, 1983, p. 58-9.

ancient Egypt as in late Victorian Britain. To quote one prison inspector in the latter, "women [were] punished more lightly than men for a similar offence and... the public and police [were] less disposed to charge them."[54] Sometimes laws and regulations were changed or watered down specifically in order to prevent women from being treated as severely as men. No sooner did women form a considerable percentage of those who committed any given offense or crime then that crime and that offense started to lose their gravity. This, incidentally, may explain people's fascination with the witch-hunting episode. It is perhaps the only time in history when more women than men were charged with a serious crime and executed for it.

Far from serving to enforce patriarchy, very often the law was used specifically to provide women with extra protection. Often it prevented the harsh attitudes that governed relations between men from being applied to women. In other cases it was actually designed to punish men in *lieu* of women. Among those who benefited from the lax arm of the law was the American suffragette Susan B. Anthony. Along with 50 other women, she was arrested in 1872 for casting her vote illegally in that year's elections. Put on trial, she harangued the judge in a way that would have earned a lesser mortal a charge of contempt. Instead of spending a possible three years in jail, she was let off with a fine. In the end, she did not even have to pay that.[55] A contemporary of hers, the famous English physician Henry Maudsley, once remarked that the feminist movement owes what successes it had less to widespread female discontent than to men's reluctance to suppress it.[56] Had Ms. Anthony heard him, perhaps she would have agreed.

3. The 20th Century

An overwhelming absence of data dooms any real attempt to quantify the different ways in which the justice system has treated the two sexes over the course of history. As regards our own time, however, a vast amount of statistics is available to prove the degree to which women are favored. This analysis is

[54] Vernon Harris, "The Female Prisoner," *The Nineteenth Century and After*, No. 363, May 1907, p. 783.

[55] See Eleanor Flexner, *Century of Struggle: The Woman's Rights Movement in the United States*, Cambridge, MA, Harvard University Press, 1975, pp. 169-71.

[56] Henry Maudesley, *Responsibility in Mental Disease*, London, Kegan Paul, 1874, p. 28.

limited mainly to the Britain and the United States, as recounting the relevant statistics country by country would be unnecessarily repetitive.

In the words of one female legal scholar:

> Women certainly do not fit the stereotype of a criminal. Such preconceptions might enable the criminal justice system to take their crimes less seriously, helping them avoid arrest and severe punishment. These attitudes... are likely to receive support from the wider public, who are less fearful of women criminals. Moreover, due to their traditional roles as wives and mothers, the 'weaker sex' might not only evoke the sympathy of officials but avoid suspicion altogether... [This may explain why] women maintain low levels of criminal involvement, and even return to non-deviant lives more easily.[57]

Even today, "attitudes toward women have not changed drastically."[58] For this, one supposes, women can only thank their stars — or men.

Do "preconceptions" about criminality still cause men and women to be treated differently? Most experts believe the answer to this question is a decided yes. As one American scholar put it, "Police officers dislike to arrest [women], district attorneys to prosecute them, judges and juries to find them guilty."[59] "A large body of research exists which at least suggests that women receive more lenient treatment than men at various stages of the criminal justice process."[60] As one scholar has noted, "for each category of offense women received shorter average maximum sentences."[61] And another one: "The most persistent findings about the treatment of men and women are that women are given more lenient treatment than are men in decisions about sentencing, especially in response to serious offenses."[62] The list of quotations could be

---

[57] Leonard, *Women, Crime and Society*, p. 82.

[58] Leonard, *Women, Crime and Society*, p. 84.

[59] Otto Pollack, *The Criminality of Women*, Westport, CT, Greenwood Press, 1978, p. 151.

[60] U.S. Department of Justice, *Survey of State Prison Inmates—1991, Women in Prison*, Bureau of Justice Statistics Special Report NCJ 145321, Washington, Government Printing Office, March 1994, p. 4.

[61] Frank H. Julian, "Gender and Crime: Different Sex, Different Treatment?" in Concetta C. Culliver, ed., *Female Criminality: The State of the Art*, New York, Garland, 1993, p. 358.

[62] Chesney-Lind, "Female Offenders: Paternalism Reexamined," in L. L. Crites and W. L Hepperle, eds., *Women, the Courts and Equality*, Newbury Park, Ca, Sage, 1987, pp. 114-39.

extended at will. Many come from female investigators.[63] Each year there are tens, perhaps hundreds, of thousands of women who are given privileges. And there are tens, possibly hundreds, of thousands of men who are discriminated against merely because they are not women.

An examination of the process by which the justice system operates is instructive here. First, having responded to a call, a policeman or policewoman on the spot will have to determine whether what he or she saw or heard is sufficiently serious to warrant an arrest. Already at this stage women are treated "paternalistically" — read, less harshly and more kindly — than are their male counterparts.[64] For example, in England and Wales, for every single offense, in every single age category, in every single year, women are much more likely to be let off with a warning than are men.[65] The same is true in the United States.[66] This is true even when factors other than sex, such as age, race and prior arrest records, are controlled for.[67]

Once the decision to arrest has been made, women are considerably more likely to receive bail.[68] There is, however, a tendency to discriminate between married women and single ones. Unmarried women are presumed to be in difficult financial circumstances, and not surprisingly are 43 percent more likely to be let off without bail. Married women are presumed to have somebody who can shoulder the burden — in other words, a man. Consequently, they are 69 percent more likely to pay.[69] Some countries exercise even more blatant discrimination by prohibiting persons accused of certain serious crimes from receiving bail at all. Once arrested, they will be remanded in custody for months or years. However, the system only applies to men; women, as usual, are exempt.[70]

---

[63] Belknap, *The Invisible Woman*, p. 85.

[64] Leonard, *Women, Crime and Society: A Critique of Theoretical Criminology*, New York, Longman, 198, p. 9.

[65] Dougherty, "Female Offenders," in McLean and Burrows, eds., *The Legal Relevance of Gender*, p. 186; Home Office, *Criminal Statistics*, London, HMSO, 1983, table 5.5.

[66] M. D. Krohn et al., "Is Chivalry Dead? An Analysis of the Changes in Police Disposition of Males and Females," *Criminology*, 21, 1983, pp. 417-38.

[67] E. Mould, "Chivalry and Paternalism—Disparities of Treatment in the Criminal Justice System," *Western Political Quarterly*, 31, 1978, pp. 416-30.

[68] I. H. Nagel et al., "Sex Differences in the Processing of Criminal Defendants," in D. K. Weisberg, ed., *Women and the Law: A Social Historical Perspective*, Cambridge, MA, Schenkman, 1982, vol. 1, pp. 259-82.

[69] Noreen L. Channels and Sharon D. Herzberger, "The Role of Gender in Pretrial Decision Making," in Culliver, ed., *Female Criminality*, p. 330.

[70] Kant, *Women and the Law*, p. 140.

Assuming a decision has been made to press charges, a woman whose case comes before a court can continue to expect preferential treatment. This is especially true if her crime has been directed against a man who has been close to her, and especially if it is very serious. In assault or murder cases, we are told, "the prosecutor must work against the sympathy she may arouse in the jury, while the defense attorney must work within the criminal law of excuse and responsibility."[71] As the case of Medea demonstrates, women who have killed their children also tend to be treated with sympathy. The presumption is that women naturally love their children and that they *must* have been deranged.[72]

Thus, a woman who has committed certain types of crimes is likely to be regarded as suffering from diminished capacity and treated accordingly. A woman who has broken the law at certain times is also likely to be so regarded. This is particularly true if she did so in Britain, and particularly if she had the good sense to do so after the publication of a best-selling volume entitled *Once a Month* (1969). The author, Katherine Dalton, argued that menstruation turns women into raging maniacs, predisposing them to suicide, homicide and child abuse. This got her invited to act as a star witness at several murder trials. In one of the cases, a woman used her car to smash her former lover into a telephone pole. Tried for murder; the so-called "Pre-Menstrual Syndrome Defense" got her off with a conditional discharge from prison and a permanent driving ban. In another case, a barmaid who had killed a male co-worker in a fit of jealousy escaped punishment altogether. One might almost conclude that the lives of men do not count— provided, of course, they are killed by the right woman at the right time.[73]

A woman standing trial along with a man is doubly privileged. In the 19th century, Britain even had a famous case when the jury was asked to consider whether a crippled and bedridden husband should be held responsible for a murder his wife committed in his presence.[74] Even today one can still find the presumption that, if a man and a woman commit a crime together, the woman

---

[71] Baer, *Women in American Law*, p. 283.

[72] See Ronald B. Flowers, *Women and Criminality: The Woman as Victim, Offender and Practitioner*, Westport, CT, Greenwood, 1987, pp. 108-9.

[73] See G. A. Samspon, "Premenstrual Syndrome: A Double Blind Controlled Trial of Progesterone and Placebo," *British Journal of Psychiatry*, 135, 1979, pp. 209-15; P. A. Buchon and K. Calhoun, "Menstrual Cycle Symptomatology: The Role of Social Expectancy and Experimental Characteristics," *Psychosomatic Medicine*, 47, 1985, pp. 35-45.

[74] Doggett, *Marriage, Wife Beating and the Law in Victorian England*, pp. 51-3.

should be held less responsible, or not responsible at all. So strong is that presumption that it has acquired a name, the "Svengali Defense," after a famous novel in which the wicked hero corrupts an innocent girl. Among the beneficiaries were several female Nazi doctors and nurses who participated in the euthanasia program, administering lethal injections to handicapped people. As a German court put it, a woman's "feminine character" and "shy love" for her murderous male superior can justify or at least mitigate any deed, however horrible.[75]

Since 1980 or so, a great deal of attention has been paid to sexual abuse of children. Yet even in regard to this particularly heinous crime, society treats men and women differently. According to Simone de Beauvoir,[76] breastfeeding mothers often maintain an "intimate animal relationship" with their babies. Some women's magazines even recommend that they should be aware of their sexual feelings and enjoy them.[77] What would happen to a man who is caught, or alleged to be, sexually aroused while washing his daughter need not be spelled out here. Though some surveys indicate that one out of six people who sexually abuse children is female,[78] the public is almost completely ignorant of this fact. So strong is the presumption that this just does not happen that when a boy complains about the problem, the *first* question he is likely to be asked is whether he is sure the perpetrator was not his father.[79]

So manifest is the tendency to treat women more leniently than men that it has been the subject of several detailed studies. One reason behind the phenomenon seems to be that, at a time when the principal penalty society has at its disposal is imprisonment, the social and economic costs of punishing women with families are considered to be too high. The prosecutor who will charge a single mother with a crime likely to cause her to be locked up is hard to find.[80] Another may be that the psychiatrists called upon to assist the court regard women differently from men. A female defendant is much more likely to have such adjectives as "deprived," "damaged," "victimized" and "insecure" applied to her.

---

[75] Jörg Friedrich, *Die kalte Amnestie: NS Täter in der Bundesrepublik*, Munich, Piper, 1994 ed., pp. 190, 193, 228.

[76] *The Second Sex*, p. 478.

[77] See Farrell, *Why Men Are the Way They Are*, pp. 239.

[78] See Naomi Wolf, *Fire with Fire: The New Female Power and How To Use It*, New York, Ballantine, 1994, p. 221.

[79] See Michele Elliott, *Frauen als Täterinnen: Sexueller Missbrauch an Mädchen und Jungen*, Ruhmark, Donna Vita, 1995, pp. 99, 102, 155, 159, 306.

[80] Channels and Herzberger, "The Role of Gender in Pretrial Decision Making," p. 323.

Researching the cases brought before British courts between 1950 and 1983, one investigator found that men are discriminated against not once but twice. First, a woman, having had one of the above adjectives applied to her, is much more likely to be referred to treatment than to punishment. And once she has reached that stage, she is more likely to be diagnosed as mentally sound. That applies even if she has been charged with a serious crime, and even if she has a decade-long history of violent assault.[81] With men, things work the other way around. Once they have been diagnosed as mentally disturbed, any possibility that they will be let off lightly is gone. Such men are *more* likely to receive punishment in addition to, or instead of, treatment. In other words, a man who is mentally sound is punished, while a man who is mentally disturbed is *also* likely to be punished — at any rate, more so than a woman.

The idea that women are less responsible for their actions may explain why, in Britain between 1984 and 1992, proportionally *six times* more women who were accused of manslaughter were acquitted.[82] Between 1982 and 1989, 50 percent of females in Britain tried for murder succeeded in convincing juries that they had acted on "provocation," as compared to just 30 percent of males. As a result, proportionally almost twice as many men as women accused of this crime were convicted.[83] When it comes to sentencing, the difference between the sexes is greater still. In California between 1978 and 1980, out of 1,164 defendants convicted of first- or second-degree murder, 5.5 percent were female. However, of the 98 defendants sentenced to death, all — without exception — were male.[84] For the United States as a whole, women comprised only 1.5 percent of those sentenced to death for murder, despite the fact that 12.5 percent of those convicted of the crime were women. Of the roughly 16,000 "lawful executions" that took place in America before the turn of the millennium, just 2.5 percent involved women.[85]

The same trend repeats itself with respect to other serious crimes. In the United States in 1979, 21.8 percent of those arrested for murder, non-negligent

---

[81] Hilary Allen, *Justice Unbalanced: Gender, Psychiatry, and Judicial Decisions*, Milton Keynes, Open University, 1987, pp. xii-xiii, 4-5, 7, 100-1, 106-7.

[82] Carol Hedderman and Mike Hough, *Does the Criminal System Treat Men and Women Differently?* London, HMSO, 1994, pp. 3-4.

[83] Jo Bridgeman and Susan Millins, eds., *Feminist Perspectives on Law: Law's Engagement with the Female Body*, London, Sweet & Maxwell, 1998, pp. 624-5.

[84] Nancy Levit, *The Gender Line: Men, Women and the Law*, New York, New York University Press, 1998, p. 107.

[85] Levit, *The Gender Line*, p. 107.

manslaughter, forcible rape, robbery, aggravated assault, burglary, larceny-theft, motor vehicle theft, arson and other such serious crimes were women — 377,108 women, as compared to 1,351,416 men. That same year, women comprised 14.6 percent of those arrested for less serious crimes, 1,076,310 women to 7,343,045 men. It would thus appear that, contrary to the common belief that women's transgressions tend to be less grave, members of the female sex were actually over-represented among those arrested for the worst crimes of all. Nevertheless, as of 1977 only 3.9 percent of convicted criminals in American jails, 11,044 out of 278,141, were female.[86] Today, women arrested for serious crimes are only half as likely as men to end up in jail. In federal prison, the gap is larger still.[87] Compared with imprisoned men, and controlling for the type of offense and previous arrest records, American prisons only contain about one-half to one-quarter as many women as there should have been had they been treated on a par with men.[88]

When women *are* sent to jail, their terms tend to be much shorter than those of men. Among those convicted of property offenses, the mean difference was found to be 42 months. The difference for drug offenders was 18 months, while that of violent offenders was 39 months.[89] Even if one calculates the severity of the punishment based not on the number of months, but instead in terms of the sentences imposed as a proportion of the maximum prescribed for any given offense, the same difference emerges. One author used a sample of convicted male and female offenders incarcerated between 1983 and 1988 and matched for race, offense, prior criminal record and several other demographic and socioeconomic variables. He found that, taking all offenses into account, men were sentenced to 24 percent of the maximum prison time permissible by law. The figure for women was just 9 percent. As he says, "the primary conclusion" is that women get much lighter sentences than do matched samples of men convicted of the same crimes.[90]

Once criminals of the two sexes are sent to prison, men continue to be discriminated against. During most of the 20th century, one female researcher

---

[86] See Leonard, *Women, Crime and Society*, pp. 30, table 10; 31; 37, table 2.

[87] Rita J. Simon, "Women in Prison," in Culliver, ed., *Female Criminality*, p. 375.

[88] Frank H. Julian, "Gender and Crime: Different Sex, Different Treatment?" in Culliver, ed., *Female Criminality*, p. 346.

[89] U.S. Department of Justice, *Survey of State Prison Inmates—1991*, p. 4; also see M. Zingraff and R. Thomsen, "Differential Sentencing of Women and Men in the USA," *International Journal of the Sociology of Law*, 12, 1984, pp. 401-13.

[90] Culliver, ed., *Female Criminality*, pp. 368-9, 371.

explains, "women's prisons [were] much less forbidding and physically oppressive than the fortress-like... dungeons" used to hold male criminals.[91] "In terms of physical facilities and the general prison environment," a male one says, most women receive[d] better treatment than their male counterparts." No wonder, he adds, "females are... more favorable toward confinement than males."[92] One survey found that over 75 percent of incarcerated women thought institutional life was not as bad as they had anticipated; 65 percent found doing time easy. Female adolescents in particular were encouraged, and rewarded for, engaging in behavior such as acting maternal, being affectionate, showing sensitivity and crying.[93] Looking back, they tended to see their time in the institution less negatively than males did. As long ago as the second half of the 19th century, some women regarded the experience positively and listed the advantages it brought them.[94] And no wonder: In Canada, at any rate, female prisons are intended not for punishment but for "empowerment."[95]

One result of female convicts' under-representation among the prison population was that prisons for women were few and far between. In the 1970s, this state of affairs came under feminist-directed fire. It was claimed that the prisons in question did not allow inmates' relatives to visit them as often as they would like and as the inmates' own welfare demanded. Female prisons were also smaller than male facilities, with the result that educational opportunities inside them tended to be limited because of cost. The solution was to reverse the existing system — itself introduced at the behest of 19th-century feminists — and reinstitute coed prisons. Only in this way, it was argued, could the women's liberation movement reach criminal women as well as honest ones.

As in coed prisons during the early 19th century, concern for female prisoners prevented them from being locked up with all but the least serious male offenders. And as in the early 19th century, this created a situation in which all women were given privileges enjoyed by only a handful of men. Indeed, it has been argued that "the major drawback [of coed prisons] is that there is a perceived double standard of treatment for male and female inmates."

---

[91] Clemens Bartillas, "Little Girls Grow Up: the Perils of Institutionalization," in Culliver, ed., *Female Criminality,* p. 469.

[92] Ralph R. Arditi et al., "The Era and COED Prisons," in Smylka, ed., *COED Prison*, p. 270.

[93] Belknap, *The Invisible Woman*, p. 102.

[94] Bartillas, "Little Girls Grow Up: The Perils of Institutionalization," in Culliver, ed., *Female Criminality*, pp. 475, 477-8.

[95] Matthews, *Doing Time*, p. 200.

But that was not the end of the story. No sooner had the coed prison been restored to its former glory than the demand was raised that women, seeking equal opportunity employment, should be permitted to guard men.[96] American courts, it is worth noting, have consistently upheld the idea that to allow male guards to routinely watch female prison inmates engage in personal activities means violating their constitutional right to privacy. With the shoe on the other foot, however, the courts saw otherwise. In *Grummet v. Rushen*, the Ninth Circuit Court for Appeals allowed female guards to conduct pat-down searches of male inmates, including the groin. "[These] searches," the court ruled, "do not involve intimate contact with an inmate's body."

Similarly, in *Johnson v. Phelan*, the Seventh Circuit Court of Appeals did not prohibit female guards from watching naked male inmates as they washed or used the toilet in their cells. In the clash between equal-employment opportunities for women and male modesty, the court explicitly privileged the former. To quote one female expert: "Female guards can view male prisoners in various stages of undress, but male guards cannot view female prisoners similarly disrobed. Women in custody are afforded more privacy than men. Simmering under the surface are assumptions about the motivations of the viewer. Women guards would not view men as sex objects, but male guards might be inclined to leer."

In such an environment, it should come as no surprise that probation officers are guided by the same preconceived notions that policemen, prosecutors, psychiatrists, judges, juries and wardens bring to the job — namely, that the female offenders under their supervision suffer from psychological or emotional difficulties, or were victims of family problems, or escaped from bad husbands or dependent relationships. Entering the process long after everybody else has had his or her say, prison guards are likely to be derive practically everything they know about the person under consideration from evidence collected by their predecessors. Controlling for other factors, the result is that a male offender stands a 25 percent greater chance of being re-incarcerated than a female one.[97]

In summary, the evidence that modern justice systems discriminate against men is overwhelming. This is as true at the beginning of the process as at its end, as true at the point where a police officer has to decide whether or not to

[96] See Levit, *The Gender Line*, pp. 109-11.

[97] C. Frazier et al., "The Role of Probation Officers in Determining Gender Differences in Sentencing Severity," *Sociological Quarterly*, 24, 1983, pp. 305-18.

make an arrest as at the point where probation officers have to decide whether or not to re-commit a prisoner. And the fact that women can expect superior treatment has hardly been a secret from female offenders or the lawyers who represent them. Some have used pre-menstrual syndrome in order to receive better treatment. Others have resorted to the Svengali Defense, pretending to be "dependent," "misled" or "influenced" and blaming their male acquaintances for crimes they themselves committed.

Provided the perpetrator is a woman, even the most malicious of crimes are capable of being diminished or dismissed as acts of devotion. This is made evident by the aforementioned case of acquitted female Nazi doctors and nurses. In places where women are locked up together with men, they enjoy privileges. And in places where they are locked up separately, women also enjoy privileges. All this applies to retributive justice, i.e. situations in which men and women are accused of having committed crimes and are facing trial and punishment. As we shall presently see, though, it is even truer when men and women are confronted not by the justice system but by each other.

4. Women vs. Men

Cases in which men find themselves accused by women have a long and dishonorable history. Already in the Old Testament the normal rules of evidence — which required that, to establish a fact, two witnesses were needed — were suspended in rape cases. Provided only that the alleged act took place "in the country" and not in a town, it was *presumed* that a betrothed woman had cried out but that there had been nobody around to come to her aid.[98] The same was also true of Byzantine law.[99]

Similarly, during the late middle and early Modern Ages, wife-beaters were frowned upon by the community.[100] Conversely, men whose wives beat them might be humiliated in a festival known as *charivari*.[101] In medieval England, proportionally more than three times as many men as women — 50 percent, compared to 15 percent — convicted for killing people of the other sex were

---

[98] *Deuteronomy*, 22.25-6.

[99] Laiou, "Sex, Consent and Coercion in Byzantium," pp. 165, 188.

[100] David W. Sabean, *Property, Family and Production in Neckarhausen, 1700-1870*, Cambridge, Cambridge University Press, 1990, p. 191.

[101] Suzanne Steinmetz, "The Battered Husband Syndrome," *Victimology*, 2, 1977, p. 499; Fletcher, *Sex, Gender and Subordination*, p. 271.

executed.[102] A famous 18th-century English law ordained that a husband beating his wife should use a rod or switch no thicker than the base of his right thumb. This law is often quoted as an example of what some wicked men permitted other wicked men to do to their wives. Yet its purpose was just the opposite — namely, to impose a limit on those things. The proof of this particular pudding is in the eating. In rural England, a husband convicted of beating his wife and breaking the peace was fined. If, on the other hand, it was the wife who was found guilty, *he* would also be fined, this time for having failed to restrain her.[103] Meanwhile, wives' right to resort to any instrument to beat their husbands was taken for granted. Islamic tradition is governed by a similar logic.[104]

In cases involving violence between men and women, the rationale for treating men more harshly than women was their superior physical strength. In cases involving sexual acts, the rationale was men's supposed greater sexual aggressiveness, including their ability to commit rape, as well as their greater physical strength. Being rooted in biology, physical strength cannot be historically constructed, and hence it should come as no surprise that most present-day courts see things much as their predecessors did. He we shall proceed in three stages. First we shall examine cases involving sexual harassment, assault (committed against adults, not children), and rape. Second we shall take a look at cases involving domestic violence. Third we shall deal with divorce, the assumption being that it often results from the aforementioned two offenses.

Over the past several decades, sexual harassment has turned into a growth industry. Right from the beginning, it was regarded as self-evident that practically all harassers are male and practically all victims female. Indeed, the Equal Opportunity Commission, wishing "to avoid cumbersome use of both masculine and feminine pronouns," decided it would "refer to harassers as males and victims as females" in the documents that it published.[105] Today the United States has strict laws prohibiting the use of anything but gender-neutral language in job advertisements and the like. Clearly, therefore, discrimination is only a problem as long as it is directed against women.

---

[102] Given, *Society and Homicide*, pp. 48, 117, 134-49.

[103] John R. Gillis, *For Better, for Worse*, p. 76.

[104] See Muhammad Ali, *Translation of the Holy Quran*, p. 86 footnote 5.

[105] Equal Employment Opportunity Commission, *Policy Guidance on Current Issues of Sexual Harassment*, No. N-915-050, March 1990, p. 3.

Since almost anything — and the absence of almost anything — can constitute harassment, ascertaining exactly how many women have been victimized is very difficult. Likewise, since reports about men being harassed are said to have "a 'man bites dog' ring to them,"[106] ascertaining exactly how many men have been victimized is even more difficult. Whatever the latter figure — and the estimates range from 15 percent to 60 percent — it is clear that men claiming to have suffered from so-called reverse sexual harassment stand a very small chance of being vindicated in court. Homosexuality aside, in practice sexual harassment is an offense only to the extent that it is committed by men against women.

The fact that a man who complains about sexual assault is more likely to be laughed out of court than to win his case is probably a major reason why such cases are also extremely rare. Until the 1970s, sexual assault as a legal category barely existed. Introduced specifically in order to deal with cases when penetration was *not* achieved,[107] it has since achieved star status. Contemporary women are constantly being exhorted to report any sexual assaults to which they have been subjected. As a result, those who do so are very likely to be believed. The reception most women receive stands in stark contrast to what men, including young men, encounter. As one female researcher put it, their complaints are said to be "guffaw engendering" and likely to be mocked "to the hilt."[108] For example, when filmwriter Lara Flynn-Boyl wanted to do a film about a female psychiatrist who had turned her male patients into sex slaves, she could not find a producer.[109]

Everything said about sexual harassment and sexual assault applies *a fortiori* to rape. Rape is usually defined as sexual assault — itself defined as a sexual act committed against the victim's will — with penetration achieved. The result is that a woman, not having a penis, can hardly be accused of rape to begin with. So biased in favor of women is the law of most countries that, until recently, it did not even admit the possibility that a man might be raped by another man.[110] Again, the conclusion is clear: In our Western society, and by no means only in our Western society, rape is considered a crime exclusively, or almost exclusively, when it is committed by a man against a woman.

---

[106] See Andrea P. Baridon and David R. Eyler, *Working Together: The New Rules and Realities for Managing Men and Women at Work*, New York, McGraw-Hill, 1994, p. 127.
[107] See Belknap, *The Invisible Woman,* p. 265.
[108] Levit, *The Gender Line*, pp. 109, 113.
[109] See (in Hebrew) *Yediot Acharonot*, Arutzim, 9.2.2001, p. 15.
[110] Baer, *Women in American Law*, p. 258.

The tendency to ignore all forms of rape except those committed by men against women is rooted in prevalent stereotypes as to what constitutes a woman and what constitutes a man. First, women continue to be seen as gentle, inoffensive creatures. Second, very often it is assumed that abuse, as long as it is committed against men — even, some would say, young men — is not abuse at all. Third, since men cannot become pregnant, the consequences both to the victim and to society at large are supposed to be less serious. Concerning the validity of the first two explanations, no words need be wasted. Concerning the third, it is worth noting that, even when the victim is a woman, the severity of the consequences can vary substantially. A woman who is sexually experienced, or who does not resist the attack (thereby reducing the likelihood of the rapist using violence and minimizing her own chances of being injured), will suffer less than some others. Another variable is community support — the more it supports a woman who has been raped, the lesser her sufferings will be. Yet society *still* treats such cases much more gravely than those committed against men.[111]

Discrimination against men is even more blatant in cases involving so-called date rape. Any discussion of the topic ought to begin by noting that, by some definitions and for some age groups, date rape comprises roughly 97 percent of all alleged rapes.[112] Beginning in the 1970s, feminists began claiming that rape is a crime involving not sex but violence.[113] By the same logic, since date rape hardly ever involves violence, properly speaking most cases are not rape at all.

In the days when the Inquisition hunted witches, an underlying assumption was that the latter had it in their power to harm witnesses and judges who, accordingly, had to be protected from them.[114] At a time when men are being accused of sexual assault and rape, it is often assumed that those men have the power to influence their accusers. Apparently they have such a compelling presence that, by merely attending the court proceedings in which their fate will be decided, they can drive the woman who accuses them of sexual assault or rape to relive her experience, burst into tears and become distracted. To prevent

---

[111] According to Patricia Lucie, "Discrimination Against Males in the USA," in McLean and Burrows, *The Legal Relevance of Gender*, p. 228.

[112] According to Suzanne S. Ageton, *Sexual Assault Among Adolescents*, Lexington, MA, Heath, 1983, p. 155.

[113] See Brownmiller, *Against Our Will*, p. 377, where rape is defined as "falling midway between robbery and assault."

[114] Kramer and Sprenger, *Malleus Maleficarum*, p. 228.

such an unfortunate experience, but also because distracted people make bad witnesses and may fail to convince juries, the accusers have to be protected from the accused. This is true even if the latter has never set his eyes on the victim since the alleged act; and even if he was remanded in prison until his trial. Indeed, one reason why he may be so remanded is precisely to protect her. Needless to say, this reading of the law is based, once again, on the assumption that even while women demand equality, they remain weak and helpless in relation to men.

Too often, the need to protect victims means that the woman who makes the accusation cannot be subjected to the kind of cross-examination normally considered necessary in court. Depending on the country in which a trial takes place, the requirement for corroboration may also be dropped. In such cases, therefore, the issue is decided solely on the basis of the victim's own testimony.[115] To make it even easier for a woman to accuse men with impunity, inquiries concerning her prior sexual behavior — whether, for example, she likes to drink before having sex, or whether she likes to walk about half-naked — have been ruled out of order. Sometimes the determination *not* to see what women are doing is taken to the point of absurdity. For example, in Britain the law does not even recognize the possibility that she may commit indecent exposure.[116] Are we to understand that only men's private parts are indecent?

Historically speaking, a good way to rebut the cry of rape was to accuse a woman of promiscuity. It is therefore ironic that, at the same time the so-called sexual revolution was supposedly making women behave more promiscuously than ever, the forward march of history was turned back. Courts were prevented from looking into the sexual history of women who accused men of sexually assaulting or raping them. The law's treatment of women who engage in group sex is illustrative. The very fact that more than one man was present when the alleged sexual assault or rape took place is now taken as evidence that she was intimidated. In other words, the woman was able to make her complaint heard *because* she had been promiscuous; should the accusation stick, then it may well lead to a verdict for gang rape.

Whereas inquiring into a woman's sexual behavior — even her sexual behavior *during* the alleged incident — is decreed humiliating, irrelevant, or both, the situation of the man or men being accused is exactly the opposite. Precisely because rape and sexual assault usually take place in private, the *first*

[115] See Belknap, *The Invisible Woman*, p. 265

[116] Greer, *The Whole Woman*, p. 289.

thing prosecutors do is to look into the history of the accused and establish a "pattern." As might be expected, this method will often lead to some interesting detective work. As might be expected, too, it can cause women to step forward years and even decades after an alleged incident and claim to have been assaulted or raped. Once such a woman has been located, armies of psychologists, social workers and police officers, many of them female, will coax, cajole and convince her to gather her courage and complain. Once enough women — the minimum number needed seems to be three — have done so, obtaining a conviction is child's play. Thus men are expected to behave according to a pattern; but women may do what they please.

In some societies, ancient Rome in particular, a man who had been accused of rape but found innocent was allowed to retaliate by bringing a suit for defamation.[117] Not so in most modern countries, where women are often considered the only persons with a reputation to lose. As a result, whereas the identity of the victim is concealed either by court order or by law, that of the accused is published. Once this happens, his good name is gone, and it will never be completely restored, even should he live to 100. This is true even if, after months and perhaps years of judicial torture, he is acquitted. When Judge Clarence Thomas said that he would "rather die" than admit to having harassed Anita Hill, he knew what he was talking about.[118] Some pundits argue that modern societies should penalize women who have failed to prove their case.[119] As such a development is rather unlikely, the parade of accusations can be expected to continue.

Like sexual harassment and sexual abuse, the legal offense known as domestic violence is largely a creation of the past several decades. As with sexual harassment and sexual abuse, the charge of domestic violence has the potential to enable women to get at men. To help women in so doing, some police departments in the United States specifically prohibit policemen called upon to deal with such cases from fully investigating the facts, as they would with any other allegation. Groups of self-styled battered women have even won court cases against police officers who did *not* arrest their alleged batterers.[120] Simply by saying she *feels* threatened, a woman can have any man arrested — even if she later admits that the threat was not meant seriously, and or that the claim was false. Another word on her part, this time in court, and a restraining

[117] Gardner, *Woman in Roman Law and Society*, p. 121.
[118] Quoted in *Chicago Tribune*, 13.10.1991.
[119] See Paglia, *Vamps and Tramps*, p. 48.
[120] Belknap, *The Invisible Woman*, pp. 159, 187.

order is issued. Needless to say, a man who has lost his home in this way is still obliged to support the woman who threw him out. Worse still, the court that issues the order is not the same as the one responsible for visitation. Therefore, from then on, merely to be allowed to see his children may well cost a man a small fortune.[121]

Like sexual assault and rape, domestic violence is usually perceived as something men perpetrate against women. However, this assumption is not borne out by the facts. In a sample of 55,000 U.S. Army soldiers, between 39 percent and 40 percent of the women reported having been involved in domestic violence at one point or another. The figure for men was between 29 percent and 43 percent. The most common pattern — some two-thirds of all cases — was for people of both sexes to hit each other reciprocally. Interestingly, however, almost *twice* as many female soldiers admitted to being sole aggressors — that is, to hitting without being hit back — than did male ones. This was quite possibly so, it must be acknowledged, because the women knew that, for them, the admission would not carry any consequences.[122]

What is true of the military is equally true for society at large. In 1975, and again in 1985, the National Institute of Mental Health studied a national sample of 2,143 married and cohabiting couples. In both years, the number of attacks which spouses of either sex directed at the other was practically equal.[123] Another study discovered that, each year, American wives were one-fifth *more* likely to "severely attack" their husbands than vice versa.[124] In Canada, according to yet another study, the discrepancy is greater still. Of the women interviewed, 6.2 percent admitted to having beaten up their partners during the preceding year, as compared to 2.5 percent of men. In the same study, more women than men admitted to having used "severe" violence, and more women than men admitted to having used a knife or a gun.[125] And the more severe the

---

[121] James Ptacek, *Battered Women in the Courtroom*, Boston, Northeastern University Press, 1999, p. 124.

[122] Peter H. Neidig, "Executive Summary Family Advocacy Prevention/Survey Project Update: Overview and Preliminary Findings," Behavioral Science Associates, unpublished paper prepared for U.S. Army, Stony Brook, NY, 1993, p. 3.

[123] M. Straus and R. Gelles, "Societal Change and Change in Family Violence from 1975 to 1985 as Revealed by Two National Surveys," *Journal of Marriage and the Family*, 48, August 1986, pp. 465-79.

[124] M. Straus, "Physical Assaults by Wives: A Major Social Problem," in R. J. Gelles and D. R. Loseke, eds., *Current Controversies on Family Violence*, Newbury Park, CA, Sage, 1983, p. 74.

[125] Reported in E. Lupri, "Harmonie und Aggression: Über die Dialektik Ehelicher Gewalt," *Kölner Zeitschrift für Soziologie und Sozialpsychologie*, 42, 3, 1990, pp. 479-501.

violence, the more likely it is to be directed by women against men. One study of police records found that women were three times *more* likely to threaten or use weapons, such as knives and guns, against their spouses than men.[126]

So-called reverse spouse abuse — note the terminology, which makes clear that the real thing refers to men abusing women — is the most under-reported form of all domestic violence.[127] Some of the reasons for this may be methodological. It stands to reason that at least some men are being hit or pushed, have things thrown at them or are kicked or whipped, just as some women are. But this does not prevent most investigators from ignoring that possibility. They assume that men's "accounts of the violence cannot be taken at face value," while registering what women say as if it were gospel truth.[128] For example, 30 percent of women questioned in one emergency room between 1976 and 1979 blamed their injuries on domestic abuse. Since men were not questioned on the matter, they could not have reported it even if it had taken place.[129] Conversely, when one study *did* compare the percentage of people of both sexes admitted to hospital emergency rooms as a result of injuries allegedly caused by domestic violence, it turned out that there was little difference between men and women.[130]

Another reason why female-on-male domestic violence is under-reported is the lenient way such cases are treated. In the movies, women who commit violence against men are often applauded by the audience. The reverse happens rarely, if ever.[131] In real life, men who dare to complain are likely to be despised, derided, or both. One does not have to be a criminologist or sociologist to know that, as long as it is perpetrated by a woman against a man,

---

[126] M. McLeod, "Women Against Men: An Examination of Domestic Violence Based on an Analysis of Official Data and National Victimization Data," *Justice Quarterly*, 1, 1984, p. 185.
[127] See Flowers, *Women and Criminality*, p. 111-2.
[128] For men disbelieved, Ptacek, see *Battered Women in the Courtroom*, p. 71; for women believed, see Jalna Hanmer, "Out of Control: Men, Violence and Family Life," in Popay et al., eds., *Men, Gender Divisions, and Welfare*, pp. 128-45; also see William R. Blunt et al., "Intimate Abuse Within an Incarcerated Female Population," in Culliver, ed., *Female Criminality*, pp. 413-68.
[129] S. V. McLeer and R. Anwar, "A Study of Battered Women Presenting in an Emergency Department," *American Journal of Public Health*, 79, 1, January 1989, pp. 65-6.
[130] W. Goldberg and M. Tomlanovich, "Domestic Violence Victims in the Emergency Department," *Journal of the American Medical Association*, 251, 24, 28, 9.6.1984, pp. 359-64.
[131] C. S. Greenblat, "A Hit Is a Hit Is a Hit... or Is It? Approval and Tolerance of the Use of Physical Force by Spouses," in D. Finkelohr et al., eds., *The Dark Side of Families: Current Family Evidence Research*, Beverly Hills, CA, Sage, 1983, pp. 235-60.

domestic violence "tends to be... victim precipitated."[132] Stripped of jargon, this means that a woman is much more likely to be regarded as having acted in self-defense. This applies even when, as happens in no fewer than 70 percent of all known cases,[133] the violence is applied at a time when the man is helpless. Lorena Bobbitt was not the only woman whose male partner was asleep at the time of the attack. Other men were drunk or bound.

As former New York governor Mario Cuomo, the father of current New York Governor Andrew Cuomo, said when he decided to pardon a woman who shot her estranged husband after driving several hundred miles, when it comes to women who kills "there are no rules."[134] In a single act of clemency in 1990, the governor of Ohio, Richard Celeste, pardoned no fewer than 27 women convicted of murdering their husbands. The leniency exercised toward women who have killed their relatives may explain why 15.9 percent of imprisoned female killers, but only 9.6 percent of male ones, are where they are for that offense.[135] It may also explain why adult women are 24 percent *more* likely to kill their children than are men, and why under-age women are 32 percent more likely to kill relatives, small children included, than are under-age men.[136]

So strong is the presumption that "mothers don't kill" that it has even formed the basis for a legal defense strategy. One offender who resorted to such a defense, a Virginia female convicted in 2000 of cooking her baby in a microwave oven, got off with a mere five years in jail.[137] With good behavior, she could have gotten off in three. Later she was joined by several more microwave-mothers, all of whom cited various psychological symptoms in the hope of receiving similarly lenient treatment.[138]

Thus, when a woman accuses a man to whom she is not married of using violence against her, or of sexual harassment, or sexual assault, or rape, then the man in question is disproportionally likely to suffer punishment. When a

---

[132] See Donald Nicolson, "Telling Tales: Gender Discrimination, Gender Construction and Battered Women Who Kill," (1953), in Jo Bridgeman and Susan Millins, eds., *Feminist Perspectives on Law: Law's Engagement with the Female Body*, London, Sweet & Maxwell, 1998, p. 630.

[133] See C. Martin, "Getting Even? Women Who Kill in Domestic Encounters," *Justice Quarterly*, 5, 1, 1988, pp. 40-1.

[134] Quoted in Naomi Wolf, *Fire with Fire*, p. 199.

[135] U.S Department of Justice, *Survey of State Prison Inmates—1991*, p. 3.

[136] Chesney-Lind, *The Female Offender*, p. 40.

[137] ABC News. (13.12.2000). "Woman Sentenced for Microwaving Baby," retrieved from http://abcnews.go.com/US/story?id=94713&page=1

[138] See Bad Breeders. (27.6.2011). "Ka Yang nuked her newborn," retrieved from http://badbreeders.net/tag/elizabeth-renee-otte/

woman accuses a man of domestic abuse, then the outcome is likely be divorce as well as punishment. And with divorce come issues related to child custody, several of which deserve further examination here.

Debate over which sex deserves custody of children in divorce cases is probably just as old as the institution of marriage itself. Sometimes children were entrusted to the parent of their sex — in other words, boys went with their father and girls with their mother. In other cases, the father got custody of both boys and girls above a certain age, the reason being that he and not the mother would be responsible for feeding them. As noted previously, some societies, including Christian ones, regarded adultery as the only grounds on which men could divorce their wives. In those societies, in other words, a divorced woman was adulterous by definition. Being adulterous, she was considered unfit to raise her children and often even to see them.[139] On the other hand, illegitimate children always belonged to their mother. That, in turn, meant that the father was not responsible for feeding them.[140]

Until 1800 or so, it was believed that the thing children needed most was economic support and an education to enable them to stand on their own feet. Beginning in the early 19th century, however, the emphasis was put on a child's need for "love." To separate children from their mothers began to be constructed as "cruel" behavior. In England,[141] from 1839 onward a separated mother could petition for access to her children. If they were under 8 years old, she could ask for custody. In 1873, the Infant Custody Act raised the age to 16 and the rule that denied custody and access to adulterous mothers was abolished. As fathers lost ground before the onslaught of motherly love, clearly the day when women would claim, and obtain, almost automatic custody over young children in particular could not be far off. This, in fact, was what happened. Beginning around 1890, notwithstanding evidence that mothers were much more likely to abuse and kill babies than fathers, the idea that the bond between mother and child was the strongest of all asserted itself.

The result was that, both in Britain and the United States, women began to obtain custody in practically all cases. Almost a full century would pass before

---

139 McKendrick, "Home Demand and Economic Growth," p. 155.

140 Shirley W. Kram and Neil A. Frank, *The Law of Child Custody*, Lexington, MA, Lexington Books, 1982, p. 79.

141 Doggett, *Marriage, Wife Beating and the Law in Victorian England*, p. 102; Juliet Mitchell, and Jack Goody, "Feminism, Fatherhood and the Family in Britain," in Ann Oakley and Juliet Mitchell, eds., *Who is Afraid of Feminism? Seeing Through the Backlash*, New York, New Press, 1997, pp. 218-20.

the United States moved to rectify the imbalance, with the Supreme Court declaring in 1979 that discrimination against fathers involved in custody cases was unconstitutional. It was, however, to no avail; to this day, most courts still use the idea of "primary caretaker" to grant custody to women. Taking care of a child's economic needs, which is what most fathers do, simply does not carry a corresponding amount of weight in court. Fathers who ask for custody are often interrogated about their involvement with the child, but the same line of questioning is rarely applied to mothers.[142] Apparently even to ask a mother whether she knows the name of her child's teacher is considered, if not technically out of order, at least reprehensible.

The results, not surprisingly, point to an overwhelming bias against entrusting children to their fathers. In California, for example, more than 10 times as many mothers as fathers receive sole custody.[143] In the words of one expert, "[fathers] asking for joint custody is like asking for the sun and the moon."[144] As a result, men who separate from their children's mother almost always face loss of custody. Since each partner can now obtain a divorce even without the other's consent, fatherhood has been made conditional. On pain of losing their children, many men have been trapped in their marriages — even if it was the wife who was violent, and even if she lost her mind not just once a month but all the time.

If the men *were* separated from their wives, and if the children *were* taken away from them, then who would pay for those children's upkeep? Before 1840, divorced men usually obtained custody. In return they were obliged to support their children. Once motherly love had triumphed and men no longer stood a chance of obtaining custody, they were still obliged to do so. No was that the end of the matter. In the 1960s, growing numbers of men and women started living together without being officially married. The result was a very steep rise in the number of children who, by the standards applied during most of history until then, were illegitimate and thus not entitled to be supported by their fathers in case the couple broke up. Driven partly by concern for the children, and partly by pressure brought about by feminist groups, the state soon rose to the occasion. The traditional distinction between legitimate and illegitimate children was all but abolished. On the one hand, fathers were obliged to pay regardless of whether or not they had been married to the mothers. On the other, women retained an almost absolute right to custody over

[142] Lucie, "Discrimination Against Males in the USA," p. 226.

[143] Levit, *The Gender Line*, p. 120.

[144] Seidenberg, *The Father's Emergency Guide*, p. 39.

the children in question. As so often, women could have their cake and eat it too.

As has been said, the new laws turned men into “divorceable sperm donors and disposable cheque-signing machines.”[145] Is it any wonder that, discriminated against in every possible way, many men try to evade their financial responsibilities? This is particularly true if they are denied the right to visit their children, as more than one-third of divorced men in the United States are.[146] No wonder that, over time, most divorced men lose contact with their children, to say nothing of the effect on the children themselves.[147] Women, in turn, did, as they always have done, what they could to obtain payments. In this they had the law on their side, even if its enforcement was not always effective. However, women who for one reason or another could not compel fathers to pay did not have to unduly worry. In most modern countries, the Social Security system has picked up where deadbeat fathers left off. Even in the United States, where the welfare state is not nearly as developed as it is in its European counterparts, such a woman could always sign up for Aid to Families with Dependent Children or its successor program, Temporary Assistance for Needy Families.

In short, there is no question that, facing a man in court, a woman very often finds the dice loaded in her favor. In cases involving sex, to quote one British judge, “charges... are so easily made, but so difficult to refute.”[148] This is all the more so because the act normally takes place in private, where, absent witnesses, it is her word against his. This is all the more so because, under normal circumstances, it brings pleasure to both sides. What one side understands as harmless flirtation the other may construct as harassment and worse. These characteristics have not prevented numerous men from being convicted of rapes that they never committed. Beginning around 1970, moreover, a whole category of offenses went on the books involving cases in which penetration was *not* achieved. To protect women — in other words, to enable them to make their accusations stick without risk to themselves — the rules of arrest were changed. Often policemen are actually prohibited from establishing the facts of the case. Due process is put aside or perverted, and the

---

[145] D. Cohen, "It's a Guy Thing," *Guardian Weekend*, 14.5.1996, p. 30.

[146] Sylvia Ann Hewett and Cornel West, "A Parents' Bill of Rights Would End a 30 Years War," *The New York Times*, 12.4.1998.

[147] See Judith S. Wallerstein et al., *The Unexpected Legacy of Divorce*, New York, Hyperion, 2000, pp. 136, 250-3.

[148] See Toner, *The Facts of Rape*, p. 218.

media permitted, if not actually ordered, to publicize the name of the alleged perpetrator only. Only those who have gone through the process can imagine the injustice and suffering it causes. As long as the victims are men, though, few care.

What is true in cases involving sex is equally true in those involving violence. One of the greatest feminist "achievements" has been to make many people believe that rape is centered on violence, rather than on sex. Yet at the same time, the statistics show that women are almost as likely to engage in domestic violence as men — and indeed, are *more* likely to engage in severe domestic violence.[149] But whereas a man convicted of having battered his spouse is quite likely to end up in prison, a woman who has done the same can expect to enter a shelter and live at taxpayers' expense. The paradox is that, according to one survey, 77 percent of battered women admitted to having been violent toward their spouse during the year before admission to the shelter. Perhaps even more telling, 58 percent admitted to having been violent during the six months after leaving .[150] In one survey conducted in a Kentucky shelter, 38 percent admitted they had been the ones who had initiated the violence.[151] In England, 62 percent of women in a shelter admitted that the violence was mutual.[152] It seems that, to obtain lodging and a sympathetic ear, all a woman has to do is attack the man with whom she lives.

When it comes to family law, the bias in favor of women is stronger still. That may be one reason why eight out of 10 divorce lawsuits are served by women.[153] Some of the above-mentioned cases may have slightly tarnished the idea that mothers are particularly fond of their children. On the whole, however, the bias against men persists. In an age when many women leave the home for work, one could justifiably argue that the *only* thing that still remains from much-maligned Victorian ideals of domesticity is the tendency of courts to deny custody while saddling divorced men with child support payments. As has so often been the case, women are able to get the best of both worlds.

---

[149] See Murray Strauss et al., *Behind Closed Doors: Violence in the American Family*, New Brunswick, NJ, Transaction, 2006 [1981].

[150] J. Giles-Sims, *Wife Battering: A Systems Theory Approach*, New York, Guilford Press, 1983, p. 49.

[151] C. A. Hornung et al., "Status Relationships in Marriage Risk Factors in Spouse Abuse," *Journal of Marriage and the Family*, 43, 1981, pp. 675-92.

[152] See Cook, *Abused Men*, p. 121.

[153] Maureen Greene, "Men and Marriage," *Woman*, 14.1.1984.

5. Conclusions

The legal advantages that women enjoy over men are far too numerous to be recounted here. The obvious bias — and, quite often, blatant misguidedness —inherent in many relevant laws are perhaps best captured by a law that was on the books in Oklahoma until the mid-1970s. Under state law, the sale of beer was prohibited to females under 18 and males under 21. As a result, a 20-year-old male could invite a young woman of the exact same age to have a drink, but could not have one himself. The clear bias is made all the more absurd by the fact that women, owing to their smaller body mass and possibly to other factors, are more susceptible to alcohol than men. Indeed, had the law been designed to assist a young man seduce his female date by getting her drunk, it could have thought of no better way. Yet so firmly entrenched is the legal principle that favors women over men that the Supreme Court had a very difficult time striking down the Oklahoma law. In the end the nation's highest court did so, but only after instituting an entirely new "middle tier" of rationality ranking between "minimum rationality" and "strict scrutiny."[154]

In nearly every area of society, a signed contract must be honored and, if necessary, enforced by the courts and the police, unless fraud can be shown to have been involved. Not so, however, when it comes to surrogate motherhood. To quote one female expert on the subject: "Currently a contracted mother may breach a contract in a least four ways. She may (1) refuse, after all, to be inseminated; (2) either abort or fail to abort the fetus against the commissioning couple's wishes; (3) negligently harm the fetus during the pregnancy; and/or (4) refuse to give up the child at birth."[155] The willingness to permit women to renege on their commitments is equally evident in custody cases. A man who has signed a notarized agreement in which he surrenders custody can wave his child or children goodbye. Not so a woman, in whose case a similar document may not be binding.[156]

Anecdotes plucked from every period in America's history can easily give the impression that "discrimination" itself only exists as long as it works against women. An excellent case in point was that of Joe Hogan. In 1982, he

[154] See Lucie, "Discrimination Against Males in the USA," p. 220.

[155] Rosemary Tong, *Feminist Thought: A Comprehensive Introduction*, Boulder, CO, Westview, 1997, p. 93.

[156] Seidenberg, *The Father's Emergency Guide*, p. 2.

asked to be admitted to the nursing program at the University of Mississippi, and was rejected. The Mississippi Supreme Court finally ruled in his favor, but not because the university had been discriminating against men. Instead, the argument used was that, by admitting only women, the school had lent "credibility to the old view that women, not men, should become nurses, and [made] the assumption that nursing is a field for women a self-fulfilling prophecy."[157] In other words, the court granted Hogan's plea not because he was discriminated against as a man, but because the prohibition discriminated against women.

In fact, so strong is the social bias in favor of women that it even affects legislation intended to establish "equality" between the sexes. For example, when the United States Senate passed the Equal Rights Amendment in 1972, it added a clause known as the "Hayden Rider" after its sponsor, Carl Hayden. The clause ruled that the rights amendment "shall not be constituted to impair any rights, benefits, or exemptions now or hereafter conferred by law, upon persons of the female sex" — in other words, that it should not deny the privileges that women already enjoyed.[158] A similar logic prevails in India, a country that accounts for one-sixth of the world's population. In interpreting that country's Constitution, Chief Justice M. C. Chagla held that a state was permitted to discriminate in favor of women against men. However, it could not discriminate in favor of men against women.[159]

Today, in nearly every country women's legal privileges are at least as extensive as they have always been. As certain authors never tire of telling us, in patriarchal societies it is men who lay down the law. Since all known societies have been patriarchal, one can only conclude that women should thank men for their privileges. This interpretation is supported by the fact that the more "feminine" the woman's behavior at the time she is arrested or put on trial, the more lenient the treatment she can expect.[160] In court, her best tactic is to wear a skirt — not, however, a miniskirt — and a blouse. The latter, while clearly showing that she is a woman, should avoid any hint of cleavage. The next, all-but-obligatory step is to burst into tears at an appropriate moment during the trial. That is what both Lorena Bobbitt and the microwave-oven lady did. Compared with the way they treat women, men have only themselves to

[157] Lucie, "Discrimination Against Males in the USA," p. 225.

[158] Baer, *Women in American Law*, p.56.

[159] Kant, *Women and the Law*, pp. 138, 141

[160] E. H. Steury and N. Frank, "Gender Bias and Pretrial Release: More Pieces of the Puzzle," *Journal of Criminal Justice*, 18, 1990, pp. 417-32.

thank for the way they treat each other. So it has always been, and so, it can confidently be predicted, it will always be.

Chapter 6: In the Maw of Mars

1. The Principle of the Thing

In regard to the way they are raised, the work they do, the economic support they receive, and their position vis-à-vis the law, women have always enjoyed and still enjoy considerable privileges. Likewise, when it comes to fulfilling their obligation to society, women also have enjoyed and still enjoy considerable privileges. The greatest single privilege is that they are hardly ever expected to shed blood for their people.

As is well known, insofar as women do not participate in war they are very often exempt, or supposed to be exempt, from its horrors. As is far less well known, there were and still are certain situations in which women are exempt, or supposed to be exempt, from the horrors of war even though they *do* participate in it. Occasionally one can even find instances when women volunteered for war *because* they were, or believed themselves to be, more or less immune to its horrors. Insofar as life is the most precious commodity of all, it is precisely in war that women's privileges stand out most clearly. So it has always been — and so, let us hope — it will always be.

2. A History of Military Service

A list of all the ways in which society has selected those whom it commanded to fight and die on its behalf would be all but equivalent to a history of civilization. Even when presented in mere outline, such a history shows the way in which women always have been and still are privileged. To the extent that women did not have to participate in war, they were privileged. And to the very limited extent that they did participate in war, they were also privileged.

In the simplest known tribal societies, every adult male was a warrior by definition. This fact is reflected in the Bible, in which a sharp distinction is drawn between men, who are members of the host, and women, who are not.[1] The same applies to many North American Indian languages, where the standard term for "man" is "brave." Men who for one reason or another could not or would not fight were exposed to contempt and derision at the hand of men *and* women. Alternatively, they might declare themselves, or be declared, holy. However, doing so this made their situation even worse; witness the pathetic figure of the priest Charises in the *Iliad*, begging for his daughter's freedom and being sent away empty-handed. In classical Greece, once the popular assembly had declared war, the magistrates would hold a levy. First volunteers were called, then other citizens. The same method was used in Rome, where the standard penalty for willful non-participation in war was death.[2]

In medieval Konstanz, and presumably other European towns as well, "men" — but not women — had to join the militia at the age of 12.[3] In most modern countries, the system under which every able-bodied male citizen is *ipso facto* a warrior and keeps his weapon at home has been obsolete for centuries past. Not so in Switzerland, where it is only now starting to be modified. The Swiss military obliges every man to do a period of service, which is followed by regular refresher training. The system enables the country to maintain armed forces wholly out of proportion to the size of its population. More important for our purpose, it explains why Switzerland waited until 1976 before it finally enfranchised women. Originally women, who were not obliged to bear arms, did not participate in the popular assemblies which themselves consisted of arms-bearing men. For the many years that they were not obliged to bear arms, Swiss women were privileged. After 1976, when they still did not have to bear arms but were entitled to vote, they became doubly privileged.

In empires such as Egypt and China, the bulk of the troops consisted of conscripted peasants. Normally their period of service was timed to coincide with the season when there was little agricultural work to be done. However, should the campaign become extended, then the men might find themselves with the regulars for years on end. Military service was a kind of *corvée*. Such an arrangement still existed in 18th-century Prussia. So harsh was Prussian discipline that it gave rise to the term *Kadavergehorsam*, "corpse-like

---

[1] *Exodus*, 12.36.

[2] See G. R. Watson, *The Roman Soldier*, Ithaca, NY, Cornell University Press, 1969, pp. 120-1.

[3] Wunder, *He Is the Sun, She Is the Moon*, p. 17.

obedience." In wartime deserters might be shot out of hand. Women, as usual, did not share in the joys.

Beginning in some pre-literate societies, a very common method of raising armies was feudal, in the literal sense of the word. "Feudal" comes from *feudum*, or "fief," and the system of distributing land in return for military service was already used by some of the larger and better-organized tribal societies. It rose to prominence in medieval Europe and also in ancient Persia, the Ottoman Empire, and pre-modern Japan.[4] How onerous such service could be is evident from numerous disputes between rulers and vassals. The former were always trying to make the latter do more. The vassals, for their part, insisted that they only had to serve under such and such circumstances, against such and such enemies, and for so and so many days a year.[5] Once again women — even those, and there were always some, who had inherited land and were holding it in their own right — were exempt.

At times, those who received land were not individuals but entire communities. Seeking to strengthen their hold over newly conquered territories, Hellenistic kings established numerous military colonies.[6] Later the Romans used a similar system, both in Italy and elsewhere; that is how many European cities were established. As late as the second half of the 17th century, the Russian, Swedish and Austrian governments still used similar methods.[7] In return for parcels of land, colonists were obliged to do military service. Colonists' sons lived under the same obligation. Thus, men, by virtue of having been born on the king's land, were destined to die for him. As one ancient Egyptian poem put it, "when [a male child] reaches manhood, his bones are scattered."[8] Daughters were exempt, as a matter of course. Nevertheless, as far as can be determined, that fact did not necessarily prevent them from inheriting land.[9]

In more sophisticated societies, and in Europe from the end of the Middle Ages, income from land as a way of maintaining an army was replaced by cash payment. Mercenaries began to be hired for campaigns. Once the fighting was

---

[4] See Gabor Agoston, "Ottoman Warfare in Europe, 1453-1826," in Jeremy Black, ed., *European Warfare, 1453-1815*, New York, St. Martin's Press, 1999, pp. 122, 138, 155.

[5] Philippe Contamine, *War in the Middle Ages*, Oxford, Blackwell, 1988, pp. 78-90.

[6] Getzel M. Cohen, *The Seleucid Colonies*, Wiesbaden, Steiner, 1978, pp. 51-2.

[7] Brian L. Davis, "The Development of Russian Military Power, 1453-1815," in Black, ed., *European Warfare*, p. 165.

[8] Jacques J. Janssen and Rosalind M. Janssen, *Growing Up in Ancient Egypt*, London, Stacey/Rubicon, 1996, pp. 103-4.

[9] Cohen, *The Seleucid Colonies*, p. 51.

over, the hired troops would be discharged. If only because they were often foreigners, such troops were regarded as expendable. An extreme example of this attitude may be found in Thomas More's *Utopia*. Here the fighting was done by a barbaric people known as "Venalians." They were a stand-in for the Swiss, who in More's time were the mercenary people *par excellence*. He called them "filthy scum" and wrote that, the more of them were killed, the better for humanity.[10] Mercenaries' pay was notoriously low and unreliable, which explains why they often deserted, rebelled or switched sides. Many of them ended, if not dead, then mutilated or destitute. Women, of course, never formed part of the system. If they did not enjoy its dubious benefits, at any rate they did not suffer from its disadvantages

In some cases mercenaries ended up by being put on retainer, and their numbers were maintained not merely during war but in peacetime as well. It was in this way that regulars and standing armies emerged. Even some of the oldest known empires, including those of Egypt, Mesopotamia and China, had armies whose cores consisted of regulars. Others maintained smaller bodies of regulars, like the Roman Praetorians, whose task was to guard the capital. In theory, service in a standing army might very well be voluntary. But in practice it was often compulsory, as Voltaire's Candide, having been tricked into joining the "Bulgarian" — read, Prussian — Army, found out to his detriment. Compulsory enlistment was even more common at sea. In Rome, Venice and France, down to the days of Louis XIV, navies got their manpower partly from among slaves and convicts. Even Britain, the least tyrannical among the major powers of the 18th century, regularly used the press gang to obtain sailors. That practice, incidentally, was denounced by none other than Mary Wollstonecraft.[11]

During the first half of the 19th century, some countries, notably France, adopted a system of selective service to find the military manpower they needed.[12] A lottery was held, and youths unlucky enough to be picked were made to serve for as many as six to eight years. It was, however, possible for those who had drawn a *mauvais numero* to buy themselves out by hiring a substitute at a tariff fixed by the state. The system was designed to help members of the middle and upper classes. The resulting economic burden could be quite considerable, equivalent to supporting a laborer for a number of years.

---

[10] Thomas More, *Utopia*, Harmondsworth, Middlesex, Penguin, 1965 [1516], p. 11.

[11] "A Vindication of the Rights of Men," in Janet Todd and Marylin Butler, eds., *The Works of Mary Wollstonecraft*, London, Pickering, vol. 5, p. 15.

[12] John Gooch, *Armies in Europe*, London, Routledge, 1980, p. 52.

Once again, that burden was carried exclusively by men. To put it differently, women were regarded as having won the lottery by virtue of their sex. The possibility of making them pay was never considered, even if they were physically fit, and even if they had property of their own.

Finally, following the example set by the French Revolution in 1792 but largely abandoned after 1815, most countries adopted general conscription from about 1870 onward. The normal period of service was two or three years. So onerous was the burden that it became one of the driving forces behind the emigration of young European men to the United States.[13] Some mutilated themselves to avoid service. In principle, and often in practice as well, conscription was capable of taking every single man who was physically fit. And during total war, it often took men who were not physically fit. A famous cartoon by the German expressionist painter Georg Grosz graphically illustrates the point: It shows a corpse that has been dug up from its grave being examined by doctors and declared *Kriegsverwendungsfähig*, or "capable of being used in war."[14] In World War II, the Wehrmacht had entire battalions comprised of deaf soldiers, of soldiers who suffered from stomach ulcers, and of soldiers who were under 18 years old. Needless to say, women were not affected by any of this. As developments after 1970 were to show, one reason why conscription could be adopted was precisely *because* women were unaffected by any of this.

Precisely *because* Israeli women are the only ones in history to have been conscripted for military service, their privileges are more pronounced than anywhere else.[15] Compared with men, Israeli women find it easier to avoid the draft, with the result that fewer of them actually serve. They can obtain a discharge by simply declaring that they are religious; merely questioning a woman's beliefs is considered injurious to her dignity and is prohibited by law. Unlike religious men, being exempt does not oblige them to spend time studying in a *yeshiva*, or religious high school, or to refrain from making a living while so engaged. Married women, too, are exempt. As Prime Minister David Ben-Gurion put it when he passed the relevant legislation in 1949, men

[13] Bebel, *Die Frau und der Sozialismus*, p. 163.

[14] Uwe M. Schneider, *George Grosz: Der Künstler in seiner Gesellschaft*, Cologne, Dumont, 1977, p. 123.

[15] See Martin van Creveld, *The Sword and the Olive: A Critical History of the Israel Defense Force*, New York, Public Affairs, 1998, pp. 120-3.

could serve first and marry later. However, tearing away "an 18-year-old newlywed" from her husband's embrace was little short of a crime.[16]

Female conscripts in Israel serve for 22 months, 14 months less than their male comrades. The vast majority of them holds comfortable jobs and spends practically every night at home, rather than at a base. Following a 1997 proposal by the Knesset's women's lobby, female conscripts were given extra pay to enable them to buy contraceptives. Since female conscripts are by definition single, it was almost as if they were being encouraged to be promiscuous at public expense. In addition, female soldiers are specifically exempted from some jobs. One is driving trucks, because doing so is heavy work, and drivers are always the first to be called up and the last to go home. Another is cooking, considered hard and unpleasant work. And once they have done their duty as conscripts, Israeli women hardly ever serve in the reserves, as do nearly all their male comrades. This means they are free from a duty which, over the course of several decades, can take up several years of Israeli men's lives. In my entire 40 years as a teacher at Israeli Universities, not a single woman has missed a single class for this reason.

In 2000, after decades when not a single woman served in a combat unit, female soldiers began to be permitted to serve in them.[17] Even then, the Knesset hastened to add a rider that no woman could be *obliged* to serve in such a unit. Women, in other words, can and do have it both ways. The outcome is plainly visible on the countless war memorials that dot the Israeli countryside. He who looks for women's names will do so almost entirely in vain. That is true even of the 1948 War of Independence, the one major Israeli conflict in which some women did fight.[18] Nor does it look as if this situation will change. When a female fighter was badly injured in the summer of 2001, Israeli feminists did not celebrate. Instead, a well-known female journalist wrote that military women should compete with military men with brain, not brawn — in other words, that women should get the cushy jobs while men fight and die.[19]

The fact that, from the beginning of history, hardly any women has been obliged to serve does not mean that field armies were altogether without women. Rather, such armies have always been trailed by female "camp-

---

[16] David Ben-Gurion, *Yichud Ve'yeud: Devarim al Bitchon Yisrael*, Tel Aviv, Maarachot, 1971, p. 79.

[17] See on this Martin van Creveld, *Men, Women and War*, London, Cassell, 2001, p. 208.

[18] See van Creveld, *The Sword and the Olive*, p. 99.

[19] *Yediot Acharonot*, 6.8.01, p. 5.

followers."[20] From the time of Scipio Africanus to that of Napoleon two millennia later, they carried out many of the tasks which, today, are performed by the so-called rear services. These tasks included provisioning, cooking, laundering, nursing and, of course, providing the troops with paid or unpaid sex. At times the number of women on campaigns approached that of the men. To be sure, going into the field was not all fun and games. Yet female camp-followers differed from soldiers in that they were invariably volunteers. Not being bound by martial law, they were permitted to leave at will. Now it should be remembered that, from ancient Rome through the end of World War II, by far the single most important crime for which soldiers were executed was desertion. Women, simply because they were women, were exempt. To anybody in the least bit familiar with military life, a greater privilege could hardly be imagined.

Here and there a handful of women took up arms, fought and died. Most, it is worth noting, were transvestites — namely, women who dressed as men and took to soldiering either temporarily or permanently, as a way of life.[21] Some did what they did out of love for some man. Others were driven by economic reasons; others still, by a lust for adventure. Particularly during America's Revolutionary War and the Napoleonic Wars, such women's motives were sometimes mixed with patriotism. The way contemporaries saw it, on occasion they themselves were mixed up. Not only did they put on male clothes and adopt the most male profession of all, some also tried to marry and bed other women.

Disguised women whose true identity became known were discharged. Women who voluntarily revealed themselves as such were also discharged, though a few cases are known when, begging not to be sent home and pulling strings, they were permitted to stay and even put under special protection.[22] Thus, to the very limited extent that women did enlist, they could leave the colors at any time they chose. Often women were sent home at a time when, having committed some offense, they were scheduled to receive punishment, such as flogging and the like. Commanders simply did not want to punish women as barbarously as they did men. Once again, to anybody familiar with military life, a greater privilege could scarcely be imagined.

---

[20] See van Creveld, *Men, Women and War*, pp. 88-98.

[21] See Rudolf M. Dekker and Lotte C. van de Pol, *The Tradition of Female Transvestism in Early Modern Europe*, New York, St. Martin's, 1989.

[22] See Nadezha Durova, *The Cavalry Maiden: Journals of a Female Russian Officer in the Napoleonic Wars*, London, Paladin, 1990.

During World War I, the situation changed again. As men enlisted, fought and died by the millions, all the belligerents found themselves critically short of manpower. They tried to employ women, mainly in the fields, factories and offices, but sometimes resorted to putting them into uniform. The first experiments were made in Britain, where the Women's Emergency Corps was established in late 1914.[23] It acted as a clearinghouse for women who wanted to "do their bit." The Corps registered the women, classified them, and referred them to forces which might have an interest in hiring them *as civilians*. The largest single group consisted of nurses, of which it was impossible to have enough. Other women ran canteens, or operated communications equipment, or acted as drivers. Unlike the camp-followers of old, they neither followed individual male soldiers nor acted as entrepreneurs. Instead, they were employed by the army itself. Like the camp-followers of old, they did not come under martial law. Nor were they supposed to enter war zones.

Early in 1917, a year after the beginning of male conscription, the British forces finally felt ready to permit volunteer women to wear the uniform. From then until the end of the war, some 100,000 did so. However, neither in Britain nor in the United States, which followed the British example, were women treated as male soldiers were. In the first place, they could only be sent abroad with their own consent. If they did go abroad, they were concentrated in the zone of communications well behind the front. This put them out of harm's way; which explains why, out of the 38 female American soldiers who died during World War I, most lost their lives to the flu.[24] Second, unlike men — conscripts or volunteers — women were permitted to desert practically at will. They were thus simultaneously inside the forces and outside them. This was made clear when American navy officers tried to court-martial some women in the service, only to have Secretary Josephus Daniels tell them to back off, since "[one] cannot deal with women as with men."[25]

In all that concerns the employment of women, World War II was to a large extent a repetition of the first. In both Britain and the United States, any ideas of conscripting women — even for labor, let alone for military service — came

---

[23] Nancy Loring Goldman and Richard Stites, "Great Britain and the World Wars," in Nancy Loring Goldman, ed., *Female Soldiers, Combatants or Noncombatants?* Westport, CT, Greenwood Press, 1982, p. 24-6.

[24] Data from Jeanne Holm, *Women in the Military: An Unfinished Revolution*, Novato, CA, Presidio, 1992, pp. 10-1.

25 Jean Ebert and Marie-Beth Hall, *Crossed Currents: Navy Women from World War II to Tailhook*, London, Brassey's, 1993, p. 14.

to nothing. In both countries, women were called on to volunteer for the forces. The number of those who did so in both countries together may have amounted to 850,000 or so. Some British women worked in anti-aircraft defense.[26] In that field, as in others, often the first sign of the women's impending arrival was that the male troops were "asked" to give up their quarters for them.[27] Or as one female American navy officer put it, "There are certain niceties it would be lovely for men to have too, but if women don't have them their efficiency is jeopardized."[28] As in World War I, the forces much preferred letting female soldiers desert over court-martialing them. Women, in other words, could get a discharge simply by breaking the law.[29] That, in turn, may help explain how those women who did stay in gained a reputation for being more disciplined than men.

As in World War I, female soldiers could be sent abroad only if they volunteered. As a result, very few became casualties. British servicemen were about 55 times more likely to be killed as British servicewomen.[30] On the other side of the Atlantic, out of 350,000 American women who wore the uniform at some point between 1941 and 1945, only 4.7 percent served "in or near combat zones." Just 3.5 percent had been fired upon, and only 2 percent had been in "serious combat" — that is, had been injured or saw other Americans being killed and wounded.[31] Except for one episode early in the war, no American women were taken prisoner.[32] The equivalent British figure was 20.

Not counting resistance movements, the only country where any number of women — just how many is disputed[33] — saw combat during World War II was the Soviet Union. From the end of the Russian Civil War to the outbreak of the "Great Patriotic War" in 1941, the Red Army hardly had any female

[26] See Frederick Pile, *Ack Ack*, London, Harrap, 1949, p. 186-7, 190-2.

[27] Gerard J. DeGroot, "Whose Finger on the Trigger? Mixed Anti-Aircraft Batteries and the Female Combat Taboo," *War in History*, 4, 4, November 1997, p. 441.

[28] See Weatherford, *American Women and World War II*, p. 57.

[29] See Cf. DeGroot, "Whose Finger on the Trigger?" p. 437; Pile, *Ack-Ack,* pp. 190-9; Ebert and Hall, *Crossed Currents*, 1993, p. 78.

[30] Based on the fact that 624 women, as against 380,000 men, were killed, and that women at peak formed about 9 percent of the British Armed Forces.

[31] Stephen J. Diensterey, "Women Veterans' Exposure to Combat," *Armed Forces and Society*, 14, 4, summer 1988, pp. 593, 599.

[32] See Helen Rogan, *Mixed Company; Women in the Modern Army*, New York, Putnam, 1981, p. 266; also see Linda B. Francke, *Ground Zero: The Gender Wars in the Military*, New York, Simon & Schuster, 1997, p. 83 ff..

[33] See van Creveld, *Men, Women and War*, pp. 140-1.

soldiers.[34] However, after the German invasion began women were permitted to volunteer. As in all other armies, the vast majority served as caterers, communicators, administrators and medics. However, a few thousand served as snipers, tank crew(wo)men, and even combat pilots.[35] The self-sacrifice and heroism of Soviet women, like that of many of their sisters in other countries, are beyond question. Still, even in the Soviet Union the conditions under which they worked and lived were incomparably better than those imposed on men. Tens of thousands of Red Army men were executed, but to see a military woman under arrest was cause for surprise.[36]

After World War I the British and American women's corps were dissolved. The aftermath of World War II, however, followed a different course. Politicians and commanders believed that the next war would again require the total mobilization of all available manpower and resources.[37] This caused several countries to establish permanent women's corps, so as to organize and train the female soldiers who would be coming in. By the 1960s, women accounted for 1.2 percent of American military personnel. As in World War II, though, they could only be sent overseas if they volunteered to go. As a result, whereas well over 2 million American men served in Southeast Asia, for women the equivalent figure was 8,000. Since women at that time did not join combat units, the discrepancy in terms of casualties suffered by service personnel of both sexes was greater still. Of the 57,000 Americans who died in Vietnam, only 8 — 0.014 percent — were female.[38]

Partly because they were bowing to feminist pressures, partly because men were becoming increasingly reluctant to take up the profession of arms,[39]

---

[34] Gaby Gorodetsky, *The Myth of 'Icebreaker'* (in Russian), Moscow, Progress Academia, 1995, p. 21. For assistance with the Russian material I wish to thank Mr. Alexander Epstein.

[35] See Ann Griesse and Richard Stites, "Russia: Revolution and War," in Loring Goldman, *ed., Female Soldiers*, pp. 68-78; V. V. Pachlopkin, *The Great War and the Peace that did not Come, 1941-1945* (in Russian), Moscow, Art Center, 1997, p. 96; Anne Noggle, *Dance with Death: Soviet Airwomen in World War II*, College Station, TX, Texas University Press, 1994.

[36] Svetlana Alexijewitsch, *Der Krieg hat kein weibliches Gesicht*, Hamburg, Galgenberg, 1989, p. 138.

[37] See Patrick M. S. Blackett, *The Military and Political Consequences of Atomic Energy*, London, Turnstile Press, 1948, chapter 10.

[38] See William B. Breuer, *War and American Women*, Westport, CT, Praeger, 1997, pp. 72, 76, 82.

[39] For Japan see K. M. Wiegand, "Japan: Cautious Utilization," in Goldman Loring, ed., *Female Soldiers*, pp. 184, 187; for Australia see V. H. Billington, "Broadening the Recruiting Base for ARA Soldiers," Fort Queenscliff Papers, 1991, pp. 56-7; for Sweden see Kurt Tornqvist, "Sweden, the Neutral Nation," in *ibid*, p. 208; for Greece see J. Brown and C. Safilios-Rothschild, "Greece: Reluctant Presence," *ibid*, p. 168; for Britain see Christopher Dandeker, "New Times for the

during the 1970s many other countries began to setting up women's corps. However, compared to their male comrades the women in question were privileged in many ways. Even in the Soviet Union, where the authorities showed no mercy to young men who refused to be drafted, female soldiers were not conscripts but volunteers. Even in the Soviet Union, female soldiers were not obliged to do combat duty. In fact, they were kept far from any conceivable danger short of nuclear war. Even in the Soviet Union, the discipline under which they worked was much more relaxed. They also enjoyed a whole series of other privileges. The same applied in other countries, among them Greece, Belgium, Switzerland and Canada. In Canada, female soldiers could not even be arrested. The rationale was that a facility that would cater to their special needs did not exist. Nor, owing to the cost, could one be built.[40] In short, when an armed force has many women, the women are privileged — and when an armed force has few women, women are also privileged.

By the time these changes started taking place in the early 1970s, at least five countries had built nuclear weapons. Several others were thought to be capable of doing so, if they so chose. On both sides of the Iron Curtain, an entire generation had passed since any developed country had fought an opponent who was even remotely capable of putting its own existence at risk. Major war between major powers was clearly on the decline,[41] and this decline was to continue during the ensuing decades. The process goes a long way to explain why women suddenly wanted to enter combat units. To put it differently, as long as armed forces were meant for combat and occasionally engaged in it, the few women who served were not expected to fight and hardly ever did. But as the armed forces' role as fighting machines all but came to an end, the number of female soldiers who served in them rapidly rose.

As the percentage of servicewomen rose, they demanded, and in most cases obtained, equal treatment in regard to pay, fringe benefits and promotion, among others.[42] Equal work, they claimed, deserves equal pay. The fact that women were *not* doing equal work was deliberately ignored both by the women

---

Military," *British Journal of Sociology*, 45, 4, December 1994, p. 649; for The Netherlands see Loes van Tuyl, "Vrouwen tegen Vergrjizing," *ARMEX*, December 1997, pp. 16; for Belgium see Seidler, *Frauen zu den Waffen*, p. 243; FGR: *ibid*, p. 223.

[40] For Greece see Brown and Safilios-Rothschild, "Greece: Reluctant Presence," in Goldman, ed., *Female Soldiers*, p. 173; for Belgium see Jeanne Klick, "Utilization of Women in the NATO Military," p. 675 as well as *Moniteur belge*, 7.5.1977, p. 62-3; for see Switzerland Seidler, *Frauen zu den Waffen*, p. 381; and for Canada Seidler, *Frauen zu den Waffen*, p. 324.

[41] See van Creveld, *The Rise and Decline of the State*, pp. 337-53.

[42] See van Creveld, *Men, Women and War*, pp. 196-97.

themselves and by the courts to which they turned. The results first became clear during the 1991 Gulf War, when servicewomen turned out to be four times as likely as servicemen to experience problems that prevented them from being deployed.[43] Some women were unavailable because they were pregnant. Indeed, at any one time, one in 10 women in the services is likely to be pregnant.[44] Others could not go because they were seven times more likely than men to be single parents.[45] On that and other occasions, even those women who did get to the theater of operations did not pull their weight. During the first decade of the 21st century, both in Iraq and in Afghanistan, proportionally eight times as many American male as female soldiers died.

In every armed force that has them, women continue to enjoy privileges which, as long as those forces consisted solely of men, had been practically unheard of. Whereas some countries still conscript men, women only serve as volunteers. In the United States during the 1970s, attempts to end this discrimination and force the military to conscript, or at least register, women were repeatedly rejected by the courts as well as by the Senate.[46] Since women are on average less suitable for combat, physically speaking, in all the militaries that take them they tend to get the less demanding, cleaner and safer jobs. In truth, they are only soldiers as long as it suits them. For example, when the Russian army went to war in Chechnya in 1994-95, its female officers — some 14 percent of the officer corps — simply refused to go. Well understanding the outcry that would follow, the army did not try to force them to.[47]

Furthermore, women's living conditions are often better and the duties they are asked to perform less arduous. Often the training they get is so lax as to border on the ridiculous. For example, when it comes to throwing hand grenades,[48] or when Israeli female conscripts go through a "basic training"

---

[43] *News Weekly*, 23.8.1997, p. 10; Mike Lynch Testimony to the Presidential Commission on the Assignment of Women in the Armed Forces, *Report to the President*, p. 59.

[44] See P. J. Edwards and J. E. Edwards, *Incidence of Pregnancy and Single Parenthood Among Enlisted Personnel in the Navy,* San Diego, CA, Navy Personnel Research and Development Center, Report TN-92-8, February 1992. Other sources give slightly higher figures.

[45] Office of the Assistant Secretary of Defense for Manpower, Reserve Affairs and Logistics, *Background Review: Women in the Military*, Washington, Department of Defense, 10.1981, p. 7.

[46] Levit, *The Gender Line*, p. 107; Baer, *Women in American Law*, pp. 39-40; Kaminer, *A Fearful Freedom*, p. 2.

[47] Oral communication from Dr. Sergei Rogov, head of the US-Canada Institute, Moscow, Bonn, 22-3.9.1999.

[48] See the examples in Stephanie Guttmann, *The Kinder, Gentler Military: Can America's Gender-Neutral Fighting Force Still Win Wars?* New York, Scribner, 2000, pp. 253-66.

course that lasts all of 10 days. Often women's privileges even apply when they are trained for serving in very high-quality, high-prestige, military occupation specialties such as pilots.[49] Especially in the United States, so good are the terms under which military women serve that the forces have become a haven for single mothers. For millennia, men have died so that women would live. Now that substantial numbers of women are wearing the uniform as well, it will be interesting to observe whether the sacrifice will be reciprocated. One could be forgiven for having doubts, if only because repeated surveys have shown that very few female soldiers want to be in combat in the first place.[50]

3. The Protected Sex

If women have very seldom fought in war, then probably the most important reason for this is not because they are discriminated against. Rather, it is because one of the reasons why men fight — some would say, the most important reason — is precisely to protect women. To have women participate in war while at the same time protecting them is folly, the more so because it is not only the women who have to be protected, but their children as well.

As previously mentioned, the male imperative to protect women by fighting on their behalf may have some kind of biological basis. Often it is inspired by love, and often it is reinforced by women's own behavior. After all, if men cannot protect their women, then whatever else they may do is of questionable value. Men's need to protect women explains why, in the *Iliad*, the Trojan leader Hector preferred "going to hell and being covered by soil and ashes" rather than witness his wife, Andromache, "being led away, crying, by one of the copper-armored Achaeans."[51] Some of the reliefs of the Athenian Parthenon show Lapiths defending their women against Centaur attacks. About 500 years after those reliefs were made, Elazar ben Yair, commander of the Jewish Zealots at Masada, tried to persuade his men to commit mass suicide in the face

[49] For the United States, see the testimony of Lt. John Calgett, USN, Presidential Commission, 15.11.1992; also David Hackworth, "War and the Second Sex," *Newsweek*, 5.8.1991, p. 26. For Israel see *Yediot Aharonot*, 8.5.1996, p. 17, and *ibid*, 9.5.1996, p. 6.

[50] See Judith H. Stiehm, *Arms and the Enlisted Woman*, Philadelphia, Temple University Press, 1989, p. 100; *Newsweek*, 5.8.991; and Laura Miller, "Feminism and the Exclusion of Army Women from Combat," Harvard University, John M. Olin Institute for Strategic Studies, 1997-8, p. 19.

[51] 6.445-60.

of inevitable defeat. First he spoke about the delights of freedom, but did not carry conviction. Next he described their wives' and daughters' "shame" if they should fall into the hands of the Romans, "while they themselves were tied up and helpless." This time his words had the intended effect. The Zealots cast lots, selected five among their number, lay down at their families' side, and died to the last man.[52]

The annals of the American West bristle with accounts of lascivious redskins lusting for white ladies' flesh.[53] On the other side, one of the main reasons why the settlers fought was allegedly to protect their women. Throughout World War I, troops of all nations saw an urgent need to protect their womenfolk against rape.[54] At various times during the Arab-Israeli conflict, Israeli determination to fight was fueled by what people saw as the threat that sex-starved hordes of Arab savages presented to their women. At these and many other points in history, there is always a ferocious enemy positively slavering after one's own women. Those women, depending on the fashion of the society at hand, are portrayed as exceptionally thin, exceptionally thick, exceptionally modest, exceptionally forthcoming — in short, exceptionally beautiful and exceptionally desirable. One of the objectives of war is always to save them from being raped, even at the cost of one's own life, and even if, as occasionally happens, the women themselves do not want to be saved.

Whereas male prisoners were routinely killed, often after having suffered the most horrible forms of torture, women, valued both for their sexuality and for their labor, were normally spared. In California, the Pomo and the Nisenan while they still enjoyed some independence regularly incorporated captive women into their own tribes by way of marriage. So did many other tribal societies. On the whole, females have received better treatment and fared better than males. Indeed, some scholars have suggested that this possibly applies to chimpanzee "warfare" as well.[55] Be that as it may, the best available figures for male versus female casualties in tribal warfare are as follows:[56]

---

[52] Josephus Flavius, *The Jewish War*, 7.8.7.

[53] See Glenda Riley, *Women and Indians on the Frontier, 1825-1915*, Albuquerque, NM, University of New Mexico Press, 1984.

[54] Magnus Hirschfeld, *Sittengeschichte des Weltkrieges*, Berlin, Schneider, 1930, vol. 2, pp. 298-305.

[55] Richard Wrangham and Dale Peterson, *Demonic Males: Apes and the Origins of Human Violence*, Boston, Houghton Mifflin, 1996, pp. 167-8.

[56] Lawrence H. Keeley, *War Before Civilization: The Myth of the Peaceful Savage*, New York, Oxford University Press, 1997, appendix, table 6.2.

Society	Male deaths as a % of total	Female deaths as a % of total	Deaths in war as a % of all deaths	Ratio of deaths, female to male
Jivaro	59.0	27.0	32.7	1:2.8
Yanomamo-Shamatari	37.4	4.4	20.9	1:8.5
Mae Enga	34.8	2.3	18.6	1:15.1
Dugm Dani	28.5	2.4	15.5	1:11.9
Yanomamo-Nanowei	23.7	6.9	15.3	1:3.4
Huli	19.6	6.1	13.2	1:3.2
Gebusi	8.3	8.2	8.3	1:1.02

The mean ratio of female deaths to male deaths for all seven societies is 1:6.1. In other words, for every woman who died as a result of war, just over six men met the same fate. Moreover, there is no correlation between a tribe's ferocity, as expressed by the figure for deaths in war as a percentage of all deaths, and the ratio in question. Warlike societies do not lose proportionally more women than do peaceful ones. The only society in which as many women as men are killed is the Gebusi. It is far and away the most peaceful of all, as indeed it would have to be in order to avoid extermination. Conversely, one could argue that the only societies in which the death rate of men and women are even nearly equal are those which for one reason or another refuse to fight. This refusal may be connected with the fact that, at last count, there were only 500

Gebusi.[57] One can fairly conclude that the road to demographic success, as to so much else in life, is littered with male corpses.

Partly because women did not participate in war, partly because the enemy saw them as a potential asset, history is full of attempts to protect them against the worst that war can do. One of the earliest known codes for doing so is *Deuteronomy* 21.10-15. Going on "optional war," meaning a war not explicitly ordered by the Lord, the Israelites were enjoined to kill all male captives. However, the law required that they not "torment" female ones. On the face of it, this is an injunction to refrain from forcible rape. However, a passage in *Genesis* seems to indicate that this is not the correct interpretation. The verb *inah* stood, or could stand, for sex that took place with the woman's own consent, but without that of her male relatives, who were responsible for her.[58] By definition, the male relatives of women taken in war were dead and had nothing more to say in this or any other matter. Hence, the injunction may have meant that the women be allowed adequate time to grieve before being married to their captors in due form; only then could sex follow.

All over the ancient Middle East and Mediterranean, from roughly 2500 B.C. onward, women were spared the worst of war.[59] Thus, shortly after 705 B.C, Assyrian King Sanherib commemorated his capture of the town of Lachish in Judea by commissioning a number of reliefs. They were used to decorate his palace at Nineveh, and are now at the British Museum. Step by step, the reliefs show the army and the siege operations that it conducted. At the end comes the moment where, the town having fallen, the severed heads of its male defenders are piled up in heaps in front of Sanherib's throne. Other men are shown impaled on stakes. Not so, however, the women, who apparently unharmed are led away together with their children.

In ancient Greece, examples abound of the softer fist wielded against women. When the Athenians recaptured the tributary city of Scione, the men were executed, while the women were sold off as slaves.[60] The same happened when Melos, another city which the Athenians chose to treat as rebellious, was captured and destroyed.[61] Originally the Athenians had decided to do the same in regard to the city of Mytilene. In the end, however, they relented, and only

---

[57] Amiram Gonen, ed., *The Encyclopedia of the Peoples of the World*, New York, Holt, 1993, p. 218.

[58] *Genesis*, 34.2-3.

[59] See Gerda Lerner, *The Creation of Patriarchy*, Oxford, Oxford University Press, 1986, pp. 81-4.

[60] *The Peloponnesian War*, 4.122.

[61] *The Peloponnesian War*, 5.116.4.

1,000 of the wealthiest male citizens were executed. For women, it ought to be noted, not being members of the Greek citizen body had its advantages as well as its disadvantages.[62] Throughout the entire Peloponnesian War, which as Thucydides points out was the greatest and most ferocious waged in Greece to that date, the only time women are certainly known to have been put to death was during the plundering of Mycalessus by Thracian mercenaries. If Thucydides bothered to mention the occasion at all, then this was precisely because of its exceptional barbarity.[63]

As one might expect, codes of chivalry often contained provisions aimed at protecting women from the horrors of war. A typical example is the Muslim commandment, attributed to the first khalif, that children, old men and women not be killed, nor trees burnt, nor houses destroyed. Medieval knights followed a similar body of rules. For example, rape, along with the use of firearms, was prohibited by the Golden Bull of 1356, which among other things sought to regulate the things that German princes might and might not do when they went to war.[64] Around 1400 the French monk Honoré Bonnet published *The Tree of Battles*.[65] The work bristles with injunctions concerning the need to spare women who, along with ecclesiastics and domestic animals such as cows and asses, were classified as "innocent" and thus deserving of Christian mercy.

A 15th-century French document includes noblemen "who violate women" among those who are barred from participating in tournaments.[66] Given that tournaments were the occasion *par excellence* for nobles to put their martial prowess on display and perhaps catch the eye of a prospective employer, this was a serious punishment indeed. As late as the 16th century, German articles of war still included strong exhortations not to harm young mothers, pregnant women and "*Mädchen*," which can alternatively be translated as either "virgins" or "young girls."[67] Between them, these categories must have embraced virtually all women of an age at which they could be considered sexually attractive. That, perhaps, was just the intention.

Beginning around the middle of the 17th century, as far as legal theory is concerned, Western warfare stopped being waged either by individual rulers or

---

[62] *The Peloponnesian War*, 3.36.2, 3.50.1

[63] *The Peloponnesian War*, 3.50.1.

[64] See Robert Ward, *The Law of Nations*, Dublin, Wogan, 1795, p. 126.

[65] Honoré Bonnet, *The Tree of Battles*, Liverpool, Liverpool University Press, 1949.

[66] See Philippe Jacomin, *War in the Middle Ages*, Oxford, Blackwell, 1984, p. 290.

[67] See Peter H. Wilson, "German Women and War, 1500-1800," *War in History*, 3, 1996, p. 129.

by peoples. More and more it became the exclusive responsibility of states,[68] causing the distinction by age and sex to be replaced by one between soldiers, who were permitted to fight on behalf of the state, and civilians, who were not. Since women never wore the uniform and were not considered to be part of the military, even when they went on campaign, in theory they were better protected than ever before. Another new concept, "military necessity," worked in the same direction. As defined by the late-16th-century Spanish jurist Balthazar Ayala,[69] among others, the original purpose of the term was to serve as a loophole that would enable King Philip II's commanders to do whatever was necessary to achieve victory. Since even the broadest interpretation of "military necessity" could hardly be said to include having forcible sex with women, however, as far as women were concerned the effect of the loophole was exactly the opposite.

Depending on the occasion, entire provinces could be "devastated," cities bombarded and villages set on fire. On such occasions both men and women might be killed, but as far as sex was concerned, the bodies of women remained sacrosanct. A particularly good example of the way things worked, or at any rate were supposed to work, comes from the American Civil War, when General William Tecumseh Sherman made Georgia howl. The economy of the Confederacy was systematically destroyed, to the point that railway tracks were torn up, heated and wound around trees like corkscrews. Yet even as the sky was darkened by the smoke of burning farmhouses, the honor, as well as the life, of the southern belle remained intact.

Needless to say, the injunctions against killing women, as well as taking them prisoner and sexually mistreating them, have often been violated. In the ancient world, Alexander and Scipio Africanus were specifically commended for *not* abusing the fair captives delivered to them.[70] The former's behavior in this respect led some to suspect that he might have been a homosexual. The latter was commemorated in a special painting produced by the 16th-century painter Domenico Beccafumi.[71] Beccafumi's contemporary Pierre de Bayard owed part of his reputation as "the cavalier without reproach and without fear"

[68] See on these changes van Creveld, *The Transformation of War*, chapter 2.

[69] Balthazar Ayala, *Three Books on the Law of War and on the Duties Connected with War*, J. Westlake ed., Washington, Bate, 1912, p. 7.

[70] Arrian, *Anabasis*, 2.12.3-8; Livy, *The History of Rome*, 26.50.

[71] Alberto Pinelli, "Il 'picciol vetro' e il 'maggior vaso': I due grandi cicli profani di Domenico Beccafumi in Palazzo Venturi," in A.A.V.V, *Domenico Beccafumi e il suo tempo*, Milan, Electa, 1990, pp. 626-7.

to his unusual chastity.[72] By contrast, mass rape accompanied the sack of Rome in 1527 and the destruction of Magdeburg in 1631. On both occasions, the perpetrators were imperial troops who had gone out of control. Mass rape took place at the hands of the Japanese army at Nanking in 1938, and mass rape was practiced by the Red Army as it invaded Germany in 1945.[73] It was with these events in mind that the obligation to treat female prisoners "with all the regard due to their sex" was written into the Second Geneva Convention of 1949.[74] Needless to say, no similar injunction regarding men has ever been considered necessary. In war as in peace, often offenses committed against men are not considered offenses at all.

In peace and in war, whether carried out on an individual basis or in an organized way as a matter of policy, the maltreatment of women — including, above all, rape — is a hideous and unfortunately all too prevalent crime. Still, whether because women are less dangerous, owing to their relative physical weakness, or because of their value for breeding purposes, on the whole they seem to have come out of war much better than men. Even the medieval Celts, notorious for their refusal to grant quarter, preferred to capture "soft, youthful, bright, matchless girls" and "blooming, silk-clad, young women" rather than kill them out of hand.[75] Centuries later a Belgian volunteer, Léon Degrelle, noted how, amid the immense carnage that took place on the Eastern Front in 1942, both sides permitted Ukrainian women to work the fields between the lines.[76] Female prisoners could also expect to be treated less harshly than men. Allied troops captured by the Japanese during World War II died like flies. Though the U.S. Army nurses captured at Bataan were also ravaged by hunger and disease, every single one survived.[77] Here is the Reverend A. E.

---

[72] Luigi Lenzi, "Fanti e cavalieri nelle prime guerre d'Italia, 1494-1527," in *Ricerche Storiche*, 8, 2, 1978, Club Cooperative Editrice Universitaria, Florence, 1978, p. 359.

[73] The number of victims in Berlin alone has been put at 100,000, comprising some 7 percent of the entire female population; see Barbara Johr, "Die Ereignisse in Zahlen," in Helke Sander and Barbara Johr, eds., *Befreier und Befreite: Krieg, Vergewaltigungen, Kinder*, Munich, Kunstman, 1992, pp. 54-5.

[74] See Wayne E. Dillingham, "The Possibility of American Women Becoming POWs: Justification for Combat Exclusion Rules?" *Federal Bar News and Journal*, May 1990, p. 228.

[75] *Annale Uladh*: *Annals of Ulster*, William H. Hennessey and Brian MacCarthy, eds., Dublin, A. Thom, 1887, vol. 1, pp. 482-3, as quoted by Matthew Strickland, *War and Chivalry: The Conduct and Perception of War in England and Normandy, 1066-1217*, Cambridge, Cambridge University Press, 1996, p. 306.

[76] Leon Degrelle, *Die verlorene Legion*, Oldendorff, Schütz, 1972, p. 93.

[77] See Rogan, *Mixed Company*, p. 266; also Francke, *Ground Zero*, p. 83 ff.

Winnington, the bishop of London, as he was exhorting his countrymen to wage war against Germany in the autumn of 1914:[78]

> Kill Germans — to kill them, not for the sake of killing, but to save the world, to kill the good as well as the bad, to kill the young men as well as the old, to kill those who have shewn kindness to our wounded as well as those fiends who crucified the Canadian Sergeant [referring to a widely circulated propaganda myth]...

Note that, even in this ferocious outburst of anti-Teutonic propaganda, German women are not mentioned.

4. The Chivalrous Male

Having noted the treatment meted out to women who did not participate in combat, it is also necessary to say something about the handful of women who *did* participate. The starting point for such an examination begins with the fact that, in war as well as in sport, men are reluctant to fight women. In sport this reluctance has always led, and for the most part still leads, to separate teams for people of the two sexes. Occasionally it also led to mock fights, as when men and women bombarded each with cakes during medieval tournaments. Had the fight been conducted in earnest, then the field would have been littered with female bodies. Conversely, reluctance on the part of both men and women to see a field so littered is a cardinal reason why women have very seldom fought in war.

At all times and places, war has been a contest of force — the one occasion in life in which all of the participants' strength, mental and physical, may be brought to bear with hardly any restraints. By definition, though, such a contest can only be of value if it takes place between people or groups whose strength is roughly equal. A boxer who knocks out a much weaker opponent in the first round, or a large army that quickly demolishes a far smaller enemy, will earn humiliation, not glory. Conversely, a weak army that suffers defeat at the hands

[78] See R. H. Bainton, *Christian Attitudes Toward War and Peace: A Historical Survey and Critical Re-Evaluation*, New York, Abingdon, 1960, p. 207.

of much stronger one will readily be excused. As the Confederate Army and the German Africa Corps show, it may very well be admired for its heroism.

Applying this logic to the problem at hand, it is undeniable that men are considerably stronger than women.[79] This difference continues to be extremely important, even in an age of advanced weaponry. Whatever some people may say, push-button warfare has not yet arrived — and it probably never will. Since men are considerably stronger than women, if they win they will be humiliated. If they lose, they will be humiliated even more. In the language of game theory, for them to enter the contest creates a lose-lose situation, one which, if they are wise, they will do well to avoid.

Ever since ancient times, few people have doubted that the Amazons were a myth.[80] Yet even myths, by acting as distorting mirrors, may have their uses in helping us understand reality. The earliest mention of the Amazons is in the *Iliad,* which, while resting on much older foundations, was probably written shortly before 700 B.C. From the first, the Amazons' gender was problematic. King Priam describes them as *antianeirai*, "equivalent to men."[81] In all of Greek literature, the Amazons are the only noun to which this adjective is applied. The form *amazones* itself is masculine, being prefixed by the definite article in its plural masculine form and corresponding with the normal way in which Greek designates groups of people made up of both men and women. The same form may also be used to describe armies, in which case it refers exclusively to men. Judging solely by Homer, and ignoring subsequent traditions, had it not been for the epithet *antianeirai* there would have been no way of knowing that Priam was talking about women. Numerous other sources also emphasize that the Amazons, though they were not men, were somehow equivalent to them.

For the Amazons to be "equivalent to men" was extremely important. Take the poem *Aethiopis*, written by the poet Arctinus at some time early in the 6th century A.D. Here we find the hero Achilles killing the villain Theristes. What occasioned the act was the latter's suggestion that Achilles was sexually attracted to the Amazon queen Penthesilea, whom he had unknowingly just killed in battle. Achilles' fury is easily explained: Had the accusation been true and Penthesilea been primarily a woman, then her death would have been transformed from a glorious feat of arms into mere murder.

---

[79] See van Creveld, *Men, Women and War*, pp. 152-3.

[80] Strabo, *Geography*, 11.5.1-2.

[81] *Iliad*, 3.184.

The same reasoning may explain why, in all representations until the middle of the 6th century B.C, no Amazon, alive or dead, was ever shown naked, as many male warriors were. Instead, they are always dressed and armed as hoplites. They wield spears, carry shields and wear body armor that hides their breasts. Had it not been for their given names, the white color of their faces and bodies, and sometimes a characteristic piece of attire, it would be impossible to know they were female. The fact that the Amazons were "equivalent to men" served a double purpose. On the one hand, it permitted them to fight. On the other, it enabled those who fought against them, and on most occasions killed them, to earn glory for their actions — something which, had the Amazons simply been women like all the rest, would not have been possible.

At some point during the 5th century B.C, Greek ideas about the Amazons began to change.[82] The first evidence for the change is iconographic. Instead of being presented as hoplites, more and more the Amazons began to be depicted as women. To achieve this, much of the armor that they used to wear on their bodies had to be discarded. Its place was taken by loosely fitting clothes that often left one or even two breasts exposed. With their identity as women fully revealed, the Amazons suffered one defeat after the next. More often than not, they are shown desperately seeking shelter behind their shields as their male enemies prepare to run them through with the spear, a scene depicted famously on a vase now in the Mansell collection in London.[83] Alternatively, they are being pulled off their horses, as on a frieze from the temple of Apollo at Bassae,[84] or being seized by the hair while trying to escape, as on Phidias' shield of Athene Parthenos that has survived only as a Roman copy.[85]

Later still, Amazons began to be shown in all kinds of lively scenes. They don armor, leave for the fray, return from battle with their dead, lead, ride or dismount from horses, equip chariots or ride in them, or simply wash themselves as their weapons lean nearby. The more varied the activities in which they are shown, the less often they fight. Subsequently this pacification of the Amazons spread from painting to literature. To put it a different way, the Amazons could fight — and men would fight them — only as long as they

[82] See Thomas H. Carpenter, *Art and Myth in Ancient Greece*, London, Thames & Hudson, 1991, pp. 125-6.
[83] See Fraser, *The Warrior Queens*.
[84] See Blundell, *Women in Ancient Greece*, No. 10.
[85] See Michael Avi Yonah and Israel Shtazman, *Illustrated Encyclopaedia of the Classical World*, New York, Harper & Row, 1975, p. 344.

were not, and could not be identified as, women. No sooner did they start being women than they ceased to fight. By the end of the 4th century B.C., the "golden-shielded, silver-axed host" of fighting women was becoming decidedly "friendly to men."

Even during the Amazons' heyday, when they were said to have won many battles and overrun many countries, to triumph over them was not exactly a great honor. Witness the death of the Amazon queen, Penthesilea, as recounted by the Greek poet Quintus Smyrnaeus during the second half of the 4th century A.D.:[86]

> Though she lay fallen in dirt and gore, beneath her lovely eyebrows shone her beautiful face, even in death. The Argives, crowding about, were amazed when they saw her; she seemed like the blessed immortals. She lay on the ground in her armor like tireless Artemis, daughter of Zeus, sleeping when weary from chasing swift lions in the lofty mountains. Aphrodite, beautiful garlanded wife of mighty Ares, made Penthesilea radiant even in death to cause the son of blameless Peleus [i.e. Achilles, her killer] to grieve. Many men prayed that when they came home they would sleep in the bed of a wife like her. Achilles suffered greatly in his heart, that he slew her and did not bring her to Phthia as his shining wife, since in height and beauty she was blameless like the immortals.

To have killed a woman, even one who had borne arms and fought like the devil, was an occasion for sorrow rather than for joy. Achilles' sole excuse was that he did not know what he was doing. This may explain why the Amazons who came after Penthesilea tended to fight, if at all, with one of their breasts exposed — as, for instance, Virgil's Camilla did.

The combination of combat and cleavage remains as fascinating today as it was in ancient Greece. One need only take a look at the popular roleplaying game *Dungeons and Dragons*, or watch Hollywood films such as *Barbarella*, *Xena the Warrior Queen* or *Barbed Wire*. The same is true of blockbuster computer games like *Tomb Raider*. The larger and more exposed the breasts, it appears, the more exciting the game is to its target audience, male teenagers. Both in the movies and on the computer screen, part of the fascination may be

---

[86] *Ta met' homeron*, Leizpig, Teubner, 1891, 659-74.

the artistic challenge of creating a female figure that is both sexy and battle-worthy at the same time. In part, however, what many of these fantasy females are really doing when they expose or emphasize their breasts is to claim immunity even as they fight. As a result, very few of them are ever killed. If they are, then their deaths are presented as tragic, either the result of an accident or the handiwork of a man who is even more wicked than the rest.

Men's dislike for killing women also explains why, as in the case of Penthesilea, women whose real identity was discovered only after they had been killed were normally pitied rather than hated. Fighting women could also expect to receive quarter, if not always then at any rate more often than men. The female villain in *The Tain*,[87] Medb, instigates an unjust war — the objective of which is to prove that she is richer than anybody else — by offering the male champion who will fight for her *both* her daughter's "thighs" and her own. Next, she raises an army and assumes command over it. Defeated at a loss of thousands of men, she begs for quarter — and the hero Cuchulainn, "not being a killer of women," agrees.

Such attitudes can also readily be found in accounts of the late Middle Ages. According to one female historian:

> [One] reason why the extent of the participation by women in the [German] Peasants' War had been underestimated is because women do not appear in the punishment lists that document the peasant defeat... When women were punished for their participation, their punishments were different from those imposed on their husbands... for example, in July of 1525 all women of the village of Dettwang [in Bavaria] were locked up in the local madhouse. What women more likely had to expect was one of the traditional milder 'women's punishments,' such as being pilloried or put to public shame.[88]

Elsewhere in history, some fighting women received quarter even though they had *not* asked for it. An interesting case in point comes from Romania during World War II. In the last year of the war, Romania changed sides, terminating its alliance with Germany and joining with the Soviet Union instead. This led on several occasions to face-to-face encounters between male Romanian pilots

---

[87] *The Tain*, pp. 169, 250-1.

[88] Wunder, *He Is the Sun, She Is the Moon*, p. 180.

and female Soviet aviators who had previously fought on opposite sides of the front. In at least one known instance, the Romanians admitted to their new Soviet comrades that they could have shot them down, but, having recognized their opponents as women, refrained from doing so. It is possible that the Romanian pilots were trying to ingratiate themselves with their new allies (or masters), or else were trying to impress the women themselves. On the other hand, the Soviet female pilots involved, Galina Burdina and Nina Slovokhtova, would scarcely have had reason to repeat the stories 45 years later had they not believed them to be true. Or perhaps they were merely proud that their charms had been judged capable of overcoming the enmity of war.

Even female irregulars —rebels, insurgents, terrorists, guerrillas and freedom fighters — can expect better treatment at the hands of the enemy. For example, following the 1916 Easter Rising in Ireland, the British executed 14 male leaders of Sinn Fein. Not so the gun-toting Constance Markievicz, the "Rebel Countess" who was reprieved "due only to her sex."[89] Later she joined the Irish Parliament and became the first woman minister in any modern democracy — proof, if anything can be, that for rebels to be female has its advantages. That even the Germans on the Eastern Front hesitated to treat women as they did men is illustrated by a directive issued by General Walter von Reichenau. By German army standards, Reichenau was more of a Nazi than most, which made him one of Hitler's favorite commanders. In October 1941 he ordered "draconian measures" to be taken against *male* Russian civilians who could have prevented sabotage but failed to do so;[90] females, however, are not mentioned.

Examples elsewhere abound. If Palestinian Jewish women under the British Mandate were often used to hide arms on their bodies, it was primarily because British soldiers were not permitted to search them. Initially, at least, the same was also true during the Algerian uprising against the French during the 1950s. Another example comes from the Seychelles. In 1982, the islands witnessed an attempted coup. After its failure the men involved were at first sentenced to death, then reprieved and finally given stiff prison sentences. Not so the sole female conspirator, a South African national by the name of Sue Ingle. She spent just one single night under arrest before being released along with her pet

---

[89] Jessica A. Salmonson, *The Encyclopedia of Amazons*, New York, Anchor, 1992, p. 170; Peter B. Ellis, *Celtic Women*, n.p., Trans-Atlantic, 1996, p. 14.

[90] Armeebefehl des Oberbefehlhabers der 6. Armee, 10.10.1941, printed in Gerd R. Überschär and Wolfram Wette, eds., *Unternehmen Barbarossa*, Paderborn, Schöningh, 1985, p. 33.

cat.[91] Had the consequences for the male perpetrators not been so serious, the entire incident would have been comic.

To cite one more example, one reason why the Palestinian uprisings so often saw women at the forefront of demonstrations was because women being sprayed with gravel or beaten with truncheons looks bad on television. According to a former military prosecutor, in the city of Hebron, the normal prison sentence meted out to a Palestinian man caught trying to knife an Israeli soldier was 15 to 17 years. A woman convicted of the same offense would get just one year, if that.[92]

Acting as rebels, revolutionaries or insurgents, women will no doubt continue to prove that they can be as courageous, as determined, and as capable of withstanding the greatest stress, and the most grueling conditions, as men. At the same time, acting as rebels, revolutionaries or insurgents, women will usually expect to be treated better than men. Quite often they will see their expectations met. In some cases, indeed, they will participate precisely *because* they expect to be treated better than men. Such, for example, is what happened in Nigeria in 1929, when women, refusing to pay taxes, started a riot in the expectation, which proved to be false, that they would not be fired upon by British troops.[93]

Women who do not participate in war are usually treated better than men. Women who do participate in war also stand a good chance of being treated better than men. This is the case even if they are armed, even if they are involved in terrorism or try to perpetrate bloody attacks, and even if they are convicted for those attacks. All this is as true in war as it is in peace, as true during a state of emergency as it is under ordinary civilian law. The reason is that men are chivalrous by nature, and that most men do not like either punishing women or fighting them. In both law and war, the fact that the criminal or the opponent is a woman can cause even some of the worst actions to be expiated or mitigated.

---

[91] Anthony Mackler, *The New Mercenaries*, London, Sidgwick & Jackson, 1985, pp. 284-6, 335-6.

[92] Oral communication from IDF Captain (res.) Amit Perl, 23.4.2001.

[93] See Peggy R. Sanday, *Female Power and Male Dominance: On the Origin of Sexual Inequality*, Cambridge, Cambridge University Press, 1981, p. 136 ff.

5. Conclusions

If some scientists are to be believed, the male reluctance to hit women is biologically rooted. Even if those scientists are not to be believed, there is no doubt that the prohibition against hitting girls is drummed into boys from the moment they are old enough to understand the meaning of "no." As long as they are small, their weak attempts to hit girls who are larger than themselves are regarded with amused tolerance. But no sooner do they become as strong as, or stronger than, girls than the prohibition against hitting comes into effect. From this point onward, the only woman a man is allowed to touch is his wife, and even here we have seen how, at all times and places, society sought to limit what he might do to her.

What is true of one-on-one encounters is equally true of the collective use of violence known as war. To be sure, for women as well as for men, war is for the most part hell. That said, women, unlike men, have hardly ever been conscripted to serve; since one of the most important, if not *the* most important, objective of war is to preserve the life of the community, doing so would be both absurd and counterproductive. To the extent that women do serve at all, they do so — as in the past, whether as camp-followers or soldiers — solely out of their own free will. Having signed up as volunteers, they continue to enjoy many privileges. In peacetime, those privileges may range from superior quarters to cushier jobs, extra pay and laxer discipline. In wartime, no country has ever obliged, or is likely to oblige, women to participate in combat.

Another difference between female and male volunteers is that once the latter signs up for service, those who subsequently seek to escape their commitment are heavily punished. Not so women who, in practice if not in theory, may withdraw their consent at any time they choose. Should they encounter any difficulty in doing so, then they can achieve the same result by committing an offense, which will result in a discharge, or else by becoming pregnant. In all probability, such women will be permitted to go home. In military *and* civilian life alike, it is nearly impossible to find a greater privilege.

In return for not participating in war, women have to some extent been immune from its horrors. Sometimes this was because they were not considered members of the political community, as in tribes and ancient city states. Sometimes this was because they were considered "innocent," as in the Middle Ages. And sometimes this was because they were classified as civilians, as in Europe from about 1700 onward. In tribal warfare, as in the ancient empires, this immunity "only" consisted of the right not to be killed. However, very often it also included other things. In instances when men were taken prisoner rather than killed, women were set free. Historically women have only very rarely been designated as hostages to vouch for their relatives' good behavior. When they are taken as hostages — as, for example, in bank robberies, aircraft hijackings and the like — they are invariably released before the men. Often men volunteer to become hostages *in order* that the women may be released. A man who obtains his release by having a woman take his place will be treated with contempt, and rightly so. That is why he only exists in Greek mythology.

Sometimes, and to some extent, women are immune to the horrors of war even when they do participate in it. Should women's immunity be accidentally violated — as happened to women who dressed as men in order to be allowed to fight, and also to those unfortunate enough to be designated "collateral damage" — then this fact is more likely to be regretted, to be turned into an occasion for sorrow, and to be explained away. Should their immunity be deliberately violated, then this fact is more likely to lead to the perpetrators being despised, ostracized or punished. Some of these differences are incorporated into formal law. Others are merely embedded in custom. Yet the end result is always the same: Women are likely to emerge from war, in all its forms, in much better shape than men do.

So great is the difference that, the more frequent and ferocious the conflict, the more the demographic balance tends to tilt in women's favor. During the 17th century, so many North American Indian men were killed as to tilt the demographic balance inside the tribes in question.[94] The same applied to the American South after the Civil War,[95] the Soviet Union after World War II, and as a result of Cambodia's "killing fields" during the 1970s.[96] In whichever way one looks at it, women's privileges in regard to war are both numerous and indisputable. So it has always been — and so, let us hope, it will always be.

---

[94] David Courtwright, *Violent Land: Single Men and Social Disorder*, Cambridge, MA, Harvard University Press, 1996, p. 111.

[95] Guttentag and Secord, *Too Many Women?*, p. 135, figure 5.3.

[96] See Ovesen et al., *When Every Household Is an Island*, 1996, p. 5.

Chapter 7: The Quality of Life

1. Once Upon a Time...

Once upon a time — in fact, during more than 90 percent of human existence, and in many places to this very day — life for most people of both sexes was often nasty and short. For the majority, neither a reasonable standard of living nor adequate medical care could be taken for granted. It was only the Industrial Revolution that put a sufficient and balanced diet, appropriate clothing and reasonable housing within the reach of the masses. The same applies to the factors that make for health and longevity. These include access to clean drinking water, sufficient hot water for cleaning both clothes and in many climates the body itself, and last but not least, scientifically-based medical care.[1]

Physiologically speaking, the greatest advantages men enjoy over women are greater strength and robustness,[2] as well as lesser susceptibility to diseases of the genitourinary tract. Men, in other words, are more resistant to the hard, dirty life than women. This may explain why, as long as most people lived by agriculture and spent a great part of their time working outdoors in the muck, most men seem to have outlived most women. Findings in seven out of eight Paleolithic sites in Central Europe and Eastern Europe indicate that, from the age of 20 onward, males enjoyed a longer life expectancy than did females.[3] An examination of human remains found in a late Neolithic cemetery in Spain also shows that men lived longer than women. The same was true at Catal Huyuk, a Hittite city that stood from roughly 8000 B.C. to 6000 B.C.[4] Among the Copper

---

[1] See Thomas McKeown, *The Modern Rise in Population*, London, Edward Arnold, 1976.

[2] See Karen J. Colson, Stephanie A. Eisenstadt, Terra Ziporyn, *The Harvard Guide to Women's Health*, Cambridge, MA, Harvard University Press, 1996, pp. 238, 241, 322, 379, 388.

[3] G. Ascasi and J. Neneskeri, *History of Human Life Span and Mortality*, Budapest, Akadémiai Kiadó, 1970, p. 184, table 55; p. 213, table 70.

[4] Lawrence Angel, "Neolithic Skeletons from Catal Huyuk," *Anatolian Studies*, 21, 1971, p. 80.

Age population of Tiszapolgár-Basatanya in Hungary, meanwhile, females had a higher mortality rate than males did.[5]

As best as can be ascertained today, ancient Greek men outlived women by a considerable margin.[6] Likewise, two different methods used to study life expectancy in ancient Rome yielded broadly similar results. First, a comparison of the ages at which, based on their epitaphs, men and women died leads to the conclusion that men outlived women.[7] The second method relies on the tables produced by a famous lawyer, Ulpian, early in the 2nd century A.D. Apparently Ulpian's objective was to calculate the pensions paid to people of both sexes. On the basis of his figures, a modern researched concluded that, for males aged 5-45, and for females aged 5-55, life expectancy resembled that which existed in Mauritius during the mid-1940s. Now in Mauritius, as in most developing countries at the time, men outlived women, though not by much.[8]

Among the Avarian-Frankish population that built the 9th century A.D. cemetery in Sopronkohida, Hungary, females aged 20 to 60 had a longer life expectancy than men. However, even here the mortality rate of females over 60 years old shot up, causing the curves for both sexes to become all but identical. Data based on the remains of five other medieval Hungarian cemeteries also show that males consistently outlived females.[9] In late medieval Tuscany, men apparently lived 37.2 years, as compared to 33.14 for women.[10] In English and German villages, men continued to lead longer lives even as late as the 18th century.[11]

Another reason why men probably outlived women was because of the dangers associated with pregnancy and childbirth. In part, high perinatal mortality rates reflected the low standard of living and the harsh conditions under which delivery sometimes took place. According to one authority, during

---

[5] Ascasi and Neneskeri, *History of Human Life Span and Mortality*, pp. 194, 197, 202-3.

[6] S. C. Bissel and Lawrence Angel, "Health and Nutrition in Mycenaean Greece," in Nancy C. Wilkie and William D. E. Coulson, eds., *Contributions to Aegean Archaeology*, Minneapolis, MI, University of Minnesota Press, 1985, pp. 197-210.

[7] Ascasi and Neneskeri, *History of Human Life Span and Mortality*, p. 224, table 78.

[8] Bruce Frier, "Roman Life Expectancy," *Harvard Studies in Classical Philology*, 86, 1982, pp. 232, 238.

[9] Ascasi and Neneskeri, *History of Human Life Span and Mortality*, p. 232, figure 51, p. 251, table 91.

[10] See Herlihy and Klapisch-Zuber, *Tuscans and their Families*, p. 83.

[11] Keith Wrighton and David Levine, *Poverty and Piety in an English Village: Teling, 1525-1700*, New York, Academic Press, 1979, p. 59; Alois Bek, *Die Bevölkerungsbewegung im ländischen Raum in den letzten 250 Jahren*, Hohenheimm, Landwirtschaftliche Dissertation, n.d., p. 120.

the Middle Ages, "conditions during pregnancy and parturition were intolerable... Some young girls did not even realize that they were pregnant... [and] gave birth on the bare ground."[12] In part, it resulted from the natural difficulty of the delivery process and inadequate medical knowledge. It has been calculated that proportionally 23 times as many women died of childbirth- or pregnancy-related causes in medieval Hungary as in the modern state of Hungary during the 1960s. To turn the figures around, modern medicine had reduced this particular cause of women's relative short-livedness by no less than 95.5 percent.[13] Yet perinatal deaths in 1960s Hungary still formed 0.06 percent of all female deaths. The corresponding figure during the Middle Ages was 1.38 percent, which means that roughly one woman in 72 died for reasons connected with childbirth. The Hungarian figure, in turn, was about 10 times higher than in 18th-century Germany, where complications connected with pregnancy and birth took the life of perhaps 0.005 percent of all women.[14]

Thus, during most of history, harsh conditions and inadequate medical knowledge caused men to outlive women. By contrast, civilization — especially modern civilization — has created a situation in which the more advanced a country, the more women tend to outlive men. The march of civilization is very much the story of human discovery and invention. From the forceps through the condom to the pill,[15] practically all those discoveries and inventions were made by men. Nevertheless, judging by life expectancy, the results have, first and foremost, benefited women. So it has been in the past, and so, let us hope, it will be in the foreseeable future.

2. Civilization and Its Comforts

Almost invariably, the places that offer the most favorable conditions to human life are those which have long been settled. Almost invariably, too, those that

---

[12]Shachar, *The Fourth Estate*, p. 119.

[13] Ascasi and Neneskeri, *History of Human Life Span and Mortality*, pp. 253-4.

[14] Arthur E. Imhof and Helmut Schumacher, "Todesursachen," in Arthur E. Imhof, ed., *Historische Demographie als Sozialgeschichte: Giessen und Umgebung vom 17. zum 19. Jahrhundert*, Darmstadt, Hessische Historische Kommission, 1975, part I, p. 580.

[15] Lois N. Magner, *A History of Medicine*, New York, Dekker, 1992, pp. 271-2; Anon. (n.d.) "The Birth of the Pill," retrieved from http://www-scf.usc.edu/~nicoleg/history.htm

offer the least hospitable conditions are frontier areas where human settlement is relatively recent and sparse.

The reasons why fewer women than men have undertaken the hardship of leaving their homes for some newly settled country or territory are easy to see. Unlike men, they were not primarily responsible for making a living and did not have the same economic incentive to spur them to unconquered lands. Women were also less up for the hardship of travel. Compared to men they have always married earlier, often passing straight from their parents' houses to those of their spouses. Once married, they were tied down by the cycle of pregnancy, delivery and the need to look after their children — at any rate, more so than their husbands. To be sure, at no time and place did an absolute barrier to female migration exist. On the other hand, it was certainly more difficult for women than for men to pack their belongings, pick up their roots, and leave. For example, in 19th-century Britain, male emigrants outnumbered female ones three to one.[16]

These factors explain why, the harsher and more primitive the conditions at any given time and place, the fewer the women to be found. Conversely, the relative number of women at any given place and time reflects the progress of civilization and its comforts. Throughout history, women have been all but absent from miners' and loggers' camps, construction sites and garbage dumps, among other such work sites. In our day, the same applies to offshore oil rigs, Arctic weather stations and the like. In the work pits of yore, so rare were women that when one did make an appearance, she was seen as a minor miracle. In Californian mining camps during the middle of the 19th century, men would pay large sums just to watch a (fully dressed) woman walk around.[17] The situation on America's opposite coast was no different. In the first Virginia settlements in the early 17th century, men outnumbered women seven to one.[18] In New England, the ratio was roughly three to two. As conditions improved, additional women arrived. Some did so on their own initiative, others because they had been sent for by men. By the second half of the 18th century, women were already beginning to outnumber men in New England.

---

[16] B. R. Mitchell, *Abstract of British Historical Statistics*, Cambridge, Cambridge University Press, 1962, p. 6.

[17] William F. Sprague, *Women and the West: A Short Social History*, Boston, Christopher, 1940, p. 79.

[18] Guttentag and Secord, *Too Many Women?* p. 115.

The situation in the South, where vast spaces and a less healthy climate caused development to lag behind, was entirely different. Not only were white women scarce, but among black slaves brought from Africa men outnumbered women two to one.[19] The total number of women in Dixieland only began to equal that of men around 1830 or so.[20] The smaller the relative number of women, the more precious and exalted they became in the eyes of the men who competed for their favors. As one scholar later explained,[21] this situation probably contributed to the creation of the myth of the "Southern Belle":

> This marvelous creation was... a submissive wife whose reason for being was to love, honor, obey, and occasionally amuse her husband, to bring up his children and manage his household. Physically weak, and "formed for the less laborious occupations," she depended upon male protection. To secure this protection she was endowed with the capacity to "create a magic spell" over any man in her vicinity. She was timid and modest, beautiful and graceful, "the most fascinating being in creation... the delight and charm of every circle she moves in."

What was true in the South was even truer in the West. During much of American history, the standard advice given to a young man without means was to head in that direction. Women, who could usually make a living by marrying, tended to stay behind, and if worst came to worst, they found it easier to obtain charity.[22] As early as the second half of the 18th century, these factors led to a situation in which, the farther away from the Atlantic one got, the higher the ratio of men to women. For example, in Portsmouth on the New Hampshire coast, the ratio was 0.86, and 10 percent of resident women were widows. On the colony's frontier, by comparison, Cheshire and Grafton counties had, respectively, 112 and 126 men to every 100 women. In these

---

[19] J. D. Fage, "The Effect of the Export Slave Trade on African Populations," in R. P. Moss and R. J. A. R. Rathborne, eds., *The Population Factor in African Studies*, London, University of London Press, 1975, p. 19.

[20] Guttentag, and Secord, *Too Many Women?*, p. 135, figure 5.3.

[21] Anne F. Scott, *The Southern Lady: From Pedestal to Politics, 1830-1930*, Chicago, University of Chicago Press, 1970, p. 4.

[22] Kessler-Harris, *Out to Work*, p. 24.

counties, widows only formed between 1 and 2 percent of the female population.[23]

As the West opened up during the 19th century, men continued to move there in much larger numbers than women. Some areas had a male-to-female ratio of 10 to one, or more. As late as 1900, Midwestern states including Ohio, Illinois, Iowa and Kansas still had more men than women. Further westward, in Colorado, Nevada, Montana, Idaho, Wyoming and California, the imbalance was much greater still.[24] Judging by women's reluctance to move to those states, one might justifiably conclude that they had not heard about the Western frontier being closed until several decades after renowned historian Frederick Jackson Turner had declared it so. Furthermore, before mass immigration into the United States ended in 1924, male immigrants outnumbered females by a considerable margin.[25] Only after World War II killed 300,000 American men, and hardly any American women, did the number of women exceed that of men for the first time.[26] Since then the gap has grown steadily. By the early 1990s, 50.9 percent of the population was female, 49.1 male.[27]

Outside the United States, the presence of women was likewise directly related to the degree of comfort provided by a country, region or town. Take Burma during the 1920s, as described in George Orwell's *Burmese Days*.[28] The British men who went to this remote, hot and insalubrious colony usually did so because living there was cheaper than at home. Wives apart, the few women who followed did so in the hope of catching a man. Each year a fresh "fishing fleet" arrived, yet the further from Rangoon one went, the fewer the European women one met. Darwin, Australia, is a mining town with an exceptionally harsh climate that includes cyclones and 100 inches of annual rainfall, all of which pours down in a single season. Accordingly, its population consists of migrants, rising to 70,000 in the winter but falling to a little more than half that number during the summer. Needless to say, almost all the migrants are men. No wonder that, in proportion to the town's size, its telephone directory probably lists more call girls than any in the world.

---

[23] Guttentag and Secord, *Too Many Women?*, p. 118.

[24] Guttentag and Secord, *Too Many Women?*, p. 126, figure 5.1; p. 127, figure 5.2.

[25] See Warren S. Thompson and P. K. Whelpton, *Population Trends in the United States*, New York, Gordon and Breach, 1969, pp. 172-5.

[26] See Thompson and Whelpton, *Population Trends in the United States*, pp. 172-5.

[27] U.S. Census Bureau. (May 2011). "Age and Sex Composition, 2010," retrieved from http://www.census.gov/prod/cen2010/briefs/c2010br-03.pdf

[28] San Diego, CA, Harcourt Brace, 1962 [1934].

Throughout history, whenever immigrants are numerous or conditions are hard and life difficult, women tend to be few and far between. These facts, rather than female infanticide or some other forms of male oppression of women, may explain why, as far as can be determined, men outnumbered women in the large commercial city that was ancient Athens,[29] just as they do in the modern state of Qatar.[30] To put it differently, what is usually regarded as the "normal" sex ratio — namely, women outnumbering men — is not really normal at all. Instead, it is the result of men providing women with the amenities of civilized life. Often, to do so, they had to go into the wilderness first. Often they had to engage in backbreaking labor, and often they paid the price by dying a lonely death. Indeed, quite often those who died far from home did not even get a sign to mark their grave.

Nutrition apart, the most important amenity men have provided women is housing. Since the building process usually involves heavy labor, it tends to be performed by men for women. This was as true among the Nuer of East Africa[31] as it is on the most modern construction sites, as true among the matrilineal Mosuo of China as among the Eskimo. To this day in Arab villages, when a man gets married his male relatives help him build a house. The women assist by bringing food. To this day in modern societies, bridegrooms are supposed to carry their brides across the threshold, not the other way around. Once houses are standing, both men and women share the benefit by spending at least some of their time in them. On the other hand, women have always tended to spend more time at home than did men. This is tantamount to saying that, to the extent that housing provides comfort as well as shelter against heat, cold, wind, rain, hail and snow, women have always benefited more than men did. And the more "secluded" their lives, the truer this was and is.

The fact that women were better protected from the elements explains why, in the art of many peoples, they are presented as having skins whiter than those of men. The difference is noticeable in ancient Egyptian art. If ancient Egyptian men are occasionally painted with light skin, then this probably means they had reached a point in their career at which they no longer had to work in the fields but were able to spend most of their time indoors, as women did. Thus the lives of women were shared only by a comparative handful of privileged men.[32] The same applies to India, where illustrations showing men and women together

---

[29] See Pomeroy, *Families in Classical and Hellenistic Greece*, p. 120.

[30] *Britannica Book of the Year*, Chicago, Britannica, 1993, p. 697.

[31] Edward E. Evans-Pritchard, *The Nuer*, Oxford, Oxford University Press, 1940, p. 66.

[32] Robins, *Women in Ancient Egypt*, pp. 180-1.

almost always present the latter as having lighter skin. As noted earlier, in Greek art the lighter color of the Amazons' skin is virtually the only indication that they were, indeed, female. Men worked by the sweat of their brows, suffered accordingly, and could consider themselves lucky if they were described as rugged. Not so women, who found it easier to keep their fair complexions and were extolled for doing so.

From ancient Egypt come images that show women being transported by water. Boats traveling on the Nile were outfitted with special cabins that offered shelter to their female passengers. Meanwhile, the all-male crew, wearing nothing but a loinskirt, worked the sails and rudder under a blazing sun. Perhaps it was fortunate for them that few lived long enough to develop skin cancer. Partly in order to protect their beauty, partly because crowded conditions onboard made it necessary to offer them some privacy, the tradition which dictated that women at sea should be given the most secluded and comfortable quarters available has continued for thousands of years. This was even true when they were of low social rank, and even in the much-maligned Islamic civilization. For example, Ibn Battuta once traveled from India to China by sea. He insisted that his female slaves be given a cabin, whereas he and the other men apparently slept on the open deck.[33]

What was true on water was equally true on land. Fleeing Laban, Jacob made his wives ride camels. However, he himself "drove" all his cattle and property;[34] the implication is that he went on foot and worked hard, even as he walked. To this day among the Bedouin, when men and women travel together it is the former who must march whereas the latter are mounted. The need to make women's travel as comfortable as possible was considered important enough to be recommended by Mohammed in person. On one occasion, meeting some women who were riding camels, he admonished the driver, who went on foot, to proceed gently so as not to damage the "glass cases" under his care.[35] Ibn Battuta, for his part, noted in his travels in India that whereas men walked or rode, ladies traveled in litters carried by eight men.[36] To this day in the Indian countryside, whenever one comes across a cart with its curtains drawn, one may be almost certain that the passenger inside is a well-to-do

---

[33] *The Rehlah of Ibn Battuta*, p. 191.

[34] *Genesis*, 31.17-8.

[35] Al Bukhari, *Sahih, Kitab an-Nikah* (*Fath al-Bari*, 10/454), quoted in Wahiduddin Khan, *Women between Islam and Western Society*, p. 135.

[36] *The Rehlah of Ibn Battuta*, pp. 122, 224.

woman. In traditional China, the standard means of transport used by upper-class women used to be the sedan chair.

Women have likewise been privileged over men when it comes to their health. A cursory look into history shows that women have always received more, if not necessarily better, medical attention than men. In ancient Egypt, numerous books were written about female-specific diseases.[37] However, when it comes to male-specific ones, all there is is blank papyrus. The Greek Hippocratic Corpus, meanwhile, contains several treatises on women's health, but not a single one devoted exclusively to that of men.

Perhaps the civilization that paid the greatest relative attention to female health was that of China.[38] Partly because of the problems attending reproduction, partly because women's ailments were considered "10 times more difficult to cure than those of males,"[39] physicians devoted an entire medical specialty to women's health. Known as *fuke*, it comprised both gynecology and obstetrics. Some *fuke* practitioners were male, others, particularly those who attended childbirth, female. Together they developed a large number of drugs specifically aimed at women. By the Song dynasty, *fuke* had become one of the nine disciplines comprising medical science. One medical encyclopedia, the *Imperial Grace Formulary*, devoted 12 of 100 chapters to *fuke*. Another, the *All Inclusive Good Prescriptions for Women*, dealt exclusively with them. In China, as in all other countries, practically the only type of the medical knowledge that is gender specific is that which deals with women. And in China, as in all other countries, there is no question that women received far more medical attention than men.

To be sure, very often so rudimentary was the medical knowledge that it could do little to help men and women alike. In Europe until the 17th century, and in other cultures until much later, the process of delivery had been an all-female affair. It was a mysterious rite that took place at home, and from which men were almost entirely excluded. Many villages did not even have a professional midwife. As a result, the only available assistance came from experienced female relatives and neighbors. Though midwives were usually

[37] Robins, *Women in Ancient Egypt*, p. 79.

[38] See Charlotte Furth, *A Flourishing Yin: Gender in China's Medical History, 960-1665*, Berkeley, CA, University of California Press, 1999, pp. 59-60, 63-4, 66, 71, 79.

[39] Sun Simiao, *Prescriptions Worth a Thousand*, quoted in Furth, *A Flourishing Yin*, p. 71.

available in the towns, the quality of their services left much to be desired. As one early 16th-century German limerick put it:[40]

> I'm talking about the midwives all
> Whose heads are empty as a hall,
> And through their dreadful negligence
> Cause babies' deaths devoid of sense.
> So thus we see far and about
> Official murder, there's no doubt.

Both midwives and moralists argued against the presence of males during delivery. The former did so out of fear for their livelihood, the latter because of their concern for female virtue. When the first male midwives made their appearance in the 17th century, they were often ridiculed. One male midwife who attended Queen Anne's numerous deliveries and was later knighted by her became known as "the rider of the cunt."

By that time, change was in the air. In 1554, Zurich ordered that midwives should be instructed by doctors, who were male. Other cities eventually followed,[41] with irrefutable results. Between 1600 and 1795, even as "English midwives were degraded into mere assistants" as one author put it,[42] perinatal mortality in London dropped by one-half, from 24 to 12 per 1,000 live births. In Berlin it declined from 11 per 1,000 births in the 1720s to 7 in the 1780s. In Edinburgh it fell from 14 in the 1750s to 6 in the 1790s, and in Königsberg from 13 in 1769-1783 to 8 in 1794-1803. Economic circumstances permitting, the more difficult any anticipated birth, the more likely it was to be attended by a male doctor rather than a female midwife. Conversely, by insisting on what one modern female historian calls "a feminist kind of delivery" — that is, without the presence of an expert male doctor — Mary Wollstonecraft may have brought about her own death.[43] The masculinization of childbirth started in the cities. It took a long time to reach the countryside, where women kept on

[40] Quoted in Edward Shorter, *A History of Women's Bodies*, Harmondsworth, Middlesex, Penguin, 1982, pp. 35-6.

[41] Shorter, *A History of Women's Bodies*, pp. 37-41.

[42] Fletcher, *Sex, Gender and Subordination*, p. 238.

[43] Margaret George, *One Woman's "Situation": A Study of Mary Wollstonecraft*, Urbana, IL, University of Illinois Press, 1970, p. 129.

as they had before. Consequently, death rates among rural mothers only started declining later and more slowly.[44]

In summary, during most of recorded history men appeared to have lived longer than women. This remained the case as long as conditions were relatively rough, thanks partly to men's greater physical robustness and partly to the fact that they did not have to bear children. Even during those times, however, women often enjoyed special protection. Very often, what feminists describe as their "oppression" at the hands of men really represented concern for their comfort and their health. Concern for women's health, and not oppression, explains why they usually stayed at home more often, and for longer, than men, and the same applies to transportation and to medical care.

3. The Demographic Revolution

As best as can be determined, given the sparseness of available data, the very first community in which women outlived men was Paris during the 9th century A.D. As one would expect, the phenomenon was most obvious among members of the upper classes.[45] That early Parisian society, it may reasonably be conjectured, was not an isolated case but the beginning of a trend that gathered momentum during the centuries that followed. Such a conjecture may help explain why, between 1100 and 1300, most European towns had already developed a low sex ratio — that is, a shortage of males — that has characterized them ever since.[46]

For example, in Frankfurt in 1385 the ratio was 90 men to 100 women. Fifty-five years later, it had risen to 85 to 100. Nuremberg in 1440 had 83 men for every 100 women. In Basel in 1454 the ratio for persons aged 14 and over was 80 to 100.[47] Speyer in 1530 had 96 adult men for every 100 adult women.[48] In London in 1694, the ratio was 77 to 100.[49] In Ansbach in 1713, meanwhile, there were 1,569 women in the 50-60 age group, as compared to 1,414 men. In the 60-70 age group, the difference was greater still, 102 to 63. The figures for

[44] Shorter, *A History of Women's Bodies*, p. 99, table 5.5.

[45] Goody, *The Development of the Family and Marriage in Europe*, p. 64.

[46] See Lester K. Little, "Evangelical Poverty, the New Money Economy and Violence," in David Flood, ed., *Poverty in the Middle Ages*, Werl, Coelde, 1975, p. 14.

[47] See Guttentag and Secord, *Too Many Women?*, p. 65.

[48] Wunder, *He Is the Sun, She Is the Moon*, p. 129-30.

[49] See Ruth Perry, *The Celebrated May Astell*, Chicago, University of Chicago Press, 1986, p. 105.

the 70-80 age group evened out at 22 women and 23 men — but whereas many of the men's wives were also alive, *all* of the 22 women were widows.[50]

By the early 18th century, women also outnumbered men in most Swedish cities.[51] The hypothesis that it was urbanization which made women outlive men — even if, at first, it sometimes caused a drop in the life expectancy of both men *and* women — can be beautifully demonstrated from a series of tables pertaining to England and Wales in the years 1813 to 1830.[52] The four counties listed in the tables with the highest percentage of people engaged in agriculture — Bedford, Hereford, Huntington and Rutland — had a male-to-female mortality rate of greater than one. The four counties with the lowest percentage of people engaged in agriculture — Derby, Lancaster, Middlesex and Surrey — had a male-to-female mortality rate of less than one. The single largest difference in mortality, 1.19:1, was found in Middlesex. Not by accident, Middlesex, with London as its center, was the most urbanized county by far, with only 4 percent of its population employed in agriculture. In the next most urbanized county, Lancaster, men's mortality exceeded that of women 1.07:1. As families moved from the countryside into the "black satanic mills," women's relative health actually improved. In the words of a contemporary demographer: "The harmful effects of industrial development that affected the mortality of English... men were less noticeable for women."[53]

Figures from 19th-century Germany, Denmark and Norway all suggest that the rural way of life is harder on women than on men.[54] Conversely, bad as the towns often were, they favored women over men. Perhaps the main way they did so was by changing women's working environment. Living in the countryside, both men and women had to do hard and dirty work outdoors, even though this was less true of women than of men. In the towns, women worked, if at all, almost exclusively indoors. Men, meanwhile, continued to be

---

[50] Herms Bahl, *Ansbach: Strukturanalyse einer Residenz am Ende des Dreissigjährigen Kriegs bis zur Mitte des 18. Jahrhunderts*, Ansbach, Max Planck Institut, 1974, pp. 169-233, quoted in Wunder, *He Is the Sun, She Is the Moon*, pp. 138-9.

[51] Anders Brandstorm et al., "Lebenserwartungen in Schweden 1750-1989," in Arthur Imhof, ed., *Lebenserwatrungen in Deutschland, Norwegen und Schweden im 19. und 20. Jahrhundert*, Berlin, Akademie Verlag, 1994, p. 360, figure 12.

[52] William Farr, "Vital Statistics or the Statistics of Health, Sickness, Disease and Death," 1837, in Richard Wall, ed., *Mortality in Nineteenth-Century Britain*, Westmead, Gregg, 1974, p. 570, table 3.

[53] Graziella Caselli, "Health Transition and Cause-Specific Mortality," in Schofield et al., eds., *The Decline of Mortality in Europe*, Oxford, Clarendon, 1991, p. 78.

[54] Shorter, *A History of Women's Bodies*, p. 238, table 9.4.

responsible for construction, transport, delivery, garbage removal, public security and the like. The difference was particularly marked in tasks which, in village life, were performed by women. The provision of drinking water offers a telling example. In early 20th-century Arab Palestinian villages, this was the task of women, who carried jars on their heads. Not so in Arab Palestinian towns, where it was done by a specialized class of men using leather bags.[55]

The first country in which women began to live longer than men seems to have been France during the 1740s. Close on its heels came Sweden.[56] Most West European countries reached the point sometime between 1800 and 1850. In 1855 the number of women over the age of 60 in Germany, which at that time was poorer than both France and England, surpassed for the first time the number of men in that cohort.[57] In Italy, which was even poorer, the shift had to wait until after unification. Since then, so self-evident has the expectation that women should live longer become that it often borders on callousness toward men. For example, in the 1820s the advantage enjoyed by French women declined from 1.9 years to 0.6 before recovering to 1.0 in the 1830s and to 2.6 in the 1870s.[58] This temporary dip was enough to make modern demographers speak of "excess" female mortality.

Women's longevity both reflected their privileged economic position — the fact that they were supported by men — and had important economic consequences. In 1860s England, an annuity bought by a 28-year-old woman was worth more annually than it was for a male of the same age. At age 58, the difference reached 1.5 years, and at age 78 it still stood at one year.[59] Observing women's growing advantage, contemporary experts had no doubt as to how,

---

[55] Tom Segev, *One Palestine, Complete: Jews and Arabs Under the British Mandate*, New York, Holt, 2000, p. 184.

[56] For France see Jacques Vallin, "Mortality in Europe from 1720 to 1914: Long Term Trends and Changes in Patterns by Age and Sex," in R. Schofield et al., eds., *The Decline of Mortality in Europe*, p. 64; for Sweden see A. Holmberg, "A Study of Mortality Among Cohorts Born in the 18th and 19th Century," in A. M. Bolander, ed., *Cohort Mortality of Sweden: Three Studies Describing Past, Present and Future Trends in Mortality*, Stockholm, Commission for Demography, 1970, pp. 71-86.

[57] Arthur Imhof, "Die neue Überlebenden," in Imhof, ed., *Lebenserwartungen in Deutschland, Norwegen und Schweden*, p. 50; also Brandstorm et al., "Lebenserwartungen in Schweden 1750-1989," in *ibid*, p. 339, figure 3.

[58] Vallin, "Mortality in Europe from 1720 to 1914," p. 64.

[59] Alexander G. Finlaison, *Report on the Mortality on the Government Life Annuities*, Westmead, Gregg, 1973 [1860], p. 65.

and at the expense of whom, it had been achieved. In the words of one observer:[60]

> It is almost certain that any material improvement in the human physical constitution will first be observed in the diminution of... the female mortality. The greater perils of life to which the male is exposed in the ordinary course of a civilized existence may neutralize his portion of the general improvement for a long time to come; but with the female it is different, from the nature of her social position.

The gap between the sexes was probably even larger than the tables showed. This was because male emigrants far outnumbered females, and more men whose births had been recorded escaped the registrars at the time of their deaths. The same applied to military personnel, numbering perhaps a quarter million. All were male, and three-quarters were stationed abroad. Thus, in many cases, their deaths did not enter the statistics at home.

Around 1900, the only Western European country in which women had not long since started outliving men was Ireland. By 1930 even that anomaly had disappeared. Since then, not a single Western life table has shown a higher male life expectancy at any age below 70.[61] During the last years of the 19th century, the spread of female longevity reached Eastern Europe. It would take several more decades, but eventually the trend reached the developing world as well. In most countries — among them Brazil, China, Costa Rica, Cuba, India, Indonesia, Kenya, Madagascar, Malawi, Malaysia, the Philippines, Somalia, Sri Lanka and Thailand — the tipping point seems to have been reached between 1950 and 1985.[62] By 1990, according to the *Encyclopedia Britannica Book of the Year*,[63] worldwide the gap had grown to four years. Only in seven poor countries — Afghanistan, Bangladesh, Bhutan, the Maldives, Morocco, Nepal and Vanuatu — did men outlive women. By 2011, even those anomalies had

---

[60] Government actuary. (10.11.1888). *Rockland County Journal*, retrieved from http://news.hrvh.org/cgi-bin/newshrvh?a=d&d=rocklandctyjournal18881110.2.5&cl=&srpos=0&st=1&e=-------20--1-----all

[61] Robert D. Retherford, *The Changing Sex Differential in Mortality*, Westport, CT, Greenwood, 1975, p.10.

[62] Imhof, "Die neue Überlebenden," pp. 96-7, 113, figures 32-8, 40-5, 47-9.

[63] Pages 757, 546, 560, 586, 662, 674, 678, 747.

disappeared, with women outliving men in every single one of the 194 countries surveyed.[64]

Considered in absolute terms, the increase in longevity brought about by modernity can only be called staggering. For example, in France during the 1740s, life expectancy stood at 24.7 years. For the years 1909 to 1913 the figure was 50.5, and by the mid-1980s it had reached 74. In Germany, the figures stood at 37.2 in 1855 and at 74.3 in 1985.[65] While both men and women have benefited from increased life expectancy, in practically all countries women have benefited more than men. The United States offers a prime example. In 1900 the overall life expectancy for people of both sexes stood at 50 years. In 1920, according to one set of statistics,[66] the life expectancy at birth of white American women was still only one year longer than that of men. By 1950, however, the difference had grown to nearly six years. By 1975, whereas white women could expect to reach 77.2 years of age, the figure for men stood at 69.4. Among black Americans, the difference greater still: 72.3 years for women, compared to 63.6 for men.

Judging by life expectancy alone, an observer might be forgiven for concluding that men and women have changed miraculously since 1750, and that they are developing into different species. On the whole, the members of one work hard, look the part, and die early. Those of the other enjoy greater comfort, take and are allowed to take better care of themselves, and receive superior or at least more medical care. In the most advanced places — those where everybody else wants to go — they live about 10 percent longer.

Since 1920, the gap between life expectancy for American women and men has grown by several hundred percent. In Germany, meanwhile, the difference increased by more than 20 percent between 1964 and 1984.[67] The extraordinary speed at which the gap has developed, as well as its spread from the richest countries to the developing world, rules out the possibility that women's greater longevity stems from their biology, as some scholars have claimed.[68] Instead, the trend shows that modernization itself tends to favor women over men, at

---

[64] For a list of countries by life expectancy, see "List of countries by life expectancy." (n.d.) Retrieved from http://en.wikipedia.org/wiki/List_of_countries_by_life_expectancy

[65] For France see Vallin, "Mortality in Europe from 1720 to 1914," p. 47; for Germany see Imhof, "Die neue Überlebenden," p. 67.

[66] Robert V. Wells, *Revolutions in Americans' Lives: A Demographic Perspective*, Westport, CT, Greenwood, 1982, p. 22.

[67] Imhof, "Die Neue Überlebenden," p. 56.

[68] See Retherford, *The Changing* Sex *Differential in Mortality*, p. 15.

least up to a certain point, and so long as women do not try to work as hard as men. As numerous studies have shown, when women do attempt to carry an equal weight, the resulting stress is substantial and relaxation hard to achieve. To compensate, growing numbers of women who carry such burdens take up drinking or smoking. This is as true of female Volvo executives as it is of senior female members of the British Civil Service.[69]

Urbanization apart, women's good fortune is also related to the biological functions of both sexes. Until 1900, virtually the only mothers who went to the hospital to give birth were unmarried ones. From the turn of the century onward, however, their numbers began to increase. In 1938, 50 percent of American babies first saw the light of day in a hospital. The figure rose to 95 percent in 1955, and to 99 percent in the late 1970s.[70] However much one may criticize the "imperialism" of doctors and their predilection for Cesareans, the attendant risk became smaller and smaller both in the hospital *and* at home. Between 1910 and 1955 alone, it went down by 90 percent.[71] The decreasing danger associated with each maternal event was accompanied by a sharp decline in fertility, a trend that was observed in developed countries in particular. Obviously an American woman who gives birth twice, on average, is less at risk than her Jordanian or Pakistani sister, who can expect to have five, six or even seven children, and who, unless she belongs to the fortunate minority, can expect to do so under far less favorable conditions. In Europe and Japan, where the average woman will have fewer than two children, the risk is smaller still.

As of 2011, the country with the highest number of perinatal maternal deaths was Chad, with 1,100 per 100,000. The country with the lowest number was Estonia, at 2 per 100,000.[72] The difference between the two ratios is more than 500 to 1. Now, it remains true that, even in the most advanced countries,

---

[69] See Bodil Bergman, *Women Among Men: Gender Related Stress and Health Hazards Affecting Women Working in a Male-Dominated Industry*, Goteborg, University of Goteborg, 1997, pp. 31, 33, 43, 45, 47; E. Haavio-Mannila, "Inequalities in Health and Gender," *Social Science and Medicine*, 22, 1986, pp. 141-9; C. Alfredson et al., "Type of Occupation and Hospitalization for Myocardial Infraction and some other Diagnoses," *International Journal of Epidemiology*, 14, 1985, pp. 378-85; Hilary Graham, "Socio-Economic Change and Inequalities," in Annandale and Hunt, eds., *Gender Inequalities in Health*, p. 100.

[70] Shorter, *A History of Women's Bodies*, pp. 156-7; Magner, *A History of Medicine*, p. 275.

[71] For Britain see John M. Munro Kerr et al., *Historical Review of British Obstetrics and Gynecology*, London, Livingstone, 1954, p. 259, table 1.

[72] See "Country Comparison: Maternal Mortality Rate." (n.d.) CIA World Factbook, retrieved from https://www.cia.gov/library/publications/the-world-factbook/rankorder/2223rank.html

about 90 percent of women will bear at least one child. What is more, the proliferation of artificial insemination and adoption agencies proves that women's desire to have offspring is as strong as ever. The clinics that provide the former are often booked for months ahead. The latter make millions out of licit and illicit traffic in children. Thus, a 500-fold improvement may not be a bad indicator of what modern medicine has done to help women. Medicine focused on men has nothing similar to show. One reason for this is that obstetrics is an extremely competitive field. Babies have a habit of appearing unexpectedly, after a process of delivery whose length cannot be foreseen, and without regard to the time of day. The long, irregular hours cause the field to be dominated by men.[73] In this, as in so much else, men seem willing to work much harder for women than women themselves are.

The growing longevity gap between males and females does not affect people of all ages equally. Take the situation as it existed in England in 1860. At age 20, the probable mean duration of life was practically equal for people of the two sexes. At age 50, however, it stood at 18.7 for men versus 20.7 for women. Women past childbearing age were forging ahead. By age 75, the gap had even widened, to 2.3 years.[74] A similar trend was observed in late 20th-century America, where the improvement in women's life expectancy relative to that of men affected mainly those past childbearing age.[75] In other words, after accounting for the improvement in women's life expectancy that was brought about by the decline in perinatal mortality, British women in the 19th century, and American ones in the 20th, *still* did considerably better than men. At least one researcher has attributed the American development to the impressive progress that has been made in the treatment of cancer of the reproductive organs. This, in turn, may be linked to the fact that research in the field has been directed almost exclusively at women, not men.[76]

Yet another indication that women continue to receive better, or at any rate more, medical attention than do men is the far greater number of publications devoted to women's health. At Hebrew University's Mount Scopus library in Jerusalem, publications on the subject outnumber those about men's health 3 to 1. Online, the ratio in early 2013 on Amazon.com was 1.4 to 1. Even those figures represent a great improvement over the situation 10 years ago, when there were *no* books on men's health at the Mount Scopus library. In part, the

[73] For Britain and Australia see Pringle, *Sex and Medicine*, pp. 53-61.

[74] Finlaison, *Report on the Mortality on the Government Life Annuities*, p. 47, table XXIV.

[75] Retherford, *The Changing Sex Differential in Mortality*, pp. 67-8, 103.

[76] Retherford, *The Changing Sex Differential in Mortality*, p. 13.

greater attention paid to female health reflects the plain fact that women-specific medical problems do, after all, exist. In part it may also be the outcome of female hypochondria. In both Britain and the United States, women's own assessment of their health is consistently worse than that of men[77] — and where demand exists, supply will usually follow.

To a growing extent, however, the greater attention paid to female health is the result of institutional arrangements that discriminate against or outright ignore men. Thus, in the 1990s America's National Institutes of Health, arguably the most important institution of its kind anywhere in the world, set up an office for women's health. A similar office for men has yet to be established. As a result, twice as much money was spent on researching diseases unique to women as on those that afflict men. Nationwide, female patients accounted for two out of every three dollars spent for health purposes.[78] The U.S. Army alone was spending $135 million a year to research breast cancer,[79] a disease that by definition only affects the roughly 10 percent of soldiers who are women. Nationwide, spending on breast cancer exceeded spending on prostate cancer more than four to one. Nationwide, too, three out of every four medical research dollars are spent on women. This fact has caused at least one investigator to wonder whether anybody cares about men at all.[80]

The much greater concern for women's health explains why today they are largely excluded from clinical drug trials. Since the late 1950s, when pregnant women were given a drug called Thalidomide, there has been a general avoidance of using women for such tests. Developed to counter morning sickness, thalidomide caused children to be born with fin-like arms and legs, or none at all. The ensuing scandal caused tests on women to be largely halted. Since women now receive medicine only after their safety has been confirmed on men, men effectively act as guinea pigs for both sexes.[81] Some scholars, however, continue to perceive things otherwise. One group of researchers published a report complaining that women's bodies were being used as

---

[77] M. Blaxter, *Health and Lifestyle*, London, Routledge, 1990; M. Whitehead, *The Health Divide: Inequalities in Health in the 1980s*, Harmondsworth, Penguin, 1988; J. Rodin and J. Ickovics, "Women's Health: Review and Research Agenda," *American Psychologist*, 45, 9, 1990, pp. 1018-34.

[78] Londa Schiebinger, *Has Feminism Changed Science?* Cambridge, MA, Harvard University Press, 1999, p. 117.

[79] Chronicle of Higher Education, 19.12.1997, quoted in Greer, *The Whole Woman*, p. 172.

[80] E. E. Bartlett, "NCQA Gender-Specific Standards: Is There a Place for Men's Health?" *Managed Care Quarterly*, 8, autumn 2000, p. 50.

[81] J. F. Lauerman, "Chivalry and Science," *Harvard Magazine*, 11/12.1997, pp. 19-21.

"testing grounds" for new drugs.[82] Others complained that drugs were *not* being tested on women.[83] Damned if they did and damned if they didn't, during the 1990s the National Institutes of Health came "under siege" by lawsuits charging them with discriminating against women.[84]

While women were receiving the medical attention, men continued to do almost all the dangerous jobs, sustaining the resulting injuries and, in a great many cases, losing their lives. In early modern Europe, far more men than women suffered from work-related accidents in the building and hauling trades, as well as occupational diseases.[85] In Breslau during the 1680s, almost five times as many men as women met an accidental death.[86] In late-19th-century Germany, some 5,000 people died in work-related accidents each year, the vast majority of them men.[87] In England, Wales and Italy between 1871 and 1901, men were two-and-a-half to three times more likely to suffer accidental death than women.[88] In the words of 19th-century statistician William Farr, "It might appear that civilization has augmented more than it has diminished the danger to mankind."[89]

Some jobs were notoriously accident prone. The worst was mining, a field in which there were few if any women after 1830. At age 18, the life expectancy of miners stood at only 39.41 years. For the entire male population, the figure was 41.26.[90] Other trades whose members led conspicuously short lives were blacksmiths, bricklayers, mill operatives, plumbers, painters, potters, printers, stonemasons and woolcombers.[91] Some workers in these trades suffered from difficult working conditions, including exposure and dust, which

---

[82] Asian Women's Research and Action Network, *Asian Women Speak Out! A 14-Country Alternative Asian Report on the Impact of the UN Decade for Women*, Davao City, The Philippines, Asian Women's Research and Action Network, 1985, p. 13.

[83] Lesley Doyal, *What Makes Women Sick: Gender and the Political Economy of Health*, London, MacMillan, 1995, p. 85.

[84] Headlee and Elfin, *The Cost of Being Female*, p. 96.

[85] According to Wunder, *He Is the Sun, She Is the Moon*, p. 117.

[86] Shorter, *A History of Women's Bodies*, p. 236.

[87] Bebel, *Die Frau und der Sozialismus*, p. 163.

[88] Graziella Caselli, "Health Transition and Cause-Specific Mortality," p. 74.

[89] Quoted in Caselli, "Health Transition and Cause-Specific Mortality," p. 77.

[90] Henry Ratcliff, "Observations on the Rate of Mortality and Sickness Existing Amongst Friendly Societies," 1850, in Wall, ed., *Mortality in Nineteenth Century Britain*, p. 11, table II; p. 101, table LIII.

[91] Ratcliff, "Observations on the Rate of Mortality and Sickness Existing Amongst Friendly Societies," p. 89, table XLI; p. 90, table XLII; p. 100, table LII; p. 102, table LIV; p. 103, table LV; p. 104, table LVI; p. 109, table LXI; p. 113, table LXV.

could lead to tuberculosis, pneumoconiosis and other lung diseases. Others were killed "by poisons unknown in the early age," to again quote William Farr. In all but two of these professions, potters and woolcombers, there were practically no women. To this day in the United States, 93 percent of all those killed on the job are men.[92]

As regards injuries resulting from violence, the difference between the sexes is larger still. As far back as the Middle Ages, women were much less likely than men to become the victims of a homicidal attack. To the extent that they did become victims, they were much less likely to be the principal targets. Instead they tended to be hit in the company of their male relatives or friends. The injuries they sustained were, practically speaking, accidental side effects of male-on-male violence.[93] In today's United States, too, men are 50 percent more likely than women to be the victims of violent crime.[94] Even during childhood, males are much more likely to be bullied, physically hit and threatened than girls. Often the tormentors receive the active support of girls, who seem to like bullies.[95]

Figures from a leading feminist, Germaine Greer, paint a similar picture:

> One thing emerges with clarity: that males are always and everywhere more likely to die a violent death than females.... Of the 606 culpable homicides recorded in Britain for 1993, 375 of the victims were male and 231 female. These figures compare with FBI statistics of 60 percent of homicides of male on male compared with 24 percent as male on female. Of the 70,000 or so people maliciously wounded in Britain each year, about two-thirds will be young males.[96]

And in the developing world, the gap between men and women is more dramatic still.[97]

Some have argued that these differences result from males' greater aggressiveness and propensity to risk-taking — in other words, that men have

---

[92] See Lance Morrow, "Men: Are They Really that Bad?" *Time*, 14.1.1994, pp. 56-7.
[93] James B. Given, *Society and Homicide*, pp. 117, 143.
[94] Levit, *The Gender Line*, p. 187.
[95] Yvette Ahmad and Peter K. Smith, "Bullying in Schools and the Issue of Sex Differences," in Archer, ed., *Male Violence*, pp. 70, 80-1.
[96] Greer, *The Whole Woman*, p. 285.
[97] Greer, *The Whole Woman*, p. 285.

only themselves to blame for their troubles. Given that more men than women are involved in car accidents, there is almost certainly some truth in this proposition. Still, there is no doubt that society as a whole considers men's lives to be more expendable than women's. This is perhaps most evident in the movies. On the silver screen, for every woman killed, no less than 200 men suffer the same fate.[98]

Another field in which men bear the brunt of pain is that of athletics. Throughout history, in all civilizations, much of sports was and is based on the destruction of men's bodies, whether attempted or actually accomplished. Formerly in gladiatorial games and in tournaments, today in football, boxing, wrestling, auto racing and the like, watching men being killed or maimed or injured is considered good fun. While a few women also practice these sports, in their case it is often less a question of inflicting violence than of sexual display.[99] The same applies to spectators. More than a few female spectators do what they can to attract attention. A good example is Pamela Anderson, whose career was launched when she was caught on camera in the stands watching a football game. The woman with the deepest cleavage gets the man with the biggest muscles, and the other way around.

In summary, in almost any way one can think of it, it is women, not men, who have the easier and better life. As examined in the preceding chapters, women are less likely to be pushed hard, less likely to work hard or long, and more likely to be provided for by someone else, be it their husband or the state. They are also much less likely to suffer the full force of the law. And as examined in this chapter, women are likely to enjoy more than their share of whatever comforts society has to offer, and are also much less likely to be accidentally or deliberately injured. To top it all off, a woman's death by accident or violence is usually considered either tragic or horrible. Not so that of a man, which is often seen as either necessary or part of the fun.

Starting in France and Sweden two centuries ago, women's life expectancy vis-à-vis that of men has been increasing decade by decade. It has now reached the point where countries in which men outlive women have all but disappeared. Conversely, when the collapse of Communism in Russia and Eastern Europe led to a drop in living standards and life expectancy during the 1990s, men's mortality rate increased much more than that of women. When society modernizes, it treats women better than men. When it regresses —

[98] Farell, *Why Men Are as They Are*, p. 362.

[99] See Martin van Creveld, *Wargames: From Gladiators to Gigabytes*, Cambridge, Cambridge University Press, 2013, pp. 285-96.

temporarily, let us hope — it also treats women better than men.[100] On top of all this there exists a special class of women who are even more privileged than the rest. It is to these women that we must now turn our attention.

4. Ladies of the Leisure Class

Except when they were favored by birth, and very often even then, men's road to fame and fortune has always led through hard work or danger. Not so women who, provided they were born into the right families, were often carefully shielded from both work *and* danger. Once married, these women still were not expected to work. The same also applies to other women who, coming from below, used their charms to attract and marry upper-class men.

If the belief that advancing civilization helps women more than men is correct, then one would expect the demographic revolution to have started with the upper classes. The little data available for the period before 1800 support this hypothesis. As noted earlier, in 9th-century Paris upper-class women probably began to outlive their menfolk long before the same process was observed among women of other classes. Likewise, while men in late medieval Tuscany outlived women by a considerable margin, as early as 1400 more upper-class women than men were living past the age of 60.[101]

More evidence on this question comes from a study of English ducal families from 1330 to 1475. It shows that men's average life expectancy at birth was 24 years, while that of women was a whopping 32.9 years. At age 20 the figure for men was 21.7, that for women 31.1.[102] The reason why so many more men than women died was because of the violent activities in which they engaged. Not for nothing does the term "duke" derive from the Latin *dux*, commander. Leading a comfortable existence — and the life of duchesses is comfortable almost by definition — while their menfolk fought and were killed, women lived longer. A study of secular peers in England between 1350

[100] See Laurent Chenet, "Gender and Socio-Economic Inequalities in Mortality," in Annandale and Hunt, eds., *Gender Inequalities in Health*, pp. 184-8.

[101] Herlihy and Klapisch-Zuber, *Tuscans and Their Families*, p. 149.

[102] T. H. Hollingworth, "A Demographic Study of the British Ducal Families," *Population Studies*, 11, 1957, pp. 3-26.

and 1500 shows that no less than 20 percent of the men died of violent causes.[103]

Later figures from the 19th century provide additional proof that civilization does, in fact, first benefit upper-class women. The numbers come from an 1874 study conducted for the National Life Assurance Society of 2 King William Street, E.C., London, by one Charles Ansell, a well-known mathematician and businessman. Among Ansell's chief concerns was comparing the mortality rate of the upper classes with that of the general population. In so doing, he arrived at the unsurprising conclusion that, when it came to both men and women, those of the upper classes fared better.

For the purposes of this examination, however, the information of interest is the *relative* advantage of upper-class men and women over their less fortunate brothers and sisters. It turned out that, until the age of 50, there was hardly any difference between the sexes. From that age onward, however, it started to increase until, by age 70, the gap in favor of women was 1.14:1.[104] At the same age, the ratio of male to females was 0.88:1 among the upper classes, but only 0.8:1 among the general population.[105] In other words, upper-class ladies led the longest lives of all. This was true in absolute terms, as well as in comparison to both other women and to men of their own class.

That this is so is closely linked to the fact that women of the upper classes, instead of having to work, have always been supported by the labor of others. In ancient Egypt, such women did not get their hands dirty, relying on underlings and servants to do their work for them.[106] If, in the *Odyssey*, Penelope engaged in weaving, this was not because she expected to wear or sell the cloth — for that she had dozens of female slaves. In neither Athens nor Sparta were upper class women expected to work.[107] In the latter, so crass was the contrast between the "Spartan" life of men and the luxurious ways of women that Aristotle blamed it for the city's decline.[108]

Throughout the Middle Ages, it was mainly noblewomen who cultivated literature, poetry and music. Whether at their own expense or that of their

---

[103] J. T. Rosenthal, "Medieval Longevity and the Secular Peerage, 1350-1500," *Population Studies*, 27, 1973, pp. 287-93.

[104] Charles Ansell, Jr., "On the Rate of Mortality... in the Upper and Professional Classes," 1874, printed in Benjamin, *Rates of Mortality*, pp. 73-4, table III.

[105] Ansell, "On the Rate of Mortality," pp. 81-2, table VII.

[106] Robins, *Women in Ancient Egypt*, p. 101.

[107] Pomeroy, *Families in Classical and Hellenistic Greece*, p. 54.

[108] Aristotle, *Politics*, 1270a23-4; Plutarch *Agis*, 7.3-4.

husbands, these ladies liked to surround themselves with artists and performers.[109] Such entertainers often lived on the premises, which may help explain why, toward the end of the Middle Ages, female heads of great English households tended to employ a larger number of servants than did male ones.[110] Bored by country life, late-16th- and early-17th-century English "fine dames" pestered their husbands to journey to London.[111] Once there they kept busy by engaging in conspicuous consumption: "to drinke choyse Wines, eate Banqueting stuffe, and play with a Parret, is the only employment of her houres."[112] Other such ladies, to quote a pamphlet written by one of them, were placed in a position where "they have nothing to do but to glorify God and to benefit their neighbors."[113]

Nor were such attitudes confined to Europe. An 18th-century Chinese scholar, Chen Hongmou, wrote of spoiled young women. Their children were raised by nurses and their needlework was done for them by maids. "All they have to think about is making themselves beautiful. Everything is done for them, so they don't know that rice comes from a stalk and that silk is unreeled from cocoons. They treat money like dirt and living creatures like bits of straw."[114] Even in the 20th century, it was a rare Chinese lady who so much as cooked a meal.[115] The surroundings in which these women lived reflected their privileges. Their rooms were furnished with elaborate alcove beds, dressing tables, other tables, comfortable chairs and a washing stand. Mirrors, toilet articles, perfumes, sewing boxes and musical instruments were always close at hand.

In 1783, one German aristocratic lady, Sophie von la Roche, tellingly boasted that she used to "go into my kitchen and give instructions, since I myself am versed in the art of cooking."[116] Evidently she thought that doing so

---

[109] Shachar, *The Fourth Estate*, pp. 160-1.
[110] Mertes, *The English Noble Household*, p. 43.
[111] Heal and Holmes, *The Gentry in England*, p. 314.
[112] Wye Saltonstal, *Picturae Locquentes*, 2nd ed., 1635, quoted in Margaret J. M. Ezell, *The Patriarch's Wife: Literary Evidence and the History of the Family*, Chapel Hill, NC, University of North Carolina Press, 1987, p. 38.
[113] Mary Astell, "A Serious Proposal" [1694], quoted in Alice Clark, *Working Life of Women in the Seventeenth Century*, London, Routledge, 1982 [1919], p. 38.
[114] See Francesca Bray, *Technology and Gender: Fabrics of Power in Late Imperial China*, Berkeley, CA, University of California Press, 1997, p. 243.
[115] Pang-Mei Natasha Chang, *Bound Feet and Western Dress*, New York, Anchor, 1997, p. 12.
[116] Michael Maurer, *"Ich bin mehr Herz als Kopf": Sophie von La Roche, ein Lebensbild in Briefen*, Munich, Beck, 1983, p. 159.

was unusual, almost heroic. And not without reason: the typical "Berlinese lady of the high classes" neither read nor worked." Instead she passed her life "babbling, dressing or undressing."[117] Working for a wealthy Anglo-Irish lady at about the same time, Mary Wollstonecraft wrote that her employer spent as many as five hours a day simply applying makeup.[118] In 1810, one American writer put the number of "females in Great Britain who are exempted by circumstances" — that is, those with money left to them by their fathers or given to them by their husbands — "from all necessary labor" at 50,000.[119] Europeans who visited the United States later in the century, for their part, often expressed astonishment at the existence of "a large class of ladies who do absolutely nothing."[120] American culture, which in many ways was built in conscious opposition to that of the English, was cut from the same mold when it came to spoiling upper class women.

An early 20th-century analysis of such women by one of their own, Emily James Putnam, speaks volumes. The Englishwoman, a self-proclaimed "female of the favored social class" who later became part of the feminist pantheon, pulled no punches in her description of fellow upper-class women:[121]

> She overshadows the rest of her sex. The gentleman has never been an analogous phenomenon, for even in countries and times where he has occupied the center of the stage, he has done so chiefly by virtue of his qualities as a man. A line of gentlemen always implies a man as its origin, and cannot indeed perpetuate itself for long without at least occasional lapses into manhood. Moreover, the gentleman... is numerically negligible. The lady, on the other hand, has until lately very nearly covered the surface of womanhood. She even occurs in great numbers in societies where the gentleman is an exception; and in societies like the feudal where ladies and gentlemen are usually found in pairs, she

[117] Count Vasili quoted in Dominic Lieven, *The Aristocracy in Europe, 1815-1914*, New York, Columbia University Press, 1992, p. 143.

[118] Miriam Brody, *Mary Wollstonecraft: Mother of Women's Rights*, Oxford, Oxford University Press, 2000, p. 54.

[119] Sydney Smith, *Writings: Female Education*, London, n.p., 1810, pp. 118-9.

[120] See Barbara J. Berg, *The Remembered Gate: Origins of American Feminism*, Oxford, Oxford University Press, 1978, p. 98.

[121] See Miriam Schneir, ed., *Feminism: The Essential Historical Writings*, New York, Vintage, 1994, pp. 294-5.

> soars so far above her mate in the development of the qualities they have in common that he sinks back relatively into the plane of ordinary humanity... Economically she is supported by the toil of others; but while this is equally true of other classes of society, the oddity in her case consists in the acquiescence of those most concerned. The lady herself feels no uneasiness in her equivocal situation, and the toilers who support her do so with enthusiasm. She is not a producer; in most communities productive labor is by consent unladylike. On the other hand she is the heaviest of consumers, and theorists have not been wanting to maintain that the more she spends the better off society is. In aristocratic societies she is required for dynastic reasons to produce offspring, but in democratic societies even this demand is often waived.

From the industrial lands of northern France comes perhaps the best study — by a female author, no less — of the lives these marvelous creatures led.[122] There, as elsewhere, what governed their existence was the physical separation of the workplace from the home. It caused bourgeois women, who until then had taken a lively part in their husband's affairs, to retreat from work. Having become "the leading consumers of industrial goods," they put their efforts into fashioning homes for themselves and their families. Initially domesticity, with its emphasis on the peaceful life, comfort and culture, was the exclusive prerogative of high-class women. Later the ideal, and to some extent the reality as well, began to trickle downward. By the end of the nineteenth century it had invaded working-class homes, reaching the point where it almost amounted to a cult.

While men worked and worked — in the early capitalist world, life was a continuous race against the clock — their womenfolk enjoyed leisure. Often husbands worked specifically in order for their wives to be able to rest. As the latter visited spas or seaside resorts, the former stayed on the job, an arrangement chronicled by Kipling during the last years of the 19th century.[123] Though my wife and I grew up in different countries — she in Chile, I in Israel

---

[122] See Bonnie G. Smith, *Ladies of the Leisure Class: The Bourgeoisie of Northern France in the Nineteenth Century*, Princeton, NJ, Princeton University Press, 1981, pp. 4, 6, 11, 21, 23, 63, 67, 71, 74, 79, 81, 84, 86, 129, 133, 138-9, 145, 159.

[123] "At the Pit's Mouth," in Rudyard Kipling, *Wee Willie Winkie*, Harmondsworth, Middlesex, Penguin, 1988 [1895], p. 89.

— both of us remember it from our own families during the 1950s. Not having to work *and* blessed with extended vacations, women had the time and ease to develop a "more humane and less economic" view of themselves. Though their day-to-day work was done for them by servants, cooks, pastry makers, flower arrangers and gardeners, it was they who got the credit. "Enormous sums" were spent on clothes and jewelry, so that a broach bought by or for a wife might cost as much as her husband's wardrobe for three years. These women might know nothing of the value of money. But they were certainly experts in spending it.

Women's physical presence in the home also gave them other advantages. It was they who mediated between their husbands and the rest of the family, deciding all questions of engagement, separation, marriage, vocation, parental largesse and parental love. That was why contemporaries spoke of a "matriarchy." At a time when business suits were becoming almost obligatory for men, women took to wearing crinolines, hoop skirts, bodices, bustles, trails and huge sleeves. All these were expressly designed to emphasize their freedom from work of any kind. The garments also increased their wearers' physical size to at least double that of men; so big were some women that they could not pass through doorways and had special seats designed for them. In so dressing, the women demonstrated power. Too refined to handle coarse foods such as fowls, roasts and vegetables, what cooking they did was limited solely to pastries and delicate desserts.

Their husbands spent their days among the noise and soot of the factories, but they had armies of servants to clean after them. Men tried to outdo each other in economic competition with all the rough-and-tumble risk-taking, and conflicts of conscience, that such work demanded. Women, meanwhile, took to religion, started seeing themselves as guardian angels, and began preaching to anyone who would (or would not) listen. Surrounded by sofas, cushions, curtains, paintings, and incredible amounts of bric à brac, their sheltered lives were all but impregnable to outside influences. Whatever the law might say, within their own world they laid down the rules. On the one hand it was a world that in many ways permitted them to lead a child-like existence, centering on the serenity of the home and devoid of real responsibility. On the other, it enabled them to govern social life with an iron hand. It was they who dictated food, fashion and rules of etiquette — in a nutshell, what was and was not considered acceptable. By using the custom of visiting others with or without prior announcement, they were also able to establish hierarchies and lord it over other women.

To marry such a woman a man had to be *very* well established. Engagements could last for years. Not infrequently were they broken off because the fiancé had not done as well, financially, as expected. On average, the higher the class to which a man belonged, the later he married.[124] Women, on the other hand, were treated as if they were silkworms, breaking their cocoons and "coming out" into society at the age of 17 or 18. From this time on, their lives were spent at picnics, parties and balls. All involved enormous expense; English girls whose fathers could not afford to show them off in London might be shipped to some other place such as Cairo. There life was cheaper and single men, though not as rich as those at home, were plentiful. Unless a girl was exceptionally plain or handicapped in some other way, two or three seasons were usually enough. The common pattern was for a woman of 20 to hitch herself, or to be hitched by her parents, to a husband in his early 30s. However, the difference in age could be much greater, and in the first years of the 20th century the gap widened even further.

Once a married woman became pregnant she had found her destiny and could afford to relax. An hour's walk per day apart, it was customary to spend the first three months in bed or on a sofa. If complications arose, then it goes without saying that the best available medical care was on hand. One late Victorian painting shows a sick lady surrounded by no fewer than 10 doctors[125] — all of whom, it is safe to assume, had been summoned and paid for by her husband. Confinement nearly always took place at home, where greater comfort could be provided than at any hospital. In at least one respect, it ought to be noted, such English ladies did indeed earn their keep: most seem to have taken contemporary scientific advice and breastfed their children. However, everything else was done for them by underlings. Once the children had been weaned at nine months or so, rare was the mother who so much as entered the nursery.

Nor was looking after children the sole purpose for which servants were employed. Even in childless households, butlers, cooks, footmen, coachmen, gardeners and sundry maids were considered a must. That is to say nothing of the kind of help that came over occasionally in order to polish floors, carry out repairs and perform other such work. This dependence on personnel made the seasonal migration from the country to London and back again into a hugely

[124] See Bebel, *Die Frau und der Sozialismus*, p. 171.

[125] Reproduced on the cover of Patricia A. Vertinsky, *The Eternally Wounded Woman: Women; Doctors and Exercise in the Late Nineteenth Century*, Urbana, IL, University of Illinois Press, 1994.

complicated operation. Referring to a particularly grand household, one contemporary described its movement as "an army on the march."

Supported by their husbands as well as having an income of their own, the women's most important functions were social. Often they specialized in throwing lavish parties. Rising living standards and advancing medical science caused the class-differentiated gap in life expectancy between the two sexes to persist and grow. During the interwar period, as during the 19th century, the better-off a woman, the more likely she was to outlive not just her own menfolk, but everybody else.[126] Not even World War II, the largest and most ferocious armed conflict of all time, was able to touch their privileges. In Germany, faced with a grave shortage of labor, one reason why the regime hesitated to compel women to work was because it feared that, if it did so, the spectacle of bosses' wives sitting in coffeehouses and shopping might be too much for the rest of the population to stomach. In Britain, as the most class-conscious society of all, wealthy women were exempted from war work because they had large houses to look after![127] One can only conclude that, by having one privilege, a woman is entitled to enjoy others as well.

Born into the class to which they belong, surrounded by beautiful things from birth on, and in firm control of family affairs, upper-class women have long resisted feminists' demands that they surrender their leisure. To the contrary, for them it has been the fact that they did *not* have to work that has made life better.[128] Unless their qualifications are particularly high, going to work would mean having to mix with their social inferiors. Consequently, in the United States during the 1980s, six out of seven wives of high-income men did not have a job.[129] Likewise, in the countries that comprised the former Soviet Union, "it is... considered prestigious when a wife does not have to work."[130] At the annual gathering of the World Economic Forum in Davos, the few career women who attend on their own account are swamped by the non-working wives of the powerful, the rich, and the famous. These women simply *cannot* work; had they done so, how could they attend?

---

[126] Michael R. Haines, "Conditions of Work and Mortality Decline," in Schofield, ed., *The Decline of Mortality in Europe*, p. 190 table 10.3.

[127] Briar, *Working for Women*, p. 73.

[128] Susan A. Ostrander, *Women of the Upper Class*, Philadelphia, Temple University Press, 1984, pp. 8, 22, 27-8.

[129] Farrell, *Why Men Are The Way They Are*, pp. 104, 219.

[130] *Torgovaya Gazetta*, 29.4.1994, quoted in Lynne Attwood, "Rape and Domestic Violence Against Women," in, Buckley, ed., *Post-Soviet Women*, p. 102.

Forming a privileged class within a privileged class, the Jacqueline Bouvier-Kennedy-Onassises, Princess Dianas and Kate Middletons of this world have tastes that can be satisfied, if at all, only by billionaires. Their great-great-grandmothers were often brought up by nuns and completed their education at exclusive "finishing schools." They themselves often breeze through some of the world's best universities. However, they are less likely to take on graduate studies where the work is harder, less time is left over for socializing, and the knowledge acquired perhaps more likely to intimidate a prospective husband than to attract him. Their great-great-grandmothers were so wedded to domesticity that everything was delivered right to their doors. These modern women, by contrast, though still certain to rely on others to look after their household needs, are more likely to jet their way around the world's most expensive department stores. Their great-great-grandmothers took pride in their delicate constitutions and white skins, themselves the result of not having to work; today's most privileged women are more likely to wear a tan as a result of spending too much time in expensive health resorts or aboard luxury yachts.

According to the *Daily Telegraph*, Princess Diana once said a job was preferable to a husband.[131] Any job she herself might have had, though, would have been purely symbolic. As the daughter of one of the wealthiest families in England, she neither depended on a job, nor ever could depend on a job, for a living. For the same reason, she was able to start and stop working at will. Now, as always, a man is successful if he makes more than his wife can spend; a woman, if she can find such a man. Now, as always, those who have done so are perhaps the most privileged group of all.

5. Conclusions

If the interpretation advanced in the preceding pages is correct, then the most basic difference between men and women is that the latter are less resistant to the hard life. Partly out of a desire for adventure, but largely because they had no choice, men have always ventured out to the hardest places, often risking their lives in the process. Partly because they are more sensible, but largely because they *did* have a choice, few women joined them. If and when they did

[131] "Once Just a Princess, Suddenly a Feminist," *Daily Telegraph*, 3.12.1995.

so, then usually it was only after conditions had greatly improved. To the present day, the harder and less comfortable the conditions in any given place, the fewer the women it harbors. It must have been clear to every society that ever existed, even before Xenophon made her views known, that men's bodies are far more suited to doing hard work than women's. Societies that did not internalize this incontrovertible fact could never have survived.

As one would expect, the demographic revolution that made women's life expectancy increase more than that of men started at society's upper levels. Often it did so at the expense of men. The first class to feel its effects was the nobility, and the first places where it took place were the towns. Both largely eliminated women's duty to engage in outdoor work. However, the process is only rarely mentioned in the history books. Possibly this is because female relative longevity has been taken for granted. Aware that women are doing better than men, people assume that it has always been that way and have invented the most nonsensical explanations for it.[132] Nothing, however, is further from the truth. In particular, during the 19th century — which happens to be the first period for which reliable nationwide statistics are available — the phenomenon gave rise to much comment. Contemporary experts working both for government and for private industry knew perfectly well that civilization and its comforts benefited women more than it did men.

Two factors brought about the demographic revolution, first in developed countries and later in developing ones. The first was an improved standard of living; the second, better medical care. For the purposes of this examination, the most important development was the transition from the countryside to towns. Others factors were better nutrition, better clothing, better housing and better hygienic facilities, among others.[133] It goes without saying that all of these have benefited both men and women. However, the female organism is more vulnerable and less resistant to the kind of infection that results from contact with dirt. Therefore, on the whole spreading civilization benefited women earlier, and more, than it did men. And the higher the social class to which people of both sexes belonged, the truer this was.

Medicine, too, has benefited both men and women — but again, the facts make clear that women have benefited more than men. The most important medical advances which, relatively speaking, favored women over men were contraceptives, on the one hand, and perinatal care, on the other. Between

---

[132] See Angier, *Woman*, p. 251.

[133] See McKeown, *The Modern Rise of Population*.

them, these two advances brought down the female mortality rate associated with childbirth so dramatically that, in today's developed countries, it can hardly be expressed in percentage points. Indeed, probably no other factor has done more to change the demographic balance between men and women.

Yet while women have gained a disproportionate share of the benefits, men have done a disproportionate share of the work. First, the transition from the countryside to towns left far more men than women doing manual labor outdoors, under difficult conditions, and sometimes in places so rough that only madmen would choose to toil there. Next the industrial revolution left more men than women exposed to occupational diseases and accidents. Thus, it is reasonable to conclude that the improvement in the quality of women's lives has for the most part been carried on the shoulders of men — to say nothing of the fact that now, as always, well over 90 percent of the discoveries and inventions that drive that improvement in life quality are made by men.

To really understand the inequity of the burden, suppose men were to oblige some radical feminists by providing women with sperm banks designed to produce nothing but girls, with the male donors dying off en masse after doing their part. Since women have for the most part always been dependent on the hard labor of men, in such a hypothetical scenario civilization as we know it would almost certainly collapse. Mining, oil extraction, heavy and chemical industry, long-distance transportation, most forms of construction, and many kinds of agriculture, such as forestry and the herding of large domestic animals, would all but cease. So would deep-sea fishing. Under such conditions, over 90 percent of the world's present-day population would die of starvation. Those women that survived such a calamity would likely revert to a primitive life based on horticulture, dwelling in huts and suffering from a permanent shortage of animal protein. Judging by historical and pre-historical precedent, their life expectancy would be reduced to less than 40 years.

Yet while the world as we know it would likely collapse without men, often instead of thanks for their efforts they get complaints. In the past, women whose prospective husbands were forced to work like slaves so as to raise the brides-wealth demanded of them complained, or at any rate had complaints raised in their name, that men were given "an automatic head-start in life."[134] Today, women whose husbands work so hard they have no time to spend time with their families complain. Women whose husbands are home all day also

---

[134] Sandra T. Barnes, "Women, Property and Power," in Peggy Reeves Sanday and Ruth Gallagher Goodenough, eds., *Beyond the Second Sex: New Directions in the Anthropology of Gender*, Philadelphia, University of Pennsylvania Press, 1990, p. 267.

complain. Women who do not receive money from Aid to Families with Dependent Children complain. Women who do receive money from the program also complain, claiming that male-designed and -directed bureaucracies are invading their lives.[135] Women whose lives have been saved by Cesareans complain that male chauvinist imperialist doctors are invading their wombs.[136] One or two have even been known to complain that they were *not* made to pay taxes[137] — surely the only time in history such a complaint has been voiced.

Given the countless privileges women enjoy, a truly complete examination of the subject must inevitably tackle the thorny question of whether there is anything in women's nature or social situation that predisposes them toward complaining. Indeed, a full appraisal of the matter must also consider the possibility that modern feminism itself may be just a manifestation, writ large, of this particular predisposition.

---

[135] Barbara Arneil, *Politics and Feminism*, Oxford, Blackwell, 1999, p. 67; Elizabeth Frazer and Nicola Lacey, *The Politics of Community: A Feminist Critique of the Liberal-Communitarian Debate*, Toronto, University of Toronto Press, 1993, pp. 75-6.

[136] Gena Corea, "The New Reproductive Technologies," in Dortchen Leidtholt and Janice G. Raymond, eds., *The Sexual Liberals*, New York, Pergamon, 1990, pp. 85-94.

[137] See Leonie J. Archer, "Notions of Community and the Exclusion of the Female in Jewish History and Historiography," in Archer et al., eds., *Women in Ancient Societies*, pp. 58-60.

Chapter 8: The Complaining Sex

1. Femininity and Its Grievances

Judged by almost any criterion, women are, and always have been, the privileged sex. As embryos they are considered more vulnerable, despite the facts indicating the contrary. As children they are treated more gently and receive more protection. As students they have long been excused, or excused themselves, from whatever subjects were considered hardest. As adults they are under less pressure to compete and perform. As workers they do rather less than half of humanity's productive labor. As economic beings they are often in the enviable position of being able to consume without having to produce. As criminals and litigants they are treated much more leniently both by the law and the courts. As members of society they are both freed from the duty to participate in the most terrible of all human activities, war, and enjoy better protection against it.

Carried on the shoulders of men — sometimes, as when escaping natural disasters and the like, literally so — women have always commanded the lion's share of whatever comforts were available to any society at any time and place. Women are much less affected by violent crime, which is both cause and effect of the fact that their lives are considered more precious than those of men. Aided by rising living standards, on the one hand, and by modern medical science on the other, during the last two centuries or so women's advantages have become more and more pronounced. The more developed the society, the earlier the change began and the greater its impact. By 2013, in all but two of the world's 194 countries women can expect to live longer than men.

Given these facts, one would expect women to be happy with their lot. Such, however, is not the case. As we shall presently see, in practically all countries, more women than men seem to be in some kind of mental trouble or suffer from mental disturbances. In practically all countries, women are a majority both among patients in mental hospitals and among those who resort to various other mental-health services that do not require hospitalization. In practically all countries, women are found endlessly complaining about their situation in society. Since 1970 or so, advocacy groups established by women have served as institutional voices for such complaints. In the words of one male historian,[1] a gap seems to have opened up between women's objective situation in society and the way many of them perceive it or experience it. The more advanced the country and the more privileged the women, the truer his words ring.

The science responsible for making people happy, or at any rate for caring for those so unhappy as to present a serious problem to themselves and to others, is psychiatry. As shall be illustrated in the coming pages, for its troubles psychiatry was rewarded with an onslaught from feminists, who attacked the field as a pillar of the patriarchal order. Some of the first shots were fired by Simone de Beauvoir. She accused psychiatry, especially psychoanalysis, of pushing women to achieve "normalcy" by identifying with their mothers rather than their fathers.[2] To Kate Millett, psychiatry, with Sigmund Freud as its totemic head, was guilty of nothing less than a diabolical plot to reestablish men's rule over women, which allegedly had been shaken by the first feminist wave.[3] Some feminists even demanded that psychiatry, as a discipline, compensate women for the harm it allegedly inflicted on them.[4]

Before we examine the problems of women's mental health, the ropes defining the arena must be first tied in place. First, a conspiracy does not exist and has never existed. From Freud on down, the vast majority of modern mental-health workers are not out to discriminate against women, oppress them or prepare them for life under patriarchy. Instead, their objective is to listen to women, understand them, diagnose them and, if possible, relieve them from their endless troubles and symptoms. The fact that doing so has proved anything but easy is hardly mental-health workers' fault. Rather, it is due to the fact that, more often than not, no sooner does one kind of complaint dissolve

---

[1] Edward Shorter, *From the Mind into the Body: The Cultural Origins of Psychological Symptoms*, New York, Free Press, 1994, p. 59.

[2] *The Second Sex*, pp. 46-7; also see Paul Roazen, *Freud and His Followers*, Harmondsworth, Middlesex, Penguin, 1971, p. 465.

[3] *Sexual Politics*, pp. 176-202.

[4] Pringle, *Sex and Medicine*, pp. 144-5.

then another takes its place. This was true back when nearly every mental-health worker, aside from nurses, was male. And it remains true today, early in the 21st century, when a large number of workers in the field are female.

Second, every mental-health worker competes not just with others in the same profession, but with anybody enterprising enough to buy a brass plaque or post his or her name online. In the field of mental health, more so than in other areas of medicine, objective symptoms are hard to define and classify. In a sense, a person who says he or she feels unwell *is* unwell. As George Bernard Shaw once put it, under such conditions water will be prescribed to teetotalers, champagne to drunkards, "uric acid free" to vegetarians, and heavy overcoats to old colonels who suffer from the cold.[5] In other words, women who go to healers get what they ask for. So it has been in the past, and so, barring a sudden and drastic change in human nature, it will be in the future.

2. Dungeons and Dragons

In Europe, the priest was historically the person entrusted with attending to people suffering from mental trouble. By recommending prayer, imposing penance, granting absolution and even simply listening, some priests may actually have helped the afflicted. Other priests specialized in exorcism. As such, they overlapped with witches of both sexes. Once again, provided people believed in them, the ceremonies may have done some good.

Most mentally troubled people probably remained on a free footing. However, there were always men and women so troublesome to themselves and to others that they could be helped by neither priest nor wizard. Provided they had not committed any crime, or had committed a crime but were obviously too deranged to take responsibility for it, they were incarcerated in special establishments.[6] In Europe, the first such establishment opened its doors in Valencia, Spain, early in the 15th century. Others soon followed. Some institutions were run by the Church, others by municipalities, others still by the state.

---

[5] "Preface" to *The Doctor's Dilemma: A Tragedy*, Harmondsworth, Penguin, 1946 [1906], p. 76.

[6] See Michel Foucault, *Madness and Civilization: A History of Insanity in the Age of Reason*, New York, New American Library, 1965, pp. 9, 38, 39, 40, 65, 72, 75, 159.

From 1650 onward there was a growing tendency to isolate deviant people from society. The outcome was that the mentally ill were often confined together with the handicapped, the vagrant and the delinquent — in other words, anybody who formed a blemish on the well-ordered picture society was trying to present. Inmates regarded as dangerous to themselves and to others were locked in dungeons, or chained to walls, or strapped to chairs. Others were put in or onto a variety of exotic devices. The purpose was to restrain them and, by so doing, to calm them down. One picture shows a man with his arms spread and chained to two opposing walls, while a third chain links his head to the ceiling.[7] It was believed that the people in question had lost what was regarded as the essence of humanity — namely, reason — and turned into brutes. As brutes, they had to be maintained and guarded, not cured. It was as brutes, too, that they were put on display.

Around 1790, attitudes toward the mentally ill began to be revised. This was, as noted earlier, the era of *bienfaisance*, of doing good, and in the field of mental health it led to rapid humanization. Often the process was accompanied by considerable fanfare. At a time when the slogan of liberty was in the air, those in charge of the reforms wasted no opportunity to jump on the bandwagon and present themselves as liberators. Some of the worst abuses were taken away. No longer were patients locked up in dungeons or restrained with the aid of instruments. Chains, whips and other paraphernalia were largely done away with. The revolution in treatment was soon followed by an even greater one in the structures where such treatment had been carried out. Most pre-1800 asylums were centuries old and notorious for the damp, dark and overcrowded conditions that prevailed in them. Owing to the cages in which patients were kept, many also resembled a zoo or menagerie.

The first half of the 19th century saw a boom in the construction of institutions for the mentally disturbed. For the first time, asylums meant for treating the mentally ill were clearly separated from those intended to house the criminal and the poor. The old buildings were replaced by hotel-like structures that offered the conveniences of the era. Pictures often show rows of beds neatly arranged in spacious halls with a potted plant near each of them. Such, in fact, remained the standard layout of a mental hospital in Western countries

---

[7] Reproduced in Hans Binnenveld, *Om de Geest van Jan Soldaat: Beknopte Geschiedenis van de Militaire Psychiatrie*, Rotterdam, Erasmus, 1995, p. 88.

until at least the 1930s. The main objective of these institutions was to provide rest against the "frantic pace" of modern life. To achieve this aim, asylums were placed in rustic environments and surrounded by gardens. Reviewing the reforms, one authority claimed that "no class of persons in the United Kingdom are so well cared for as the insane." Food and clothing were provided, and in the words of one contemporary scholar, "every sort of indulgence within reasonable bounds [was] theirs."[8] Like their 18th-century predecessors, the new asylums attracted visitors eager to take a peek inside. Now, though, they came to admire, rather than to leer.

The so-called first revolution in psychiatry led to a change in the identity of those whom society put in charge of mental patients. Though doctors had always participated, until then many asylums had been run by priests on behalf of the church. Others were supervised by officials on behalf of the state, or by lay entrepreneurs on behalf of themselves. Some of these people joined the movement and even helped initiate it. One was Francis Willis, an English cleric who successfully treated the deranged King George III. Another was William Tuke, a tea and coffee merchant who set up a model asylum for the Quaker community of York. His son took over where he left off, and caring for the insane became the family business for several generations.[9]

Most of the reformers, however, were doctors. Arguably the best known among them was Philippe Pinel.[10] Born in 1745, he studied theology before switching to medicine and mathematics, and later became a consulting physician to Napoleon himself. Pinel was a disciple of Rousseau. He saw the origin of all social evils, insanity included, as rooted in the tyranny, inequality, religiosity and superstition of the *ancien regime*. By doing away with these, the Revolution laid down the groundwork for liberating madmen as well. Freedom itself was considered the best cure for lunacy; in one day alone, Pinel deprived 40 inmates of a municipal madhouse of their chains and the attendants of their horsewhips. In the place of physical constraints he put a regime emphasizing

---

[8] Edgar Shepard, "The Modern Teaching of Insanity," *Journal of Mental Science*, 17, 1872, p. 510, quoted in Showalter, *The Female Malady*, p. 27.

[9] See Klaus Doerner, *Madmen and the Bourgeoisie: A Social History of Insanity and Psychiatry*, Oxford, Blackwell, 1981, pp. 74-80.

[10] See Doerner, *Madmen and the Bourgeoisie*, pp. 127-38; also Dora B. Weiner, "'Le Geste de Pinel': The History of a Psychiatric Myth," in Mark S. Micale and Roy Porter, eds., *Discovering the History of Psychiatry*, New York, Oxford University Press, 1994, pp. 232-47.

order, regularity, sanitary conditions and work. Those who responded were rewarded; those who resisted were punished. Such means, it was reasoned, might lead them back, step by measured step, to rationality.

Not everybody subscribed to these ideas. In Germany, the most important reformer was another doctor, Johan Reil. It was he who invented the term "psychiatry." The cures he recommended were, to say the least, peculiar. Among other things, he suggested building special apparatuses that would cause the madman to "sail through the air on fire-spewing dragons."[11] Other patients were to be immersed in water with live eels, an early form of electroshock. Still, insofar as he emphasized regular work, as well as the sheer power of the therapist's personality, Reil resembled Pinel. Most other doctors also prided themselves on the fact that "chains or strait jackets [had] never been used or provided" in the asylums they ran and that no attendant was permitted to lay hands on a patient.

Since then, explanations as to the nature of mental disease have changed every few decades. At times it was seen as originating in weakness of the will. That included the kind of weakness which led to, and resulted from, masturbation.[12] At other times it was believed to be caused by degeneration of the organism, which might or might not be hereditary. Others declared that it originated in traumatic childhood experiences, or in some mysterious electrical disturbances in the brain, or was caused by the stress of "modern" life, or by the presence or absence of certain chemicals in the patient's bloodstream. All these were held responsible for the fact that some people were desperately unhappy, or felt extremely fatigued, or acted strangely, or could not control themselves, or presented a danger to themselves and to others. Whatever the fashionable theory, the principle that mental disease — the term itself was an innovation — is primarily a medical problem became firmly established.[13] It followed that those responsible for it should be neither jailers nor disciplinarians, but therapists or healers.

From the patient's point of view, being turned from a wild animal into a sick human being did not necessarily mean that the treatment which followed

---

[11] Johan C. Reil, *Rhaphsodien über die Anwendung der psychischen Curmethode auf Geisteszerrütungen*, Berlin, Ebing, 1936 [1803], p. 209.

[12] See E. E. Hare, "Masturbatory Insanity: The History of an Idea," *British Journal of Psychiatry*, 108, 1962, pp. 1-25.

[13] See also Foucault, *Madness and Civilization*, pp. 269-70.

was always effective, let alone pleasant. Still, in theory at any rate, that treatment was now based on proper scientific principles. It was administered by people who had taken the Hippocratic Oath. They operated, or at any rate were supposed to operate, in a sympathetic spirit with the express objective of making the patient feel better about him- or herself. If dungeons were still used, then this was only because no better accommodation was available and not because darkness was considered desirable for punishing inmates or curing them. If restraint was still employed, then only in order to prevent patients from causing harm to themselves and to others, and only because less brutal means were unavailable or ineffective. The more radical a cure, the more likely it was to be monopolized by persons who, whatever else, had behind them years of training in psychiatry as well as medicine. Such has been the situation since the middle of the 19th century, and so, in spite of all the changes that have taken place, it remains today.

3. The Rise of the Female Patient

Perhaps because troubled men were more dangerous to themselves and to their surroundings than were troubled women, before 1800 most inmates in mental asylums appear to have been male. Certainly this applied to the stereotype of such institutions. Pictures and drawings of people being restrained with the aid of various instruments almost always show men. One may properly surmise that, had they been women, then the results, seen from the point of view of those who produced them, would have been counterproductive. No more than today were the people of the 18th-century immune to the sufferings of women, real or imagined. In England, the most famous representations of madness were the bronze chained male nudes known as "the brazen, brainless brothers," "Melancholy Madness" and "Raving Madness." They kept watch over the gates of Bedlam, helping those who entered the hospital lose hope.[14]

By turning the mentally disturbed from brutes into sick people and humanizing the treatment they received, the first revolution in psychiatry caused the stereotype of the lunatic as a male monster to disappear. As if to

[14] On Cibber see *Encyclopaedia Britannica*, 1993, vol. 3, p. 312.

herald the change, in 1815 the twin statues were removed from Bedlam. In a society that believed in progress, people felt ashamed of what their predecessors had done to madmen.[15] In the popular imagination, the madman's place was taken by the disturbed woman. Later in the century, that woman became something of a favorite with photographers and artists. Usually she was young, and often she was beautiful. Instead of wearing chains, she is presented as reclining on a cushion in a comfortable room. Instead of appearing brutish or dangerous, she has the haunted look of someone who is neither here nor there — out of this world, as it were. Implicitly or explicitly, she is shown begging for help.

The stereotype may have influenced reality, or perhaps things worked the other way around. Be that as it may, as more asylums were built to "dispel the wailing of the despondent," as one historian put it,[16] the percentage of female inmates rose. By mid-19th century, they formed a clear majority.[17] The English census of 1871 showed that for every 1,000 male mental patients, there were 1,182 female ones. A year later, England and Wales had 31,822 certified female lunatics, but only 26,818 male ones. By the end of the century, the share of women had risen to about two-thirds. As with men, the mental illnesses of women were attributed to the most fanciful causes. As with men, those causes changed every few decades, as psychologists and psychiatrists claimed to make new discoveries. Whatever the causes of mental illness were believed to be, women have formed the majority of inmates ever since. When feminist Phyllis Chesler conducted her landmark study of women and madness in the late 1960s, she found that American women hospitalized for mental illness outnumbered men more than two to one.[18]

Women who were referred to the asylums only formed the tip of the iceberg. They were joined by much larger numbers of those who, feeling unhappy or unable to cope, either entered institutions out of their own volition or turned to some other therapy that did not require hospitalization. Throughout

---

[15] Foucault, *Madness and Civilization*, pp. 221, 223.

[16] Edward Shorter, *A History of Psychiatry: From the Era of the Asylum to the Age of Prozac*, New York, Wiley, 1997, p. 45.

[17] Showalter, *The Female Malady*, p. 17.

[18] Calculated from Chesler, *Women and Madness*, pp. 42-3, table 1. The figures do not include alcohol addiction, alcohol intoxication and drug addiction. However, even when these are taken into account, women still outnumbered men.

the second half of the 19th century, women were the primary clientele at surgical clinics, water establishments, rest homes and a whole series of similar institutions that promised quick cures at high cost.[19] By the last quarter of the century, if not earlier, women were undoubtedly the majority of psychiatric patients. That lead has been maintained ever since.

Looking back, perhaps the most decisive — but least noted — fact about the rise of the female patient is its timing. Before 1800, people whose behavior was disturbed or troubled were locked up and tied down. If they did not obey, they were also likely to be punished in all kinds of exotic ways. But around 1800, as noted earlier, the disturbed and troubled suddenly began to be regarded as sick. This caused them to become the object of pity, to be treated with consideration and, if at all possible, to be "cured." And as noted earlier, when conditions improve, very often those who benefit are primarily female; after all, women are never supposed to endure conditions as harsh as those considered standard for men. To put it another way, no sooner had attitudes toward troubled and disturbed people begun to change — for the better, most people would agree — then women suddenly became the majority among the disturbed and the troubled.

The hypothesis that the growth in the number of female patients may have been linked to the "domestication of insanity"[20] is supported by the fact that, just as women were being referred to treatment or hospitalized, men were being criminalized. Not by accident, the first revolution in psychiatry coincided with the drawing of a very sharp line between those who lived within the law and those who lived outside it and formed part of the underworld, as it was later called. Not by accident, too, it coincided with the rise of incarceration as the principal form of punishment between fines and death.[21] Whereas the vast majority of those institutionalized by way of punishment were male, a smaller number, though still a majority, of those institutionalized in order to receive treatment were female. To this day, women facing charges in court stand a much better chance of being declared "troubled" and referred to treatment than do men. If they are lucky, they may escape institutionalization altogether;

[19] Showalter, *The Female Malady*, p. 52.

[20] Showalter, *The Female Malady*, p. 52.

[21] See on this above all Michel Foucault, *Discipline and Punish*: *The Birth of the Prison*, London, Penguin, 1979.

instead they will spend their sentence talking to another woman with the title "therapist" in front of her name.[22]

By the 1870s, perhaps the most important mental disease was neurasthenia, or exhaustion of the nerves. Neurasthenia was discovered by a New York electrotherapist, George Beard, and was widely diagnosed in both North America and Europe.[23] With men, it was supposed to be the result of overwork, and included a vast array of symptoms including fatigue, depression, weak memory, lack of concentration, vertigo, insomnia, impotence and spermatorrhea (otherwise known as wet dreams). With women, its symptoms were equally wide-ranging. However, instead of impotence and spermatorrhea, they suffered from blushing, headaches, uterine irritability and that most common of female maladies, irregular menses.

The main difference, though, was that most women did not work. Leading a sheltered life, they were much less exposed to what late 19th-century people called "the struggle for existence" and what we today often call "stress." Accordingly, the origins of their problems had to be different. Doctors never stopped wondering why most of the patients who crowded their waiting rooms were female.[24] Here is a contemporary physician's description of what, in his view, might be the cause: [25]

> A woman, generally single or in some way not in a condition for performing her reproductive function, having suffered from some real or imagined trouble, or having passed through a phase of hypochondriasis of sexual character, and often being of a highly nervous stock, becomes the interesting invalid. She is surrounded by good and generally religious and sympathetic friends. She is pampered in every way. She may have lost her voice or the power of a limb. These temporary paralyses often pass off suddenly with

[22] See Foucault, *Discipline and Punish*, chapter 5.

[23] See Shorter, *A History of Psychiatry*, pp. 130-3; also George F. Drinka, *The Birth of Neurosis: Myth, Malady and the Victorians*, New York, Simon & Schuster, 1984, p. 191.

[24] Edward Shorter, *From Paralysis to Fatigue: A History of Psychosomatic Illness in the Modern Era*, New York, Free Press, 1992, p. 283.

[25] George Henry Savage and Edwin Goodall, *Insanity and Allied Neuroses*, London, Cassell, 1907, pp. 96-7.

a new doctor or a new drug; but, as a rule, they are replaced by some new neurosis.

The standard cure for neurasthenia was invented by an American surgeon, Silas Weir Mitchell. His Infirmary for Nervous Diseases became a mecca for patients from all over the world, including some of the most famous "new women" of the age. Among them were the social worker Jane Addams and the feminist writer Charlotte Perkins Gilman. He recommended, and did not hesitate to enforce, extended bed rests lasting for weeks or months. Such rest entailed the suspension of all activity — including, of course, economic activity. Normally it took place not at home, but in a sanitarium or spa. This made it very expensive indeed; no wonder women, who were not expected to work, could afford to become sick more easily, and to stay sick for longer, than men.[26] The works of Mitchell and his fellow doctors bristle with accounts of women who clung to their diseases and did whatever they could *not* to be rid of their afflictions. In the end, some were only "cured," if at all, by the heroic will of doctors.[27]

The other two main mental diseases of the period, *anorexia nervosa* and hysteria, were distributed even less evenly between the sexes. Anorexia, which first received its name in 1874, was and remains between 95 percent and 98 percent a female disease.[28] Female hysterics, meanwhile, were estimated in the 1970s to outnumber males by between two and four to one.[29] And that was an improvement over the late 19th century, when doctors put the difference at 20 to one.[30] Worse, whereas anybody knew how refusal to eat led to anorexia, hysteria, like neurasthenia, seemed to have no discernible organic causes. Instead, it manifested itself in a vast range of symptoms — including

[26] Shorter, *From the Mind into the Body*, p. 83.

[27] See Gerald N. Grob, *Mental Illness and American Society, 1875-1940*, Princeton, NJ, Princeton University Press, 1983, pp. 127-31; also David K. Henderson, *The Evolution of Psychiatry in Scotland*, Edinburgh, Livingstone, 1964, pp. 156-67.

[28] John Carlat et al., "Eating Disorders in Meals: A Report on 135 Patients," *American Journal of Psychiatry*, 8, 1997, pp. 1127-32.

[29] Dianne L. Chambless and Alan J. Goldstein, "Anxieties: Agoraphobia and Hysteria," in Anette M. Brodsky and Rachel T. Hare-Mustin, eds., *Women and Psychotherapy*, New York, Guilford, 1980, p. 116.

[30] Charles K. Mills, "Hysteria," in William Pepper and Louis Starr, eds., *A System of Practical Medicine*, Philadelphia, Lea, 1886, vol. 5, p. 215.

headaches, fainting spells, paralysis, mutism and uncontrollable screaming — for no apparent reason.

Why neurasthenia and hysteria should be mainly female diseases was, and is, by no means clear. From his perch as the foremost expert of his age, Mitchell proclaimed that "for the most entire capacity to make a household wretched there is no more complete human receipt than a silly woman who is to a high degree nervous and feeble, and who craves pity and likes power."[31] A late 20th-century male psychiatrist who authored a major study on hysteria blamed women's greater "search for emotional reactivity."[32] Others thought that "men may be less likely than women to present symptoms in a histrionic fashion;" others still, that the "sick" role was more acceptable for women than for men.[33]

Some of these explanations were adduced by male experts. Others were advanced by female ones. On the whole, the latter agreed with their male colleagues. In the words of one late 20th-century female historian of madness in women:

> When the hysterical woman became sick... she demanded service and attention from others. The families of hysterics found themselves reorganized around the patient, who had to be constantly nursed, indulged with special delicacies, and excused from ordinary duties... Physicians were concerned that hysterical women were indeed enjoying their freedom from domestic and conjugal duties, as well as their power over the family and the doctor himself.[34]

Anorexia, which meant refusing to take the very stuff of life and which was normally acted out in front of the entire family at mealtimes, was even more useful. In the words of the same historian, it gave the girls who suffered from it "the perfect means" to control their families, making "fathers storm, mothers

---

[31] Silas Weir Mitchell, *Doctor and Patient*, Philadelphia, Lippincott, 1901 [1887] p. 117.

[32] Hersch Wolowitz, "Hysterical Character and Feminine Identity," in Judith Bardwick, ed., *Readings on the Psychology of Women*, New York, Harper & Row, 1971, p. 309.

[33] Bruce Rousnaville et al., "Briquest's Syndrome in a Man," *Journal of Nervous and Mental Disease*, 167, 1979, pp. 364-67.

[34] Showalter, *The Female Malady*, p. 133.

cry" and turning themselves into "the sole object of preoccupation and conversation."[35] Not for nothing has it been called "the classic fashionable disease of the *belle époque*."[36]

Perceptive female patients such as Florence Nightingale sometimes ended up by admitting that what they wanted was attention.[37] Others denounced the doctors who had done their best to provide a cure; others still made their symptoms into the focus of their lives. Some women, "having never done anything that ought to tire [them],"[38] spent half their lives in bed. Others went from one clinic to another, demanding that their ovaries, or uteruses, or clitorises be operated on or removed.[39] Nor was it simply a case of male doctors abusing hapless female patients, as some have claimed. First, many such operations, clitoridectomies in particular, were carried out by female doctors who, in this respect as in so many others, simply followed where men led. Second, similar operations were carried out on males. In 1923 Freud himself, in the hope of concentrating his body's energies on combating cancer, had his seminal vesicles severed.

Many doctors were well aware that the operations in question were unnecessary, useless or both. They often warned each other both against individual patients and against "active" and "passive" "*mania operatoria*."[40] Many of their female patients, however, refused to listen. For example, Freud's follower and subsequent benefactor Marie Bonaparte had her clitoris operated on. But she did so in spite, not because, of the advice he gave her.[41] Some women faked symptoms by putting feces in their mouth and then vomiting it back out, in order to simulate an injury to the digestive tract.[42] Others talked and talked. Of the latter, the best known was Freud's "Dora."[43] Dora, whose

---

[35] Showalter, *The Female Malady*, p. 137.

[36] Lisa Appiganesi and John Forrester, *Die Frauen Sigmund Freuds*, Munich, Econ, 2000, p. 93. The German edition was used because the original English edition is out of print.

[37] Florence Nightingale, *Cassandra* [1860], Old Westbury, NY, Feminist Press, 1979, pp. 41-2.

[38] Robert T. Edes, "The New England Invalid," *Boston Medical and Surgical Journal*, 133, 1.8.1895, p. 102.

[39] Shorter, *From Paralysis to Fatigue*, pp. 73, 81-2, 87, 91.

[40] Albert Krecke, "Die weibliche Asthenie und die Mania operatoria activa und passiva," *Wiener medizinische Wochenschrift*, 72, 24.7.1925, pp. 1231-32.

[41] Appignanesi and Forrester, *Die Frauen Sigmund Freuds*, p. 470.

[42] Shorter, *From Paralysis to Fatigue*, p. 92.

[43] See Showalter, *The Female Malady*, p. 160-1.

real name was Ida Bauer, was the daughter of an upper-middle-class family. She was referred for a variety of symptoms, including the inability to speak her native language (though she retained her other linguistic abilities). So much did she like being a famous case study that her disease, such as it was, became the center of her existence.[44] After being treated by Freud she tried to repeat her triumph, displaying new symptoms and moving from one doctor to the next in an endless quest for attention. She was still "sick" when she died in New York in 1945, much to her family's relief.

Still, it was not every woman who could afford a Mitchell or a Freud. Most of their less fortunate sisters likely made do without any treatment. Others entered public institutions. These asylums specialized in paupers who were also diagnosed as suffering from mental illness. Or perhaps things worked the other way around, and it was mentally diseased people unable to afford private care who were admitted. As in the 17th and 18th centuries, to some extent the asylums presented an alternative to the workhouse or the street. While this was true for both men and for women, women dominated public asylums, as they did private ones. In 1871 in England and Wales, for every 1,000 male pauper lunatics there were 1,242 female ones. Women who, if they had been men, might have been sent to prison were joined by those who, if they had been men, might have been sent to the workhouse. Aware of what was going on, some asylum superintendents warned against housing hysterics for too long. Such women, they claimed, "sometimes get too fond of the place, preferring the dances, amusements, and general liveliness of asylum life... to the humdrum and hard work of poor homes."[45]

The history of diagnoses over the past two centuries, since the advent of psychiatry, strongly suggests that mental diseases are simply labels invented to fit patients' complaints into whatever intellectual framework exists at any given time and place. Hence it is not surprising that they follow a similar trajectory, exploding into public view and then, over time, losing their appeal and import. Borrowing the metaphor of the logistic curve from the business world is instructive here. A successful commercial product usually starts out with a slow, gradual rise in business, followed by a steep jump indicating a

[44] Felix Deutsch, "A Footnote on Freud's Fragment of an Analysis of a Case of Hysteria," *Psychoanalytic Quarterly*, 26, 1957, pp. 159-67.

[45] Thomas S. Clouston, *Clinical Lectures on Mental Diseases*, London, Churchill, 1898, pp. 530-1.

tremendous expansion in sales. As competitors catch up and the market becomes saturated, however, the curve drops and then flattens out. The logistic curve is a fitting framework for understanding why new ways of expressing and classifying unhappiness are constantly being invented, and why few mental diseases have retained their hold for very long. Indeed, it was in this way that neurasthenia and hysteria were condemned to disappear.

Of the aforementioned diseases, the only one that has succeeded in evading extinction is anorexia. Its longevity may be due to the clear physical symptoms that it presents. Alternatively, it is proof of how useful the disease is to both patients and doctors. In the words of one "victim" who for 16 years made her own life and that of her family a misery: "The more they tried to take anorexia away, the more I hung onto it... it kept me strong... without it, I would have nothing... do nothing... be nothing." She expected her relatives to discuss it constantly. When her family talked about anything else, she felt offended.[46] No wonder the "epidemic"[47] spread of this disease has given birth to an entire industry.

Another factor that may have contributed to the decline of neurasthenia and hysteria was World War I.[48] As long as they were regarded as female maladies *par excellence*, these diseases were treated by means which — as befitted females, most of whom visited the doctor out of their own free will — were comparatively mild. Even if an operation was involved, it was carried out under the influence of anesthetics. However, the war upset the balance between the sexes. In all armies that fought in the war, hundreds of thousands of young men began to suffer from what was known as shell shock. Their symptoms included extreme fatigue, insomnia, weeping, trembling, bedwetting, impotence and its opposite priapismus, blindness, stuttering, mutism, and paralysis of the limbs. The German Army alone registered 613,047 cases of shell shock, amounting to almost one in 20 of all those who passed through its ranks during the war.[49]

The appearance of vast numbers of male neurasthenics and hysterics shook the medical wisdom of the age. Men were supposed to cope; now, however, those affected were not women but soldiers who, having been examined and found healthy, engaged in the manliest activity of all. Partly because of the

[46] Cynthia N. Bitter, *Good Enough*, Penfield, NY, HopeLines, 1998, pp. 91, 143, 165.
[47] Shorter, *From the Mind into the Body*, p. 191.
[48] See Showalter, *The Female Malady*, p. 181.
[49] Unsigned, undated note, Bundesarchiv/Militärarchiv, Freiburg i.B., H20/480.

sheer number of cases, partly because of the effect which men who evaded battle by displaying the symptoms of a mental breakdown might have on the morale of those still in the trenches, armies could not afford to treat them with kid gloves. Some armies insisted on keeping them in camps close to the front. Others evacuated them and concentrated them in rear-area bases. Most gave them a few days' rest and then subjected them to fairly tough regimes, including drill and fatigues. Those who did not recover were subjected to electric shocks applied to various parts of the body.

In both England and Germany, so severe were the shocks administered by some doctors that they amounted to real torture. The real objective of the treatment was less to bring about a "cure" than to suggest to the recipients that the doctor would do whatever was necessary to bring it about. Hence there could be no question of using anesthetics; on the contrary, the idea was to inflict as much pain as the soldier could stand, perhaps a little more. Gradually it became clear that the best way to treat these patients — best in the sense that they could resume their function as cannon fodder, regardless of how terrible they may have felt — was *not* to permit them to rest far away from the battlefield.[50]

From the point of view of female neurasthenics and hysterics, the appearance of large numbers of male ones whose symptoms resembled their own spelled disaster. No doubt the causes that gave rise to women's troubles — be they oppression, discrimination or abuse — were deep, serious and deserving of all respect. Still, such personal tragedies were dwarfed by the terrible ordeal men underwent. These men, often quite young, faced the horror of a comrade's brains being blown up all over their body, or the very real possibility of being buried alive in a collapsing trench. Some neurasthenic and hysterical soldiers suffered concussions as shells burst nearby, perhaps slamming them against a wall, showering them with debris, and taking away their breath before they could recover. Others were temporarily blinded by gas — hysteria was a well-known aftereffect of exposure to this weapon — or had their lungs permanently damaged by it. Relative to such hellish experiences, the use of the term "survive" in the context of problems such as sexual harassment is simply obscene.

---

[50] See Peter Watson, *War on the Mind,* London, Hutchinson, 1978, p. 235.

Several contemporary female novelists described the soldiers' symptoms in lurid detail, shocking a public largely insulated from the mental horrors of the battlefield. One such writer, Dorothy Sayers, declared that once neurasthenia began to attack young, healthy men, it ceased to be presentable and became "indecent." Informed by doctors that their problems were quite similar to "cases of functional disorder observed by soldiers during the war,"[51] female patients had their thunder stolen, so to speak. Worse still, it had been shown that a cure of sorts could be brought about by the use of some pretty brutal means.

Yet applying such rough methods to women — let alone to troubled, frail, middle-class women — was unthinkable. Instead of being talked to and soothed, they might actually find themselves twisting and screaming with pain as an electrical current was passed through their bodies and a hard-faced doctor told them that this proved they could, after all, walk or speak. Much to the surprise of doctors,[52] both the number of female hysterics and the severity of the symptoms of those who remained decreased very sharply.[53]

As hysteria all but disappeared, a need was felt for another outlet for female complaints. Rising to the occasion, psychiatric science provided it in the form of schizophrenia. The founding fathers of schizophrenia were three German "mad doctors," as psychiatrists were popularly known: Emil Kräpelin, Eugen Bleuler and Kurt Schneider.[54] At first it met with only moderate success, but after 1920 schizophrenia took off, and its subsequent rise was spectacular. Along with bipolar disorder, also known as manic depression, it became one of the two pillars of psychiatric practice. As with neurasthenia and hysteria, though perhaps to a lesser extent, the majority of patients were female.[55] More than in the case of neurasthenia and hysteria, its symptoms — including a tendency to isolation, incoherence, delusions, hallucination and violence directed against the self and against others — were considered dangerous. Clearly schizophrenia was not to be trifled with. Patients were almost always institutionalized. Between 1966 and 1968, the number of Americans diagnosed

---

[51] Charles P. Symonds, "Two Cases of Hysterical Paraplegia," *Guy's Hospital Gazette*, 42, 1928, quoted in Shorter, *From the Mind into the* Body, p. 62.

[52] See Ernst Jones, *Free Associations*, New Brunswick, NJ, Transaction, 1990 [1959], pp. 124-5.

[53] See Shorter, *From Paralysis to Fatigue*, pp. 268-9, 272.

[54] See Mary Boyle, *Schizophrenia: A Scientific Delusion?* London, Routledge, 1990, pp. 16-75.

[55] See Chesler, *Women and Madness*, pp. 42-4, table 1.

and hospitalized as schizophrenics stood at no less than 850,000. Had psychiatrists had their way and the logistic curve been allowed to continue rising, then the point would have come where half the population was institutionalized under the care of the other half.

The other major mental disease that replaced neurasthenia and hysteria was depression. Whereas schizophrenia never reached more than 2 percent of the population,[56] depression affected as many as one in four people. The worst depressives were hospitalized. However, the vast majority walked the streets, and if they did commit themselves to getting help, did so voluntarily. Depression, like most afflictions, struck people of both sexes. However, as with other such mental diseases, the majority of those who suffered from it, or who claimed to suffer from it, were female.[57] In Britain it was considered to be "the paradigmatic female illness."[58]

Those were the years when psychoanalysis spread like wildfire. The key selling point about the method of treatment is that it is essentially a talking cure — the attention-getter *par excellence*, one might say. By its very nature it cannot and does not involve any coercion. Ordinarily patients are encouraged, even expected, to be at ease. Lying on the couch so that nothing can disturb them, they must let themselves go and say whatever enters their heads. Even if the therapist is unsympathetic, ultimately all he or she has at his or her disposal is words which the patient is free to accept or reject. Perhaps because women are better at "networking" — the politically-correct term for small talk — than men,[59] they were attracted to psychoanalysis like moths to a fire. Freud's own early clientele consisted almost entirely of women; one, indeed, presented him with the famous couch.[60] At London's Tavistock Clinic during the 1930s, nearly two out of three patients were female.[61]

---

[56] Shorter, *A History of Psychiatry*, p. 258.

[57] In 1966-8 manic-depressive women outnumbered men in American hospitals by just over two to one; Chesler, *Women and Madness*, pp. 42-3, table 1.

[58] Ludmilla J. Jordanova, "Mental Illness, Mental Health: Changing Norms and Expectations," in *Women in Society: Interdisciplinary Essays*, London, Virago, 1981, p. 106.

[59] See Carol Gilligan, *In a Different Voice: Psychological Theory and Women's Development*, Cambridge, MA, Harvard University Press, 1982, pp. 29, 43, 53-5, 57, 77.

[60] Appignanesi and Forrester, *Die Frauen Sigmund Freuds*, p. 235.

[61] Showalter, *The Female Malady*, p. 175-6.

Psychoanalysts, as one might expect, responded by pampering their female patients. Freud himself had to be warned by his daughter Anna, herself a renowned psychoanalyst, against sacrificing himself to his patients. As she saw it, the "millionairesses" might as well stay mad since that was their only occupation.[62] Probably another reason why women were over-represented among those taking the talking cure was the sheer amount of time it demanded. Originally psychoanalysis was a comparatively brief affair. Even a serious problem was supposed to be cured in about three months.[63] Later it stretched like chewing gum, and a standard analysis might involve six sessions a week and last for several years.

All these sessions had to be paid for even if they did not take place. So great were the demands of psychoanalysis in terms of both money and time that access to it was limited to members of the middle and upper classes. But whereas the interwar period all but eliminated the kind of upper class man who enjoyed leisure, this was much less the case with women. The higher the class to which a woman belonged, the less likely she was to work outside the home and the more likely she was to have servants work for her inside it. That left such women with more time to devote to talking through their complaints.

At first, practically all psychiatrists and similarly qualified therapists were male. During the 1880s they were joined by a trickle of women. Taught and, to some extent, overseen by the men at the head of the profession, women practitioners treated women patients with the same amount of sympathy, and by the same methods, as male doctors. Few if any of them developed an alternative view, let alone tried to empower their sisters and deliver them from the domination of men.[64] Freud's own followers included many women. He treated them as adopted daughters and judged them based on the quality of their ideas. Perhaps because he did not see them as rivals, if anything he was *more* open to their ideas than to those of his male students.[65] Women were proportionally

---

[62] Anna Freud to Freud, 20.7.1922, cited in Gay, *Freud*, p. 492.

[63] See Freud's own comment in Wilhelm Reich, *The Function of the Orgasm*, London, Panther, 1968, p. 68.

[64] See Regina Morantz, "The Lady and Her Physician," in Mary Hartmann and Lois Banner, eds., *Clio's Consciousness Raised: New Perspectives on the History of Women*, New York, Harper & Row, 1974, pp. 50-1.

[65] Roazen, *Freud and His Followers*, pp. 415, 416, 417, 444, 463.

more numerous among psychoanalysts than in many other professions.[66] One of them, Karen Horney, caused Freud some uneasiness by suggesting that "the flight from womanhood" and penis envy were the result, rather than the cause, of women's position in society. Still, even Horney objected only to one part of psychoanalysis, rather than to the system as a whole — let alone saw it as designed to oppress women, as her feminist successors did decades later.[67]

Freud's other female students accepted his tenets. One, Jeanne Lampl de Groot, insisted that "the absence of a penis cannot be regarded as a matter of secondary and trifling significance for the little girl, as Karen Horney [thinks]."[68] Rather, "the material" — meaning her own clinical experiences and that which others brought to her attention — proved that "penis envy is a central point." It is "from this point that the development into normal femininity begins."[69] Woman's "wish for a penis is the consequence of a biological datum that underlies her psychic reaction of feeling inferior and is 'rock bottom.'"[70] A similar line was taken by Helene Deutsch. As one of the first Austrian women to obtain a medical degree, Deutsch considered herself, not without reason, "a leader in female emancipation."[71] Good looking, highly intelligent and very hard working, for 30 years she was considered the world's foremost authority on the psychology of women. To Deutsch, the clitoris was "an inadequate substitute" for a penis.[72]

Freud's teachings garnered a wide following, particularly in the United States. The climax came around 1970, a time when no middle-class family

---

[66] See Appignanesi and Forrester, *Die Frauen Sigmund Freuds*, p. 17.

[67] See Karen Horney, "The Flight from Womanhood" [1926], in Harold Kelman, ed., *Feminine Psychology*, New York, Norton, 1967; and, for Freud's reaction, Marie Jo Buhle, *Feminism and Its Discontents: A Century of Struggle with Psychoanalysis*, Cambridge, MA, Harvard University Press, 1998, pp. 70-81.

[68] "Problems of Femininity" [1931], in Jeanne Lampl de Groot, *The Development of the Mind: Psychoanalytic Papers on Clinical and Theoretical Problems*, n.p., International Universities Press, 1965, p. 27.

[69] "Masochism and Narcissism" [1937], in Lampl de Groot, *The Development of the Mind*, p. 91.

[70] "Superego, Ego, Ideal and Masochistic Fantasies" [1963], in Lampl de Groot, *The Development of the Mind*, p. 358.

[71] Roazen, *Freud and His Followers*, p. 453.

[72] See Susan Quinn, *A Mind of Her Own: The Life of Karen Horney*, Reading, MA, Addison-Wesley, 1987, p. 218.

seemed complete without at least one psychoanalyst in the mix[73] — "yours, mine and ours," as a popular joke went. At $50 per 50-minute hour, the going price in New York City at the time, it was horrendously expensive. It drained people's pockets without necessarily giving anything but jargon in return. If ever a profession was subject to the logic of the logistic curve, it was psychoanalysis. In time, even the most obtuse patients started wondering why they should spend years discussing the origins of depression or anxiety or obsessive-compulsive disorder if a psycho-pharmaceutical drug such as Trophanil, Elatrol or Prozac could relieve the symptoms in a few weeks.

These doubts were reinforced by the rising second wave of feminism. In the eyes of many, the Nazis in particular, psychoanalysis had always been a racket. During the 1970s it was further decried as a racket directed against women. Freud himself was pulled down from his pedestal. Instead, he came to be seen as a man who had refused to take seriously the complaints of women such as "Dora." Some even suggested that he had abused his patients.[74] His colleagues came under similar fire. By defining women as weaker and more dependent than men, it was claimed, some psychoanalysts had belittled women. By defining women as strong and resistant to men, other psychoanalysts had failed to take women's complaints seriously. Yet others had had the impudence to suggest that children need a father as well as a mother.[75] In an age when divorce rates were soaring and divorced women were almost certain to obtain custody, this last transgression on the part of psychoanalysts may have been the worst of all.

Throughout these changes, which space only allows for presenting in the barest outline, far more women than men continued to suffer from, or at least ask to be treated for, most kinds of mental and psychosomatic problems.[76]

---

[73] See Shorter, *A History of Psychiatry*, pp. 166, 180-1.

[74] See Florence Rush, "The Freudian Cover-up: Sexual Abuse of Children," *Chrysalis*, 1, 1977, pp. 39-44; also Jeffrey M. Mason, *The Assault on Truth: Freud's Suppression of the Seduction Theory*, New York, Viking, 1985, *passim*.

[75] See Nancy Friday, *My Mother/My Self: The Daughter's Search for Identity*, New York, Delta, 1997, p. xviii.

[76] See William Coryell and George Winokur, "Course and Outcome," in Eugene Paykel, ed., *Handbook of Affective Disorders*, Edinburgh, Churchill Livingstone, 1992, pp. 89-108; Noreen Coldman and Renee Ravid, "Community Surveys: Sex Differences in Mental Illness," in Guttentag et al., eds., *The Mental Health of Women*, pp. 33, 45; Nancy F. Russo, "Women in the Mental Health Delivery System," in Lenore E. Walker, ed., *Women and Mental Health Policy*, Beverly

Women formed the majority of patients at a time when most of them did not work outside the home. Perhaps not surprisingly, now that most women work outside the home, they still form a majority of patients. In England in 1955 and 1956, almost twice as many women as men complained of "debility and fatigue." Among those suffering from "neuralgia and neuritis," the disproportion was similar.[77] In the United States in 1967, proportionally twice as many women as men were under psychiatric care in general hospitals for "psychophysiologic and psychosomatic disorders."[78] Later women accounted for 70 percent to 92 percent of depressives, and 73 percent of those suffering from "delusional parasitism" — that is, the feeling that they were infected by some imaginary germs or bugs.[79] As one female psychiatrist explained in 1989, patients with "such popular non-scientifically documented disorders" as total allergy syndrome and chronic fatigue syndrome are usually "psychologically disturbed, well-educated, single women, aged 30-50, in unhappy life circumstances."[80]

Among agoraphobics, women outnumbered men four to one.[81] Indeed, agoraphobia has been called a "housewives' disease." Hysteria and neurasthenia having gone out of favor, few other syndromes were so useful in disrupting family life and turning it into a misery. To quote a famous female expert on the history of women's mental afflictions,[82] what women were after

---

Hills, CA, Sage, 1984, p. 27-8; Myrna M. Weissman, "Depression," in Brodsky and Hare-Mustin, eds., *Women and Psychotherapy*, pp. 98-9; Joseph Veroff et al., *Mental Health in America: Patterns of Help-Seeking from 1957 to 1976*, New York, Basic Books, 1981, pp. 47, 159, 201; Lilli S. Horning, "Affirmative Action Through Affirmative Attitudes," in Elga Wasserman et al., eds., *Women in Academia*, New York, Praeger, 1975, p. 9; Headlee and Elfin, *The Cost of Being Female*, p. 98; Greer, *The Whole Woman*, pp. 181-2, 184; Veroff et al., *Mental Health in America*, p. 47.

[77] General Register Office, *Morbidity Statistics from General Practice*, London, HMSO, 1958, vol. 1, pp. 72, 86.

[78] Walter R. Gove and Jeanette F. Tudor, "Adult Sex Roles and Mental Illness," *American Journal of Sociology*, 78, 1973, p. 826.

[79] George Winokur and Ming T. Tsuang, *The Natural History of Mania, Depression, and Schizophrenia*, Washington, American Psychiatry Press, 1996, pp. 227, 295.

[80] Dona Steward, "Unusual Presentations of Psychiatric Disease," *Medicine North America*, 37, 1989, p. 718.

[81] Chambles and Goldstein, "Agoraphobia and Hysteria," p. 122. The number of women suffering from agoraphobia is said to be in excess of 1 million.

[82] Chesler, *Women and Madness*, p. 109.

was "attention, understanding, merciful relief, a *personal solution*" to their troubles. Whether because men are conditioned to aggressiveness and competition or simply because they were too busy making a living, she says, women were unable to get it "in the arms of the right husband."[83]

In reality, perhaps the greatest shortcoming of psychoanalysis was its insistence on absolute honesty. Proceeding under the motto "truth will make you free," and using a technique — free association — designed to generate as much liberty as a human being is capable of achieving, psychoanalysis by its very nature is a voyage into the self. To feminists, however, trying to make a woman — an "unsuspecting creature" — "seek the cause [of her unhappiness] in herself" was an "extraordinary confidence trick."[84] Much as they differed in other respects, all feminists wanted to see women's troubles placed on the shoulders of men. Once the premise that patriarchy was to blame for women's troubles was accepted, it followed that male therapists were useless, or worse. Though caused by men, women's troubles were unique to them. Accordingly, troubled women should be cared for by other women who could empathize and sympathize with them, act as role models for them, and open up to them about their own feminine troubles, which of course no man could fully comprehend.[85]

The idea that the world was a male conspiracy and that only women could properly understand women led to a massive shift in the personnel that made up the profession. Even as the number of psychiatrists began to decline, that of psychiatric social workers began to rise. By 1985 it had reached 55,000 in the United States alone. Five years later, America had no fewer than 80,000 clinical social workers.[86] Women formed the majority among both psychiatric and clinical social workers. The shift was accompanied by a massive outpouring of popular literature. It bore titles such as *Women Who Love Too Much*, *Men Who Hate Women*, and *The First Wives Club*. Regardless of whether they were meant to offer "serious" advice or comic relief, all told their female readers that many, perhaps most, men were louts. To get rid of them was the best a woman

---

[83] Gerald L. Klerman and Myrna M. Weissmann, "Depression Among Women," in Guttentag et al., eds., *The Mental Health of Women*, p. 75.

[84] Greer, *The Female Eunuch*, p. 91.

[85] Lucia Albino-Gilbert, "Feminist Therapy," in Brodsky and Hare-Mustin, eds., *Women and Psychotherapy*, pp. 249-50, 257-9; Linda Gordon, *Heroes of Their Own Lives: The Politics and History of Family Violence*, New York, Penguin, 1988, pp. 25, 282-5.

[86] Shorter, *A History of Psychiatry*, p. 293.

could do. This was all the more the case if she could milk them for money as well, or even better, make money by writing about the process and telling other women how to follow in her footsteps.

Yet some problems have remained. In the brave new world of psycho-pharmaceuticals, instead of patients getting the doctor's attention for years on end — as with psychoanalysis during its heyday — a visit to today's clinic takes only a few minutes. As one woman treated for obsessive-compulsive disorder recounted.[87]

> I wanted to tell the Prozac doctor about my hands. I wanted to splay them across his desk and say: "Look at them. What are they seeking?" I wanted him to touch my hands, not really an odd desire, the laying on of hands a practice as ancient as the Bible itself.... Instead, he reached down, opened a desk drawer, and pulled out a sample pill packet.

As she herself says, this was "asking a lot" from a busy doctor working for an insurance company. Worse still, after years of treatment and several hospitalizations that had resulted in a file "as thick as an urban telephone book," presumably it was impossible to know if and when she would turn around and accuse the doctor of sexual assault. No wonder he kept his distance and always stayed behind his desk. As of 2013, women who still hanker for a "laying on of hands" — and there are a lot of them — must turn either to a female therapist or to a husband.

For those still seeking a doctor interested in what their hands are saying — one who would be "not only technician, but poet, priest, theologian, and friend" — the choices are endless. While some therapists still stick to Freud, most have now adopted other methods. They rang from that of Carl Gustav Jung to that of Maharishi Siva Nadi Jothida Nilayam of Poona. Therapists include, and treat, people of both sexes. Still, the majority among both patients and, increasingly, therapists are women. Unsurprisingly, an estimated 20 percent to 25 percent of therapists are lesbian.[88] It has also been claimed that, psychological disease by

[87] Lauren Slater, *Prozac Diary*, New York, Penguin, 1999, p. 7.

[88] See Pringle, *Sex and Medicine*, p. 151.

psychological disease, women receive more attention and more treatment than their “otherwise indistinguishable” male counterparts.[89]

Therapists may receive patients either privately, for pay, or as part of the myriad welfare schemes that are financed by the state. As usual, women find it easier than men to attract welfare. The more lonely, abused, battered or batty she is, the more likely she is to be treated for free. In Quebec, and perhaps some other places as well, the State Health Service will even pay for a woman to have cosmetic surgery — breast implants — if she decides that her psychological well-being depends on it.[90] In this way, much of the mental health care business has turned into a system whereby the state or various other organizations pay some *bijoux indiscrets* to commiserate with others of their kind. Even general practice has often turned into a talking session, with female doctors spending on average twice as long with their patients as their male counterparts.[91] Men, as usual, pay either by supporting their female relatives or indirectly, by way of their taxes. That, after all, is the role nature has destined them for.

4. The Anorgasmic Woman

In society at large, women who for one reason or another feel they do not get the attention they deserve conjure up a variety of mental health symptoms and turn to therapists to have those symptoms treated. In conjugal life, with or without a ring, women who for one reason or another feel they do not get the attention they deserve can always deploy the ultimate weapon in the war between the sexes: frigidity. For men it is the cause of endless unhappiness. For women it is both a cause of unhappiness and, as often as not, a means of expressing it.

The fact that frigidity is *not* the result of Western culture refusing to grant the human female orgasm “undeniable status”[92] should be clear from its

[89] Blechman, "Behavior Therapies," p. 235, quoting L. S. Stein et al., "Comparison of Male and Female Neurotic Depressives," *Journal of Clinical Psychology*, 32, 1976, pp. 19-21.
[90] *Yediot Acharonot*, 11.1.2001, p. 7.
[91] Pringle, *Sex and Medicine*, pp. 179-80.
[92] See Masters and Johnson, *Human Sexual Response*, p. 138.

prevalence in a culture as different from the West as China. The fact that it is *not* a Victorian invention intended to help men "contain their hidden panic at the secret female appetite they feared"[93] is evident from its antiquity. Its existence was already known to Aristotle. More detailed information comes from the Roman poet Ovid. Judging by his self-description Ovid, who lived around the time of the birth of Christ, was a playboy and a man about town. He spent as much time as he could seeking women, seducing them, and making love to them. He celebrated his activities in some of the finest poetry ever written. As regards female frigidity, he had this to say:[94]

> So, then, my dear ones, feel the pleasure in the very marrow of your bones; share it fairly with your lover, say pleasant, naughty things the while. And if Nature has withheld from you the sensation of pleasure, then teach your lips to lie and say you feel it all. Unhappy is the woman who feels no answering thrill. But, if you have to pretend, don't betray yourself by over-acting. Let your movements and your eyes combine to deceive us, and, gasping, panting, complete the illusion. Alas that the temple of bliss should have its secrets and mysteries.

Nor can the matter really be cleared up by studying other animals. Since insemination is vital to reproduction, why the males of sexually-reproducing species ejaculate and why evolution has caused them to experience that activity as pleasurable is perfectly clear. In the case of females, however, orgasm is not biologically necessary. That leaves open the question as to why it has evolved at all — *if* it did. Particularly in the case of primates as our closest relatives, the question has given rise to much controversy.[95] In recent years, however, it seems to have been settled by a series of studies. Judging by their behavior, expression and heartbeat, among other indicators, it seems that female monkeys can experience orgasm and do so regularly. Primate females, like human ones, like to have sex at least partly because doing so is fun.[96] But that fact only

[93] Gay, *Freud*, p. 513.
[94] Ovid, *The Art of Love*, London, Private Edition, 1930, p. 179.
[95] See Small, *Female Choice*, pp. 143-7; also see Angier, *Woman*, pp. 69-70.
[96] Small, *Female Choice*, pp. 117-50.

makes the question why some human females do not have fun, or only do so rarely, even harder to answer.

The male orgasm is brought about by applying friction to the erogenous zones surrounding the penis. Aristotle knew the female orgasm is also brought about by applying friction, but just how and to what end is not entirely clear from his writings. In 1559, Renaldus Colombus, a doctor at the University of Padua, told his "most gentle reader" of his discovery that the clitoris was "preeminently the seat of woman's delight." His claim was promptly disputed by his successor, Gabriele Fallopius (of Fallopian tubes fame), who asserted that he, Fallopius, had discovered the clitoris first. In the next century, both Fallopius and Colombus were taken to task by yet another doctor, the Dane Kaspar Bartolin. He argued that the clitoris had been known about since it was discovered by Galen in the 2nd century, if not earlier.[97]

To "discover" the clitoris' existence is one thing, but to proclaim its importance as the "preeminent seat of woman's delight" is another entirely, and in that respect Colombus was clearly the first. Others soon came to agree with him. In 1668 *Bartholin's Anatomy*, a standard textbook used in English universities, described the clitoris as women's "chief seat of delight in carnal copulation" and as crucial to orgasm. Twenty years later, yet another doctor, the Frenchman Nicholas Venette, wrote that it provided "the fury and rage of love... the seat of pleasure and lust."[98] Yet another reference dates from 1836. Expressing the general consensus,[99] an English manual noted that "the lower part of the vagina and the clitoris" were "the seat of venereal feelings from excitement."[100]

Neither Ovid nor the 1836 handbook explained what they meant when they said that "some" women did not experience orgasm. Subsequent doctors tried to be more precise. In 1844, the Englishman William Acton wrote that they were "the majority." One, the Frenchman Adam Raciborski, claimed that as many as three-quarters of all women merely endured their husbands' embraces. Throughout the 19th century, apparently the only figures based on a survey rather than on guesswork were provided by an American woman, Clelia Duel

[97] See Thomas Laqueur, *Making Sex: Body and Gender from the Greeks to Freud*, Cambridge, MA, Harvard University Press, 1990, pp. 64-5.
[98] Porter and Hall, *The Facts of Life*, p. 75; also Fletcher, *Gender, Sex and Subordination*, p. 37.
[99] See Laqueur, *Making Sex*, p. 233.
[100] See Laqueur, *Making Sex*, p. 189.

Mosher, who worked at the University of Wisconsin.[101] Using a sample of 47 women, most of them faculty wives, she concluded that about 20 percent of them had never had an orgasm.[102] Mosher's conclusion was not that much different from the results Alfred Kinsey obtained from his much larger survey of American married women during the late 1940s. He found that 25 percent did not experience orgasm during their first year of marriage. After 20 years together, however, the number was down to 11 percent.[103] These figures were in line with subsequent findings dating to the 1970s.[104]

The more the 19th century advanced, the more frigidity tended to be seen as a major social problem. Such was the view of Martin Charcot in the 1880s, Richard Krafft-Ebing in the 1890s and, from that period onward, Freud. All three agreed that women's psychological troubles were largely a result of their inability to achieve orgasm. As Freud put it, psychoanalysis showed that a woman's entire psychological makeup depended on whether or not she enjoyed sex.[105] Karen Horney, the famous feminist, agreed. In her entire career, she claimed, she had not seen even "one [female] case without some functional disturbance of their genital system," including, above all, "frigidity in all degrees."[106] Left unsaid by virtually all, of course, was the added unhappiness the women's sexual problems caused among the unfortunate men condemned by the vows of marriage to live and sleep with them.

Some of the difficulties experienced by women were clearly the fault of husbands who lacked a *penis normalis*, as one of Freud's colleagues, referring a patient, once put it.[107] However, many difficulties could by no means be attributed to male impotence, insensitivity or other assorted defects. Presented with an endless parade of neurotic or frigid females, each doctor according to

---

[101] See on her Vern L. Bullough, "The Development of Sexology in the USA," in Porter and Teich, eds., *Sexual Knowledge, Sexual Science*, pp. 308-9.

[102] See Laqueur, *Making Sex*, pp. 190-1.

[103] *Sexual Behavior in the Human Female*, Philadelphia, Saunders, 1953, p. 408, table 112.

[104] See Golombok and Fivush, *Gender Development*, p. 137.

[105] For Charcot and Freud see Gay, *Freud*, pp. 91-2; for Krafft-Ebing, his "Neuropathia sexualis feminarum," in W. Zülzer, *Klinisches Handbuch der Harn- und Sexualorgane*, Leipzig, Vogel, 1894, pp. 80-103; also see Krafft-Ebing, "Über das Zustandkommen der Wollustempfindung und deren Mangel (Anaprhodisie) beim Sexuellen Akt," *Internationales Centralblatt für Psychologie und Pathologie der Harn und Sexualorgane*, 2, 1891, p. 105.

[106] See Quinn, *A Mind of Her Own*, p. 255.

[107] See Gay, *Freud*, p. 92.

his, and increasingly her, lights did what he or she could to help — and do so, what is more, without causing them to run away as "Dora" had. Some doctors took Galen's advice and masturbated their patients to orgasm. This skill they found hard to master and unpleasant to perform; that was why one of them, hoping to rid himself of the "chore," invented the vibrator.[108] Others spent countless hours of crushing boredom trying to make sense of their patients' complaints, only to find that, all too often, new symptoms appeared as fast as old ones could be cured. The fact that the doctors' efforts were not without merit, or at any rate not considered without merit, is proved by the ability of some of them to attract a large, primarily female following.

By that time Darwinism had come to rule the intellectual world. Darwinism led to the idea that each biological phenomenon served a function which accounted for its existence and without which it could not, or should not, have evolved. In contrast to earlier times, it was now clearly realized that conception did not depend on a woman reaching orgasm. This raised the question of why the female orgasm existed in the first place. The same question was also raised about the clitoris itself, which, after all, plays no role in reproduction. In fact it may be, and often has been, excised without impairing a woman's fertility. It was Freud's belief in evolution, not his "patriarchal" views, which gave rise to his famous theory about the two different kinds of orgasm. Decades before his findings were confirmed by that great researcher, Shere Hite,[109] Freud knew that the penis invites masturbation in a way that the clitoris, which is hidden from view, may not.[110]

More than most people, Freud admired and tried to model himself on "the great Darwin."[111] Confronted with a riddle that had long baffled his predecessors and continues to baffle his successors, male and female alike,[112] he tried to identify the origins of a woman's orgasm by splitting female sexual awakening into two stages. A girl, he reasoned, starts her sexual life by discovering the clitoris in the same way as a boy discovers his penis, though

[108] See Rachel P. Maines, *The Technology of Orgasm*, Baltimore, MD, Johns Hopkins University Press, 1999, pp. 3-4, 6, 11.

[109] See Golombok and Fivush, *Gender Development*, pp. 137-8.

[110] Sigmund Freud, *Standard Edition of the Complete Psychological Works of Sigmund Freud*, London, Hogarth Press, 1955-74, vol. 15, p. 155.

[111] See Gay, *Freud*, pp. 26, 36, 333, 603.

[112] See Angier, *Woman*, pp. 70-5.

perhaps at a later stage. Once she has discovered her clitoris, she focuses her sexual pleasure on it. However, his reasoning went, since stimulating the clitoris was not essential for reproduction, doing so was an immature act. For a woman to become fully mature, therefore, she had to move the center of her sexuality to the vagina, where the penis could reach it. Doing so was a difficult feat, one which by no means all women successfully accomplished.[113]

For what it is worth, most of Freud's female followers agreed with him. To Jeanne Lampl-de Groot, abandoning the clitoris in favor of the vagina was "an arduous task."[114] To Helene Deutsch, "the awakening of the vagina to full sexual functioning is entirely dependent on the man's activity."[115] To Simone de Beauvoir, who did not study with Freud but was strongly influenced by him, "the clitorid system" was "only indirectly connected with normal coition." To her, sexual maturity in a woman could be produced "only through the intervention of the male."[116] All this may prove that women, even when studying their own anatomy and pleasure, tend to be "schooled"[117] by men. That, or else those who hail de Beauvoir as the herald of female sexual emancipation have never read her book.

Over the years, perhaps no other part of Freud's doctrines has been subjected to so many attacks. The climax came in the years immediately after 1966. It was then that William Masters and Virginia Johnson showed that "clitoral and vaginal orgasms are not separate biological entities."[118] Echoes of "the great orgasm debate" are still being heard today.[119] The discovery gladdened the hearts of feminists. They quickly claimed that women were much more orgasmic than men — after all, they could achieve orgasm many times in succession.[120] Better still, they did not even require the help of a penis

[113] Sigmund Freud, "Femininity," in Sigmund Freud, *The Complete Introductory Lectures on Psychoanalysis*, James Strachey ed., New York, Norton, 1966, pp. 580, 596.
[114] "Masochism and Narcissism," p. 92.
[115] *The Psychology of Women*, vol. 1, 233.
[116] *The Second Sex*, p. 348.
[117] Angier, *Woman*, p. 131.
[118] *Human Sexual Response*, pp. 21, 67.
[119] See Buhle, *Feminism and Its Discontents*, pp. 212-20; also Small, *Female Choices*, pp. 137-8; Laqueur, *Making Sex*, pp. 234-5; Maines, *The Technology of Orgasm*, pp. 5-6, 111-24.
[120] See Angier, *Woman*, p. 66.

to do so.[121] The result was an entire literature that turned the clitoris into the glory of creation. In fact, by concentrating on the clitoris and pretending that the penis was unnecessary, feminists deliberately falsified Masters and Johnson. This is because, in the words of one female sexologist, the clitoris does not stand on its own; instead it forms part of an "erotic network" that also comprises the labia and the perineum.[122] That is why, the sexologist added, women who masturbate "usually stimulate the entire mons area rather than concentrating on the clitoral body."[123]

Furthermore, to quote Masters and Johnson, "The fact that the clitoral glans rarely is contacted by the penis in intravaginal thrusting does not preclude the coital development of indirect clitoral involvement." "Direct or primary stimulation of the clitoris" by the penis is particularly easy in the "female superior and lateral coital positions." Still, "clitoral response" was observed even during "coital activity" in the "knee chest" position, which is what Masters and Johnson called a woman being penetrated from behind. In other words, the fact that "the primary focus for sexual response in the human female's pelvis is the clitoral body" does not obviate the "female... demand for continued active male pelvic thrusting during the woman's orgasmic experience."[124] Other researchers believe this "demand" may explain why human males have the largest penises of any primates.[125]

But as Masters and Johnson recognized,[126] Freud was right when he said that sex cannot be understood without taking into account the part played by emotions. On average, sex probably is more of an emotional experience for a woman than it is for a man. One need only note the vast industry specializing in selling real or imaginary sex to total strangers, an industry that caters almost exclusively to men. Further proof has been provided by the introduction of Viagra. Viagra's success shows that men's impotence is largely due to organic causes, particularly those that prevent blood from flowing into the penis. By

---

[121] See Millet, *Sexual Politics*, pp. 117-8; also see Harriet G. Lerner, "Early Origins of Envy and Devaluation of Women: Implications of Sex-Role Stereotypes," *Bulletin of the Meninger Clinic*, 38, 1974, pp. 538-53.

[122] See Mary J. Sherfey, *The Nature and Evolution of Female Sexuality*, New York, Random House, 1972, p. 94.

[123] See Masters and Johnson, *Human Sexual Response*, pp. 53, 59, 64.

[124] Masters and Johnson, *Human Sexual Response*, pp. 61, 65.

[125] Fisher, *The Sex Contract*, p. 96.

[126] Masters and Johnson, *Human Sexual Response*, p. 135.

contrast, female orgasmic capacity does not depend on either the size or the position of the clitoris.[127] Countless studies have failed to explain why 43 percent of women are said not to enjoy sex to the fullest.[128] Experiments in administering Viagra to anorgasmic women only showed that placebos can do equally well.[129] To be satisfied, it seems, women need more than a pill.

There are several logical explanations for why emotionally achieving sexual satisfaction is more difficult for women than for men. Women, for one, are on average physically weaker. Secluding themselves with a man, they are more vulnerable than he is, to say nothing about the need to open up their bodies and be penetrated. Second, more than men they have the consequences of sex to consider. Not only can they become pregnant, but they are more at risk of contracting venereal disease than are heterosexual men. In the 1990s, AIDS became the fifth-leading cause of death for American women of childbearing age.[130] Thus, women have excellent reason not to abandon themselves — the term speaks volumes — before establishing "the most absolute trust in the transcendence of life," as a French feminist philosopher somewhat bombastically put it.[131]

Should a woman fail to reach climax, then to the extent that medical science can determine, almost certainly the problem is not physiological but psychological.[132] And the exact nature of women's psychological problems has given rise to an enormous body of literature. Freud himself originally believed that such problems were due to excitation of girls' genitals at too early an age — in plain English, sexual abuse. But as Freud's first and most important biographer noted, he tended to be much too credulous when listening to his female patients.[133] Later the sessions he had with those patients caused him to abandon his sexual abuse theory. "I was at last obliged to recognize that these

[127] Masters and Johnson, *Human Sexual Response*, p. 57.

[128] Martindale, "What Women Want," p. 28.

[129] See Rosemary R. Basson et al., "Efficacy and Safety of Sildenafil in Estrogenized Women with Sexual Disjunction Associated with Female Sexual Arousal Disorder," *Obstetrics and Gynecology*, 95, 2000, 4 Suppl. 1: S54.

[130] Richard Davenport-Hines and Christopher Phipps, "Tainted Love," in Porter and Teich, eds., *Sexual Knowledge, Sexual Science*, p. 371.

[131] Lucy Iragary, *An Ethics of Sexual Difference*, Ithaca, NY, Cornell University Press, 1993, p. 197.

[132] See Martindale, "What Women Want," pp. 31-2.

[133] See Appignanesi and Forrester, *Die Frauen Sigmund Freuds*, pp. 249-50.

scenes of seduction had never taken place, and that they were only fantasies my patients had made up."[134] In his later days, Freud simply gave up. He admitted that 30 years of research into "the feminine soul" had not taught him "what women want." "The sexual life of adult women," he lamented, was "a dark continent" for psychology.[135]

Others, however, did not hesitate to venture where Freud had been reluctant to go. They came up with all kinds of explanations, proffering advice to those who turned to them for treatment or bought their books.[136] Most such experts were male. However some, such as the bestselling writers and activists Isabel Hutton and Marie Stopes, were female. Remarkably enough, Stopes produced her principal work on the subject of sex while she was still a virgin. More remarkable still, she managed to remain a virgin and married at the same time.[137]

Broadly speaking, the answers proffered by these experts on sex were of one of two types. Some continued emphasizing abuse, both that which had taken place years previous during childhood and that perpetrated against a woman by her sexual partner. The difficulty of defining what exactly constituted sexual abuse perpetrated against a woman by her sexual partner made it a challenge to ascertain the validity of the charge. One is reminded of a story writer Stefan Zweig told about one of his aunts. Several hours after her wedding she stormed into her parents' house, screaming that her husband was a madman and had tried to take her clothes off.[138] And accounts of abuse that took place years previous, based as they are on what psychologists termed "repressed memory," are more problematic still. The minimum one can say about such charges is that they are often unreliable — as Freud, to his chagrin,

[134] Sigmund Freud, "An Autobiographical Study," in *Standard Edition*, 1959, vol. 20, p. 34. See also Gay, *Freud*, pp. 93-8; and Alan Krohn, *Hysteria: The Elusive Neurosis*, New York, International Universities Press, 1978, pp. 19-21.

[135] Gay, *Freud*, p. 501; Freud, *Standard Edition*, vol. 20, p. 212.

[136] See Porter and Hall, *The Facts of Life*, pp. 212-6.

[137] See Hall, "'The English Have Hot-water Bottles': The Morganatic Marriage between Medicine and Sexology in Britain since William Acton," in Porter and Teich, eds., *Sexual Knowledge, Sexual Science*, p. 358.

[138] *Die Welt von Gestern*, Frankfurt/Main, Fischer, 2000 [1944] p. 98.

discovered. Often, and some would say not often enough, such charges are regarded with skepticism by psychologists, policemen, lawyers and judges.[139]

The second type of answers proffered by the experts blames the difficulties many women have in reaching orgasm on the way they were educated. Partly because most people in modern societies consider themselves enlightened, and partly because contraceptives are so easily available, notions of chastity as a woman's paramount virtue have lost some of their force. Still, even in developed countries, the upbringing of young women continues to reflect their vulnerability and the consequences that sex may entail. The parent who recommends that his or her daughter sleep with any man as long as he agrees to wear a condom has yet to be born. However good the intentions behind educating girls in such a manner may be, there is little doubt that it can be overdone and turned into a form of abuse. It stands to reason that some women who, from childhood on, have been subjected to endless tales of wicked men and the need to resist them may find it hard to enjoy sex when they reach the point where they are permitted to actually have it. Indeed, mothers have been known to "castrate" their daughters, causing frigidity to pass from one generation to the next.[140]

Both these interpretations assume that frigidity is something from which women suffer, a condition that, created by external pressures, affects them against their will, persists through no fault of their own, and causes them nothing but pain and embarrassment. But this assumption may be incorrect, or only partly correct. For a great deal of women, frigidity can very well be seen as part of their sex's greater tendency to complain about psychological problems from hysteria and depression to neurasthenia and anorexia. Though there is no objective evidence that women's lives are harder than those of men, more women complain about mental troubles in order to attract attention. Though only a very small percentage of frigid women display an organic defect, a much larger number complain about frigidity in order to get the attention of their husbands or sexual partners.

Since many frigid women *do* reach orgasm by masturbation, consciously or not their inability to do so during coitus may very well be a punishment they

[139] See Elizabeth Loftus and Katherine Ketcham, *The Myth of Repressed Memory: False Memories and Allegations of Sexual Abuse*, New York, St. Martin's, 1994, *passim*.

[140] Julian de Ajuriaguerra, "Le Probleme de hystérie," *L'Encephale*, 40, 1951, p. 76; Friday, *My Mother/My Self*, pp. 5-6, 13, 21-2, 69-72.

inflict on men for the sins the latter may have committed. Whether those sins are real or imaginary is, in the end, both unprovable and irrelevant. After all, there is a sense in which she (or he) who feels sinned against has been. Some women, we are told, deliberately use their frigidity as "a useful tool with which [they] could gain leverage in sexual relations."[141] Far from being ashamed of it or trying to overcome it, they speak of it with "self-righteous complacency."[142] They even reproach other women for not using it in order to crack the whip. At least one wrote a book about her distaste for "genital thrashing about."[143] Another believes that the vaginal orgasm has been forced on women as part of "the androcentric model of sexuality."[144] For such women, being brought to orgasm by a man, and especially by a man's penis, is a sign of weakness. Or else, by convincing him it is all his fault, they make sure, or try to make sure, that he stay with them.

The doyenne of modern feminists, Simone de Beauvoir, knew these problems first hand.[145] Like many other feminists from Mary Wollstonecraft on down,[146] de Beauvoir grew up in a middle-class family whose male head found it hard to provide and became the object of his wife's resentment. Determined never to be in her mother's position, the dutiful daughter decided to stand on her own economic feet and directed her studies toward that end. Next she met Jean-Paul Sartre, fell in love, and wished to marry him as the only man she considered worthy of her. He, however, did not think he could be faithful, and was honest enough to tell her so.[147] That led to the famous pact under which each was free to do as he or she pleased, as long as they told one another everything. If she could not have him entirely for herself, at any rate she could share his adventures.

---

[141] See John d'Emilio and Estelle Freedman, *Intimate Matters: A History of Sexuality in America*, Chicago, University of Chicago Press, 1997, p. 71.

[142] Eliot Slaterand Moya Woodside, *Patterns of Marriage: A Study of Marriage Relationships Among the Urban Working Classes*, London, Cassell, 1951, p. 21.

[143] Sally Cline, *Women, Celibacy and Passion*, London, Deutsch, 1993.

[144] Maines, *The Technology of Orgasm*, pp. 5-6.

[145] See Barbara Klaw, "Simone de Beauvoir and Nelson Algren," in Melanie C. Hawthorne, ed., *Contingent Loves; Simone de Beauvoir and Sexuality*, Charlottesville, VA, University of Virginia Press, 2000, pp. 127-8, 142.

[146] See Edna Nixon, *Mary Wollstonecraft, Her Life and Times*, London, Dent, 1971, pp. 1-13.

[147] See *The Prime of Life*, Harmondsworth, Middlesex, Penguin, 1965 [1960], pp. 22-5.

From this point on, de Beauvoir was forced to keep up with her soulmate's *petites camerades.* She would have been inhuman if she had not resented the arrangement, and indeed in her first novel, the main character — based on herself — ends up by murdering her competition.[148] Though de Beauvoir had several affairs, she was unable to find love with others. Approaching 40 years of age, she had still not discovered the true joy of sex. Like so many others in her position, on occasion she must have faked it.[149] No wonder that, over time, she and Sartre lost their sexual interest in each other.

In the end, de Beauvoir was rescued by an American writer, Nelson Algren. She met him while touring the United States in 1947, and for several years she kept up a relationship with him. In *The Mandarins*, which was produced not long after her affair with him ended and which is autobiographical in all but name, she wrote: "His desire transformed me. I who for a long time had been without taste, without form, again possessed breasts, a belly, a sex, flesh; I was as nourishing as bread, as fragrant as earth. It was so miraculous that I didn't think of measuring my time or my pleasure; I know only that before we fell asleep I could hear the gentle chirpings of dawn."[150]

No longer handicapped by her personal problem, de Beauvoir found the courage to write about the essence of womanhood. The result was her first bestseller, *The Second Sex*, in which she delved into the topic of frigidity:[151]

> Resentment is the most common cause of feminine frigidity; in bed the woman punishes the man for all the wrongs she feels she has endured, by offering him an insulting coldness. There is often an aggressive inferiority complex apparent in her attitudes... She is thus revenged at once upon him and upon herself if he has humiliated her by neglect, if he has made her jealous, if he was slow in declaring his intentions, if he took her as a mistress while she wanted marriage. The grievance can flare up suddenly and set off this reaction even in a liaison that began happily... Frigidity... would appear to be a punishment that woman imposes as much

---

[148] *She Came to Stay*, Harmondsworth, Middlesex, Penguin, 1959 [1943].

[149] See Asa Moberg, "Sensuality and Brutality; Contradictions in Simone de Beauvoir's Writings about Sexuality," in Hawthorne, ed., *Contingent Loves*, p. 104.

[150] *The Mandarins*, London, Fontana, 1960, p. 341.

[151] *The Second Sex*, pp. 369, 375.

> upon herself as upon her partner; wounded in her vanity, she feels resentment against him and against herself, and she denies herself pleasure.

Many men, de Beauvoir continued, suffer "torment" from their wives' failure to be sexually responsive. And what starts from an inability to climax, she noted, might easily result in women refusing to have any sex at all.[152] Meanwhile "many married women find amusement in confiding to one another the 'tricks' they use in simulating a pleasure that they deny feeling in reality; and they laugh cruelly at the conceited simplicity of their dupes. Such confidences may often represent still more play-acting, for the boundary between frigidity and the will to frigidity is an uncertain one." "In any case," the oracle of feminism concluded, "they consider themselves to lack sex feeling and thus they satisfy their resentment."[153]

5. Conclusions

While everything in the this book indicates that women are indeed the privileged sex, everything in the present chapter indicates that women are the complaining sex. To paraphrase Nietzsche in *Thus Spoke Zarathustra*, everything about women, and feminists in particular, is a complaint, and the complaint has one cause: namely, the plain fact that a woman stands a much better chance of getting her way by complaining than a man.

Thus understood, women's greater tendency to complain about real and imagined troubles follows directly from their relative physical weakness and lesser degree of competitiveness. He whom God, nature or hormones has made competitive and strong will, more often than not, take what he can. She whom hormones, nature or God has made less competitive and less strong is, more often than not, better off begging, wheedling, maneuvering or complaining. And if all else fails, she can always weep. For most women in most situations, experience shows this tactic usually works. All other things being equal, the more readily she can squeeze water out of her eyes, the better her prospects.

---

[152] D. Claire Hutchins, *Five Minutes to Orgasm Every Time You Make Love*, n.p., JPS, 2000, p. 21.
[153] *The Second Sex*, pp. 417-8, 440.

Such histrionics have earned perhaps the greatest ire from those women who (while otherwise privileged) did not live off of the privileges of their sex. Indeed, history abounds with examples of successful women expressing nothing but contempt for their weaker sisters. Queen Artemisia of Caria — the first known female commander, and a very successful to boot — told her lord, Emperor Xerxes of Persia, that Greeks were as superior to Persians as men to women.[154] Queen Elizabeth I of England cracked jokes about women.[155] Mary Wollstonecraft, for her part, called female authors "timid sheep."[156]

Timid sheep that they might be, women are hardly passive, unknowing participants in their own drama. Women's greater inclination to complain about their troubles does *not* indicate that "the course of a woman's mental illness, be it schizophrenia or manic-depression, often is more unpredictable and labile than that of a man." Nor does it indicate that a woman's mind is, as one modern author put it, "truly a syncopated pulse,"[157] whatever that might mean. On the contrary, by developing symptoms and clinging to them, women have proved they have an excellent understanding both of the advantages and disadvantages that result from their physical structure, on the one hand, and on the other their position in society. If you cannot beat him who, on average, is stronger and more competitive than you, you can always "manipulate"[158] him by making him feel guilty.

Normally the first prerequisite for a woman's complaint to be crowned with success is for her to be without a man. Should she have one, then unless he abuses her it is assumed her main difficulty is over, given that responsibility for her rests primarily on his shoulders. As long as she is not a "whore" or a "slut" — and under the new rules of cross-examination, even if she is — being without a man makes a woman helpless by definition. If she is also seen as weak or sick, then so much the better for her chances of getting help. From the time of Moses to that of Aid to Families with Dependent Children, having children was often the joker in the deck of cards. An unattached woman with children earns a much bigger bonus than does her male counterpart. That is

[154] Herodotus, *The Histories*, 8.8.

[155] Fraser, *The Warrior Queens*, p. 269.

[156] See Harriet D. Jump, *Mary Wollstonecraft, Writer*, New York, Harvester Wheatsheaf, 1994, p. 32.

[157] Angier, *Woman*, p. 27.

[158] Friday, *My Mother/My Self*, p. 81.

probably one reason why most widowed and divorced fathers remarry as soon as they can. Conversely, women sometimes have had children specifically in order to obtain aid That aid might take the form of a man who was forced to marry them; or of charity; or of social security; or of a variety of other benefits. Finally, a woman whose troubles can be attributed to other people is more likely than anybody else to receive assistance.

Underlying all such complaints, whether personal or societal, is an unending quest for attention. Attention is something people of both sexes crave, and there is no reason to believe that women do so more than men. However, their paths to receiving attention differ fundamentally. In the eyes of both men and women, almost the sole way men can attract attention is by succeeding. In the eyes of both women and men, women can attract attention almost equally well by failure or by complaining about it. This may explain why, among those with an MBA, women are said to be four times more likely to seek psychological help than men.[159] Behavior tolerated and even praised in the goose is, quite simply, not acceptable in the gander. In the words of one female historian of women,[160] "If 'depression' is soon viewed as a meaningless catchall category, another female malady will appear to take its place for another generation." Since psychoactive drugs took the drama out of most kinds of mental trouble, her prophecy came to pass. A new way of drawing attention had to be found. Various attempts were made, but none really caught on.[161] A change of course was called for; and sexual harassment duly appeared.

Like mental trouble, women's complaints about sexual harassment often involve "a desire for recognition." Such a desire runs "throughout the interviews" conducted with them, reported one otherwise empathetic male writer.[162] Unlike mental trouble, this kind of complaining is played out not in the privacy of the clinic but in the courtroom. And the courts have become a safe haven for women; witness the fact that they are often given the choice between a public trial and one conducted behind closed doors.[163] But like anything else, complaints about sexual harassment are subject to the logistic

---

[159] Oren Harari, "What Do Women Want Anyway?" *Management Review*, 81, 3, March 1992, p. 43.

[160] Showalter, *The Female Malady*, p. 249.

[161] See Shorter, *From the Mind into the Body*, pp. 86-7.

[162] Ptacek, *Battered Women in the Courtroom*, p. 152.

[163] See Ptacek, *Battered Women in the Courtroom*, Chapter 5.

curve, and as they, too, grow into a meaningless catchall category, they will eventually recede in prominence. As for what will come after sexual harassment, heaven knows. Who would have guessed that, out of the attempts during the 1970s to prove that women can do anything as well as men, there would be born the teary-eyed, hapless victims of sexual harassment of the 1990s and 2000s?

So strong is the determination to complain at all costs that "patriarchy" is often damned if it does and damned if it doesn't. If women are said to be the second sex, then this is wrong. But if they are said to be the first sex, then this is also wrong.[164] If fathers embrace their daughters, they may be accused guilty of child sexual abuse. But if they "ignore the little girl's sexuality," then those girls will become "insecure about it."[165] If fewer girls than boys go to school, then they are discriminated against. If more girls go to school than boys, the girls' options are being limited.[166] If women who sleep around are frowned upon, then there is a double standard. If they are encouraged to do so, then "there's license, there's terror."[167] If husbands do not give money to their wives, then this is cause for complaint. But if they give them an allowance, then this is "economic abuse."[168]

And there is more. If child allowances are instituted, then women are discouraged from working.[169] If corporations offer women paid maternity leave, their jobs guaranteed upon return from a period of absence which may last for years, part-time jobs, flexible hours, special training courses, and opportunities to work from home, then they are deploying these devices to prevent women from getting ahead.[170] If there are no laws protecting women at work, then this is oppression. When there are such laws, then this proves that

---

[164] Angier, *Woman*, pp. 43-4.

[165] Friday, *My Mother/My Self*, pp. 87, 91.

[166] Julia Wrigley, "Gender and Education in the Welfare State," in Wrigley, ed., *Education and Gender Equality*, p. 9.

[167] Naomi Wolf, *Promiscuities: The Secret Struggle for Womanhood*, New York, Fascett Columbine, 1997, p. 81.

[168]See Ptacek, *Battered Women in the Courtroom*, p. 173.

[169] Yvonne Hirdman, "State Policy and Gender Contracts: The Swedish Experience," in Eileen Drew et al., eds., *Women, Work and the Family in Europe*, London, Routledge, 1998, p. 44.

[170] Daliah Moore, *Labor Market Segmentation and its Implications*, New York, Garland, 1992, p. 78; Dienel, *Frauen in Führungspositionen in Europa*, pp. 46-7.

men are trying to justify "domination" in the name of chivalry.[171] Women who are not given their day in court against men who allegedly harassed or abused them complain. Women who *are* given their day in court also complain, this time about the "psychic strain" that testifying implies.[172] Some feminists have even complained that the law's much more lenient treatment of women is a male tactic designed to "slight," "pathologize" "depoliticize" and "trivialize" them.[173] As the late novelist Doris Lessing, herself a feminist, put it:[174] "Generally it is the most stupid and ignorant women who throw mud at the most courteous and intelligent men."

The supreme form of complaint is attempted suicide. Worldwide, about four times as many women as men try to kill themselves. That does not prove they really want to die; rather, we are told, many if not most such attempts are directed "toward human contact and life."[175] If it is true that one in six British women try to kill themselves before they are 25 years old, they seem to be remarkably incompetent at it.[176] With men, the situation is different indeed. Knowing that if they complain they are much more likely to be met with indifference or contempt, far more of them pretend they are well.[177] Men who do see a mental health worker often start by saying that they "do not want to talk about it."[178] Instead, using drugs or alcohol, they self-destruct far more often than women do.[179] Ever since statistics on suicide began to be compiled at the end of the 19th century, it has been clear that men are more likely to kill

[171] Wendy Kaminer, *A Fearful Freedom*, pp. 7-8.

[172] Judith L. Herman, *Trauma and Recovery*, New York, Basic Books, 1992, p. 165.

[173] E. Anderson, "The 'Chivalrous' Treatment of the Female Offender in the Arms of the Criminal Justice System: A Review of the Literature," *Social Problems*, 3, 23, 1976,

[174] See (in Hebrew) *Haaretz*, 15.8.01, page D2.

[175] Edwin S. Schneidman and Norman L. Farberow, "Statistical Comparisons between Attempted and Committed Suicide," in Norman L. Farberow and Edwin S. Schneidmann, eds., *The Cry for Help*, New York, McGraw Hill, 1965, pp. 26-7, 34-6; Stengel, *Suicide and Attempted Suicide*, p. 90, table 11.

[176] Greer, *The Whole Woman*, p. 181.

[177] See Jennie Popeigh and Keleigh Groves, "'Narrative' in Research on Gender Equalities in Health," in Annandale and Hunt, eds., *Gender Inequalities in Health*, p. 83.

[178] Terence Real, *I Do not Want to Talk About It: Overcoming the Legacy of Male Depression*, New York, Fireside, 1997.

[179] Chesler, *Women and Madness*, pp. 42-3; Gerald L. Kleinman and Myrna M. Weissman, "Depression Among Women," in Guttentag et al., eds., *The Mental Health of Women*, p. 75.

themselves than women.[180] By the 1960s, the phenomenon had been documented in Australia, Austria, Czechoslovakia, Denmark, England, Finland, France, Germany, Hungary, Israel, Italy, Japan, Norway, Scotland, Sweden, Switzerland and the United States.[181] Worldwide, in the first years of the 21st century three-and-a-half times as many men as women committed suicide.[182]

In that they are free to complain, as in so much else, women are the privileged sex. That is especially the case if they are young, if they are beautiful, and if they have mastered the fine art of appearing vulnerable. And for those who can blame their troubles on a man, all the better for them. Such a woman obtains license to engage in the craziest behavior; in the case of Princess Diana that included such misguided acts as self-induced vomiting, throwing herself down stairs while pregnant, cutting herself with a lemon slicer, stabbing herself in the arms and chest with a penknife, or crashing into the glass door of a cupboard. The crazier she acts, the more attractive she becomes, and the larger the number of males who dream about rescuing her. As to her man husband — the supposed cause of all her troubles — his one sin was that he was prohibited from marrying the woman he loved. Still, he was supposed to keep a stiff upper lip; his pain simply did not count. So it has always been, and so — unless the nature of people of both sexes changes suddenly and fundamentally — it will always be.

---

[180] Emile Durkheim, *Suicide*, New York, Free Press, 1966 [1897], pp. 70-1, 101

[181] Erwin Stengel, *Suicide and Attempted Suicide*, Harmondsworth, Middlesex, Penguin, 1973, p. 22, table 2.

[182] "Gender and Mental Health." (June 2002). World Health Organization, retrieved from http://www.who.int/gender/other_health/en/genderMH/pdf

Conclusion

The most important conclusion from this study is that women, though not the equals of men in some respects, always and everywhere have been more than equal in others. For every disadvantage under which women labor, there is a privilege they alone enjoy. For every man who has to bear hardship, there was and is a woman who did not share in it, or who only shared in it to a lesser extent. Some of women's privileges seem to be biologically based, but many others are socially constructed.

Another possible conclusion from the present study is that penis envy really exists. How else to explain why it is that, in the face of overwhelming evidence and often enough their own personal experience,[1] millions of women claim that men have it better? How else to explain why women insist on participating in any and all male vices, from killing defenseless animals[2] to getting an "ego boost" by watching naked strangers of the opposite sex dance?[3] Or why women do whatever they can to enter even the most unpleasant male occupations, from climbing telephone poles to fighting in war, and in so doing sometimes risk life and limb? Or why, for that matter, at least one well-known feminist has expressed joy at the "genderquake" which, in some advertisements, caused "phallic objects... to emerge... from *women's* groins?"[4] One can only surmise that Freud may have been right after all — that is, that women do in fact crave "the obvious 'extra' that [men] have."[5]

If the campaign to show that women are oppressed is so riddled with nonsense, then why has it succeeded to the point that, in today's developed countries, most people can no longer even imagine that much of it might be false? One reason is the sheer persistence with which it has been conducted. Ours, after all, is a democratic age. Since we are all supposedly equal, a failure

---

[1] See Valian, *Why So Slow?*, pp. 164-5.

[2] See van Creveld, *Men, Women and War*, pp. 82-3.

[3] Wolf, *Fire with Fire*, p. 244.

[4] Wolf, *Fire with Fire*, p. 29.

[5] Friday, *My Mother/My Self*, p. 109.

by some people to achieve as much as others *must* result from discrimination, and not from other factors such as hormonal differences. While feminists did not invent this strategy, perhaps the reason why they have been more successful than most in using it is precisely because they are women. In other words, their success is itself one more proof of their privileged position in society.

Perhaps more important still, it is now almost 70 years since any developed country has engaged in a serious war of the kind that could even remotely endanger its national existence. Now if there is anything in the world that can lead to a truce in the battle between the sexes, it is war. When Simone de Beauvoir visited Israel in the spring of 1967, she was surprised, and not a little angered, to find that Israeli women would not listen to what at the time struck them as outrageous nonsense.[6] War is an unfavorable breeding ground for feminism because, as long as it lasts, most women sit safely at home while men are obliged to fight and die. War is an unfavorable breeding ground for feminism because, as long as it lasts, women desperately need men to defend them. Finally, war is an unfavorable breeding ground for feminism because, as Aristotle wrote of Sparta,[7] while the men are away on campaign women do exactly as they please.

In other words, feminism is a tree that will only grow in the luxury of peace. That is as true today as it was as under the *Pax Romana*, when women enjoyed greater rights than they had under the Republic. It was equally true during the last years before World War I, when suffragettes argued that, since war was on its way out, women deserved to vote.[8] If the price of peace is indeed the rise of feminism, as some 19th century philosophers thought, then perhaps it is a price well worth paying.

As of 2013, no threat that would seriously disturb the peace of any developed country looms on the horizon. In such an environment, one of two very different outcomes can be expected: Either women and men grow further apart, or feminism as we know it collapses under the weight of its own contradictions.

First, the former. The ongoing barrage of feminist complaints, in particular those concerning sexual harassment, may very well lead to a growing

---

[6] Claude Francis and Fernande Gontier, *Simone de Beauvoir*, London, Mandarin, 1986, p. 318.

[7] *Politics*, 1267b-70a; also Xenophon, *Lacedaemonium Politeia*, 1.9.

[8] Aileen S. Kraditor, *The Ideas of the Woman Suffrage Movement, 1890-1920*, Garden City, NJ, Anchor Books, 1965, pp. 54, 56, 157.

separation between the sexes. In some spheres, integration has already been replaced by its opposite. Even as some women use the courts to force their way into men's schools, others are demanding schools that will cater exclusively to women.[9] Perhaps the day is not far off when we will again see separate workplaces (as in the late 19th century); separate transport (as in Orthodox Jewish communities and in some Indian cities); separate schools (as during most of history); separate religious institutions (as in Christian and Buddhist monasteries); and separate medical treatment, as when doctors treating the womenfolk of Muslim rulers were only allowed to see an arm stuck through a hole in the wall.

Already now, it is a brave male doctor who agrees to treat female patients unless a female nurse is present in the room and other precautions are taken. Already now, it is a brave male university professor who allows his female student to close his office door while he advises her on her paper or thesis. Though most would be loath to admit it, many professors would prefer that female students disappear from their classrooms, so that they can concentrate on their work without fear of being accused of harassment. U.S. Marines are likewise terrified that the new regulations concerning women in combat will lead to such charges.[10] In these and other fields, the only people not aware of the danger are those who will soon find out.

Society's rules already prevent both men and women from communicating as freely as they did several decades ago. At school, the lesson that females are frail flowers and will suffer permanent psychological damage if they so much as overhear a naughty word being said now starts to be hammered in when children are 5 years old. At the other extreme, the U.S. Air Force once went so far as to jail a married couple because, during their courtship, the woman had been under the man's command. Instead of trying to improve communication between the sexes, in many ways we are doing what we can to prevent it from taking place.

Instead of liberating women, we assume they are so vulnerable that they cannot look at a picture of a naked person without suffering a hysteric fit. Instead of empowering them, we present them as too foolish to know what a

---

[9] Hoff Sommer, *The War against Boys*, pp. 39, 176.

[10] Julie Watson. (1.2.2013) "Marine Survey Lists Concerns on Women in Combat," *Yahoo News*, retrieved from http://news.yahoo.com/marine-survey-lists-concerns-women-combat-002047180.html

male acquaintance wants of them and too weak to tell him so. Observing the way things have changed since the 1970s, one might conclude that advanced countries have decided to go back to Victorian times when, among the upper classes, for an unmarried woman to be alone with a man was considered scandalous. Or perhaps that, given the inability of people of both sexes to keep out of each other's way and avoid misunderstandings as to what constitutes consent, the Victorian doctrine of separate spheres is, in fact, the best there is.

Since boys tend to do better in single-sex schools than in mixed ones,[11] in case separate spheres make a comeback it is boys who have the most to gain. Since men will still be needed to do most of society's productive work, as well as to defend it against internal and external enemies, it is women who have more to lose. The higher the class to which any woman belongs, the greater the likelihood that renewed segregation will cause her to retreat into the home — if she left it in the first place, that is, since of all members of the human race, these ladies are the least likely to work for a living. The process may well cause women to lose both their earning power and the freedom to go out and about. Women may also be forced to submit to restrictions on the clothes they can wear and the behavior they can engage in. The more vulnerable to harassment they claim to be, the more likely this is to happen.

The second possible outcome from the peace that by and large reigns over today's developed countries is that feminism will collapse under the weight of its own contradictions. Today, as in the past, men and women want each other and cannot live without each other. Today, as in the past, for a woman to succeed in her career while also looking after her home is a challenge only a minority can successfully meet — and those who do meet the challenge are often left very, very tired. Today, as in the past, few women, and feminists least of all, want to have men who "do not aim for occupational pinnacles or positions of authority and... do not want to head households or be husbands and fathers"[12] — let alone want to have men who are economically dependent on them. And today, as in the past, the more successful a woman, the less likely

---

[11] John O'Leary, "A Level Analysis Finds Boys do Better in Single Sex Schools," *Times*, 14.7.1997; Rachel Williams, "Single-Sex Schools Help Boys to Enjoy Arts," The Guardian, 20.1.2010.

[12] Jean Sinoda Bohlen, *Goddesses in Everywoman: A New Psychology of Women*, New York, Harper Perennial, 1985, p. 247.

she is to have either a husband or children.[13] It is almost as if these women do what they can to wage war against their own genes.

As far as the great majority of women are concerned, feminism seems to be coming up against the fundamental clash between equality and privilege.[14] He or she who demands the former cannot have the latter. She or he who demands the latter cannot have the former. Should women achieve true equality, then many of their privileges will be lost. Many, perhaps most, can expect both their quality of life and life expectancy to drop sharply. This is especially true of married women who, as long as they stayed married and often even if they did not, have always been carried on the shoulders of men. From Alexandra Kollontai and Simone de Beauvoir to Germaine Greer and Andrea Dworkin, perhaps much of feminism should be understood as an attempt by women who failed to attract and keep a man to avenge themselves on their more fortunate sisters. Mary Wollstonecraft did it by making those who preferred raising children over a career to feel as if they were a cross between nincompoops and criminals. Adrianna Rich did it by trying to turn them into lesbians. And Gloria Steinem did it by convincing them that marriage was bad for them (before she got married, that is).

Many women, in short, would first sacrifice equality before giving up on their sex's privileges. At least some female authors have begun to demand that women be given "more than equal treatment" in a whole variety of areas from reserved parking spaces and child custody to special rights in educational institutions and courts of law.[15] In the United States, millions of women turned against the Equal Rights Amendment, a key reason it was never ratified.[16] Today many women fear, with good reason, that equality before the law may cause the number of female offenders who are sent to prison to increase, and the conditions under which they are held to deteriorate.[17] It has even been suggested that girls from traditional homes are less likely to be arrested than

[13] See Catalyst. (May 2000). "Women and the MBA: Gateway to Opportunity," retrieved from http://www.catalyst.org/knowledge/women-and-mba-gateway-opportunity

[14] Danielle Crittenden, *What Our Mothers Didn't Tell Us*, New York, Touchstone, 1999, pp. 51-4.

[15] Kaminer, *A Fearful Freedom*, p. 5.

[16] See Phyllis Schafly, *The Power of the Positive Woman*, New Rochelle, NY, 1977, pp. 68-138; Jean J. Mansbridge, *Why We Lost the Era, Chicago*, University of Chicago Press, 1986, p. 72.

[17] Baer, *Women in American Law*, p. 281; Belknap, *The Invisible Woman*, p. 39; Chesney-Lind, *The Female Offender*, pp. 152, 161.

those raised in egalitarian ones or by women on their own.[18] If this is true, then "patriarchy" may actually be good for young females.

At the same time, some women are realizing — perhaps because so many women have taken up paid work and begun to see men's lives close up — that those lives are not all fun and games. To misquote three leading feminists, the great majority of women do not want to play in the male "ballfield."[19] Nor do they demand a share in male "potency" and the "agony" of men.[20] Rather, many of them are content to enjoy their privileges; stay at, or return to, their homes; spend their days raising their children and cultivating their gardens; and come as close to the Platonic idea of happiness in contemplation as anybody can. For these women, feminism — in all its variations — holds little appeal. This is in part so because very often it demands that they betray their trust as the daughters, sisters, wives and mothers of men.

Another reason why feminism may eventually implode is because of the way feminists treat women who refuse to follow their call (and vice versa). Working women accuse non-working women of not pulling their weight in the cause of liberation. Non-working women, for their part, accuse working ones of not being women at all.[21] In some surveys, over half of women say that other women had treated them unethically in the workplace. Four out of five women claim that "female bosses [are] often unsupportive" and prefer not to work for them.[22] Women often devalue their sisters' work, as by calling household work a "pseudoscience"[23] and referring to "caring for the young" as "animal functions."[24] Finally, it was self-styled "power feminists" who invented the term "victim feminists" to pejoratively describe women who did nothing but

---

[18] John Hagan, "Class in the Household: A Power-Control Theory of Gender and Delinquency," *American Journal of Sociology*, 92, 1987, pp. 788-816.

[19] Friedan, *The Second Stage*, p. 30.

[20] Sinoda Bohlen, *Goddesses in Everywoman*, p. 284; Wolf, *Fire with Fire*, p. 207.

[21] Feroza Jussawalla, "Mothers, Work and the Media: How Women Don't Support Other Women," in Lynne B. Welch, ed., *Women in Higher Education: Changes and Challenges*, New York, Praeger, 1990, pp. 84-93.

[22] Crittenden, *The Price of Motherhood*, p. 251; Jussawalla, "Mothers, Work and the Media," p. 92; Hakim, *Key Issues in Women's Work*, pp. 108, 115, 117.

[23] Marjorie Theobald, *Knowing Women: Origins of Women's Education in Nineteenth-Century Australia*, Cambridge, Cambridge University Press, 1996, p. 27.

[24] Millett, *Sexual Politics*, p. 119.

complain.[25] As no less a figure than Simone de Beauvoir declared, "Women are pitiless toward each other."[26]

If feminism does indeed recede into the dustbin of history, then perhaps the loss to both men and women, but especially to women, will not be all that great. Listen to Betty Friedan, who may have done more to jumpstart the modern feminist movement than any single other person, describing what her life looked like in the late 1950s, before she and others raised the standard of revolt:[27]

> All the years I was working on *The Feminist Mystique*, I would blithely stop writing when my little daughter came home from school or my boys were in a Little League or basketball game, or to make a martini when my husband got home, fix dinner, argue, go to the movies, make love, join an expedition to the supermarket or a country-auction on Saturday, organize a clambake on the beach at Fire Island, take the kids over the battlefield at Gettysburg, or camping on Cape Hatteras — the stuff of family life.

To more than a few people of both sexes, this might not sound like such a bad deal. It might actually sound rather appealing, particularly if the alternative is wasting several hours each day battling other drivers on the highway, spending the time between commutes in some factory or office doing work that one does not like for a boss whom one cannot stand, all in return for wages that always feel as if they are just sufficient to keep one functioning with little left to spare.

Whatever the future may hold for women, what it has in store for men is perfectly clear: Men will continue the pursuit of power, fame and riches so that they can lay their gains at the feet of one or more women. They will continue to be treated more harshly by parents, at school and by other institutions whose purpose is to prepare people for adult life. They will also continue to work more, and harder than, women, carrying out a wholly disproportionate number of dirty, dangerous tasks and suffering a wholly disproportionate number of accidents as a result. Whether individually or collectively, or both, men will

---

[25] Wolf, *Fire with Fire*, pp. xx, 154, 156, 177, 179, 244.

[26] See Hawthorne, *Contingent Loves*, p. 60.

[27] *The Second Stage*, p. 46.

continue to support women economically by means of whatever mechanisms exist at any time and place. Without public money, which is made up overwhelmingly of the contributions of men, most feminist organizations would go bankrupt. Faced by the rigor of law, men will continue to be treated much more harshly than women. Faced by the horror of war, men will continue to die so that women may live. In these and countless other ways, men will continue to do what they can to give women easier, better, more comfortable and longer lives than men themselves enjoy. All the while, listening — or quite often, trying not to listen — to women's complaints about anything and everything, including them.

We men well realize that nature, having made us, as Nietzsche put it, the "unfruitful animal"[28] and forced us to compete for women, has turned us into the superfluous sex. Giving us larger and more robust bodies, it has also destined us to act as beasts of burden. Our need of, and love for, women being as strong as it is, most of the time we do not really mind the fact that they are privileged in so many ways. Nor, in our heart of hearts, would we like the situation to change. After all, it was women who gave us life. In a way, all we are doing is returning a debt. This is true even if the burden is occasionally heavy, and even if while carrying it we sometimes have to lay down our lives. Ceasing to support women, we would lose not just our existence but our self-respect. Perhaps the real reason why women have never fought in war is because, as Hector told his wife, we men would rather die than watch them dying. To quote an Indian proverb, where women are worshipped, there the gods dwell. It would be nice, though, if from time to time, amid the torrents of invective feminists spew at us, we occasionally heard a pleasant female voice saying "thank you, Mate."

---

[28] *Beyond Good and Evil*, p. 83.

Index

Made in the USA
Lexington, KY
08 April 2015